Claude Reignier Conder

**The Survey of Eastern Palestine**

Memoirs of the Topography, Orography, Hydrography and Archaeology

Claude Reignier Conder

**The Survey of Eastern Palestine**
*Memoirs of the Topography, Orography, Hydrography and Archaeology*

ISBN/EAN: 9783337292492

Printed in Europe, USA, Canada, Australia, Japan

Cover: Foto ©ninafisch / pixelio.de

More available books at **www.hansebooks.com**

# THE SURVEY
## OF
# EASTERN PALESTINE.

## MEMOIRS
### OF THE
## TOPOGRAPHY, OROGRAPHY, HYDROGRAPHY, ARCHÆOLOGY, ETC.

*VOLUME I.—THE 'ADWÂN COUNTRY.*

BY

MAJOR C. R. CONDER, D.C.L., R.E.

FOR
THE COMMITTEE OF THE PALESTINE EXPLORATION FUND,
1, ADAM STREET, ADELPHI, LONDON, W.C.
1889.

# PREFACE.

THIS Survey was conducted in the months of August, September, and October, 1881, by a party consisting of Lieutenant A. M. Mantell, R.E., and Messrs. T. Black and G. Armstrong, under the command of Captain C. R. Conder, R.E. Five hundred and ten square miles were triangulated and completed, and 610 names obtained. The difficulties due to Government opposition on the part of the Turks are detailed in 'Heth and Moab' (Chapter iv., pp. 103-119, 1st edition), and in Appendix A of this Memoir.

The names are here given exactly as they were written down by Mikhail Kassatly, the scribe of the party. A large proportion are familiar geographical terms, concerning the meaning of which no hesitation can be felt, as they have been ascertained beyond dispute. Some of the rarer and more peculiar names are given in accordance with the meaning ascertained by careful questioning on the spot, and these also must be regarded as beyond dispute. A small number remain which are doubtful, and, as a last resource, a dictionary was used, as referred to in the text. In these cases it has only been considered safe to give the most probable meaning of the root, partly because these names present very unusual grammatical forms, and partly because every Arabic root has so many well-known meanings that no certainty can be felt unless the word is actually known by its use in Syria. Thus, for instance, *Bedd* in literary Arabic means an 'idol-temple,' but in Syria it is the usual name for a millstone—as is clear in the case of Kefeir Abu Bedd in the present list. From the instance of er Rekiáiyeh in the present list it will be possible to judge how vague and uncertain information merely obtained by consulting a dictionary of literary Arabic must always be. The Syrian dialects preserve many Aramaic and Hebrew words with their original meaning, and many archaisms of both language and pronunciation. It is only in the case of ascertained meanings noted in the field that any certainty can be attained.

The illustrations in this volume are either from photographs, or from sketches made on the spot, and drawings with dimensions. The drawings of dolmens are to one scale; so that the comparative size of the monuments can be seen at a glance.

C. R. C.

# LIST OF ILLUSTRATIONS.

|  | PAGE |
|---|---|
| PLAN AND SECTIONS, SARCOPHAGUS AT 'AIN HESBÁN | 6 |
| RELIEFS ON ARAB TOMB AT 'AIN HESBÁN | 7 |
| ARAB TOMB CIRCLE AT 'AIN HESBÁN | 8 |
| PLAN AND VIEW OF STONE CIRCLE AT 'AIN EL MINYEH | 11 |
| PLAN OF CHAPEL AND DETAILS AT EL 'ÁL | 17 |
| CAPITALS AND STANDING STONE AT EL 'ÁL | 18 |
| PLAN OF DOLMEN A AT 'AMMÁN | 20 |
| VIEWS OF DOLMEN A AT 'AMMÁN | 21 |
| VIEWS OF DOLMENS A AND B AT 'AMMÁN | 22 |
| VIEWS OF DOLMENS C AND D AT 'AMMÁN | 23 |
| VIEW OF MENHIR O AT 'AMMÁN | 23 |
| VIEWS OF MENHIRS M AND N AT 'AMMÁN | 24 |
| SURVEY OF 'AMMÁN | to face 24 |
| VIEWS OF DOLMENS L, G, H, AND I AT 'AMMÁN | 25 |
| VIEW OF MENHIR J AT 'AMMÁN | 26 |
| PLANS OF HEBREW TOMBS (FIGS. 1, 2, 3) AT 'AMMÁN | 28 |
| LETTERS ON PILLAR-BASES AT 'AMMÁN | 31 |
| PLAN OF PRONAOS OF TEMPLE AT 'AMMÁN | 32 |
| PROFILE OF TEMPLE PILLARS AT 'AMMÁN | 32 |
| LETTERS ON PILLAR-BASES AT 'AMMÁN | 32 |
| INSCRIPTION ON PILLAR AT SIDON | 32 |
| INSCRIPTIONS ON FLAGSTONES AT STA. SOPHIA, CONSTANTINOPLE | 32 |
| INSCRIPTION ON TEMPLE CORNICE AT 'AMMÁN | 33 |
| PLAN OF THEATRE AND ODEUM AT 'AMMÁN | to face 36 |
| PLAN OF SUPPOSED FORUM AT 'AMMÁN | 37 |
| PROFILE OF PILLAR A IN SUPPOSED FORUM AT 'AMMÁN | 37 |
| PLAN OF SUPPOSED ROMAN BATHS AT 'AMMÁN | 40 |
| PROFILE OF PILLAR B IN SUPPOSED BATHS AT 'AMMÁN | 40 |
| PLAN OF KABR ES SULTÁN AT 'AMMÁN | 42 |
| PLAN OF WESTERN TOMB AT 'AMMÁN | 43 |
| SKETCH OF DOME OF WESTERN TOMB AT 'AMMÁN | 44 |
| PLAN OF RUIN NEAR WESTERN BRIDGE AT 'AMMÁN | 45 |
| PROFILE OF PILLAR A IN PRECEDING PLAN | 46 |
| ELEVATION OF SARCOPHAGUS WEST OF 'AMMÁN | 47 |

## LIST OF ILLUSTRATIONS

|  | PAGE |
|---|---|
| PLANS OF TOMBS AND DETAILS AT 'AMMĀN | 48 |
| PLAN OF ROCK-CUT TOMB AT 'AMMĀN | 50 |
| COVERS OF SARCOPHAGI IN PRECEDING TOMB | 51 |
| PLAN AND DETAIL OF SOUTH-EASTERN TOMB AT 'AMMĀN | 51 |
| ARAB TRIBE-MARKS | 52 |
| PLAN OF PRINCIPAL CHURCH AT 'AMMĀN | 55 |
| PLAN OF TWO SMALLER CHURCHES AT 'AMMĀN | 56 |
| PLAN OF MOSQUE AND DETAILS OF ARCHES AT 'AMMĀN | 57 |
| SKETCH OF NORTH WALL OF MOSQUE AT 'AMMĀN | 58 |
| ARAB TRIBE-MARKS IN MOSQUE AT 'AMMĀN | 58 |
| PLAN OF TOMB OF URIAH (SO CALLED) AT 'AMMĀN | 60 |
| DETAILS OF SUPPOSED SASSANIAN BUILDING (TOMB OF URIAH) | to face 60 |
| SECTION OF TOMB OF URIAH (SO CALLED) AT 'AMMĀN | 61 |
| ROCK WITH NICHES, AND DETAIL OF NICHES (FIGS. 1, 2), AT 'ARĀK EL EMĪR | 68 |
| PLANS OF CAVES (FIGS. 3, 4, 5, 6) AT 'ARĀK EL EMĪR | 69 |
| PLAN OF EL HOSN (FIG. 7) AT 'ARĀK EL EMĪR | 70 |
| DETAIL OF MANGERS (FIG. 8) IN EL HOSN AT 'ARĀK EL EMĪR | 71 |
| PLANS OF CAVE AND CISTERNS (FIGS. 9, 10, 11, 12) AT 'ARĀK EL EMĪR | 72 |
| PLAN OF CAVE (FIG. 13) AT 'ARĀK EL EMĪR | 73 |
| PLANS OF CAVES (FIGS. 14, 15, 16) AT 'ARĀK EL EMĪR | 74 |
| SECTIONS OF CAVE, EL WEIBDEH (FIGS. 17, 18) AT 'ARĀK EL EMĪR | 75 |
| PLAN OF CAVE (FIG. 19) AT 'ARĀK EL EMĪR | 75 |
| VIEW OF INSCRIBED ROCK AT 'ARĀK EL EMĪR | 76 |
| INSCRIPTION AT 'ARĀK EL EMĪR | 77 |
| COMPARATIVE ALPHABETS TO ILLUSTRATE THE PRECEDING | 77 |
| PLANS OF CAVES (FIGS. 21, 22) AT 'ARĀK EL EMĪR | 78 |
| PLAN OF KUSR EL 'ABD AT 'ARĀK EL EMĪR | 79 |
| VIEW OF EAST WALL OF KUSR EL 'ABD | 80 |
| SITE PLAN OF KUSR EL 'ABD | to face 80 |
| PROFILE OF CORNICE AT KUSR EL 'ABD | 81 |
| DETAIL OF SCULPTURED LIONS AT KUSR EL 'ABD | 81 |
| DETAIL OF CORNICE AND WINDOW AT KUSR EL 'ABD | 82 |
| PLAN AND ELEVATION OF CAPITAL AT KUSR EL 'ABD | 82 |
| DETAILS OF PILLARS AND FRIEZE AT KUSR EL 'ABD | 83 |
| ELEVATION OF EASTERN GATE AT KUSR EL 'ABD | 84 |
| DETAIL OF CORNICE AT KUSR EL 'ABD | 84 |
| ELEVATIONS AND SECTION OF CIPPI AT 'ARĀK EL EMĪR | 85 |
| FAÇADE OF ROCK-CUT HERMITAGE AT ED DEIR | 94 |
| PLAN OF ROCK-CUT HERMITAGE AT ED DEIR | 95 |
| DETAILS OF NICHES IN ROCK-CUT HERMITAGE AT ED DEIR | 95 |
| SECTION OF GROUND-FLOOR OF ROCK-CUT HERMITAGE AT ED DEIR | 96 |
| PLAN OF HADANIEH CIRCLE AND LINTEL | to face 100 |
| SKETCH OF CAPITAL AT HESBĀN | 105 |
| PLAN OF THE KAL'AH AT HESBĀN | 106 |
| PROFILE OF PILLAR BASE IN THE KAL'AH AT HESBĀN | 106 |
| DETAILS OF MASONRY, LINTEL AND PILASTER AT HESBĀN | 107 |
| DETAILS OF CORNICE AND LINTEL AT HESBĀN | 108 |
| VIEWS OF KABR FENDI EL FĀIZ | 114 |
| PLAN AND SECTION, EASTERN TOMB AT EL KAHF | 117 |
| PLAN OF WESTERN TOMB AT EL KAHF | 118 |

# LIST OF ILLUSTRATIONS

| | PAGE |
|---|---|
| SKETCH OF DETAILS OF FAÇADE OF WESTERN TOMB AT EL KAHF | 119 |
| DETAILS IN INTERIOR OF WESTERN TOMB AT EL KAHF | 120 |
| ARAB TRIBE-MARKS | 121 |
| PLAN AND ELEVATION OF SARCOPHAGUS AT EL KAHF | 121 |
| SECTIONS OF WESTERN TOMB AT EL KAHF | 123 |
| ARAB TRIBE-MARKS AT KAL'AT UMMEH | 125 |
| PLAN AND VIEW OF DOLMEN, NO. 1 AT EL KALÛ'A | 126 |
| VIEWS OF DOLMENS NOS. 2, 3, 4, 5 AT EL KALÛ'A | 127 |
| VIEWS OF DOLMENS NOS. 6, 7, 8, 9 AT EL KALÛ'A | 128 |
| VIEWS OF DOLMENS NOS. 10, 11, 12, 13, 14 AT EL KALÛ'A | 129 |
| VIEW OF DOLMEN NO. 15 AT EL KALÛ'A | 130 |
| VIEWS OF DOLMENS NOS. 17, 18 AT EL KALÛ'A | 131 |
| VIEWS AND PLANS OF DOLMENS, NOS. 19, 20 AT EL KALÛ'A | 132 |
| PLAN OF BUILDING AT KEFEIR ABU SARBÛT | 135 |
| ELEVATION AND SECTION OF PILLAR AT KEFEIR ABU SARBÛT | 135 |
| CAPITALS AND BASES AT KEFEIR ABU SARBÛT | 136 |
| VIEW OF RUINED TOWER AT KEFEIR ABU SARBÛT | 136 |
| TRIBE-MARKS | 137 |
| LINTEL WITH CROSS AT KEFEIR ABU SARBÛT | 137 |
| FURCATED CROSS FROM APHRODISIAS | 138 |
| LINTEL, ETC., AT KEFEIR EL WUSTA | 139 |
| PLAN AND SECTIONS OF CISTERN AT KEFEIR EL WUSTA | 139 |
| PLAN OF TEMPLE AT KHAREIBET ES SÛK | 142 |
| CAPITAL IN TEMPLE AT KHAREIBET ES SÛK | 143 |
| PLAN AND DETAILS, EASTERN TOMB AT KHAREIBET ES SÛK | 143 |
| PLAN OF TANK AT KHAREIBET ES SÛK | 144 |
| PLAN OF NORTHERN TOMB AT KHAREIBET ES SÛK | 144 |
| PLAN OF WINEPRESS, KHURBET EL 'AMRÎVEH | 146 |
| PLAN OF WINEPRESS, KHURBET EL MESHUKKAR | 151 |
| CAPITALS AND MOULDING, KHURBET SIÂGHAH | 154 |
| PLAN OF WINEPRESS, KHURBET UMM HADAWÎVEH | 157 |
| SITE PLAN, EL KURMÎYEH | 159 |
| PLAN AND VIEW DOLMEN NO. 1, EL KURMÎVEH | 161 |
| PLAN AND VIEW DOLMEN NO. 2, EL KURMÎVEH | 162 |
| PLAN AND VIEW DOLMEN NO. 3, EL KURMÎVEH | 163 |
| VIEW OF DOLMEN NO. 4, EL KURMÎVEH | 163 |
| PLAN OF DOLMEN NO. 4, EL KURMÎVEH | 164 |
| VIEWS OF DOLMEN NO. 5 | 164 |
| PLAN AND SECTION OF WINEPRESS AT EL KURMÎVEH | 164 |
| PLAN OF DOLMEN NO. 6, EL KURMÎVEH | 165 |
| VIEW OF DOLMEN NO. 7, EL KURMÎVEH | 165 |
| VIEW OF DOLMEN NO. 8, EL KURMÎVEH | 166 |
| SITE PLAN DOLMENS NOS. 9, 10, 11, EL KURMÎVEH | 166 |
| VIEW OF DOLMEN NO. 12, EL KURMÎVEH | 167 |
| VIEW AND SECTION OF MENHIR NO. 13, EL KURMÎVEH | 167 |
| VIEWS OF DOLMENS NOS. 14, 15, EL KURMÎVEH | 167 |
| VIEWS OF DOLMENS NOS. 16, 17, 18, EL KURMÎVEH | 168 |
| VIEWS OF DOLMENS NOS. 19, 20, 21, 22, EL KURMÎVEH | 169 |
| VIEWS OF DOLMENS NOS. 23, 24, 25, 26, EL KURMÎVEH | 170 |
| PLAN AND SECTION, KUSR EN NÛEIJIS | 172 |

## LIST OF ILLUSTRATIONS

|  | PAGE |
|---|---|
| ENTABLATURE AND DETAILS KUSR EN NÚEIJÍS | 173 |
| PLAN AND SECTION, KUSR ES SEB'AH | 174 |
| SIDE-VIEWS AND SECTIONS OF SARCOPHAGI IN KUSR ES SEB'AH | 175 |
| LINTEL AND SCULPTURED STONE AT MÁ'AÍN | 177 |
| PLAN OF CHURCH AND CAPITAL, MÁDEBA | 179 |
| LINTEL WITH CROSSES AT MÁDEBA | 180 |
| PLAN OF NORTH-EAST GATE AT MÁDEBA | 181 |
| MOULDINGS OF GATE-TOWER AT MÁDEBA | 181 |
| LINTEL AND PLAN OF LARGE RESERVOIR AT MÁDEBA | 182 |
| LINTEL OF DOOR IN TOWER OF LARGE RESERVOIR AT MÁDEBA | 183 |
| PLAN OF WINEPRESS, EL MAREIGHÁT | 185 |
| PLAN AND VIEWS OF HAJR EL MANSÚB | 186 |
| VIEW OF PRINCIPAL MENHIR GROUP, EL MAREIGHÁT | 187 |
| VIEW OF GROUP OF MENHIRS AT EL MAREIGHÁT | 187 |
| VIEWS OF DOLMENS NOS. 1, 2, 3, AT EL MAREIGHÁT | 188 |
| VIEWS OF DOLMENS NOS. 4, 5, AT EL MAREIGHÁT | 189 |
| PLAN OF TOMB AT EL MEKHEIVIT | 192 |
| PLAN AND SECTION OF TOMB AND OF NICHE, MUGHÁIR EL 'ADEISÍYEH | 196 |
| MONUMENT AT MUNTÁR EL MESHUKKAR | 197 |
| VIEW OF DOLMEN NO. 1 AT NEBA | 202 |
| PLAN AND ELEVATION OF DOLMEN NO. 1 AT NEBA | 203 |
| VIEW OF DOLMEN NO. 2 AT NEBA | 203 |
| ARAB TRIBE-MARKS AT ES SÁMIK | 211 |
| ELEVATIONS OF PILLARS AT SERABÍT EL MESHUKKAR | 212 |
| ELEVATIONS OF PILLARS AT SERABÍT EL MEHATTAH | 213 |
| PLAN AND SECTIONS OF TOMB AT SHÚNET EDH DHIÁBEH | 217 |
| ELEVATION OF LINTEL-STONES AT SHÚNET SUKR | 219 |
| BLOCK PLAN OF BUILDING AT SÚMIA | 221 |
| ELEVATIONS OF DRAFTED STONES AT SÚMIA | 222 |
| ELEVATIONS OF LINTEL-STONE AT SÚMIA | 223 |
| ELEVATIONS OF SCULPTURED STONES AT SÚMIA | 223 |
| ELEVATIONS OF DOORWAY AT SÚMIA | 223 |
| ORNAMENTATION ON A LINTEL-STONE AT SÚMIA | 224 |
| PLANS OF ROCK-CUT TOMBS AT SÚMIA | 225 |
| PLANS OF ROCK-CUT SARCOPHAGI AT SÚMIA | 226 |
| VIEW AND PLAN OF DOLMEN NEAR SÚMIA | 226 |
| VIEWS OF DOLMENS AT TELL EL HAMMÁM | 229 |
| VIEW OF TWO DOLMENS AT TELL EL HAMMÁM | 230 |
| VIEW AND PLAN OF MONUMENT NO. 1 AT TELL EL MATÁB'A | 232 |
| PLAN OF CIRCLE AND MENHIR NO. 2 AT TELL EL MATÁB'A | 233 |
| ELEVATION OF MENHIR A IN PRECEDING PLAN | 233 |
| PLAN OF MONUMENT NO. 3 AT TELL EL MATÁB'A | 234 |
| SKETCH OF MENHIR NO. 4 AT TELL EL MATÁB'A | 234 |
| PLAN OF MONUMENT NO. 5 AT TELL EL MATÁB'A | 234 |
| VIEW OF DOLMEN NO. 6 AT TELL EL MATÁB'A | 235 |
| PLAN OF TANK AT UMM EL BURUK | 242 |
| ROCK-CUT STABLE AND TOMBS (FIGS. 1, 2, 3) AT UMM EL BURUK | 243 |
| TOMBS AND SARCOPHAGI AT UMM EL HANÁFÍSH (FIGS. 4, 5, 6) | 243 |
| INSCRIPTION OF ANTONIUS RUFUS AT UMM EL BURUK | 244 |
| FRAGMENT OF LINTEL AT UMM EL HANÁFÍSH | 246 |

## LIST OF ILLUSTRATIONS

|  | PAGE |
|---|---|
| PLAN OF EL KUSR AT UMM EL HANÂFÎSH | 247 |
| BASE AND CAPITALS AT KHURBET HAMZEH | 247 |
| PLAN AND SECTION OF TOMB AT UMM EL KENÂFID | 249 |
| VIEW OF DOLMEN NO. 4 IN WÂDY JIDEID | 254 |
| VIEWS OF DOLMENS NOS. 14, 16, IN WÂDY JIDEID | 256 |
| VIEWS OF DOLMENS NOS. 17, 20, IN WÂDY JIDEID | 257 |
| VIEWS OF DOLMENS NOS. 21, 22, IN WÂDY JIDEID | 258 |
| VIEWS OF DOLMENS NOS. 27, 28, IN WÂDY JIDEID | 259 |
| VIEWS OF DOLMENS NOS. 33, 40, IN WÂDY JIDEID | 260 |
| VIEWS OF DOLMENS NOS. 43, 44, IN WÂDY JIDEID | 261 |
| VIEWS OF DOLMENS NOS. 48, 50, 52, IN WÂDY JIDEID | 262 |
| VIEWS OF DOLMENS NOS. 54, 55, 56, IN WÂDY JIDEID | 263 |
| VIEWS OF DOLMENS NOS. 60, 61, IN WÂDY JIDEID | 264 |
| VIEWS OF DOLMENS NOS. 70, 80, 91, IN WÂDY JIDEID | 265 |
| VIEWS OF DOLMENS NOS. 92, 93, 100, IN WÂDY JIDEID | 266 |
| VIEWS OF DOLMENS NOS. 101, 102, 107, IN WÂDY JIDEID | 267 |
| VIEWS OF DOLMENS NOS. 112, 113 (AND PLAN OF 113), IN WÂDY JIDEID | 268 |
| VIEWS OF DOLMENS NOS. 114, 116, IN WÂDY JIDEID | 269 |
| VIEWS OF DOLMENS NOS. 117, 118, 119 (AND PLAN OF 117), IN WÂDY JIDEID | 270 |
| VIEWS OF DOLMENS NOS. 120, 121, 124, 125, IN WÂDY JIDEID | 271 |
| VIEWS OF DOLMENS NOS. 126, 127, 134, IN WÂDY JIDEID | 272 |
| VIEWS OF DOLMENS NOS. 144, 146, IN WÂDY JIDEID | 273 |
| VIEW OF DOLMEN IN WÂDY UMM SHUÂMIR | 277 |
| DIAGRAM OF CONSTRUCTION OF HESBÂN BASE-LINE | 284 |
| DIAGRAM OF TRIANGULATION | 287 |

---

ERRATA.

Page 196, line 11, *for* 'as' *read* 'was.'
Page 205, line 6, *for* '1883' *read* '1881.'
Page 209, line 12 from foot, *for* 'AVRELVS' *read* 'AVRELIVS.'
Page 215, line 1, *for* 'el 'Al' *read* 'el 'Âl.'

# LIST OF PHOTOGRAPHIC VIEWS.

*(From Negatives taken by Lieutenant A. M. Mantell, R.E.)*

|  | PAGE |
|---|---|
| SUPPOSED ROMAN BATHS AT 'AMMÁN | *frontispiece* |
| SUPPOSED FORUM AT 'AMMÁN | *to face* 32 |
| ODEUM AT 'AMMÁN | 40 |
| WESTERN TOMB AT 'AMMÁN | 44 |
| VIEW OF CLIFF AT 'ARÁK EL EMÍR | 72 |
| INSCRIPTION ON THE ROCK AT 'ARÁK EL EMÍR | 84 |
| ARAB TOMB AT HADÁNIEH | 104 |
| TEMPLE AT KHAREIBET ES SÛK | 140 |
| NORTHERN TOMB AT KHAREIBET ES SÛK | 144 |
| KUSR ES SEB'AH | 176 |

THE

# SURVEY OF EASTERN PALESTINE

'A b d  e l   J u w â d  (عبد الجواد, 'servant of the bountiful'—one of the names of the deity).—This is the grave of one of the Hasâsineh (see K a b û r  e l  H a s â s i n e h). It is a large modern tomb, now held sacred, and surrounded by stone piles, or Kehakir. Visited September 13, 1881.

'A b d û n  (عبدون).—This name is similar to the Hebrew Abdon עבדון, applying to a town in Galilee (Joshua xxi. 30), and to Eboda, south of Beersheba, and 'Abdûn ('Western Survey,' Sheet VII.). It is also a man's name, 'the worshipper' of God. The name applies to a group of three ruins west of 'Ammân, built, like most in the vicinity, of rude flint blocks of no great size. A few walls are standing, and are conspicuous dark objects. There are also foundations, and at the principal ruin, to which the name is written, are remains of a small dolmen (compare those under head 'A m m â n,  G. H. I., p. 25).

A b u  e l  'A d i s  (ابو العدس, perhaps 'father of lentils ').—A hill-top near Minyeh, in the southern part of the work.

A b u  e l  H a s n  (ابو الحسن, 'father of grace').—The name, said to have been that of a Sultan who visited the spot, is apparently applied to a spur close to the last.

A b u  e l  K e r r â m  (ابو الكرّم, 'father of stumps').—On the edge of the forest north of 'Arâk el Emir, where the local Arabs have cut down many oaks and terebinths for fire-wood.

I

Abu el Kâuwûkah (ابوالكاووقه, 'father of hootings of owls').—
This is a sacred place—a tomb enclosed in a circle, with a lintel or altar on the west like those described at 'Ain Hesbân. It stands in flat ground with trees in the valley north of Umm Kuseir. It is omitted on the reduced map for want of space.

Abu Lôzeh (ابو لوزه, 'father of the almond-tree ').—This is a similar sacred place beside the road due east of 'Arâk el Emir. The lintel-stone is on the west, and ploughs, etc., were stored inside the circle. There are some rude cave tombs in the rock to the north.

Abu en Naml (ابو النمل, 'father of ants ').—A plot of ground in the valley west of 'Arâk el Emir (compare Wâdy Abu en Naml).

Abu Nuseir (ابو نصير, proper name. The term Nusr, of which this is the diminutive, is specially applied in the Korân to those who were converted to Islam in Medina after the Hejira. Sura lxi. 14, etc.)— This name applies to a sacred tree near Shânab, on the north-west. It is omitted from the reduced map for want of space, and because unimportant.

Abu Raghif (ابو رغيف, 'father of the cake ').—A small Arab graveyard near Minyeh.

Abu Safa (ابو صفا, 'father of clearness,' or of 'shining').—Applies to a cliff on the south side of West Kefrein.

Abu Shiyâh (ابو شياح, perhaps 'father of the wormwood plants,' Artemisia Judaica شيح).—A hillside south of Wâdy Jideid.

Abu Tineh (ابو تينه, 'father of the fig-tree ').—A hillside north of Wâdy Bahhâth, probably from a wild fig, many of which occur in the district. This spur is south of Khûrbet ed Dubbeh. It is omitted from the reduced map for want of space.

Abu Zagheileh (ابو زغيله, 'father of squirting').—Traces of ruins east of Minyeh.

El 'Adeimeh (العضيمه, 'the streak,' i.e., a patch of colour differing from the rest, Lane).—A cliff at the edge of the Jordan plain, with a clump of canes in the valley-bed below. In autumn there is no water, but in spring the supply is said to be good.

## Springs.

In addition to 'Ain and Ayûn, see under the heads el Bassah, Bir, Hammâm, el 'Ameireh, Barrakât, 'Adeimeh, Dereibeh, el Gharbeh. The fine water supply is one of the great features of the country. Every large valley has a stream, generally perennial, including the Zerka Mâ'ain, Wâdy Jideid, Wâdy 'Ayûn Mûsa, Wâdy Hesbân, Wâdy Nâ'aûr, Wâdy Sir, Wâdy Nimrin, and Wâdy 'Ammân. There are upwards of seventy springs and perennial wells in the district, and in most of these the water is good, cool, and perennial. The plateau of Moab consists of soft chalk; and the springs are found on the slopes some 500 feet lower down, where the hard dolomitic limestone crops out. The 'Ammân stream (the head of the Jabbok) issues in the same way on the surface of the harder formation, about the same level, 2,440 feet above the Mediterranean.

'Ain el 'Abbâdeh (عين العبّادة, 'spring of the 'Abbâdeh Arabs,' a small branch of the 'Adwân).—A very small spring in Wâdy Jeriâh.

'Ain Abu Turfah (عين ابو طرفة, 'spring of the tamarisk ').—A small spring dripping down the rocks in the valley of the same name, and supplying el Bassah farther down. The water is said to be good and cold.

'Ain Abu 'Oneiz (عين ابو عنيز, 'spring of little goats ').—A small spring north of Shânab. The water is cold and good.

'Ain 'Adeisiyeh (عين عديسة, perhaps 'spring of lentils ').—Near the last. A perennial spring of fair supply, flowing from the rock. The water is cold and good. A dolmen, or cromlech, was found near it by Mr. Armstrong. Near the spring, also, Lieutenant Mantell found six rock-cut tombs, like those near Sûmia. The first was $5\frac{1}{2}$ feet long, 1 foot 10 inches broad, $2\frac{1}{2}$ feet high, and roughly cut; a second was $7\frac{1}{2}$ feet long, $3\frac{1}{2}$ feet broad, and $3\frac{1}{2}$ feet high; the other four were of the same class. The doors in each case were at the north end of the chambers, which are cut in a cliff on the south side of the valley. On the hill to the south are traces of an old rujm, or cairn, and there are rough steps quarried in the hillside.

'Ain 'Ajeirmân (عين عجيرمان, 'spring of the 'Ajermeh Arabs '— a small tribe under the 'Adwân).—This is in the valley of the same name, south of Minyeh, and was found to contain a perennial supply of fairly good water rising among rushes and bushes.

'Ain 'Ammân.—This, with its perennial stream, is specially described under 'Ammân.

'Ain 'Arûs (عين عروس, 'bride's spring').—Near the Dead Sea. Only a very small supply was found in October, but the water is cold and good; and the growth of canes which covers it shows that in spring there must be a large supply. It is curious to note how many springs in Western Palestine have this same name. One occurs in the Jordan valley nearly opposite that now noticed.

'Ain el Baheirah (عين البحيرة, 'spring of the pool,' or 'lake'). —A small supply of good water on the north side of Wâdy Nâaûr.

'Ain el Bahhâth (عين البحّاث, 'spring of the scrapers-up of earth,' Lane).—In the valley of the same name; a good perennial supply, sufficient to turn a mill. The ruins of several mills occur in the valley lower down, and some are yet worked by the Bedawîn for grinding flour. There is a waterfall in the valley near them. The stream joins that of Wâdy Nâaûr.

'Ain el Bawâti (عين البواطي, 'spring of the wooden bowls'—as explained on the spot).—Near 'Ain 'Adeisîyeh; a very small supply. It is omitted from the reduced map for want of space.

'Ain el Beida (عين البيضا, 'white spring').—A small spring at the extreme north edge of the Survey. It is perennial, and the water is cold but not very good.

'Ain el Bûeirdeh (عين البويردة, 'the cold spring').—Just below the mill at Sûmia; a small perennial supply of cold water issuing from the rock in the ravine.

'Ain el Fejîreh (عين الفجيرة, 'spring of the stream').—A small supply of good water was found here in September, beside the stream of Wâdy Nâaûr.

'Ain el Fudeili (عين الفضيلي, 'the excellent spring').—A very fine supply of clear, cold water issuing under rocks and boulders, making a small pool with gravelly bottom, and running to the brook of Wâdy Hesbân. This is the favourite autumn camp of Sheikh Kablân en Nimr, and the Survey camp was established near it from September 10 to 20. There are remains of the foundations of a small building west of the spring, which issues in a flat open part of the valley, with coarse turf round it. Numerous dams and lades lead from the spring towards the remains of former irrigated places. Traces of one little aqueduct lead to the Jineinet Belkis, or 'Zenobia's garden,' which is a mere barren plot. About 300 yards farther west on the south side of the valley is a rock-cut wine-press. Though now so barren, this spot was once cultivated, and probably covered with vineyards, as the hills on the south appear also to have been. This may have been in the Roman or Byzantine ages, when the settled population was evidently a thick one. Explored September 20, 1881.

RIVER JABBOK.

'Ain el Ghazâl (عين الغزال, 'gazelle's spring ').—A large supply of water, perennial and fresh, issuing in a pool with a pebbly bottom surrounded with oleander bushes. This, with 'Ain 'Ammân and 'Ain er Raseifeh, is the principal supply of the Jabbok. In autumn, the stream from 'Ain 'Ammân disappears in the rocky bed of the valley about a mile and a half from the town. The stream recommences at 'Ain Ghazâl, and flows about 5 miles, when it again sinks into the ground; and the stream from 'Ain er Raseifeh disappears in the same way. The flow from the 'Ain ez Zerka to Jordan is perennial. In the early spring the stream is continuous all the way from 'Ain 'Ammân. It is called Wâdy 'Ammân as far as 'Ain ez Zerka, and from that point it becomes Wâdy Zerka Shebib.

'Ain el Hammâm (عين الحمّام, 'spring of the bath ').—A good supply of cold water, not perennial, and found quite dry on October 11, 1881. It is in the valley of the same name, at the north edge of the Survey. In winter it produces a good stream down the ravine.

'Ain Hebbeseh (عين حبسه). The root means to 'enclose,' or 'imprison ').—A small supply close to Tell Hebbeseh, whence it is apparently named. The water trickles towards Wâdy Kefrein. It was visited in October.

'Ain el Hekr (عين الحكر, 'spring of the enclosed land,' Lane\*).— A little pit containing muddy water at the head of the valley called Hekr. There is turf in the vicinity, and it is at the edge of the 'Amrîyeh wood of oak and terebinth. Probably in spring the supply is more abundant.

\* Hakûrah is a Syrian word for a 'garden.'

# THE SURVEY OF EASTERN PALESTINE

'Ain Hesbân (عين حسبان, 'spring of Heshbon').—The Survey camp was fixed south of this spring from August 17, 1881, to September 10. The water rises at the foot of a low cliff in the west side of a narrow valley, and forms a shallow pool amid large boulders. It flows thence in a stream about 10 feet wide, southwards, at the rate of some 2 or 3 miles an hour. The brook is shallow, but very clear, with a shingly bed, and it is full of small fish. Near the spring are clumps of oleander, and an Arab graveyard. The surrounding hills are very barren, consisting of

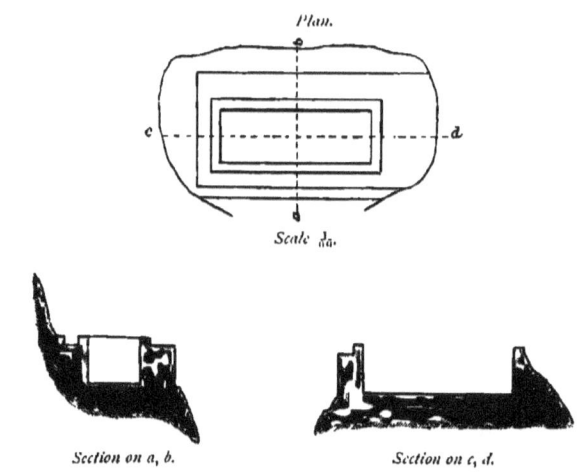

Section on a, b.   Section on c, d.
Rock Sarcophagus, 'Ain Hesbân.

gray chalky limestone. In the upper part of the valley are the ruins of Shûnet edh Dhiâbeh and Shûnet Sukr, mentioned under those heads respectively. Higher up the stream are remains of masonry channels, which may have led to pools or mills now destroyed; but there is no indication of the date of these remains. A sarcophagus cut in the rock was found in the same vicinity.

The cemetery is on the east, or left bank, close to the spring. In addition to some rude graves resembling those common in the Moslem towns west of Jordan, there are two graves of greater importance, surrounded with circles. Of one of these (the southern) Lieutenant Mantell obtained a photograph. The northern circle is 9 paces in diameter, and is formed by a dry stone wall some 3 feet high of unshaped stones rudely piled up. On the west is a little trilithon, consisting of three stones taken from some ruin in the vicinity, and dressed for their original purpose. The side stones are 2 feet high, and 2 feet apart; the top stone is about 3 feet long. The second, or southern circle, is about

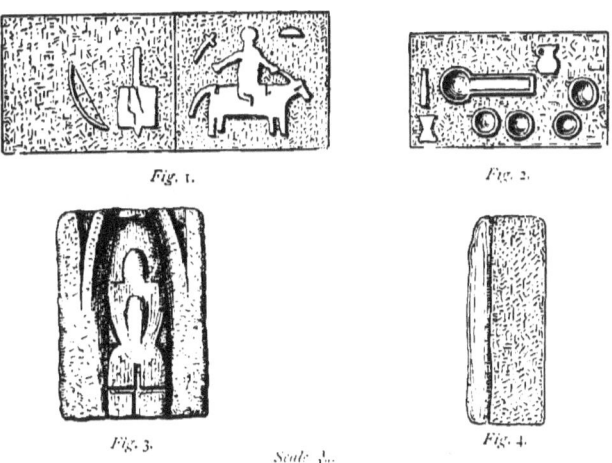

*Fig.* 1.   *Fig.* 2.

*Fig.* 3.   *Fig.* 4.
Scale 1/12.

FIGS. 1, 2.—RELIEFS ON ARAB TOMB.   FIGS. 3, 4.—RELIEFS ON HEADSTONE.

9 paces in diameter, and consists of large blocks (as shown in the photograph) measuring in some cases 4 feet in length by 2½ feet in height. This has also a trilithon altar, or gate, on the west, on which were found small offerings consisting of glass beads and pottery chips. A wooden coffee-mortar had been placed on the same capstone, whether as a votive offering or for protection was not ascertained. The trilithon stones were squared ashlar in this as in the former case, and in each instance the W u s m, or tribe-mark, of the 'Ajermeh Arabs (who inhabit the surrounding district) was cut on the altar-stones—ارْ جل. It is cut either way up, and is called the Mehjan, or 'crook.' This title applies apparently to the

hook-shaped figure, while the single stroke is intended for a numeral, showing that the dead man belonged to the eldest family of the tribe.

Near the northern circle (which, like the southern, encloses an ordinary grave) there is a peculiar headstone to a grave with a pattern carved on it. The stone is well hewn, 7 inches thick, 18 inches high, and 13 inches wide; the carving projects 2 inches, and seems rudely to suggest a human figure, with a cross below. The cross is also found on an Arab grave at 'Ain 'Ammân. Close by is a well-built modern tomb of Sheikh Shehâb el Fuliyeh, who has been buried beside the older sacred circles. His tomb resembles those at Kefrein and Kabr 'Abdallah. This tomb has

ARAB CIRCLE NEAR HESHBON.

also the same tribe-mark upon it—that of the 'Ajermeh ; it is built of cut stones, but not whitewashed or plastered. On one side is a stone 2¼ feet long and 1 foot high, on which are carved in relief—projecting about a quarter of an inch—rude designs representing a bow, a coffee-mortar and pestle, and finally a man on a horse with a sword and a bow above him. There are traces of geometrical designs and raised bosses on other stones, which probably come from some older building. At the end of the tomb lies a fallen stone 1½ feet long and 10 inches high, and on this are rudely carved representations of a coffee-mortar and pestle, four coffee-cups, or finâjîn, and a spoon (Mihmasah) for roasting, and a little jug or pot for boiling the coffee

These designs are modern Arab work, and are interesting, first because they are intended by an illiterate people to be symbols of the warlike valour and of the hospitable character of the chief here buried, and secondly because the representation of the man and horse shows that the 'Ajermeh at least are not strict Moslems. The symbols were explained by the Bedawîn. The spring, like others, appears to be a sacred spot.

On the banks of the stream many flint chips were found, and a few of these seemed possibly to be artificial flakes.

'Ain el Jâmûs (عين الجاموس, 'spring of the buffalo ').—A green patch of turf with a small spring of bad water.

'Ain el Jemmâleh (عين الجمّالة, 'spring of the camel-drivers '). —A small patch of grass with bad water. The supply is not perennial.

'Ain Jeriâh (عين جريعه, 'spring of the single draught of water '). —A small spring in the bottom of the valley surrounded by a few reeds and rushes. A muddy stream was found in October flowing thence some 30 or 40 yards. The pool is dammed up with stones. Close by is the Hajr ed Dûmîyeh, which see. This is close to Kh. es Sûr, west of 'Arâk el Emîr.

'Ain Jideid (عين جديد).—In Arabic this means ' the new spring.' The Arabic root also means ' to be great or plentiful.' Professor Palmer (Name Lists, p. 2) suggests ' a vein, or dyke ' (geologically so called); but this never applies to the springs so named. The best rendering is probably ' the copious.' The description of 'Ain Jideid and its ruins is given under Hadânieh.

'Ain Jûrat el Haiyeh (عين جورة الحية, 'spring of the snake's hole ').—This was not visited; it is quite a small spring, with a little patch of green round it.

'Ain el Khalfeh (عين الخلفة; see el Khalfeh).—A little spring south of a group of dolmens on north side of Wâdy Hesbân. It rises in open ground, and the supply is perennial, with good water.

'Ain el Khalifeh (عين الخليفة, ' the Khalif's spring ').—A small spring in Wâdy Jeriâh. Khalifeh may, however, mean ' valley ' (Freytag Lex.).

'Ain el Kharrâr (عين الخرّار, 'murmuring spring ').—A small spring close to Jordan, not visited. It is in the jungle at the edge of the Zôr, or lower bed of the river.

'Ain Kuseib (عين قصيب, 'spring of the cane,' diminutive form).—A very small spring, not visited.

'Ain Máit (عين معيط, apparently 'the spring sometimes dry;' see Freytag Lex.).—In Wády Zerka Máǎin, close to el Habis; a small spring, not visited.

'Ain Matábá (عين مطابع; see Tell el Matábá).—A small supply, with water trickling into Wády er Rámeh.

'Ain el Meheiyineh (عين المهيّنة, apparently from a plant).—A small spring, with water trickling into Wády el Kefrein.

'Ain el Meiyiteh (عين الميّتة, 'dead spring').—A green patch, with water said to be good and perennial. It is marked 'Ain on the reduced map west of Shánab.

'Ain el Merussus (عين المرصّص, 'spring of the place of pebbles').—A small supply of good cold water, apparently perennial. It is in a small valley-head west of Kh. el Merussus, and is marked 'Ain on the reduced map.

'Ain el Meshabbah (عين المشبّة, apparently 'spring of the lioness,' Lane).—A small spring, not visited. See Wády el Meshabbeh.

'Ain el Minyeh (عين المنية, 'spring of desire').—This is a perennial spring of good cold water. The supply in autumn is small, and it rises in a shallow masonry well on the slope of the hill. A stunted thorn-tree grows beside it. Rather higher up on the slope, on the south, is a modern white tomb of one of the Sheikhs of the 'Awâzim Arabs.

The crest of the ridge is 400 feet above the spring towards the east, and a conspicuous knoll, called Tuweiyil el 'Azzâm (طويل العزّام, 'the lion's peak'), here exists south of the spring, commanding a fine view of the Dead Sea and of the Jordan Valley. About ¾ mile north-east of this knoll is the highest point of the ridge, called Talât el Benât, or 'Ascent of the Maidens,' and between these two points there is a line of seven monuments extending in a north-east direction over a distance of about ½ mile. No name is given to them by the Arabs, nor do they seem to know of any tradition connected with them. They regard them simply as Munâtir, or 'watch-towers,' of great antiquity, and the same term is applied by many of the 'Adwân to the dolmens.

The number of these monuments, as counted by Mr. G. Armstrong, is seven; but most of them are in a very confused condition of ruin. The most distinguishable is the seventh from the north, which was photographed by Lieutenant Mantell (No. 8 of his series). He draws attention

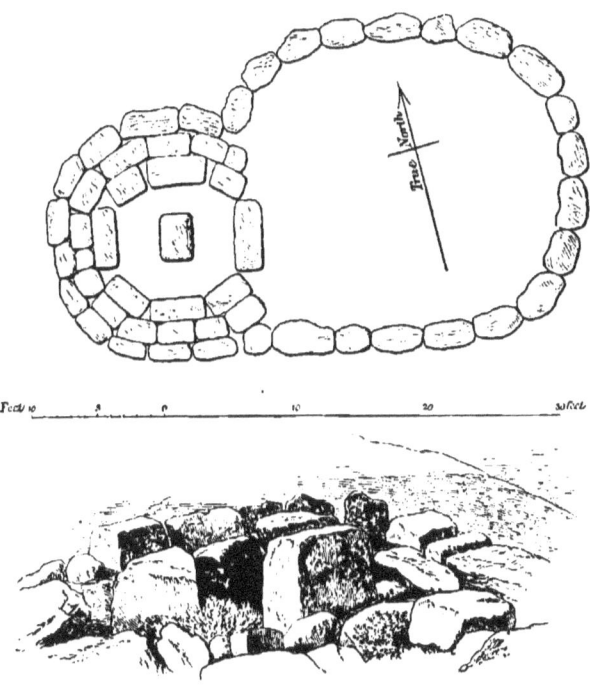

el Minyeh
PLAN of Stone Circle

in his remarks ('Quarterly Statement,' July, 1882, p. 173) to the fact that a similar monument (which he discovered) exists in the Jordan Valley (see el Mâberah). The four southern monuments are close together; the three others are rather further to the north, and more widely separated from each other (as shown on the Survey map).

2—2

The monument measured is a rude polygon (see Plan) about 8 feet in interior diameter, with a central cubical stone measuring 3 feet 4 inches by 2 feet 5 inches, and 3½ feet high. The central stone, and many of those in the enclosure, appear to be rudely hewn. The thickness of the wall is about 5 feet, and the present height 3 feet. The original height appears to have been at least 4 feet, with two courses of stones. The blocks used are as large as, or larger than, the central stone. On the east is a little enclosure, or court, made by a single line of stones, about 30 feet in diameter. The stones in this enclosure are rather smaller.

In other examples, the central cubical stone was also still visible, and near one of the circles, just outside, is a flat rock, in which was sunk a cavity, evidently artificial, 1½ feet long, 1 foot broad, and 3 inches deep, resembling the hollows found in rocks beside dolmens, or in the capstone of the dolmen itself.

The theories suggested by these remains are fully noticed in 'Heth and Moab' (chap. iv., pp. 143, 252). The site is appropriate topographically for that of Baal Peor (Numbers xxiii. 28). The 'spring of desire' gets its name from a tradition that it was made by the spear of Imâm 'Aly.

'Seated on the edge of the cliff of Minyeh, beside the seven circles with altar-stones, we looked down on the brown and utterly arid plateau which runs to the top of the eastern cliffs, beyond which the Dead Sea lies calm and shining.

'In this plateau is the black basalt outbreak called Hammet Minyeh; and not far below us, on the slope, is the spring-well of Minyeh, with its stunted thorn. It was here that Abu Wundi, the hale and cheerful old Sheikh of the 'Awâzim Arabs, began to tell us the first fairy-tales we had heard beyond Jordan. The black natural fortress, he said, was once the city of 'Antar, the black hero whose woes and dolorous love-songs are said to fill forty-five volumes of Arab poetry. To the spot on which we sat came once the wandering 'Aly, "the Lion of God," son of Abu Taleb, and husband of the Prophet's daughter Fatimah, one of the first converts to Islam, whose claims to the Khalifate originated the great schism of Shi'ah and Sunnee. He has become in Persia, and even in Syria, a mythical hero whose name is often substituted for that of Moses, Joshua, or Samson in perverted versions of Old Testament histories. 'Aly, riding his horse Maimûn, reached Minyeh in a state of exhaustion, and prayed to Allah that he might die. He was, however, commanded to strike the earth with his spear, when at once the fountain of Minyeh welled up, and 'Aly drank and was refreshed. Minyeh signifies "desire" or "wish," and the wishing-well was here so named, according to the Arabs, because it arose at the desire of 'Aly.

'Further instructed by Allah, 'Aly descended to the Hammet Minyeh and cried out for 'Antar ("the Spearer"), when suddenly fifteen hundred black men rose up, each saying, "I

LEGEND OF 'ALY 13

am 'Antar! We are all 'Antars!" 'Aly, again divinely instructed, asked for the 'Antar whose father was Shadid ("the Strong One"), and his mother Zebibeh, or the 'Sea Foam,' and this host he at length found, and was invited to enter his house. Here he perceived a woman hanging to the beam of the roof, to which she was tied by her long eyelashes, and, being astonished at such cruelty, he demanded who she was. "She is my mother," said 'Antar, "and I hung her up because she hates and curses strangers." 'Aly begged that she might be taken down, which was no sooner done than she began to revile the guest at whose asking she had been released. "Hang her up again!" said 'Aly; and this was also done, after which 'Aly and Maimûn were alike courteously treated, and he remained the guest of 'Antar for three days, according to the law of the Prophet.

'"It was after this," said Abu Wundi, "that he went forth and took the City of Copper" —a legend we had already heard at Jericho. Here (as I have previously related) stood the copper or brazen city of the infidels, where now the single enormous tamarisk marks the site of Gilgal. Round the brazen walls (as the Abu Nuseir Arabs told us in 1873) 'Aly rode on Maimûn seven times, and, blowing upon them with his breath, they at once disappeared, and the faithful pursued the infidel westwards to Koruntil. The sun was about to set behind the cliff of that mountain, when 'Aly cried to it, "Return, O blessed one!" and the sun stood still until the infidels were slain.

'This tale differs from others in one respect, that it presents affinities to three Old Testament episodes—namely, the Rock of Rephidim, the fall of Jericho, and the miracle of Gibeon; while many others of its features are clearly akin to the Persian mythology. It cannot well be supposed that the tradition preserved is indigenous, because the Arabs, to whom alone such tales are peculiar (none of the same class being known to the Fellahin), are a people who emigrated in post-Christian times from the Hejaz and from Yemen into Syria. There is, however, a very simple explanation possible of the existence of Bible stories among the Bedawin, and one which appears to be supported by the fact that a mediæval monkish legend is certainly preserved among the Abu Nuseir. The "high mountain" of the Temptation was shown in the twelfth century at the curious peak called 'Osh el Ghurâb, or "Raven's Nest," north of Jericho, although its summit is 300 feet below the level of the Mediterranean; and this place is still called "The Ascent of Jesus" by the Bedawin. East of Jordan, also, we must not forget that a Christian colony founded by the Crusaders still survives at Kerak; and it was, no doubt, from the priests or monks of this fortress that the Arabs first learned the history of Moses and Joshua, which they have gradually confused with legends of 'Aly and 'Antar, although retaining some indistinct remembrance of the localities which led to their belief in a city of brass or of copper, which they place at the true site of Israel's camp, and not far from the Jericho whose walls are related to have fallen before the blast of Hebrew trumpets.'—Conder's 'Heth and Moab,' pp. 347-350.

Explored October 1, 1881.

'Ain el Mûciniyeh (عين المؤنيه, 'spring of the storehouse'). —A perennial supply of water, with a small stream trickling through grass some 50 yards to join the main stream in the valley below 'Arâk el Emîr.

'Ain Nââûr (عين ناعور, 'spring of the Naurah, or water-wheel'). —A fine perennial supply of water issues from under rocks into a pool, or basin, with a gravelly bed. When visited, the temperature was 67° Fah., that of the air being about 80° Fah. The spring is north-west of the houses of Khŭrbet Nâаûr. There are several smaller springs in the valley. The stream falls over a precipice about 50 feet high, making a very picturesque waterfall near the houses. The camp was pitched here on the night of October 4, 1881.

'Ain en Nusûry (عين السوري, 'spring of eagles'; see 'Arâk en Nusûry).—A small spring under the cliff, not visited.

'Ain er Raseifeh (عين الرصيفة, 'spring of pebbles;' Hebrew רצף, 'a stone ').—A large spring like 'Ain Ghazâl. The stream hence runs for 5 miles in autumn, then sinks into the ground (see the account under 'Ain Ghazâl).

'Ain esh Shidkah (عين الشدقة, probably from شدق, the side of a valley).—A group of small springs, not visited.

'Ain (Wâdy) esh Shita (see Wâdy esh Shita).—A good perennial spring, whence in winter a stream flows down the valley. It is west of er Ramleh, and is marked 'Ain on the reduced map in the valley of Wâdy esh Shita.

'Ain es Sîr (عين السير), 'spring of the fold;' see Kh. es Sîr).—A good perennial supply of cold water, which is the head spring of the stream in Wâdy es Sîr, to which, however, other springs contribute.

'Ain es Sûeimeh (see Khŭrbet es Sûeimeh).—This is a copious salt spring. It was visited in the end of October, and was found to have a temperature of 80° Fah., the air being about 100° Fah. It was drinkable, though brackish, and is perennial.

'Ain Sûmia, see Sûmia, where this spring is described.

'Ain et Terâbîl (عين الطرابيل. The word طربيل means a threshing-sledge, called in Western Palestine Nûrej, or Mûrej).—A small spring, not visited, but seen.

'Ain et Terki, by Butmet et Terki.—A little pool of muddy water, cold and perennial.

'Ain eth Thoghrah.—A small spring near the Thoghret es Sâjûr. Not visited, but seen.

'Ain Umm 'Abâh (عين امّ عَباه, 'spring of the Aba, or cloak.' It might also mean 'spring of shining').—A small spring at the valley head, seen, but not visited.

'Ain Umm el Kenâfid (see Umm el Kenâfid).—A little pool of dirty water in the rocky bed of the valley, with a fair supply.

'Ain Umm 'Olleik (عين امّ عُلَيْق, 'spring of little cell;' see Muâllakat ed Deir).—A small marshy landspring.

'Ain Umm Tineh (عين امّ تِينَه, 'spring of the fig-tree').—This is a conspicuous spring in the cliff north of Wâdy Hesbân. A fine wild fig grows up against the rock, and is a conspicuous object. The place is almost inaccessible, and it was not visited. It is not marked on the reduced plan, but is close to 'Ain Nusûry, which is marked.

'Ain Umm Zeitûneh (عين امّ زيتونه, 'spring of the olive tree').—A good supply of cold water. It is not a large spring, but perennial.

'Ain Wasâdeh (عين وسادَه, 'spring of the pillow').—In Wâdy en Nefiâiyeh; not visited.

'Ain Yâjûz (see Khŭrbet Yâjûz).—A good supply of cold water, perennial.

'Ain ez Zerka (عين الزرقا, 'blue spring').—This is the principal supply of the Wâdy Zerka Mââin, on the south extremity of the work. The springs were visited on October 3, and were found to be distinctly thermal, the water being 89° Fah., while the air was 74° Fah. The water rises in the bed of the valley in pools, with a gravelly bed, and small fish are found in these. Fine clumps of oleanders and other small trees form a shade round the springs. The Arab women wash clothes here, and the water is also drunk. The banks of the valley are here very steep, but the horses were taken down from el Mareighât to the springs. On the north side there are caves in the hillside, which are used by the Arab shepherds. The scenery of the valley is here very bare and featureless. A good picture is given in Canon Tristram's 'Land of Moab' (p. 230).

El Ahma (الأحمى, 'the defended,' or 'the inaccessible').—This is the same name given to the plateau above the cliffs west of Tiberias. It applies in the present case, as in the former, to a flat plateau.

El 'Ajemy (العجمي, 'the stranger ').—This word 'Ajem applies to all non-Arab speaking countries, but more especially to Persia. It here marks a sacred place near Tell el Hammâm in the Jordan Valley. It is west of the Tell, and is omitted from the reduced map for want of space.

'Akweh (عكوه, 'high ').—The name of a hill with dolmens (see Tell el Matâbá) east of the Mensef Abu Zeid in the Jordan Valley.

### ELEALEH.

El 'Âl (العال).—This is recognised as the Hebrew Elealeh, עלעלה (Numbers xxxii. 37), and was known to Eusebius ('Onomasticon') as being a mile from Heshbon. The modern meaning, 'the lofty,' is derived from the conspicuous position of the Tell in the ruin, on which a Survey cairn was erected in 1881. It stands south of a very flat plateau, which also extends on the east and south. A broad camel-track from the 'Ain Hesbân approaches from the west, and a good specimen of a rock-cut winepress is to be noticed beside this road, showing that (as mentioned in the Old Testament, Isaiah xvi. 9; Jeremiah xlviii. 34) the vicinity was once cultivated.

The ruins cover the top and slopes of the Tell, or mound. On the flat summit there is a modern Arab graveyard, with two circles enclosing graves (as at 'Ain Hesbân, which see). One of these is dedicated to Sheikh Râshed. It is 8 paces in diameter, and the drystone wall is from 1 foot to 2 feet high, built of unhewn stones about 1 foot in diameter. The door, or altar, is on the west side, consisting of two jambs 1½ feet high, and a capstone, all three being of cut stone taken from the ruins. Beads, pottery, glass, china, basalt chips, are placed on the capstone, and a plough was found inside—left there for protection.

The ruin is about 100 yards in diameter; but only the foundations and lower courses of the masonry are left belonging to private houses and enclosed courts. The masonry is chiefly of unsquared stones, varying from 1 foot to 5 feet in length. On the south-east are cisterns, and a solitary pillar stands up on the slope on this side. On closer inspection, this appeared to have formed part of a basilica, or temple, with a nave 18 feet wide in the clear, and a south aisle 12 feet wide. The south wall was traceable, and the position of one pillar on the north side of the nave, but the length and north boundary of the building were not distinguishable. The pillar still standing is 7 feet 3 inches in height, and 19 inches in diameter; the capital has fallen.

There are many drystone enclosures of large stones, but these may, perhaps, be later reconstructions. Among them was found a rude capital of debased classic style, which seemed probably to have belonged to the colonnaded building just mentioned. About 130 paces south of the single pillar in this building are remains of another building, possibly a chapel, though no apse was found on the east. It measured 23 feet in width north and south, and seems to have been 35 feet long. On the north side is a door

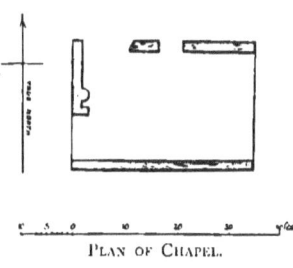

PLAN OF CHAPEL.

4 feet 7 inches wide; on the west wall, inside, a semi-column is visible, 2 feet 4 inches in diameter, and 1½ feet in projection. This seems to indicate a division into two walks by a line of pillars running east and west. There seems to have been a western entrance south of this pillar. The walls of the building are 1 foot 10 inches thick. Outside, on the north, was found the fallen lintel of the north door with an Ionic capital,

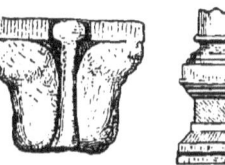 

and a pillar-base and stool. There is another Ionic capital fallen on the south. All these were measured and drawn. The lintel resembles many others in Roman and Byzantine buildings, the stone being 5 feet 1 inch long, and 1 foot 6 inches high. The principal moulding projects 1½ inches. On the under side is a hinge socket 7½ inches in diameter.

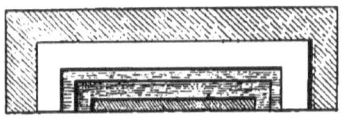

The two capitals differ from one another, both being rudely Ionic, one 10 inches in diameter of the shaft, the other 15 inches. They somewhat resemble the capital at Khûrbet Siâghah (which see), and

are quite different from the Ionic of the Kŭsr en Nueijis, which is of purer style. They may perhaps be referred to the early Christian period (fourth and fifth centuries). The stool and base recall the remains of the Byzantine Church of St. John at Beit Jibrin ('Memoirs, Western Survey,' vol. iii., p. 276). A stone was

measured in the north wall of this building 4½ feet long, 1 foot 9 inches high, 1 foot 10 inches thick. It had an irregular draft 4 inches to 5 inches wide, and a boss projecting about 1 inch, dressed smooth, but much worn.

Immediately north of this building there is a rude cave-cistern, and beside it, remains apparently of a small stone handmill. About 50 yards

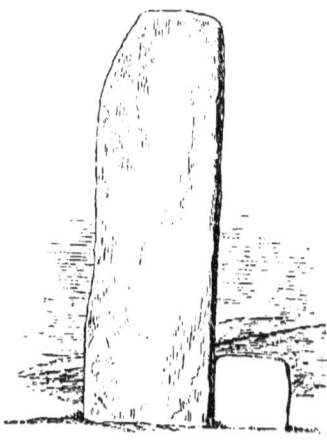

south-east of the building just described is a rude enclosure, and on its east side traces of foundations. A stone here erected like a menhir may have been the jamb of a doorway, but is, perhaps, intended as a memorial stone (cf. Kefeir Abu Sarbût, and Hajr el Mansûb). It is 1 foot 11 inches in diameter at the bottom, and 6 feet high. On the north side it is steadied by a short pillar-stump about 1½ feet in diameter.

Near this curious stone are many caves and vaults, and there seem to have been others under the Tell (as also at Mâàin). The ruin called Madowerat el 'Âl is treated under that head; it seems to have been the quarry whence the stones at el 'Âl were obtained. The ground immediately east of Elealeh is a chalky limestone, and is strewn with flints and fragments of chert. The general impression obtained by examination of the ruins at this site is that a Byzantine town here existed, as known to Eusebius; and that nothing remaining, unless it be the menhir, is of greater antiquity than the fourth century.

Visited August 23, 1881.

'A l w â n (علوان).—See Hesbân.

E l 'A m e i r e h (العميرة, 'the perpetual') is so called from the existence of a good perennial spring well at the site. It is the boundary between the Beni Sakhr (who camp here) and the 'Adwân. There are three Tells or mounds with ruins north of the well, but nothing distinguishable was observed on them. The well could not be visited, being in possession of the personal enemies of Captain Conder's guide, Sheikh Kablân en Nimr. Sir C. Warren appears to have camped here (see 'Quarterly Statement,' 1870, p. 29). The Bedawin often pronounce this name 'Amweireh, and M. Clermont Ganneau notices the same peculiar pronunciation of the Y, as in 'Obweideh for 'Obeideh, or b u e i n for b e i n ('Quarterly Statement,' 1874, p. 172).

## Rabbath Ammon.

'A m m â n (عمّان, the Hebrew רבת בני עמון, 'capital of the sons of Ammon,' Deut. iii. 11; Josh. xiii. 25; 2 Sam. xii. 26; Jer. xlix. 2; Ezek. xxi. 20; xxv. 5; Amos i. 14).—This is the later Philadelphia, under which name it was known to Ptolemy and Josephus. It was one of the chief cities of Decapolis (see Reland's 'Palestine,' vol. i., p. 203). In the fifth century it was an episcopal city; in consequence, however, of its secluded position it does not appear prominently in history. In David's time there appears to have been an upper and lower town (2 Sam. xii. 26, 27), and its palaces (אַרְמוֹן), or lofty fortifications, are mentioned by Amos (i. 14).

An epitome of what is known of the history of 'Ammân is given by Dr. Grove (Smith's 'Bible Dictionary,' vol. ii., p. 983, *et seq.*). The name Philadelphia is said to have been given in honour of Ptolemy Philadelphus (B.C. 285-247), according to Jerome (on Ezek. xxv. 1). Josephus says the surrounding district was called Philadelphene (3 'Wars,' iii. 3).

3—2

The episcopal See was subordinate to that of Bozrah (Reland's 'Palestine,' vol. i., p. 228).

Coins of the city exist, having the head of Marcus Aurelius (161-180 A.D.) and the legend 'Philadelphia of Hercules of Cœle Syria.' (Compare the inscription of the milestone at Rujûm Rafiâh, under that name.)

The remains to be described under this head are of five classes, viz.: 1st, Prehistoric monuments; 2nd, Hebrew or 'Ammonite structures; 3rd, Roman; 4th, Byzantine; 5th, Arab. There appear to be no traces of Crusading work, but with this exception all the great periods of Syrian architecture are represented at 'Ammân by important remains.

*The Prehistoric Period.*—The rude stone monuments of 'Ammân include fifteen examples in all, of which ten are dolmens and six menhirs.

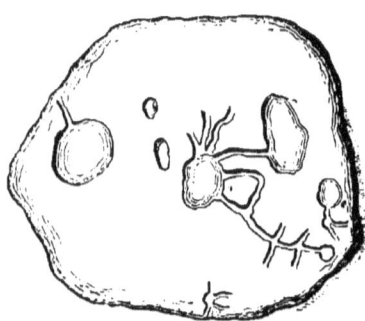

*Plan of Dolmen A.*

The first example stands alone on the south, and is marked on the hill west of Khŭrbet 'Aisheh, and east of Rujm el Misdâr. It is a demi-dolmen of great size, and was photographed by Lieutenant Mantell. The capstone measures 13 feet east and west by 11 feet north and south, and the mean thickness is about 20 inches. A curious system of channels and hollows was noticed in the capstone, and carefully drawn. Near the middle of the stone is a hollow 26 inches by 20 inches, and 12 inches deep; near the west end, which is the highest, is a hollow 1 foot square. In the flat rock beside the monument is a shallow double pan, each hollow about 20 inches in diameter, with a channel between. The western end-stone of this dolmen is 6 feet high and 5 feet broad, and the sidestone on the north is 11 feet long and 8 feet high. The monument is close to the upper part of the west slope of the hill, with a rocky ravine beneath. This dolmen is of limestone of medium hardness (see Plan and Sketches, Dolmen A).

The next group of dolmens is that shown on the special Survey of 'Ammân west of the citadel hill. They are situated on the southern slope of the hill, and built of chert or flint-like rock, which occurs in bands in the chalk. These monuments include four large dolmens and one small

*Dolmen A from S.E.*

one, and these stand in a rude circle of about 200 yards diameter, although this may be accidental. They are due east of the great menhir on the opposite hill.

The first, or furthest east, is a rough trilithon which was sketched and also unsuccessfully photographed. The capstone is 12 feet long, north and south, and 6 feet wide. The clear height beneath is $3\frac{1}{2}$ feet, and the clear width $2\frac{1}{2}$ feet. The length of the sidestones is about 10 feet. There is no floorstone or endstone, and the blocks of chert are exceedingly rough and irregular in shape. This is marked B on the special Survey.

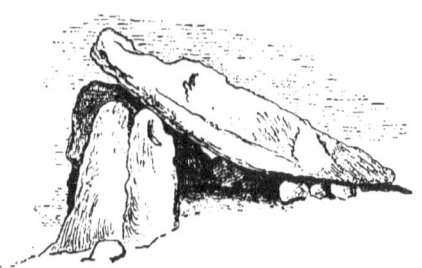

*Dolmen A from E.*

The second, further down the hill, marked C on the special Survey, and more to the west, was successfully photographed from the south-east (No. 379, P. E. Fund's list; frontispiece, 'Quarterly Statement,' 1882,

p. 176). The capstone is 8 feet square and 2 feet thick, and in its upper surface there is near the west end a large hollow 2½ feet by 1 foot, and 3 inches deep. There are several other smaller hollows as well. The clear height under the cap is 4½ feet, and the width 4 feet 3 inches.

*Dolmen A. From S.W.*

The sidestones are 8 feet long, and the endstone is 4 feet high and 3½ feet wide. This stone is scotched in place by a small pebble inserted between it and the southern or down-hill sidestone. All the blocks are of chert.

The third monument is smaller and further south-west. It resembles some of the Kurmiyeh examples (see Nos. 16, 17, 23 under that head; also see Wády Jideid).

A flat stone, 6 feet by 4 feet, is supported on the down-hill side by two little stones, and is kept in place at the other end by a stone laid over it. There is, however, no indication whatever that the structure has fallen out of its original shape (see Dolmen D, next page).

*Dolmen B*

The fourth and fifth dolmens are large and fallen, and would have been about the same size as the first of the group. They each consisted of four stones, and the endstones remain in relative position. Between them was another little specimen, a stone 8 feet by 4 feet, and supported at one end. The hillside north of this group is covered, as shown on the special Survey, with ruined drystone walls of chert or flint, and by loose stones of the same kind.

On the hill west of the group thus described is a menhir (O), or standing stone, marked on the Survey Map. It is of irregular shape, 4½ feet high, and 4 feet wide in the middle. At the base it is 6 feet wide, and the average thickness is 1½ feet. In the top of this stone is sunk a cup-hollow 6 inches in diameter, and 4 inches deep. This stone still stands erect, its broad faces being towards the north and south. The peculiar shape

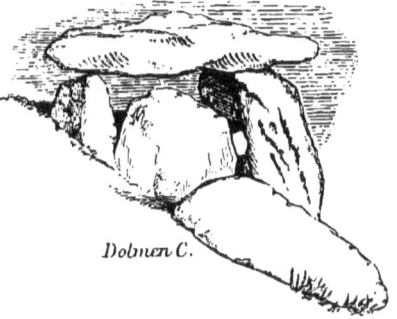
Dolmen C.

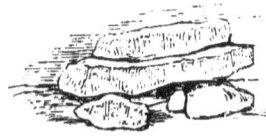
Dolmen D. End View.

Dolmen D Section.

(though this may be accidental) is like that of one of the group on the top of the knoll at el Mâreighât. There is a cave to the east of this menhir lower down. It is much weather-worn and broken, but was originally, perhaps, a tomb-chamber.

On the north-east side of the citadel is the ruin called Haddâdeh, and close to it is the stone marked N on the special Survey. It is a large fallen menhir which seems to have stood in a kind

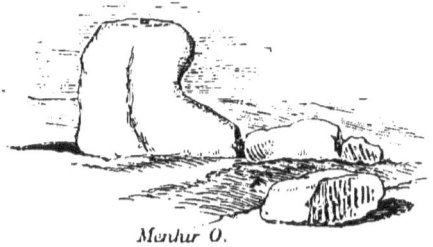
Menhir O.

of socket, which is still noticeable on the north. The stone is 12 feet long, 6½ feet broad, and 2 feet thick. It is remarkable for a hollow in one side, which measures 9 inches by 5 inches, and is 9 inches deep.[*] A similar hollow in the side of a stone (apparently a fallen menhir) was

*Menhir N.*

noticed by Lieutenant Mantell in the group south of Kefrein at Tell el Matâbâ.

On the south side of the site is another structure, marked M on the special Survey. It is near the head of the ravine, which runs out northwards at the theatre, and close to a group of tombs and sarcophagi. It is simply a stone supported in a sloping position on a very small stone. The flat table thus formed is 9 feet by 8 feet, and the stone seems possibly to have been rudely hewn. A group of three sarcophagi, close by on the west, will be specially noticed later on.

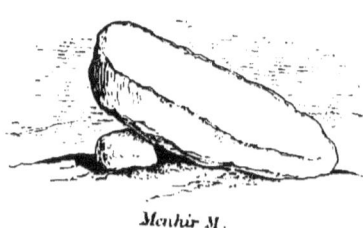

*Menhir M.*

Another structure further west is south of the limits of the special Survey. Close by is a Roman road, with a fallen milestone, marked R.M.S. on the Survey Map. The largest stone, 7½ feet high and wide,

---

[*] I have found similar hollows in the erect stones at Stonehenge, and at Kitt's Cotty House. They seem to have been made *after* the stone was erected, and are worn smooth, as though by rubbing.

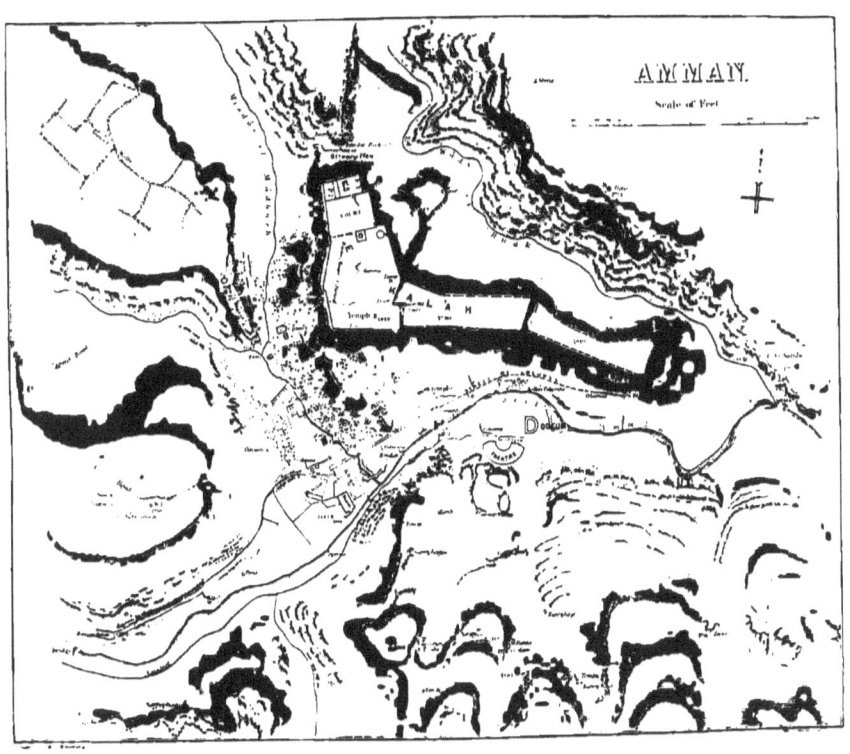

and 21 inches thick, is supported in a nearly vertical position by two others. There is a small hollow in one side near the ground.

The four remaining monuments are at some distance off on the left side of the stream (Jabbok), north-east of 'Ammân. The first (G) is in Wâdy Haddâdeh, and is close to a small cave (see Survey Map). It is a

*Dolmen L.*        *Dolmen G.*

rude structure, perhaps half fallen. The capstone is 8 feet long and 16 inches thick. In its present position one end is on the ground; the other is 9 feet above it. Close by is another little table (H), only 5 feet long, resting on a very small stone at one end. Another (I), which is constructed of chert, is to be found on the flat ground further west. It is about 200 yards east of the road to Nûeijis. East of this group there

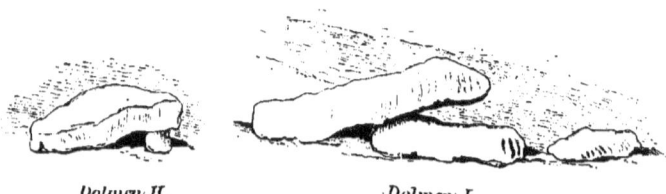

*Dolmen H.*        *Dolmen I.*

is a fine menhir (J) which was unsuccessfully photographed. It is a great block 8 feet high, 9 feet wide at the base, 1½ feet thick. There is another further west, close to the road, which is only 4 or 5 feet high, but resembles the preceding.

The monuments thus described have been called prehistoric, being of the same class with others described further south ; but perhaps some of the menhirs are boundary stones of the time of the Ammonites, or even of the Roman city. They are, however, much ruder structures than any of the buildings of the city.

*Pre-Roman Remains.*—With exception of the dolmens and menhirs, there is nothing in the way of architecture at 'Ammân which can with any certitude be referred to the pre-Roman period. There are, however, caves and tombs, no doubt of great antiquity, especially as the latter have the peculiar *kokim* of Jewish and Phœnician sepulchres. Although the citadel hill was no doubt fortified in David's time, there is nothing to show that any of the masonry in the present walls is older than (if as old

Menhir J.

as) Roman times. The Ammonite or Hebrew cemetery is, however, of great interest, and appears to have extended south-west of the fortress (on the north banks of the stream), and also on the north. The chief Roman cemetery was on the south. The *kokim* tombs at 'Ammân were with one exception (at el Mekheiyit) the only ones found by the Survey party east of Jordan. The numerous caves in Wâdy er Rûâk ('the valley of porches or vestibules') may also, perhaps, have been intended for tombs.

In the western cemetery, marked on the special Survey as 'Rock-cut tombs,' fifteen caves in all were examined. The first, on the west in the highest tier, is only a rough cave about 6 paces (15 feet) across, with four recesses in the walls, each recess 3 paces (7½ feet) across. The second, higher up, is like it. The third, west of the last, is also only a cave. The fourth is a cave 15 feet wide and 18 feet to the back; in the floor of the cave a sarcophagus is sunk near the back. The height of this cave is only about 3 feet. The sarcophagus is 6 feet 8 inches long and 2½ feet wide. The cave has no doubt become filled with *débris*.

Immediately east of the last is the fifth cave (Fig. 3), which is larger, the outer chamber measuring 33 feet to the back and 10 feet across. There is on one side a rock-cut pillar supporting the roof. At the back is an entrance to a chamber 14 feet square, which has a recess on the back wall, and another on the left-hand wall. The door to this chamber is 3½ feet wide. The cave at its entrance is 16 feet wide. The recesses are each 10 feet long, 8 feet wide, and 4 feet high.

The sixth cave is very rough, and measures 8 paces (20 feet) by 10 paces (25 feet); it has a side chamber on the west, and seems probably to be a tomb. The seventh is a cave measuring 5 paces by 10 paces (12 by 25 feet). The eighth is a chamber 12 feet by 15 feet. The ninth was found full of chopped straw. The tenth and the eleventh (Fig. 2) have between them three entrances. The eastern of the two is reached by a passage with recesses as shown in the plan, the passage being 30 feet long and 6 feet wide, with two recesses to the right and two (one converted into a passage) to the left. A door at the back leads to a chamber 12 feet by 15 feet, having nine *kokim*, three on each wall. Each *koka* is 7 feet long, 2½ feet wide, 3½ feet high. The passage to the west is 10 feet wide and 22 feet long. It has three *kokim* on its north wall, and a narrow passage on the west into the eleventh tomb. This is 18 feet wide and 17 feet to the back, and eight *kokim*—four on the north wall, four on the west—are rudely hewn in the chalk.

The twelfth tomb (Fig. 1) is east of the last, and is much decayed. It was a chamber, 16 feet wide, 21 feet to the back, with two entrances; and on the east is a recess 13 feet by 11 feet. In the larger chamber there is a sort of rude *arcosolium*, and two unfinished *kokim* occur on the west wall; while on the north wall are five *kokim* of various lengths, of which two seem to be unfinished. In the smaller chamber to the east are four *kokim* much dilapidated.

The thirteenth tomb is about 100 feet away east of the last, and is

## THE SURVEY OF EASTERN PALESTINE

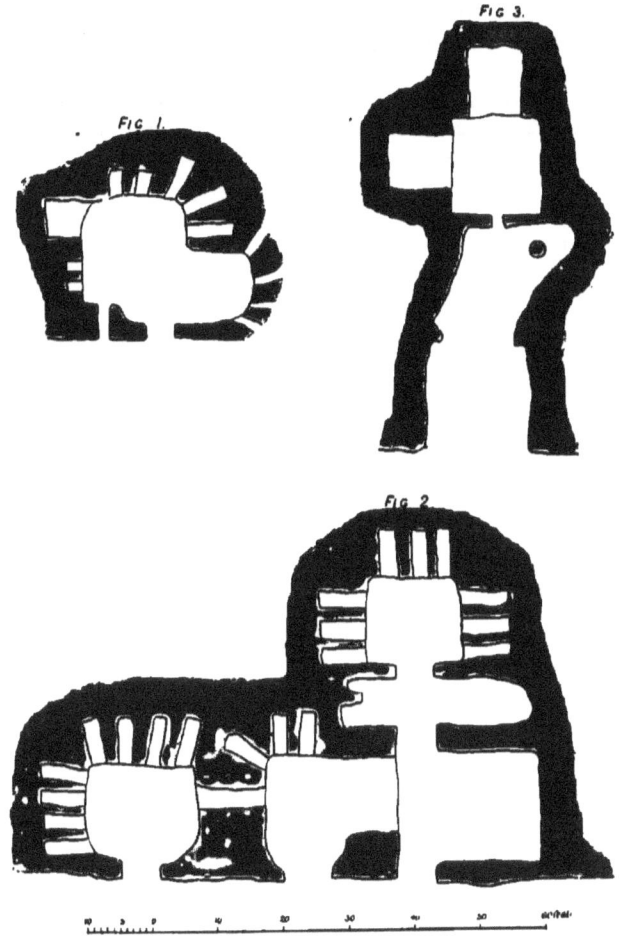

HEBREW TOMBS AT RABBATH AMMON.

entered from an outer cave 14 feet by 24 feet. The chamber to the left is 14 feet across, the entrance 8 feet across. On the walls are five radiating *kokim*. There are traces of another ruined chamber north of the entrance or porch cave. The fourteenth tomb is west of the last, a long chamber of irregular shape, 6 paces by 12 paces (15 feet by 30 feet), with two *kokim* at the east end. The fifteenth tomb is close to the first in the series, and was found full of *tibn*, or chopped straw.

To the north of the castle is another cemetery in which are many *kokim* tombs. They are cut in soft chalk below a stratum of chert, which thus forms the roof, while a second stratum forms the floor. The first visited had nine *kokim*, of which four were at the back, two to the one side, three on the other. Three other examples, in which the *kokim* were extremely rough, were also examined. Another tomb had four *kokim* at the end, and a very rude *loculus* on each side of the chamber. Another had two *loculi* under *arcosolia* at the end, and very rough *kokim* at the sides. These belong to the later Jewish, or transitional period ; and at Jerusalem the mixture of *kokim* and *loculi* in one tomb seems to belong to the second century B.C. at earliest. On the east side of the saddle north of the Kaláh there are about a dozen caves. Those on the north side of Wády er Rûâk are of the same character, and many of them were also visited ; they average from 6 to 10 paces (15 to 25 feet) in width, and are most probably tombs.

*The Roman Period.*—This is the most important period at 'Ammán, and the ruins are only surpassed in Syria by those of Jeràsh Baalbek and Palmyra, which belong to the same period—the age of the Antonines. The Roman remains include the K a l á h, or fortress, and its temple ; the theatre and odeum ; the supposed temple, or forum, north-west of the theatre ; the baths ; the street of columns and gate ; and, finally, the mausolea and masonry tombs, with the Roman cemetery on the south, and scattered tombs on the north and west.

The K a l á h, or 'castle,' of 'Ammán occupies the long tongue which runs out south and east on the north side of the stream. It is divided from the hill of which it is naturally the continuation by a saddle on the north side of the fortifications, which seems probably to have been artificially cut down. The fortress is L-shaped ; the short line north and south measuring 1,200 feet, and the long line running east for 2,700 feet.

The western part is the highest, and its surface is about 400 feet above the stream; the eastern part is divided into two terraces. The irregularities of the plan will be seen by the special Survey, and are due to the conformation of the hill plateau. The western, or upper, terrace of the Kalâh includes the remains of a temple on the south, an Arab building near the middle, with a large well east of it, a court of the Roman period further north, and additions of the Arab period. The tower on the south wall, and the gate on the east, as marked on the special Survey, also require a few words.

The exterior rampart walls of the Kalâh are standing on all sides, and at the north-west corner their height is from 30 to 40 feet. They are built of drafted stones, averaging about 2 feet in height, and from 2 feet to 4 feet in length. Each course is stepped back from the one beneath about 2 inches. In the north-west angle, where the hill rises very steeply, there are several breaks in the horizontal joint-lines. The masonry may be either Roman or Byzantine, but perhaps more probably the former. The largest stones do not exceed 5 feet in length, or 3 feet at most in height. The masonry is thus in size (and also in finish) inferior to that of the Kalâh at Baalbek, or of the Jerusalem and Hebron Harams.

The drop from the western terrace, which measures 1,200 feet north and south, by 600 feet east and west, is about 30 feet. The second terrace, 1,000 feet long east and west, by 300 feet north and south, falls gradually in its length some 50 feet more. The third, or most eastern, terrace, 1,100 feet long east and west, and 200 to 300 feet wide, is 30 feet lower on the west, where is a kind of moat 10 paces (25 feet) wide, with a very slight counterscarp, and it is 100 feet lower on the east than the level of the middle terrace at its east end. The whole area of the Kalâh plateau is thus 1,295,000 square feet, or about 29 acres, which is less than the area of the Jerusalem Haram (35 acres). The north wall of the eastern, or lowest, terrace is built of rough unshapen blocks of moderate size. It might, perhaps, be older than the ashlar of the western, or highest, terrace; but it is also possible that it is a mere retaining wall, and therefore more roughly built.

The court marked towards the north of the highest, or western, terrace appears somewhat to have resembled the great court at Baalbek on a smaller scale. The remains of the north wall, and of parts of the east wall, are clearly of the Roman period. On the north wall the south face is adorned with alcoves about 3 feet in diameter, with a round or half-dome roof which appears to have been ornamented, as at Baalbek, with a scallop-shell pattern. One alcove at the south end of the east wall still remains, showing a little sculptured pediment above its dome. On the north wall seven alcoves are visible, and the remains of two entrances. The masonry is much weathered, but was originally very well cut ; none of the stones are drafted. They are of square proportions, with fine joints. The alcoves were no doubt intended for statues. The court measured 380 feet east and west, and 300 feet north and south.

The eastern gate leads from the higher western terrace to the second terrace on the east. The gateway or porch consisted of three entrances with four pillars. The central entrance was 8 feet wide; the side entrances were 3 feet wide. Each of the four pillars stood on a base 3 feet square, and on the north a little flanking tower, 4 feet from the north side of the north pillar, projected eastwards, and was 27 feet square. This tower is at the corner of the fortress wall, which here recedes west, as will be seen on the special Survey. The bases of the four pillars remain *in situ*, and are like those of the temple further west on this hill (see Fig., next page). There are letters or signs incised on the flat surface of the bases where the shaft stood. When the pillars were erect, these signs were of course invisible, and their object is not clear; but they may be compared with the marks on pillar bases at Ascalon ('Memoirs of Western Survey,' vol. iii., p. 240). These signs were also observed by De Saulcy ('Voyage en Terre Sainte'). It seems as if the inscription was originally the same on each base.

$$\Delta \overline{\underset{\epsilon \upsilon c}{\omega}} \qquad \Delta \omega c \epsilon$$

The letters are Greek, and the uncial shape of the E and Σ is that used in inscriptions as late as the fifth to the eighth centuries in Palestine. Possibly the letters may have been cut in later Byzantine times by pilgrims or others, after the pillar shafts had fallen.

The great temple was not in the same axis with this gate, but rather further south. Only the foundation of the pronaos or porch remains, and scattered fragments of a huge cornice. The pillars have fallen, and only the bases remain, four on the east and one on the north, and another on

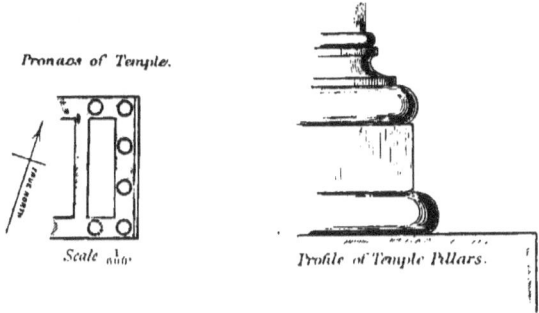

Pronaos of Temple.
Scale
Profile of Temple Pillars.

the south side of the porch. They stand on a wall 10 feet high, which is 52 feet north and south, by 23 feet 7 inches east and west. The shafts lying on the ground are 4½ feet in diameter; and battered capitals of the Corinthian order were also lying on the ground. The building must have been a very large one, as the pillars exceed in diameter any others at 'Ammân. On one of the bases again occurs the same inscription above noted on the bases of the eastern gate.*

The western part of the temple has so entirely disappeared as to suggest that the building was destroyed by the Christians of the Byzantine period. The cornices or epistylia are 3¼ feet high, and bear Greek inscriptions. It is extremely difficult, however, to read these, and De

* It should be noted that Sir Charles Warren found a somewhat similar inscription on the under side of a Corinthian capital at Sidon ('Quarterly Statement,' 1870, p. 324).

The inscriptions on the flagstones of the Sta. Sophia at Constantinople are also worth comparing ('Quarterly Statement,' 1882, p. 149). These three examples seem to be monograms. At Ascalon (see 'Memoirs, Western Palestine,' vol. iii., p. 240) I found marks cut on the flat surfaces of pillars in the same way, which are either Phœnician, or early Greek, or Arab letters.

SUPPOSED FORUM AT AMMAN, GERASA.

To face page 32.

Saulcy's reading is quite different to that now given. The name Aurelius may perhaps be distinguished with the words 'of the Gods.'

This temple may be supposed to be that of Hercules, the later representative of the Sun deity, here worshipped by the Ammonites; for the coins of Philadelpheia bear the name Heracleion. Stephanus of Byzantium calls the city Astarte, and some of the coins bear a figure of Ashtoreth. No doubt, as at Tyre and elsewhere, the male and female deity were both adored.

On the south wall of the Kalâh are two towers, as marked on the special Survey. Of these the western is the best preserved, and is a conspicuous object on the hill-top. It is about 30 feet square, and built of drafted masonry. On the north side is the door, which has a flat lintel, and a low relieving arch above the lintel. The relieving arch of five voussoirs has carefully dressed drafts to each stone, and the faces of the bosses are also dressed flat. The lintel has a winged tablet in low relief cut upon it. The whole arrangement and execution resembles that of Byzantine doorways (see Deir el Kalâh in the 'Memoirs of Western Palestine Survey,' vol. ii., pp. 317, 318), and this suggests the possibility that the walls of the Kalâh are not older than the Christian period (fourth to sixth centuries). The stones in the tower are, however, very carefully dressed, and much better finished than is usual in Byzantine work in Syria. Some are drafted, the draft being 3 inches to 6 inches wide. The corner stones, which are the largest in the walls, are

5 feet long and 3 feet to 3½ feet high. The south wall is ornamented by two discs, each 4 feet in diameter, and projecting 6 inches; these were evidently cut for their present position. The bosses of the drafted stones are carefully dressed with an adze-dressing; the drafts have a diagonal tooling with a pick.

On the saddle of the hill, outside and immediately north of the Kaláh, a very fine rock-cut tank was found by the Survey party.

The entrance is on the north, a rock-cut door 4½ feet wide, inside which a very steep slope leads down to the floor of the tank. The mouth (see special Survey) is about 50 paces (125 feet) north of the middle tower, in the north wall of the Kaláh. The tank is 20 to 30 feet high, and rough steps are cut in the descent from the entrance, and on one side is a kind of shoot with a rock-cut parapet-wall, as though for letting in water. The main part of the tank is 20 feet wide and 93 feet long, north and south. There is a recess on the west with an arch-shaped roof, and the roof of the main chamber is also rounded like a vault. The corresponding recess on the east is 18 feet wide, 25 feet to the back; and on this same side there is a third recess of about equal size. In general character this rock-cut hall resembles one at Sheikh Abreik ('Memoirs of the Western Survey,' vol. i., p. 328). There is a curious passage just inside the entrance, not far below the level of the rock surface; it runs in at first eastwards, but gradually curves round southwards. It was pursued for 40 feet, when it becomes choked. It is 4 feet wide at the entrance, but gets gradually narrower and smaller as it goes south. It seemed possible that this was a secret passage from the interior of the Kaláh, and may have led to a postern inside the tower above mentioned.

It seems probable that this tank and passage are mentioned by Polybius, who states that, when Antiochus the Great besieged Ptolemy Philopater's forces in B.C. 218 in this citadel, a communication with the external water-supply, by means of an underground passage, enabled the garrison to hold out until it was discovered to Antiochus by a prisoner (Polybius, v. 17; Ritter, 'Syrien,' 1155).

Immediately north of the tank-mouth there is a little shrine or place of prayer with low walls and no roof; it measured 8 paces (20 feet) north and south, 14 paces (35 feet) east and west. It has a Mihrab in the south wall, and appears to be of no great antiquity.

Descending from the hill, the theatre and the odeum must next be described. The theatre is built against a natural recess in the hill, and is said to be the largest in Syria. It faces northwards, and is fairly well preserved. The exterior diameter is 228 feet, and the interior 124 feet. The height to the top of the back wall, from the ground in front, is 70 feet. There are three tiers of seats (mœniana) separated by flat terraces $7\frac{1}{2}$ feet wide, running round (præcinctiones). Above the highest tier is a terrace $11\frac{1}{2}$ feet wide. The wall at the back is 5 feet thick and 12 feet high, and the imperial seat in the centre of this wall remains almost intact, though now converted into a dwelling by the Circassian exiles. There are sixteen steps in the top tier, fourteen in the second, and about five apparently in the lowest. Each step has a rise of $16\frac{1}{2}$ inches, and a tread of 2 feet; they have all a projection of 3 inches (see detail section), giving a seat 27 inches wide, and allowing room for the legs and heels. Flights of steps run up between the seats, which are thus arranged in eight blocks (cunei) in each tier; there are seven flights, and there are three steps to each tier of seats. The bottom of the lowest step of the top tier is 3 feet 10 inches above the first terrace, and the wall at the back of the lower terrace is in the same way 4 feet 9 inches high. It is calculated that this theatre would easily hold 3,000 persons.

The great side vaults, 100 feet long and 20 feet across at the narrowest end, were probably used for the gladiators and wild beasts, and supported the flat platforms where certain dignitaries were intended (as at Herculaneum) to be seated. The conformation of the hill prevented any vomitories or passages being constructed at the back of the cavea, or tiers of seats. There was no stage or scena, and, like the theatre at Beisân, the present one seems to have been intended for gladiatorial contests. There is, however, a colonnade in front of the orchestra, which seems to have run eastwards as far as the smaller theatre, or odeum, which faces westwards. The colonnade also continues northwards from its west end (see plan), though not at right angles, the obtuse angle measuring 108°. It is possible that the colonnade ran northwards, originally, as far as the stream. It also appears probable that a reservoir for *naumachia* existed in front of the theatre beyond the colonnade, for an aqueduct runs (see special Survey) along the foot of the hill, on the south of the stream, as far almost as the corner of the colonnade, on a level which would have allowed of its filling a basin in this situation.

The odeum, as it is generally called, is a theatre with stage, or proscenium, scena-wall, and postscenium gallery, partly ruined. It seems to have had a tower at each end of the proscenium, but the northern one has fallen. The term 'odeum' is properly applied to covered theatres, whereas the smaller theatre with a stage at 'Ammân does not seem to have been covered. The term is here used, however, for the sake of distinction, having been already applied by other writers.

The pillars in the colonnade already mentioned are 2 feet 8 inches in diameter, with an intercolumniation of 7 feet, and epistylia consequently of 9 feet 8 inches. The mouldings on these blocks are similar to those on the epistylia of the temple in the Kalâh. The corner pillar is double, like the double pillars at Jerâsh, at Tyre, at Khûrbet Belât (Sheet III., 'Memoirs of Western Survey,' vol. i., p. 171), and at some of the Galilean synagogues. There are eight pillars west of this, and four on the north.

The interior diameter of the so-called odeum is about 85 feet. The postscenium and south tower only remain well preserved; the proscenium is much ruined. The exterior face of the postscenium is just 100 feet long; the gallery is 13 feet wide inside, with walls 6 feet thick; and three entrances 7 feet wide exist on the west, between each of which is an alcove, as though for a statue (four in all). The roof is a barrel vault, round arched, of well-dressed stone.

The total breadth of the cavea is 24 feet, including the wall at the back, 5 feet high, and 3 feet thick. There are seven tiers of seats, each seat 15 inches high, 2 feet 4 inches wide, with a projection (see detail sketch) of 4 inches. The total height of the theatre wall at the back was 27 feet. There were three vomitories, one at the back, one on each side, being tunnels 9 feet wide and 4 feet high at the inner end (above the present surface), with vaults in shape of the segment of a hollow cone. The interior is much choked with fallen masonry, and heaps of fallen stones lie outside on the north. The scena-wall was adorned with a rich cornice on the east side. The south tower measured 25 feet north and south, by 11 feet east and west, and is built up of drafted stones of moderate size. The height can be judged from the photograph, by com-

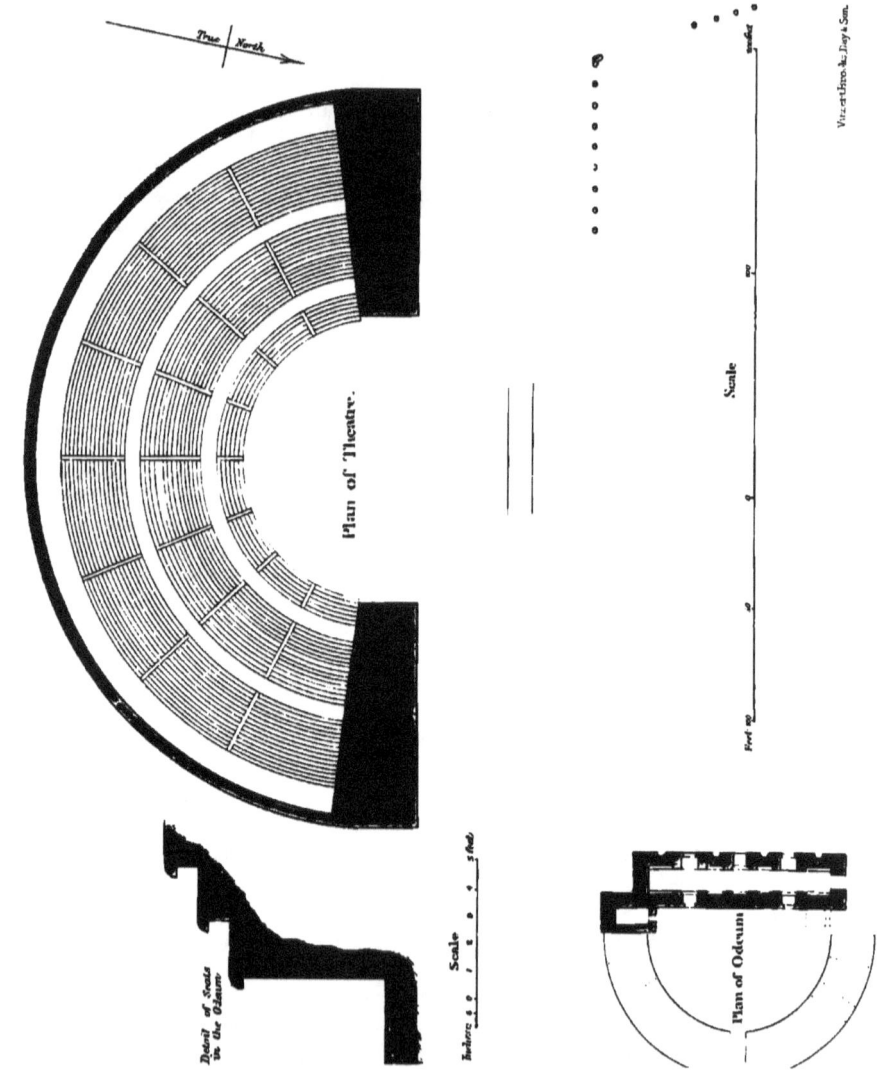

parison with the height of the theatre, to be about 50 feet. The rest of the masonry of the odeum is of well-dressed stones of square proportion and moderate size. The exterior ornamentation is simple; the vaults of the vomitories have carefully-dressed voussoirs. The building could have accommodated easily an audience of four hundred persons. It is also possible that a second tier, or mœnianum, below the præcinctio, existed

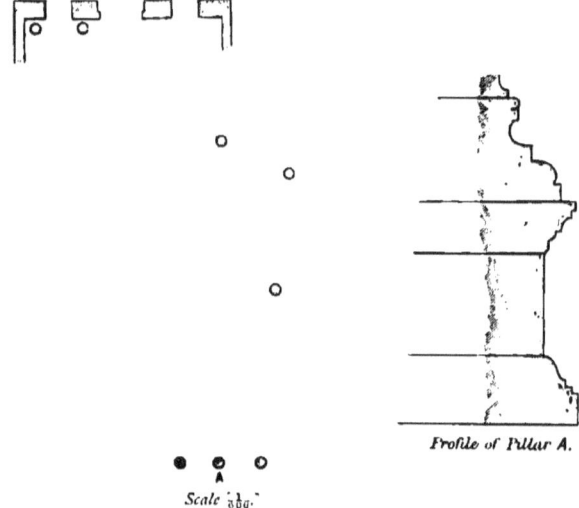

Profile of Pillar A.

Scale ₂₄₀.

under the tier already described, which is now partly ruined and covered with fallen masonry; and this second tier may have accommodated some two hundred more persons. (See P. E. Fund's Photos, Nos. 376 and 390.)

The next building to be described is generally called a temple, but its use is doubtful. The north wall, bearing 50° true bearing, is standing in parts to the full height of about 20 feet, together with pillars running south-west in continuation of the line of the wall, and three other pillars of smaller size, apparently belonging to a peristyle. The total breadth of the building (see Plan above) thus appears to have been 82 feet outside, and the length north and south 180 feet. The street of columns is just in front of the building on the south side. The north wall has three entrances, the middle one 18 feet wide, the side ones 10½ feet wide. The central door has a skewback for an arch cut at the top of each jamb; the jambs are ornamented with mouldings. The side-doors have flat lintels, with little niches above. On the inside they were flanked by pillars, of which only those by the western door remain, 3 feet 3 inches in diameter, of Corinthian order, and supporting an elaborately-carved cornice. These details are shown in the photographs (Nos. 10 and 13 of Lieutenant Mantell's series). Of the two columns shown in the first of these photographs, the eastern is marked A. They stand on stools* 6 feet square and 3 feet 3 inches high (see Profile of Pillar, A) and these are covered with Arab tribe-marks. The three pillars supposed to have belonged to a peristyle are about 3 feet in diameter, whereas the others are 3 feet 10 inches. They are also not in a parallel line with the east wall of the building, and may be out of place. The masonry in the walls is well cut, of moderate size, and not drafted. This building cannot have been roofed, and it has been suggested that it was the forum of the city. The Roman forum and the Temple of Jupiter on its north were, like the building under consideration, arranged with the length north and south. The general arrangement and details of the north wall, with its lofty central gate and lower side-entrances, very closely resemble the east wall and entrances of the Sun Temple at Kedes, in Galilee (Sheet IV., 'Western Survey Memoirs,' vol. i., p. 226).

The street of columns resembled that at Jerâsh, but on a smaller scale. Very few of the pillars remain, but it can be traced eastwards to the remains of what appears to have been a city gate, and westwards beyond the mosque, where six pillars stand in position. This gives a total length of at least 1,000 yards for the street, but not all in one straight line. The shafts are slender, and not more than 3 feet in diameter at most. There are many remains, apparently foundations of private houses, on both sides of this street, and also on the west slopes of the hill below the Kalâh.

* By stool is intended the stylobate when not continuous.—C. R. C.

The stream is spanned by two bridges. The upper one, having three small arches, is half a mile west of the mosque; the arches are semicircular. The lower or eastern bridge is immediately east of the supposed baths. It is a single arch of well-cut stones, not quite semicircular, but perhaps shaken by earthquake. The span is 33 feet, and the breadth of the remaining part is 10 feet, but it appears to have been originally broader. Below the bridge, walls, which in some cases look as if they had supported arches, confine the stream, which is clear, abundant, and full of fish. It seemed possibly to have been vaulted over for some distance north-west of the theatre—perhaps for 100 yards.

In addition to the southern aqueduct leading to the theatre as already mentioned, another aqueduct runs parallel with the stream on its north side. This was traced (see special Survey) as far as the Moslem baths north of the mosque; but it may perhaps have been first constructed in the Roman period for the supposed Roman baths east of the mosque. The present wall is of small irregular masonry, the stones about 15 inches by 9 inches. The channel is about 2 feet wide, and is fed from the spring 'Ain 'Ammân. Two side-channels 3 feet deep lead out south to little ruined mills, which have been wrongly marked on early plans as city gates. There can be no doubt as to the use of these side-channels, which are lined with cement, and give 10 feet head of water at the mills. A piece of moulding built into the mill wall shows the comparatively modern date of one of these structures.

The building east of the group of later buildings, which comprises a mosque, a khân, and a Christian church, have been suggested by Rev. J. N. Dalton to be the *Balnew*, or baths, of the Roman period. They appear, at a later period, to have been converted into a kind of fortress facing the stream on the south. Only the southern end of the building remains standing and distinguishable. Heaps of rubbish, north of this, probably cover the foundations of other parts of the structure, and a wall north of the street of columns may be connected with the same. The south wall presents a portico facing north, with three large alcoves (like apses) set in the three walls of a sort of octagonal end to the building. The portico was about 15 feet wide in the clear, and the total breadth of the building was 225 feet outside. The alcoves are 28 feet in diameter, and there are twelve smaller alcoves or niches, $4\frac{1}{2}$ feet in diameter, symmetrically arranged, as shown on the plan. Of the pillars, seven only remain, including the bases of the two semi-pillars at the ends; they are about 4 feet in diameter. The terrace wall of this portico is 26 feet high, and the ground is hollowed out north of it, the waters of the tributary valley (Misdâr el Mâdhneh) running through the building (in winter) to join the main stream. A passage 20 feet 6 inches wide runs

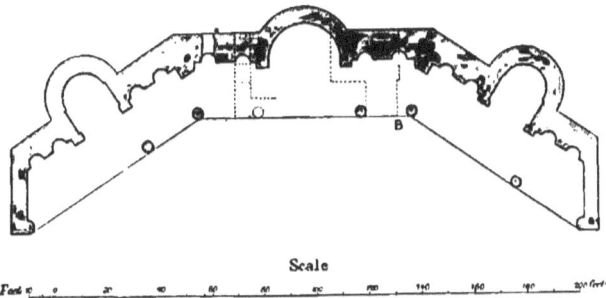

at the lower level through the south wall, as dotted on the plan, west of the central alcove. The arch of this passage is a semicircular arch; but it is not clear whether this passage does not belong to a later period, when the building was converted into a fortress, of which this formed the south gateway. East of the central alcove there is also a passage at the lower level with a small postern leading out on to the banks of the stream. This passage is 6½ feet wide, and runs in 17½ feet, when it turns round west, and no doubt originally communicated with the interior below the portico. The roof is a round-arched tunnel vault, but at a later period a pointed arch has been built inside near the entrance, probably as a further support to the roof.

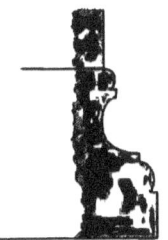

*Profile of Pillar B.*

A retaining wall runs out north, facing west, and is covered with a great heap of rubbish. It is somewhat west of the centre of the building, but pillar-shafts are built into it, and it seems to belong to a later period. The general impression is that the original portico

ODEUM, AT TARSUS.

*To face page 46.*

looked out north on a large basin 26 feet deep, which was probably filled with water by the northern aqueduct already noticed.

The pillars are of the Corinthian order. The details of one base (Pillar B) were measured carefully. The interior walls and the semi-domes of the alcoves are fitted with square holes sunk in the stones (see P. E. Fund's Photos., Nos. 316, 371). These may have been intended for fixing marble flags for casing the interior. The internal masonry is not drafted, but the stones are well dressed, from 1 foot to 3 feet long, and 1 foot to 16 inches high : all the arches are round ; the exterior masonry is drafted, the stones having a rustic boss. Over the lower western gate already described there is a pointed arch in the wall, and the upper part of the wall here appears to be a later restoration of masonry differing in character from the Roman work. Many stones in the lower courses are drafted, and all those in the upper. The latter look like Saracenic work, and the original building was evidently much injured at the time of its later conversion into a fortress. The western alcove is broken through at the back, and holes have also been punched through the wall at the back of the two smaller alcoves or niches, just east of the large central apse or alcove. These demolitions appear to be purposely effected with the view of making windows, or loops for defending the building if attacked from the south. A wall of the later period runs from this building to the church, continuing the line of defence.

The limits of this building—north of the portico—cannot be determined without excavation. What remains does not at all resemble the Roman baths at Jerâsh, or, indeed, any known building in Syria. It is possible that the portico belonged to some kind of place of justice, resembling in use, though not in plan, the pagan basilica ; but the baths are generally important buildings in a Roman city, and the aqueduct seems to lead to the building just described, which is the only one at 'Ammân which can be supposed to represent the Balnea.

The only remaining buildings of Roman 'Ammân are the mausolea and tombs, which include some of the finest public buildings yet remaining. The Kabr es Sultân is a fine tomb east of the citadel, on the north side of Wâdy Abu er Rûâk, and there is a cemetery west of the town, a few tombs to the north, and a considerable cemetery to the south.

## THE SURVEY OF EASTERN PALESTINE

The Kabr es Sultân, or 'Sultan's Tomb' (see Photo., No. 389), is a fine structural monument built against the face of the cliff at the mouth of the valley. The porch is flanked by two recesses or alcoves, 10 feet wide by 7½ feet to the back, having a smaller round-headed niche each side (3 feet in diameter), and a larger alcove or niche (7 feet in diameter), also round-headed, at the back (see plan). The central porch is 12½ feet wide, and its door is 6½ feet wide, leading to a chamber 18 feet wide, 16½

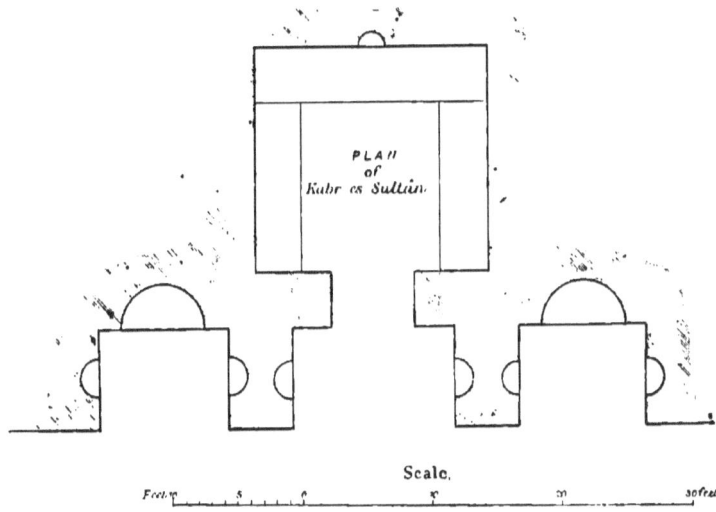

feet to the back. Round three walls of the chamber run benches; the side benches are 3½ feet wide, 1½ feet high; the bench at the back is 4 feet wide, 4¼ feet high. All these are of stone, and the bench at the back is ornamented with six little pilasters cut in low relief. On these benches stood sarcophagi, there being room for seven in all. Of these sarcophagi only two now remain on the higher bench at the back, those at the sides having disappeared, or never having been put in place. The two remaining are 21 inches high, 7¼ feet long, 3 feet wide outside, the thickness of their sides being 6 inches. They have stone head-rests or pillows at the ends, and a bold simple moulding on the side visible. The wall of the chamber is adorned with a simple string course, from which springs a round-arched tunnel-vault. At the back above the string course is a recess or niche, probably intended for a small statue, and an arrangement over the door appears to have admitted a ray of light on to this recess from outside. Like the larger alcoves and niches outside, this little shrine has a round-headed, or half-dome, roof. The keystone of the roof-vault is narrow, and the voussoirs gradually increase slightly in breadth towards the haunches. The voussoirs are all very well dressed, as is also the

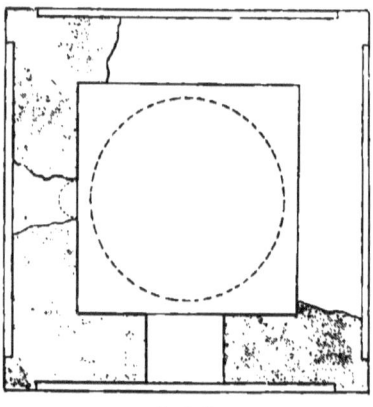

PLAN of Western Tomb.

Scale $\frac{1}{120}$.

masonry of the walls, the stones being of moderate size, not drafted, but dressed with an adze. In each of the four corners of the chamber is a bracket on the level of the string course, perhaps intended to support four other small figures, or urns, or lamps (cf. el Kahf). The details of the exterior cornice and other classic features will be seen in the photograph. The walls are thickly covered with Ausâm, or Arab tribe-marks.

The next mausoleum of importance is that in the flat ground 300 yards south-west of the mosque north of the stream (marked 'Tomb' on the special

Survey). It is the first important building which the traveller sees on approaching from the spring-head (see Lieutenant Mantell's Photos., No. 16). It is a square structure of masonry, 28 feet side, with walls 5 feet thick. It was once roofed with a dome, and had a niche in the west wall 3 feet in diameter and 4 feet high, round-headed, as usual, and adorned with scallop-shell pattern. The door, 6 feet wide, was on the north. The west wall is almost intact, though a hole has been punched

SKETCH OF WESTERN TOMB, SHOWING STRUCTURE OF DOME.

through behind the niche, perhaps in search of treasure, perhaps to make a rude window. The greater part of the south and east walls have fallen in ruins. The north wall is standing to half its full height, as also the east wall. There appears to have been a handsome arch in the south wall. The exterior of the walls is ornamented by a pilaster in low relief at each angle. They stand on a stylobate, and have Corinthian capitals supporting a simple cornice. The masonry resembles all the other masonry of this date at 'Ammán, the stones being well set and dressed,

WESTERN TOMB AT AMMÂN.

*To face page* 44.

of square proportions, and not drafted. The soffit of the arch in the south wall has a 'rose-and-coffer' pattern, like that in the roofs of some Roman basilicas (see sketch on preceding page).

The most curious feature of the building is, however, the arrangement of the dome. About three-quarters of the circle is visible, the two lowest courses alone being left. These do not spring from pendentives (see Kusr en Nûeijis), but directly from the angles—large voussoirs projecting inwards, and their faces being cut to the required arc. These, no doubt,

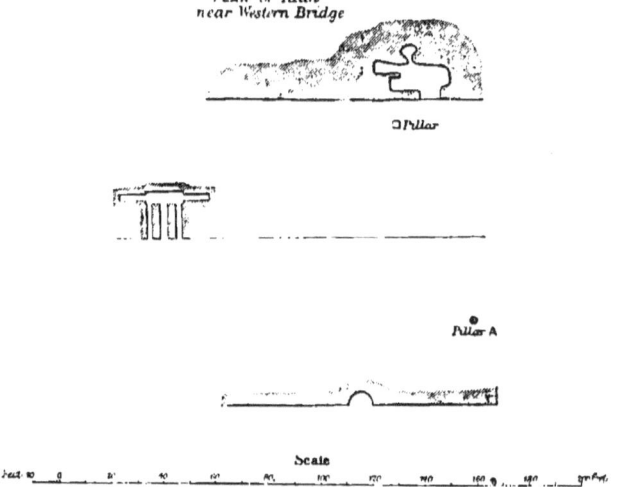

were held in place partly by the thrust, partly by the counter-weight of their own centre of gravity, or by blocks which weighted them in the wall. This arrangement is best explained by the sketch, but it is very unusual in Syrian architecture.

West of this monument, about 350 yards distant, there is a shelf of rock in which other tombs have been placed, on the hill above the aqueduct. A wall is built on the south against the rock, below the shelf or platform; it extends 105 feet, and has in it a niche or alcove, 10 feet in diameter. Above this stands a solitary pillar-base (A) on a stool, which is a conspicuous object (see Fig., Pillar A). The platform is 110 feet wide north and south, with a cliff behind, and in the cliff a rude tomb, which has tunnels on the west like *kokim*. This chamber is 18 feet wide, and 6 feet to the back. The *kokim* are two, the longest 10 feet by 4½ feet wide, the shortest 4 feet 2 inches wide, by 3 feet 10 inches to the back. These are 3 feet 10 inches above the floor, and under the northern, or longer, is a *koka* 9½ feet long, 3½ feet high, 2½ feet wide, on the level of the floor. On the back wall is a round excavation (like those sometimes found in Jewish tombs) 6½ feet in diameter, with an opening or mouth 2 feet 9 inches wide. This is 3 feet 10 inches above the chamber floor. The cave-door is 8 feet wide, and 3 feet above the floor. The total height of the chamber is 9½ feet. The drop from the door-sill to the platform outside is 4½ feet, and there seems here to have been a court, 50 feet wide, with pillars. The base of one of these remains *in situ*. Another small catacomb, built in masonry, exists west of the court, which seems to have run in front of the cave. It is a chamber 14½ feet long, 4 feet wide, with a *koka* at each end 10 feet long, 2 feet 3 inches wide. In the long side on the south are three entrance-tunnels, which might also have served as graves. Each is 2 feet 3 inches wide, and 12 feet 9 inches long, and

Pillar A.

they open out southwards in the face of a low terrace wall (see plan). The masonry is a mere facing of the rock, which is very soft and friable. In the western *koka* a skull was found. The passages and *kokim* are 3 feet high; the roofs are barrel vaults, round-arched, of well-cut masonry, but with small stones. The roof of the chamber itself has fallen in towards the east, leaving a hole visible from the surface of the platform above. Near the pillar A, east of this chamber, were observed remains of a block belonging to a cornice, sculptured with scroll-work, but too decayed to sketch. The pillar is 2 feet 4 inches in diameter; the stool below the base is 3 feet square, and 1 foot 10 inches high. An important building, perhaps intentionally destroyed, seems to have stood in the Roman period at this place.

South of this last ruin is the upper bridge already noticed, and south again, at the foot of the hills, south of the stream, there are two sarcophagi placed at right angles to one another, as though *in situ*. One of these is 7 feet long, 45 inches high (including the cover), and 3 feet wide. The rude sculpture of the lid is shown in the drawing. About 100 yards west of these, and immediately west of the path from the bridge to the Misdâr Abu 'Aisheh, another sarcophagus without any lid lies as if rudely thrown down. There is a third group of sarcophagi further east than the first noticed, as shown on the special Survey.

North of the Kalâh the early caves and tombs have already been described; among these lie sarcophagi also of the Roman period. About

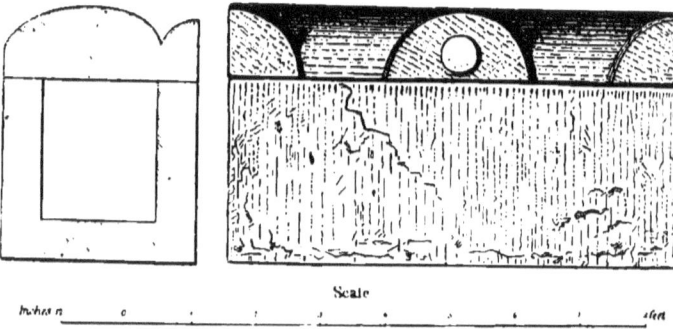

100 yards north of the north wall of the fortress are two, as shown on the special Survey. There is here a cave facing southwards in the rock of the hill-saddle. It is 18 paces (45 feet) long, and 6 paces (15 feet) wide, and contains several other sarcophagi placed under rude rock-cut arcosolia. The entrance to the cave is built up with masonry, and has a lintel-stone over the door. On the right, or east, jamb a cross is cut. There was once a semicircular court in front of this door, constructed by piling rough stones together (one course only), forming a courtyard 20 paces (50 feet) in diameter. This tomb is some 50 yards north of the fortress wall.

Immediately north-west of the Kalâh a tomb is marked on the special Survey. This is a masonry monument on the side of the hill. It is a square chamber, 15 feet 9 inches wide, 18 feet 3 inches to the back, and open on the west, with a round-arched tunnel-vault. A recess 8 feet wide, 4 feet 9 inches to the back, with an arched roof, is built in at the back of the chamber, and six sarcophagi are arranged (as shown) round the walls. The rubbish has accumulated inside to the level of the tops of the sarcophagi. The walls rise some 5 feet higher, and a simple string course runs round beneath the vaulted roof. The masonry resembles that in tombs already noticed.

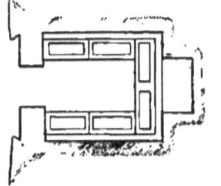

Scale 2¹⁄₁₀.

There was also a handsome mausoleum on this same spur north of 'Ammàn, and beyond the bounds of the special Survey. Only the western part of the stylobate remains, but the building seems to have resembled one on the south hill to be described immediately. It was 30 feet square and the stylobate was 8½ feet high, with a profile, which was measured. The Arabs have piled up the masonry of this

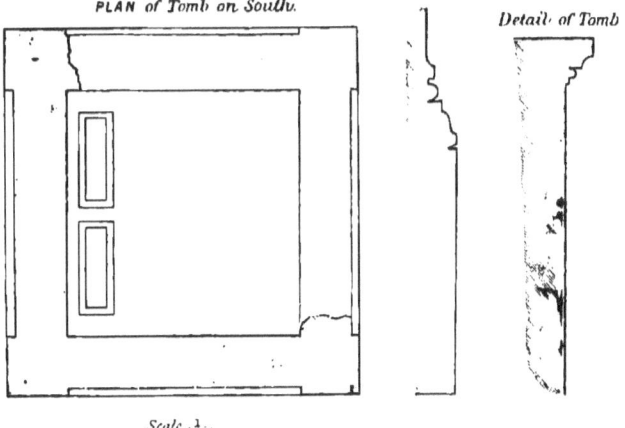

PLAN of Tomb on South.    Detail of Tomb

Scale 1²⁄₁₀.

building so as to form a rude enclosure south-east of the fragment still *in situ*.

On the western hill, where an ancient road is shown on the special

Survey, there are other sarcophagi, with cave-cisterns and remains of a watch-tower, as shown.

We must now turn to the southern cemetery, which is the most extensive and important of those belonging to the Roman period. Ascending from the sarcophagi near the western bridge already mentioned, a foundation belonging to a former mausoleum is found on the hilltop south of the limits of the special Survey. It has been partly ruined, but the plan is still distinguishable. The building resembles that in the valley below, and was 27 feet square outside, with walls 4 feet thick, and corner pilasters as in the former case. The base is solid to the top of the pilaster bases, and the stylobate is 3 feet 4 inches high. The wall is ornamented inside with a string course 7 feet above its floor, which no doubt marked the spring of the vaulting. Two sarcophagi remain *in situ* on the west side, where the wall remains perfect to the string course. On the north and east the wall is destroyed. The walls of the sarcophagi are 6 inches thick, and the interior measure is 6 feet by $1\frac{1}{2}$ feet, by 1 foot 9 inches in depth. Each, as usual, has a raised stone pillow for the head. Below the pilasters the stones of the stylobate are drafted with a rustic boss (*cf.* Kusr es Sebâh); the remaining stones are not drafted. They are on an average $2\frac{1}{2}$ feet long and 2 feet high.

About 200 yards north-east of this latter tomb a broken stele, apparently a Roman milestone, lies by the road (marked R. M. S. on the Survey map). North-east again from this, and south of the T o w e r marked on the special Survey at the end of the spur, is a group marked 'Tombs and Columns.' The most southern of these tombs is a chamber with three benches under *arcosolia*. Its door is well cut, 2 feet wide, with a simple moulding round the outside. This door faces north in a low cliff. A second tomb further north faces east, and is partly destroyed. On a sort of buttress of rock to the right are traces of a bas-relief, representing circles with arabesque patterns.

North again, and about half-way between the tombs and the tower, a single sarcophagus stands on the rock, in a conspicuous position, and perhaps *in situ*. It may have been intended to be left on the surface, as in cases in Western Palestine (*cf.* 'Memoirs,' vol. i., p. 316, Sheet V.). This sarcophagus is 6 feet 8 inches long, 3 feet wide, $2\frac{1}{2}$ feet high outside. The walls vary from 5 inches to 9 inches in thickness. The depth inside is 1½ feet, and there is the usual rest for the head. The cover lies fallen beside the sarcophagus, and is 9 inches thick, with sculptured sides.

The tower on the spur just noticed is a conspicuous object; its use is not certain. It measures 28 feet by 32 feet outside, and there is a plain round arch in the east wall, which seems to have belonged to the entrance. The interior, however, is choked with fallen stones. The masonry is well cut, and not drafted. The stones are 1½ to 3½ feet long, and 1 foot 3 inches high. A bit of moulding is built into the flat roof, showing this part of the structure to be comparatively modern. The present height above ground is only 7 feet. The exploration of the interior would be dangerous.

East of the tower a tomb is marked. This is a rude cave with an inner chamber and a narrow entrance. On the left wall of the cave is a bench under an *arcosolium*. East again, three sarcophagi lie on the ground, as marked on the special Survey.

Further south-east again, in the valley which runs down to the theatre, there are three sarcophagi—two parallel, one across at the south end. They seem to be in their destined position. The stone or menhir immediately east of them has been already described.

In these examples we find a gradual development, according to the civilization or wealth of the people.

1st. A sarcophagus standing on the ground.
2nd. A platform with sarcophagi (see el Kahf).
3rd. A mausoleum enclosing sarcophagi.

*Scale ₂¹⁄₆₀.*

In the same valley, a little further north, is a cave-tomb with one *loculus* and two sarcophagi. The cave measures 10 feet by 12 feet. The *loculus* is 7 feet long, and the sarcophagi the same. The covers are much worn, and partly destroyed, but were originally more ornamental than is usual. One had two lions rudely carved on it; the other (on the south wall) had a vine, with leaves and grapes. There are many other rude caves near this tomb, which were probably sepulchres of the poorer class.

Another large system of tombs occurs further east, near the quarries marked on the special Survey. It is partly structural and partly rock-cut. The façade was photographed, but not successfully. The courtyard in front is rock-cut, and at the back is a central chamber with an arched entrance of masonry, while to the left, or east, are a pair of rock-cut sarcophagi placed parallel, with a narrow passage between and a masonry

COVER OF SARCOPHAGUS *a*.

COVER OF SARCOPHAGUS *b*.

vault above. To the right of the chamber two other sarcophagi, cut in rock at different levels, have also a masonry vault above. These are arranged, not, as in the previous case, at right angles to, but with the length parallel to the face of the rock. To the right again, in the very corner of the courtyard, is a *loculus* under an *arcosolium*, also of rock.

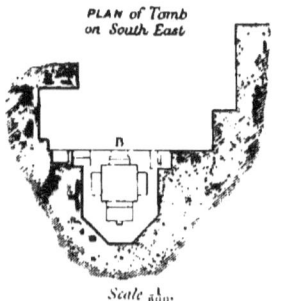

DETAIL OF VOUSSOIR AT B.

These *loculi*, or sarcophagi, are all about the same size—7 feet by 3 feet on an average.

The central chamber is 13 feet 9 inches wide, by 13 feet 2 inches to the back. It has an *arcosolium* on each side $8\frac{1}{2}$ feet long, 3 feet 9 inches wide. At the back, under an *arcosolium*, are two *loculi*, the front one 2 feet high, the back one 3½ feet higher. These have their length parallel to the chamber wall. The side-recesses, or *arcosolia*, were perhaps intended to hold separate sarcophagi. Their floors are on the same level with that of the chamber. Above and behind the back *loculus* under the end *arcosolium*, there is a niche, 2 feet wide, 1 foot 9 inches to the back. This resembles the little alcove in the Kabr es Sultân (see p. 42), and there was another like it at the end of the sarcophagi to the right. The heads of these niches are flat, not rounded. The walls of the courtyard are of rock, and about 6 feet high. The roofs above mentioned are all tunnel-vaults, round-arched, with fairly good voussoirs, though somewhat weathered.

It appears that a hexagonal or octagonal building stood above the roof of the central chamber. The foundations remain, and the stones are drafted with a rustic boss.

The entrance to the central chamber is 7½ feet wide, and is spanned by a round arch. The chamber does not appear to have been roofed, but only its *arcosolia*. The face of the entrance-arch has fallen away, and a block of octagonal shape (B) was found on the ground, ornamented with a large rosette pattern of twenty-four leaves. This no doubt stood over the keystone. Remains of a pilaster capital, too much worn to measure, were also noticed. The interior of this tomb, which contained nine bodies in all, was covered with the Ausâm, or tribe-marks, of the Arabs. As these seem to have often puzzled De Saulcy and others, those found in the present tomb are here given. They include the marks of the 'Ajermeh, the Jibbûr, and other tribes (see appendix on Tribe-marks).

### THE SPRING.

While speaking of Roman 'Ammân, the spring-head at 'Ain 'Ammân, with its ruins, may be described. The stream is perennial, of clear fresh water, and full of small fish. The water rises under the foundations of a kind of alcove or apse, facing east, and 20 feet in diameter. On the north side is a retaining wall, which faces north, and runs east 160 paces (400 feet). It is built of stones about 2 feet long, in three courses, with a total height of 4 feet. The stones are built in alternately as headers and stretchers, as in brickwork, and are well dressed, but not drafted. About the middle of this wall are remains of steps. The top course projects so as to form a kind of coping. This wall confines the waters of a stream at a lower level from springs further west.

West of the alcove a large Arab cemetery is found, and among the tombs is one said to be that of Sheikh el 'Ajemy (the Persian), which is a masonry monument about 3 feet high and 7 feet long, with an upright stone, 2 feet high, 8 inches wide, at either end. The western stone has a rude Arab inscription and a tribe-mark on it. This tomb is peculiar, because a slab has been let into its south side, evidently taken from a Byzantine building. Although the Arabs deny the resemblance, the design represents a Greek cross in a circle of 8 inches diameter, flanked below by two fish. The cross is incised, and rather roughly executed. Close by there is another tomb, with a fragment of a cross on one stone. This use of the cross should be compared with the frequent appearance of the cross among the Arab tribe-marks, for although the 'Adwân deny the fact, and attribute cross-shaped tribe-marks to the men of es Sâlt, there seems to be little doubt that it is used by the Jibbûr Arabs.*

About 100 yards east of the spring there is another Arab cemetery, south of the stream, and in it are two sacred Arab circles (*cf.* 'Ain Hesbân) which are peculiar, because the ordinary trilithon, or dolmen door, is in each case on the east side of the circle, and not, as is usual, on the west. One of these trilithons is rather larger also than usual, the legs being 3 feet high, and the space between them about the same. It thus equals in dimensions many of the ancient examples found in the great dolmen groups.

*The Byzantine Period.*—Considering that no great break occurs between the earlier non-Christian period of the Roman Empire and the later Christian period after Constantine, it is not easy to distinguish the buildings of the two periods when not of a religious character. It is possible that some of the tombs above described, especially those cut in rock with *loculi* or sarcophagi, may be Christian, and in one case north of the citadel a cross has been cut on the jamb of the entrance (as already

* As a tribe-mark, however, it is to be regarded as the letter *Tau*, and not as a Christian cross.

noted), though this may be of later date than the tomb. The only distinctively Christian buildings at 'Ammân are the cathedral, and two chapels north of it ; the so-called ' belfry ' being really the minaret of the mosque, which will be described later.

A wall (already mentioned) which runs south from the cathedral apse was found by the surveyors to be of older material, and one block covered with mortar had a Greek inscription, which appears to be the first found at 'Ammân. It was quite legible, and a squeeze was taken. The text is injured in the second line. Another stone was removed from above that bearing the inscription, and the mortar was scraped off.

ΟΡΙΚΤΩ<br>
ΝΟΝΑ ... ΕΓ<br>
ΔΕΚΑΤΗΣΦΙ<br>
ΓΟΡΔΙΑΝΗΣ<br>
ΛΥΡΟΥΙΚΤΩ

The feminine noun Gordiana appears to occur, which suggests Ulpia Gordiana, the mother of Gordianus Africanus. The Emperor Gordian, grandson of the preceding, reigned from 238 A.D. to 244 A.D., and went to the East to fight Persia. He was slain in Mesopotamia. It should be noted that the letters Σ and Ε in the original of this text are of the round form, and the Ω of the IV form. These uncial forms found in inscriptions and MSS. from the fourth to the ninth centuries A.D. (at Jerusalem, for instance) are also found in the early Antonine texts of the second century. They occur on the temple frieze at 'Ammân as well ; but some texts at Jerash have the earlier classic shapes for E, and Ω, and Σ.

The cathedral lies in a south-east direction; its length, exclusive of the apse, is 137 feet 6 inches, its breadth, 73 feet inside. The west door is 9 feet 9 inches wide, and on the outside there is a niche or alcove 2 feet in diameter each side of the door ; the walls are 2 feet 8 inches thick. There is a north door, and remains exist of a wall 20 feet from the east wall, which appears to have divided the chancel, and may have formed the foundation of the iconostasis, the church being no doubt built for the Greek rite. On each side of the main apse are two small apses or alcoves 5 feet 3 inches in diameter ; the central apse is 24 feet 9 inches in diameter, and 12 feet 6 inches to the back. This arrangement of five apses has not been found in any church west of Jordan. The apse walls are very thick; on the interior they are pitted with holes 1½ inches square and 1½ inches deep, like those in the walls of the baths already noticed. These may be compared with the holes in the outer walls of the Dome of the Rock at Jerusalem, intended for the fixing of the tiles which cover these walls, and, as at the baths, so in the cathedral of 'Ammân, they may have been intended to facilitate the attachment of either a marble casing or of glazed tiles. The cathedral (see Photo. No. 14 of Lieutenant Mantell's series) has been purposely ruined—no doubt by the Arabs. The masonry is of moderate size, the stones dressed, not with an adze, but with a pick or pointed instrument. The

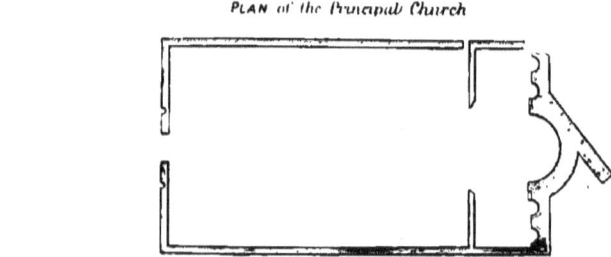

PLAN of the Principal Church

Scale

blocks are from 1 foot to 2 feet long, and 1½ feet high on an average; but some stones even 6 feet long occur in the walls. The exterior stones are drafted; the draft is 3½ inches wide, and 1½ inches deep. These stones average about 2½ feet by 1½ feet; the boss, as is usual in the Byzantine masonry, is plain, and not rustic. Two syenite pillars lie within the church, 11½ feet long, 1½ feet in diameter; and outside on the north-west lies a lintel-stone 13 feet long, 1 foot 10 inches high.

There is a wall nearly parallel to the west wall of the church, 115 feet from it, with remains of a gate 8½ feet wide. The gate is, however, not on the central axis of the cathedral, and there is a difference of 1° 30′ between the bearing of the west wall and this fragment of outer wall. The latter might belong to some sort of atrium; but it may, on the other hand, be part of a distinct building. There is nothing to show the date of the cathedral ; but we are confined between the limits 330 A.D. and 630 A.D., and the building probably belongs to the fifth or sixth centuries.

The next Christian building is a small church near the bottom of the hill west of the south-west angle of the Kalâh (see special Survey). It is a small building about 45 feet square outside, with an apse having an internal diameter of 18½ feet. Four pillar-stumps show that the chapel had a nave and two aisles ; these shafts are much weather-worn, 2 feet 3 inches in diameter. The walls of the chapel are 3 feet 9 inches thick, and it may be calculated that there were five pillars in each aisle.

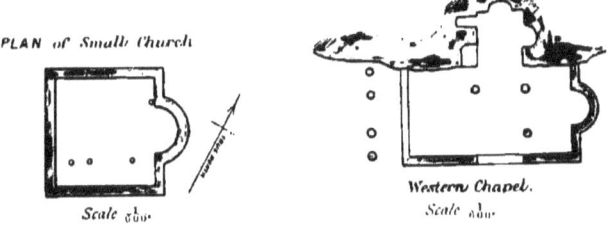

PLAN of Small Church

Scale ₆₀₀.

Western Chapel.

Scale ₆₀₀.

The third chapel is perched on the narrow spur west of Misdâr el Mâdhneh, or the valley of the 'minaret,' north-west of the last noticed (see special Survey). It is built south of and adjoining a cave. The apse, the window in the south wall, and three pillars of the aisles remain, with four which belonged to a porch 10 feet wide at the west end. The apse is 14 feet in diameter, the aisles 9 feet wide in the clear. The interior length of the chapel, not including the apse, is 63 feet. The pillars are 2 feet 2 inches in diameter in the chapel, but those in the porch only 1½ feet. There are remains of cornice mouldings in the south window, and a pillar-capital of the rude Ionic form usually found in Byzantine buildings was sketched. The cave immediately to the north, and opening into the north aisle, was perhaps sacred as the tomb or cave-dwelling of some saint. The rock rises in a cliff. The excavation is 18 feet across, and 20 feet to the back ; on the east wall is an alcove 10 feet in diameter—a kind of apse—and on the west wall in the south-west angle is a rock-cut sarcophagus. There is another recess in this wall, and one also in the north wall.

# RABBATH AMMON

*Arab Period.*—This is in some respects the most interesting building period at 'Ammân. We know that one early Persian building occurs in Moab (at Mashita), and in the present case the use of round arches in the mosque at 'Ammân seems possibly to indicate an early date. The minaret is described by Lord Linsay as the 'lofty steeple' of a church, but this is an error. The plan of the mosque is quite distinct, with its mihrab and minaret; and the brackets which supported the gallery of the Muedhdhen remain intact. The mosque is of the typical form, with a large square court to the north, and a broad, short, covered building on the south. The court is 120 feet wide east and west, by 135 feet north and south inside; the covered part is 37 feet north and south, by 120 feet east and west. The court had three entrances, about 6½ feet wide; the mosque itself had three entrances, the middle one 10 feet wide, the side ones 7 feet. The roof of the mosque was supported on narrow arches which sprung from the wall,* and were corbelled out (see 'Details,' arches *a, a*) in such a manner as to be apparently—but not structurally—of the Moorish form, or rather more than a half-circle or ellipse. The mihrab

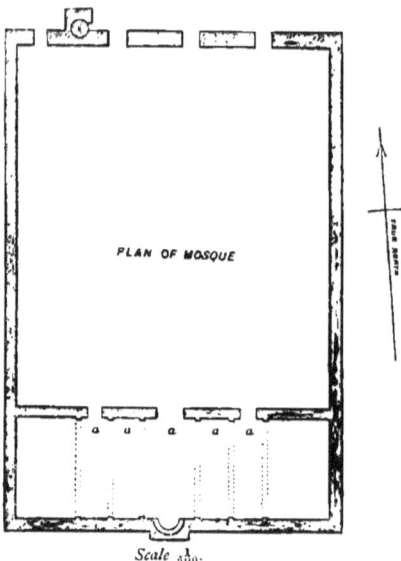

PLAN OF MOSQUE

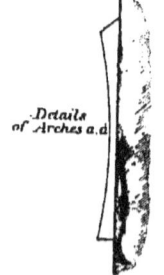

Details of Arches a.d

---

* This mosque is described about 985 A.D. by el Mukaddasy: 'In the city near the market-place stands a fine mosque, the court of which is ornamented with mosaic. I have heard it said that it resembles that of Mecca.'

S

in the south wall is 11 feet 9 inches in diameter, and a smaller mihrab has been built up inside it. The arches of the entrance-gates are semicircular in two cases, while the central one is segmental (see sketch). The segmental arch has a lintel-stone 16 feet long beneath it, and a second lintel lower again forming the head of the door. The west entrance has a lintel 9 feet long, similar to this last. The arrangement of

segmental relieving arch and lintel is similar to that so often found in Byzantine buildings (*e.g.*, the Kalàh Tower), but is also not uncommon in Arab work. There are four windows in this north wall between the entrances, also with round arches. This wall is standing to its original height, but the others are ruined in parts; the masonry is of moderate size and finish, not drafted. The Ausâm, or tribe-marks, of all the principal tribes are found on the walls. Of these, three

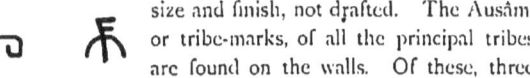

of the most distinctive were copied. The first belongs to the Nimr, a division of the 'Adwân; the second to the Shàlàn, who are an 'Anazeh clan; the third to the Jibbûr, who are a clan of the Beni Sakhr. The minaret of this mosque is on the north wall near the west end, and although the masonry in this structure is smaller than that in the walls, there seems no reason to suppose that the minaret is a later addition. The minaret is square on plan, a tower 10 feet side. A shaft of stone 14 inches in diameter in the centre supports the winding stair in a cylindrical well about 6 feet in total diameter, the stairs being only 2 feet wide. There are thirty-three steps, with a total height of $33\frac{1}{2}$ feet, leading to a platform with four windows, one in each wall. The total height is about 45 feet, and the top is crowned by a dome, which is concealed outside by an elegant octagonal shaft which springs from the corbels of the Muedhdhen's gallery above the windows. The windows are round-arched, and partly filled in with a balustrade of stone 3½ feet high. The minaret stair is reached from a low door in the east wall having a lintel above it, on which is rudely incised an Arab inscription. This, both from its character and rude execution, is no doubt late. It is merely the formula : ' No God but Allah ; Muhammed is the messenger of God.'   لا اله الا الله محمد   ورسول الله

The use of round arches in this building seems to indicate early date. The oldest parts of the Amru mosque at Cairo have round arches (642 A.D.), but Ibn Tulûn (876 A.D.) used the pointed arch, which appears to have begun to be employed by the Arabs in the ninth century. The mosque at 'Ammân would thus appear to be a building either of the time of the Ommiyeh Khalifs (661-750 A.D.), or more probably of one of the Abbaside family (750-850 A.D. at latest). The Khalif el Mamûn (died 833 A.D.) was a munificent monarch who built much in Jerusalem, and it seems not impossibly to his time that the 'Ammân mosque should be ascribed, with perhaps the building in the fortress about to be described, which may, however, be possibly later.

The Khân, which occupies all the space between the cathedral and the Roman baths, is a later building than the mosque. Its ruins are almost indistinguishable, but it consisted of a great court, with small surrounding chambers, occupying about 300 feet north and south, by 170 feet east and west. Small chambers have also been built up, apparently at the same time, within the cathedral itself. Some pointed arches remain, and in one case the keystone is nicked out below to form the point, just as in Crusading arches and in Arab work of the fourteenth and fifteenth centuries.

The small baths are marked on the special Survey north of the Khân and mosque. There are eight small low chambers, built of inferior masonry, and apparently not very ancient. The block containing them measures 40 feet east and west, 50 feet north and south. The arches are pointed. The northern aqueduct seems to have supplied these baths with water. There are several wild-figs growing in the middle of the building.

Two buildings, probably of Moslem origin, remain to be described, one standing in the middle of the highest terrace (the western) of the Kalâh enclosure, the other traceable further north. The first of these has often been mentioned as a church or as a mosque by former travellers; but no drawings of the details had been procured before the visit of the Survey party, although they are visible on the photograph taken by Sir C. Warren. The building measures $85\frac{1}{2}$ feet north and south, by $80\frac{1}{2}$ feet east and west, and has a central court 33 feet square. It is clearly all of

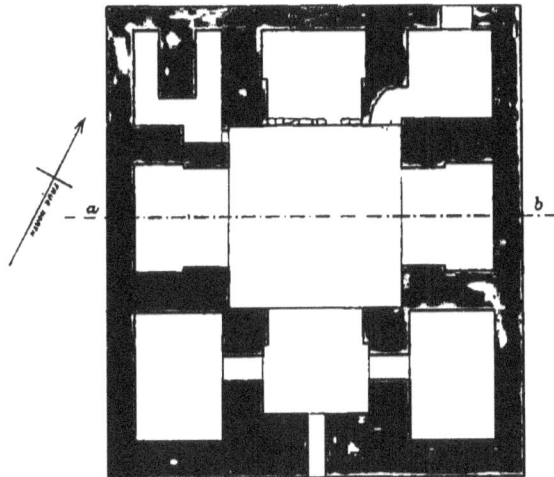

Tomb of Uriah (so called).

one period and structure, and there seems never to have been any roof to the central court. It has been erroneously called 'cruciform,' because four arched chambers run back, one from each side of the court; but the four corner chambers appear to belong to the same period, and there was certainly never any apse on the east, where the stone panels (to be described) remain intact, and exactly resemble those on the north, south, and west.

Each recess is 18 feet wide, and $17\frac{1}{2}$ feet to the back. Each has a fine

Supposed Sassanian Building

Fig 1. W. Wall, South Panel.
Fig 2. Northern Building.
Fig 3. S. Wall, West Panel.

arch rising about 9 feet, and 6½ feet thick. Behind this arch the roof is domical, but does not rise from regular pendentives, as in late Arab work, but very awkwardly from a kind of dome gradually flattened off to the angles of the recess. The total height from the roof of the recess to the floor of the court is 27 feet, and the arch springs about 14 feet from the floor. The corner chambers of the building are square (16½ feet) on the north-east and north-west. On the south-east and south-west they are 23 feet north and south, by 17 feet east and west. In the north-west chamber the staircase to the roof, now ruined, once ascended. The entrance to the court is on the south side, and is 3½ feet wide. There was also an entrance 6 feet wide into the north-east chamber from the north side, and into the west recess from the back, now closed up.

Section on A B
Scale

TOMB OF URIAH (SO CALLED).

The object of this structure is not clear. To this building el Mukaddasy seems to allude when he says: 'The castle of Goliah is on the hill overhanging the city, and therein is the tomb of Uriah, over which is built a mosque.' It cannot have been a church, and has no windows, so that the light is entirely derived from the central court, which was probably always open to the air. The building is also not suited for a mosque. It has no fountain for washing, and no mihrab, and its door is on the south. It appears to be a kiosk, or small hall or palace, connected with another, perhaps larger, further to the north.

The great interest of the building consists, however, in the detail of its stonework. A shallow panel with a round head flanks each of the great arches already described, and stands on a string course 5 feet 3 inches from the ground, supported by three small arches which spring from coupled dwarf-columns, and form the heads of three smaller panels.

This lower panelling is also carried round the walls of the recesses at the same level; and above the large panel, which is also flanked by slender coupled columns, there is a band of ornamentation, and a second string course supporting three other panels, like those in the lowest tier. This arrangement is repeated on each wall, but the designs in the panels differ; some do not appear to have been ever finished, some are of arabesque design, some geometrical. A dog-tooth moulding runs round the arches, and in one of the larger panels—that on the west half of the south wall—there is a representation of a tree, with leaves and berries, conventionally executed, which is not unlike the Assyrian tree of Asshur. None of the arches are structural; they are all carved out of one or more blocks of stone in the wall, and the panelling seems to have been cut after the walls had been built. The arches are rudely and irregularly executed, and while some are semicircular, others are of the Saracenic type, corbelled inwards at the spring, but only slightly. The details will be best explained by the drawing.

The great structural arches of the recesses appear to be very slightly pointed. The photograph shows a smaller arch at the back of the recess, also slightly pointed, whence it appears that on the north the building was originally open, and on this side the roof arrangement also differs, as will be seen in the photograph.

The arrangement of panels in different tiers, flanking large arches with recesses, resembles that of the walls of the Tak Kesra, at Ctesiphon, which is ascribed by Mr. Fergusson to the Sassanian period, about 550 A.D. The Tak Kesra arches appear to be horseshoes, while the panels have segmental and pointed arches, with coupled columns, as at 'Ammân.

It should be noted that the arches in the Dome of the Rock at Jerusalem seem to be slightly elliptical, while the structural arches at 'Ammân have only a very slight point. It should also be noted that the outer wall of the Dome of the Rock presents panels with a second tier of smaller arches, flanked by coupled dwarf pillars, just like those at 'Ammân. The similarity is so great that it seems possible that the outer walls of the Dome of the Rock and the 'Ammân building may belong to the same period. The panels and arcade in the Jerusalem example have round arches, like the majority of the arches in the 'Ammân example. The entire absence of any representation of animals in the panels at 'Ammân suggests a Moslem origin for the building, for in the case of the supposed Palace of Chosroes, at Mashita (end of the sixth century), the representations of animals are numerous.

The dog-tooth moulding was employed by Crusaders and by Arabs of the fourteenth century alike, but in their buildings it is much bolder than in the 'Ammân example, where the ornament consists merely in cutting out triangular pieces from the flat surface of the face of the arch. (See what has been said on the subject of this moulding under the head Sûmia.)

The use of round arches, the panelling details, the arrangement of the recesses (which is like that of many Persian buildings, but unlike anything Byzantine or Arab), all seems to point to a period of Persian influence as being that during which the 'Ammân building was erected. Professor Hayter Lewis is inclined to place it as late as the eleventh century; but as the pointed arch (much more defined than any at 'Ammân) appears to have been used by the Arabs in Egypt and Syria as early as the middle of the ninth century, it may perhaps be suggested that this interesting building belongs to the same time with the octagonal wall of the Dome of the Rock, which, on independent considerations, may be supposed to be the work of el Mamûn (831 A.D.).

The second building of the same kind was re-examined during the visit of the Princes, on April 11, 1882. In this case also there appears to have been a central court, 35 feet square, and three recesses (one on the north, one on the east, one on the south), about 30 feet wide, and 35 feet to the back—these measurements are, however, doubtful, as the building is much ruined. The north wall of the Kalâh formed the back wall of the north recess. On the west, a recess only 5 feet to the back and 35 feet wide existed. The southern recess or archway was probably open at the south end. The remains of a tunnel-vaulting still exist on this side.

About 50 feet south of this building is the wall (already described as the north side of the court) of a temple or enclosure of the Roman period. Upon the north side of this wall, opposite the building just described, were found remains of two panels with round heads (carved on fallen stones), resembling in general character the panels already fully noticed (see sketch). This seems to indicate a continuation of the ruined building (just described) southwards as far as the older wall in question.

There is a large round tank of perhaps the same period east of the square Sassanian or Arab building. It is 58 feet in diameter, 19 feet deep, with steps leading down.

The Survey of 'Ammân and the notes above given occupied the party for seven days. The Survey was commenced by measuring a base in the Kalâh, and fixing points with a theodolite from the ends of the same, by Messrs. Black and Armstrong. The buildings were measured with a tape, and their bearings taken. The wall of the Kalâh was plotted in the same way from measurements by Captain Conder and Lieutenant Mantell. The minor objects were interpolated with aid of the prismatic compass by Mr. Armstrong, who completed the detailed Survey. Every building described was visited by Captain Conder. Lieutenant Mantell took ten successful photographs. Plans had already been made by De Saulcy and Sir C. Warren, but the time at their command was more limited. Lieutenant Mantell's photographs of the dolmens and menhirs are the first taken, as these remains, together with the tank and secret passage, were discovered by the surveyors. The other buildings had already been photographed successfully by Sir C. Warren.*

Explored October 8, 13, 14, 15, 17, 18, and 19, 1881.

'Amûd el Inkliziyeh (عمود الانكليزية, 'pillar of the English lady').—This is the grave of Mrs. Bland, and bears the inscription beneath:

EMILY ALICIA BLAND, MARCH 16, 1868.

Mr. and Mrs. Bland were travelling with Sir C. Warren, and Mrs. Bland died on the spot. A short column of red granite with a square base is erected on high ground, and the inscription is in Egyptian capitals. The column is surrounded by a great cairn of blocks of sandstone. The grave is respected by the Arabs, and the place is sacred, for near it is one of their own sacred circles. In the valley below is the 'Ain Hamârah, or 'donkey's spring' (see Senáin el Hamârah), a copious thermal spring, which was found to be about 80° Fah. The Nubian sandstone is here close to the surface of the plateau east of the Dead Sea on which the

---

* Some idea of date may be obtained, perhaps, for the Roman buildings at 'Ammân by comparing the names of Emperors on the milestone not far east (see Rujûm Rafiah).

cairn stands, and an outbreak of black basalt occurs near the spring. By the water there are a few palms and some tamarisk bushes, but the place, when visited in autumn, is intensely bare and desolate, and the sudden discovery of an English lady's tomb thus guarded in the desert by wild Arabs was very touching. Mr. Bland has lately died; but even if the sum of £5 annually paid to Sheikh Kablân by him as guardian of the place should cease with the death of the latter, the tomb will continue to be honoured.

Visited September 30, 1881.

'Arâk 'Âisheh (عراق عيشة, 'cliff of Aisha').—Named from the wife of Muhammed, as the Arabs suppose the bas-relief bust of a woman here to be the portrait of the Prophet's wife. The site is south of 'Ammân, and the cliff facing north has here been quarried for some distance eastwards from the road (Misdâr Abu 'Âisheh). A few scattered stones form the Khurbet 'Âisheh. This latter name is the one marked on the reduced map, the 'Arâk not being written.

Towards the west end the quarry is cut back southwards for a width of about 19 feet, and square chambers are cut at the back and on the west side of this recess. They were probably tombs.

On the east of this there is an alcove in the rock about 10 feet high, and 7 feet wide, and 2 feet deep. Eastwards, again, is a second just like it. These may have been intended for statues. The little bust is on the right or west side of the eastern alcove, and the chin is $14\frac{1}{2}$ feet from the ground. A photograph was taken by Lieutenant Mantell, and a sketch made by Captain Conder. It is clearly a bit of Roman sculpture. The head is veiled, the features are obliterated, but the drapery is classic. It is larger than life-size, and cut with a sunk medallion round the face. Similar busts, but not so well executed, have been found at Abila (Sûk Wâdy Barada) in Antilebanon over tombs and at es Salt by Captain Conder. It was probably the portrait of the lady buried in the chamber close by.

Explored October 10, 1881.

## Tyrus.

'Arâk el Emir (عراق الامير, 'cliff of the Emir,' or prince).—The original name of this site, according to Josephus, was Tyrus (12 Antiq., iv. 11). The Greek would represent the Hebrew צוּר (or possibly ציר),

as in the Phœnician city Tyre, and would no doubt be derived from the 'rock' or cliff now called 'Arâk. The valley immediately south of the site is called Wâdy Sir, and a ruin called Sir exists in it north-west of the ruins about to be described. There is also an 'Ain es Sir in the valley, and a large ruin called Khûrbet Sâr on the hill above the valley-head. West of 'Arâk el Emir is the ruin called Khûrbet es Sûr, which is the closest to the original Tzur ; but all the names above quoted may probably be derived from the Hebrew original name.

The ruins to be described at this site include the excavations in the cliff, the K a s r e l 'A b d, and the remains on the plateau. The cliff faces southwards, the true bearing along its length being 67° (see Lieutenant Mantell's Photo., No. 27); it extends about 550 yards east and west; its height is from 80 to 90 feet. At its foot extends a terrace, apparently artificial, about 300 yards north and south. On this plateau are ruins, apparently of a village, and on the south side are scarps of rock. The K a s r e l 'A b d stands on the south and rather to the west of the cliff, about 600 yards from it. It is built on a raised earthen platform, surrounded by low ground. A retaining wall and bank on the south shut in this surrounding basin, which was once filled with water by an aqueduct from the stream. A raised ramp or causeway led through the water to the Kasr or palace on its island mound, and is still visible, reaching to the slopes of the hill below the great terrace north-east of the palace.

The history of the site is given by Josephus. A certain priest named Hyrcanus was the youngest son of Joseph, who was of the high priest's family. On the death of his father he made war on his brothers, but, being unsuccessful, he retired beyond Jordan, and engaged in continual strife with the Arabs. The following is the description of his buildings :

However, Hyrcanus determined not to return to Jerusalem any more, but seated himself beyond Jordan, and was at perpetual war with the Arabians, and slew many of them, and took many of them captives. He also erected a strong castle, and built it entirely of white stone to the very roof, and had animals of a prodigious magnitude engraven upon it. He also drew round it a great and deep canal of water. He also made caves of many furlongs in length by hollowing a rock that was over against him, and then he made large rooms in it, some for feasting, and some for sleeping and living in. He introduced also a vast quantity of waters, which ran along it, and which were very delightful and ornamental in the court. But, still, he made the entrance at the mouth of the caves so narrow that no more than one person could enter them at once: and the reason why he built them after that manner was a good one; it was for his own preservation, lest he should be besieged by his brethren, and run the hazard of being caught by them. Moreover, he built courts of greater magnitude than ordinary, which he adorned with vastly large gardens. And when he had brought the place to this state, he named it Tyre. This place is between Arabia and Judea, beyond Jordan, not far from the country of Heshbon. And he ruled over those parts for seven years, even all the time that Seleucus was King of Syria. . . . As for Hyrcanus, when he saw that Antiochus had a great army, and feared lest he should be caught by him and brought to punishment for what he had done to the Arabians, he ended his life, and slew himself with his own hand, while Antiochus seized upon all his substance.—Josephus, 12 Antiq. iv., 11. Whiston's Translation.

Hyrcanus committed suicide in 176 B.C. He lived seven years in Gilead (*i.e.*, from 183 B.C., when Joseph died). The ruins of his palace, and the Aramaic inscription at the caves, are thus very accurately dated, and are most valuable for comparison with other undated or vaguely-dated examples of Jewish art.

*The caves* were carefully examined, measured, and planned by Lieutenant Mantell, R.E. They are in two tiers. The lower tier is on ground-level; the upper tier is entered from an open gallery cut in the face of the cliff. The gallery extends eastwards from the west end of the cliff about 300 yards, and terminates at a point where the rock is cut back at a slope of about five over one, so as effectually to prevent anyone reaching the level of the gallery at this end. The gallery is about 46 feet above the level of the plateau; it is on an average 10 feet wide and 9 feet high to its roof. The south side is open, except at one point, where a sort of buttress projects, and through this buttress there is an arched communication to the gallery from a ledge or advanced gallery in front of the buttress. This is well shown in the sketch given by De Vogüé ('Temple de Jerusalem,' Plate XXXV.). Towards the middle of the gallery there is a sloping ramp between rock-scarps about 5 feet wide, leading up westwards from the ground-level to that of the gallery near the middle cave. The object of this ramp was clearly to allow of horses being brought up to the caves in the upper tier, one of which was, as will appear immediately, used as a stable.

At the west end of the cliff there is a curious detached block of rock standing erect. It is $16\frac{1}{2}$ feet high, $12\frac{1}{2}$ feet broad on its eastern face, and 7 feet thick. In the east face are cut 26 niches—in four upper rows of four each, and two lower rows of five. The niches average about

11 inches in height, 9 inches at the base, and 6 inches to the back (see Fig. 2), and are 15 inches from centre to centre. The object of these niches is not clear. In Jewish tombs (see 'Memoirs,' vol. ii., p. 375) niches are often found in the façade, and were intended for small lamps; these are, however, smaller than those in question. Roman columbaria are also found in Palestine (see 'Memoirs.' vol. iii., pp. 290, 358), but these are in caves or vaults. Curious niches occur in walls at Masada (see 'Memoirs,' vol. iii., p. 420), which seem to have been used for the skulls of hermits, as in the Burj er Rûs at Damascus (compare e d D e i r below); but it seems unlikely that this would be the origin of

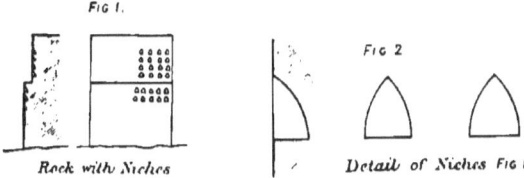

Fig. 1. Rock with Niches
Fig. 2. Detail of Niches Fig 1.

the niches at 'Arâk el Emir. On the whole, it seems most probable that the niches served to light the gallery, although its extent seems too great to be so illuminated.

The number of caves examined by Lieutenant Mantell (and by Captain Conder) was fifteen in all—six in the lower tier, nine in the upper. There are also some small caves towards the east end of the cliff, which were not entered, as there does not appear to be any means of reaching them. They are high up and inaccessible, like many of the hermit caves west of Jordan, and they may have been reached by a rope or a ladder, as in the case of the hermit caves.

The fifteen caves in and below the gallery are as follows, commencing with the most westerly of the upper tier:

No. 1 (see Fig. 3) is 49 feet to the back, and 11 feet wide, with a descent of three steps, and a narrow ledge on the side walls 6 inches to 18 inches wide. The total height of the cave is about 17 feet, and the ledge is 6 feet or 7 feet from the floor.

No. 2 (Fig. 4) is a similar chamber, with a branch to the right. The chamber is 38½ feet long, and 11 feet wide; the branch is 15½ feet to the back, 6 feet wide. A flight of eleven steps leads down 10 feet from the surface of the gallery to the cave floor. The height of the cave is about 20 feet at the further end.

No. 3 (Fig. 5), still proceeding eastwards, is a cave on the level of the ground or gallery outside. It is 30 feet to the back, and 8 feet wide at the back above the ledges of the side walls, which are each 2 feet wide. At the entrance the cave is 11 feet wide; the height could not be ascertained. On the right is a branch 7 feet wide, 14 feet to the back, with a rounded roof 7 feet from the floor in the middle.

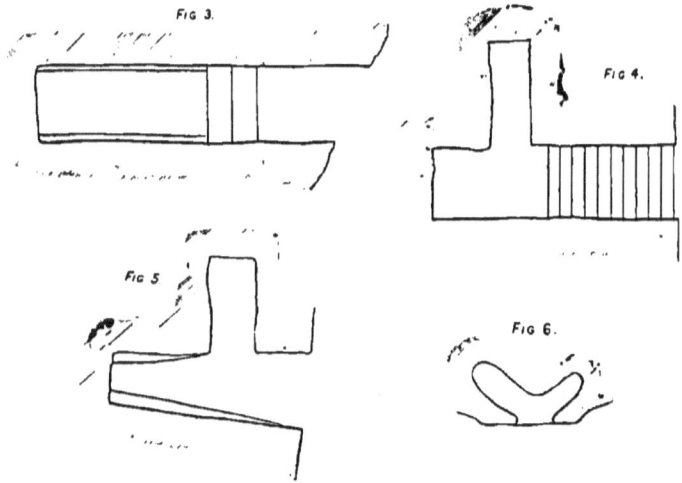

No. 4 is a cave with an entrance five feet above the gallery level (Fig. 6). It has two branches, about 12 feet and 8 feet long respectively, and the height is about 4 feet.

No. 5 is the largest cave in the upper tier (see Fig. 7), and measures 143 feet to the back. There is a kind of hall (as shown) with a gallery at the back 95 feet long, 21 feet wide, and about 12 feet high. The principal side-chamber to the left is 10 feet wide, and 20 feet to the back. Both the long gallery and the side-chamber have stone mangers, no doubt for the horses of a cavalry force employed by Hyrcanus against the Arabs.

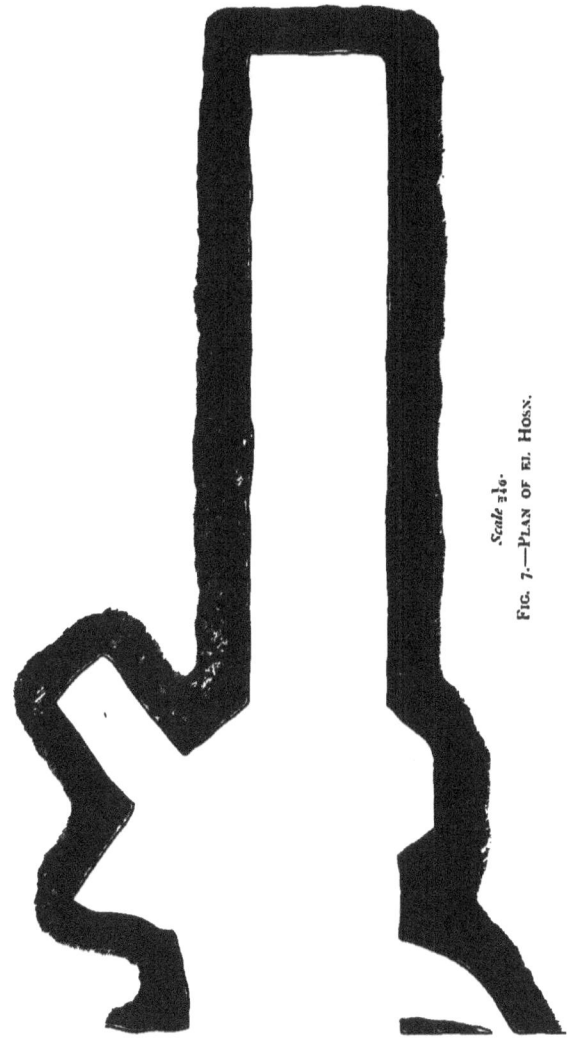

Fig. 7.—Plan of El. Hosn. Scale 1/16.

There are more than a hundred mangers in all, but many are much decayed. The best preserved specimens were measured (see Fig. 8). The rock was cut back at 3 feet from the floor to form a manger, measuring 1 foot 9 inches to the back, and 19 inches wide, and 2 feet 3 inches high in front. A ledge, 6 inches high and wide, separated each manger from the next; and in front under each manger was a rock-staple or ring for the halter, with a hole 6 inches by 3 inches through it. On the right-hand side of the cave there was one of these staples for each

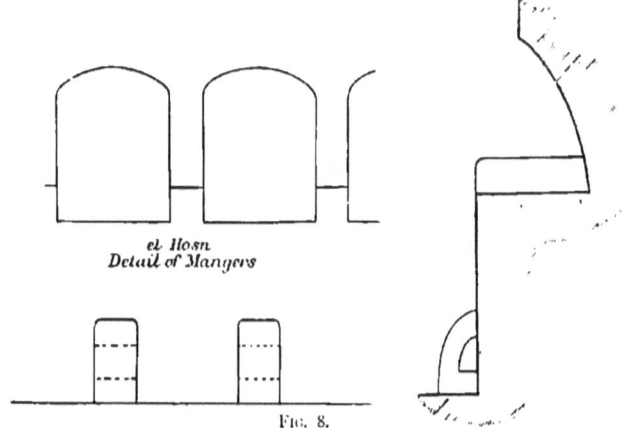

el Hosn
Detail of Mangers

Fig. 8.

manger, but on the left-hand side only one for every two mangers; but it is possible that a long rope was passed through the staples, and the halters attached to the rope, after the usual Syrian method of tethering animals at the present time. This cave receives at the present time the name el Hosn, probably meaning 'the horses' (الحصن).

Immediately west of this cave there is a sort of alcove cut in the rock. It is 4 feet across, 4½ feet to the back, and 3½ feet high. To the left is a little niche, 1 foot wide, 6 inches to the back, 1½ feet to the top; this may have held a lamp. The object of the cutting is not clear; it may have been intended to excavate another cave, which was never completed.

No. 6 cave, east of the large one No. 5 (see Fig. 9), is 52 feet to the back, and 13 feet wide. It has a recess on the right, 18 feet wide, 9 feet to the back, and a flight of seven steps, 4½ feet wide, leading down to the floor. The floor of the cave is about 12 feet below the gallery level, and the total height is about 25 feet. In the left-hand wall of this cave there are niches 1 foot 8 inches to 3 feet above ground, 2 feet 9 inches to 3 feet 9 inches apart, six in all; one of which is 1 foot wide, 9 inches high, 7 inches to the back; and a smaller one, 7 inches by 7 inches by 3 inches to the back. They are rounded at the top, and may have been used for lamps.

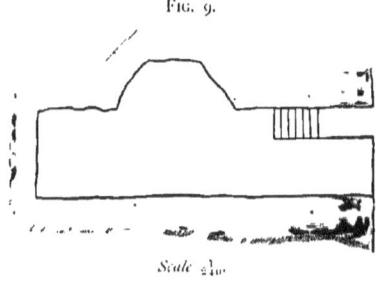

Fig. 9.

Scale ₂¹⁄₁₀.

No. 7 cave (Fig. 10) is only 11 feet wide, and 6 feet to the back. The floor is level with that of the gallery, with a rock wall 1½ feet high in

Fig. 10.

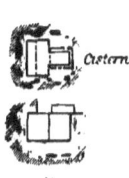

Fig. 11.

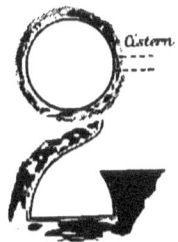

Fig. 12.

front of part. The total height is 6 feet. Near this cave are two cisterns: the first (Fig. 11) is 4 feet deep and 7 feet long; the second is round, being 13 feet in diameter and 10 feet deep. The mouth opens from the gallery, and the floor is 6½ feet below the gallery level. A recess like a *koka* runs in from one side of the circle; it is 2 feet long, and 2 feet wide (see Fig. 12).

VIEW OF CLIFF AT 'ARAK EL EMIR.

To face page 72.

No. 8 cave.—This is called e s h  S h â r i by the natives, apparently 'the elevated' (see 'Memoirs of Survey of Western Palestine,' vol. iii., p. 266), and is probably one of the living rooms described by Josephus as having very narrow entrances. There are two stories in this excavation, the lower having a doorway 4½ feet wide leading from the gallery, while the upper has a window over the door. The plan is on the level of the upper floor, which is reached from the lower by a hole (as shown) in the floor between them. The lower chamber is (at present) only 3½ feet high, and runs in 37 feet, the breadth being about 10 feet at the back; and

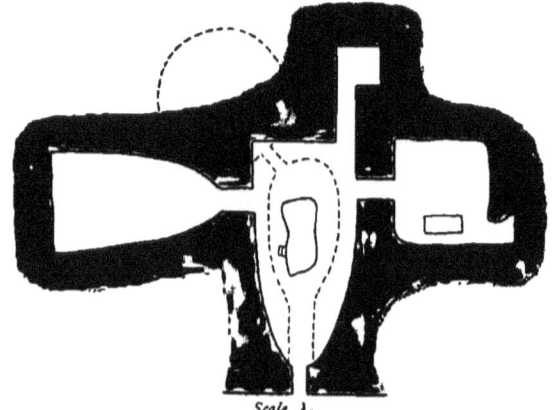

Scale 2¹⁄₄₀.
FIG. 13.

rather lower is a circular excavation, perhaps a cistern, about 20 feet in diameter. There are traces of steps at the side of the hole to the upper story, and the central chamber on this upper tier is about 30 feet by 16 feet. It has a chamber on each side. That to the left is 7 feet high, and is entered by a narrow passage 5 feet 3 inches long, 3½ feet wide; the total measurement to the back of the chamber is 31 feet, and the back wall is 15 feet long. The chamber to the right is 6 feet high, with a similar entrance; it measures 14½ feet to the back, by 15 feet across, and has in one corner (as shown) an irregular recess 4 feet by 4½ feet—in this chamber also is a sort of well sunk in the floor, 6 feet long, 3 feet wide,

6 feet deep. A *koka* or recess also runs in in the right-hand corner of the back wall of the central chamber: it is 14 feet to the back, and 3 feet wide, with an enlargement 4 feet by 6 feet on the right at the back.

Fig. 14.   Fig. 15.

The window of the central chamber is 2 feet 3 inches broad, 3½ feet high, and its ground-sill is 2 feet above the floor. The side-chambers are, of course, quite dark (see Fig. 13).

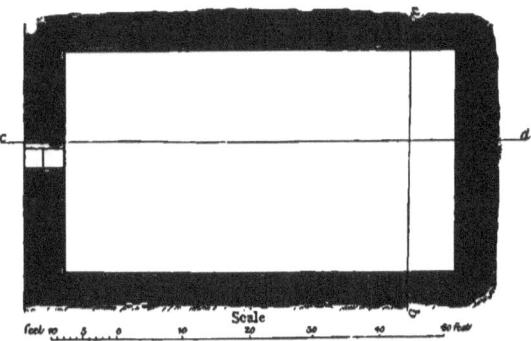

Fig. 16.—El Weibdeh.

No. 9 cave (Fig. 14) is of irregular shape, with two entrances. It is about 17 feet across, with recesses as shown on the plan, and a ledge in one angle 2½ feet above the floor.

No. 10 cave (Fig. 15), the furthest west in the lower tier of caves, is a simple chamber 14 feet wide and 22 feet to the back, and about 14 feet high.

No. 11, east of the last in the same tier, is called by the Arabs el Weibdeh ('the cutting') (see Figs. 16, 17, 18). It is a better cut than

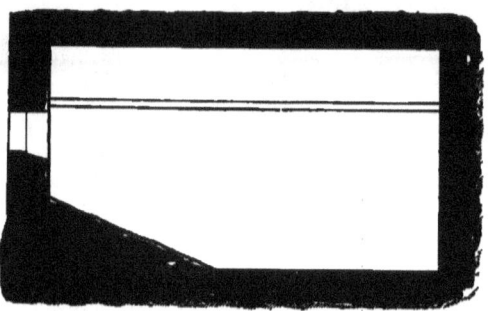

FIG. 17.—SECTION ON $c$, $d$.

most, and considerably below the present level of the ground outside, though this may in part be due to the accumulation of rubbish outside.

FIG. 18.—SECTION $a$, $b$.   FIG. 19.

It measures 60 feet to the back and 33 feet across, and is 33 feet high to the top of the arched roof, which is cut as shown. The entrance is 3 feet wide and 6 feet high, and a ramp, now covered with rubbish which may conceal rock-steps, leads down to the floor.

No. 12 cave (Fig. 19) is 22 feet to the back, 13 feet wide, with an entrance 4 feet wide.

No. 13 cave resembles No. 11, but being full of brambles and of *tibn*, it could not be properly measured. In the back wall is a niche about 3 feet high and 2 feet wide towards the left. The entrance is 4 feet wide, and is cut with a simple sculpture, as shown in the photograph (Lieutenant Mantell's Series, No. 26). To the right of the door, high up, is an inscription which also shows in the photograph. Lieutenant Mantell estimated the length and breadth of the chamber within to be

FIG. 20.

60 feet by 30 feet. This inscription is interesting and important because, with exception of the Moabite Stone and the Siloam text, no other inscription has yet been found within the limits of the Holy Land which is with certainty of as great antiquity. The tomb of the Beni Hezir at Jerusalem is probably a century later; but the Gezer stones ('Memoirs,' vol. ii., pp. 436, 438) may be nearly as old, being dated by M. Ganneau as possibly of the Hasmonean period, or about thirty years later than the present text, which is shown on next page.

The letters are very distinct, and the photograph bears out the copy, which agrees with that made by De Vogüé. There can, therefore, be no doubt that Euting was wrong in giving the form 6 to the first letter, which he read as *Teth*, making the whole to read *Turiah* for 'Tyre.' De Vogüé read *Arabiah*, and *Aduiah* has also been proposed.

The only alphabet which accounts for all the letters is the contemporary alphabet of the Hasmonean coinage (see Madden's tables in 'Coins of the Jews'). The final letter, however, is nearer to the

alphabets of the Carpentras Stone and papyri. The first letter is *Ain*; the second is found as *Vau* on the coins; the third might be *Beth*, or possibly *Caph* or *Nun* on the coins, and is like the *Resh* of the Carpentras Stone. The fourth is the *Yod* of the coinage. The last must be a *Heh* or a *Tau*.

The same alphabet occurs on contemporary Jewish coins. The most probable transliteration seems to be עוריה, the meaning of which is doubtful, as there are several roots to which it might be referred, viz.: (1) עור (Arabic, غَار), 'to bore,' whence מְעָרָה (Arab. مغارة), 'cave,' and غور, the *Ghor* or Jordan Valley; (2) עור, 'to be watchful,' etc., etc.

The following table may be useful for comparison:

| TYRUS TEXT. | JEWISH COINS. | CARPENTRAS STONE. |
|---|---|---|
| ע | ○ ○ ▽ ○ | ○ |
| ו | ל ↑ ץ | ןך |
| ר | ५ ५ ९ | ५५ |
| י | ʔ ∼ ʔ | ⅃∧ |
| ה | ⅂ ⊤ ⅂ | ∧ ⊓ |

No. 14 cave, east of the last (see Fig. 21), measures 23 feet by 9 feet, with a recess at the back, 11 feet wide, 16 feet to the back. A flight of seventeen steps, 4 feet wide, leads up to a height of 10 feet above the cave floor, where is a kind of platform with a window 6 feet wide, used, no doubt, as an outlook place. The entrance to this cave is 3 feet wide and 4 feet high.

No. 15 cave (Fig. 22) is only 9 feet by 4 feet, and 6 feet high; it is perched up 12 feet above the ground-level in the side of the cliff.

All these caves, whether excavated at one time or gradually increased in numbers, were probably older than the palace of Hyrcanus, which seems never to have been finished. It is clear both from their defensive arrangements, and from those of the palace, that the inhabitants of this site were in constant danger of sudden attack.

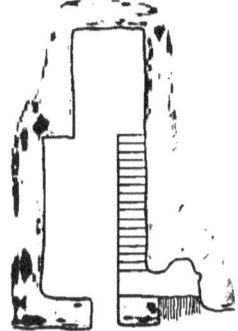

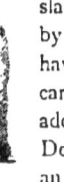

FIG. 21.   FIG. 22.

The K u s r e l 'A b d, or 'palace of the slave,' is the palace described by Josephus (see p. 66) as having been built by Hyrcanus of white stone, and adorned with sculptured lions. De Saulcy supposed it to be an Ammonite temple, but the shape is not that of a temple (either Greek, Egyptian, or Phœnician); and of Ammonite worship we have no records. The modern name is due to a legend or myth. The Emir whose name is preserved in the title 'Arâk el Emir had a daughter whom he left in charge of a black slave while he went on pilgrimage. The slave loving the daughter, she promised to marry him if he would build her a palace (as in the story of Aladdin). The slave began building the ruined palace still existing, thence called Kusr el 'Abd (palace of the slave). His superhuman power is evidenced by the enormous size of its stones. But before he completed it the Emir returned, and the place where his horse first became visible is the hill, east of the palace, still called M u t u l l e l H i s â n, 'the appearing of the horse.' He consumed the black slave with fire, and afterwards buried him (or crushed him) beneath a stone.

This tale resembles many other Arab legends, and may be supposed to be mythical. The princess freed from the black slave is perhaps the dawn; the Emir on his horse, who goes on pilgrimage and reappears in the east, is probably the sun, who in Persia (*e.g.* as Rustem) is represented as a horseman; the black man is the genius of the night slain by the first rays of the sun. The whole question of Arab mythology is discussed in 'Heth and Moab' (chap. xi.). The story was related on the occasion of the royal visit to the site by Sheikh Fellâh en Nimr, and translated by Mr. N. T. Moore, C.M.G.

The Kusr el 'Abd stands in a sunk basin formed by a retaining wall on the south and east, while on the west is a steep natural slope, and on the north a gradual ascent. The area thus enclosed still holds stagnant water in winter, and traces of an aqueduct seem to show that it was filled from the stream in the valley. The plateau measures 320 yards east and west, and the retaining wall is 100 yards south of the south wall of the palace. This wall is about 8 or 10 feet high, and outside it is a terrace, generally about 25 feet broad, beyond which is a second retaining wall.

The palace stands on a sort of island about 15 feet above the level of the surrounding court or basin. The causeway from the east is on the same level, and passes immediately north of the gateway at the north-east angle of the retaining wall, as shown on the plan. The total breadth of the palace east and west is 62½ feet from outside to outside; the total exterior length is 126 feet. The east wall is standing at its ends to the height of three courses, and the foundations of the other walls are also traceable. The retaining-wall of the platform or island on which the palace is built measures 70 yards north and south, by 50 yards east and west; it is built of

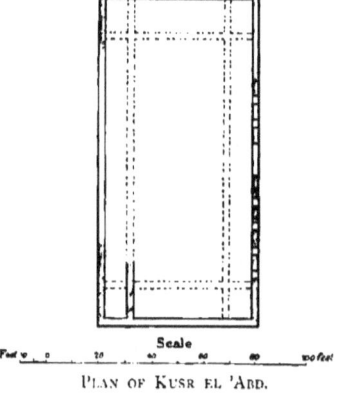

PLAN OF KUSR EL 'ABD.

rudely-squared stones of moderate size and cubic proportions. The building had a gate on the north, and probably one corresponding on the south. On the east it had a central gate 12 feet 4 inches wide, and two side-entrances north of it, and four to the south—these side-entrances are 3 feet wide. The plan of the interior is not very clearly traceable, though it seems probable that De Vogüé's restoration may be correct, showing a central court surrounded by chambers and cloisters. The remains of an inner wall are clearly visible on the north and on the west (see Plan), and the capitals of various pillars, apparently belonging to cloisters or to the entrance-gates, remain fallen in the interior of the building.

Kusr el 'Abd.   E. Wall.

The masonry is of very great size. The greatest height, which may have been the total intended height of the building, is 21 feet, as below:

|  | Feet. | Inches. |
|---|---|---|
| Lowest course | 8 | 0 |
| Second    ,, | 5 | 2 |
| Frieze    ... | 1 | 6 |
| Course with lions ... | 6 | 6 |
|  | 21 | 2 |

There is a stone on the south side of the palace fallen flat, and measuring 20 feet by 10 feet. The corner-stone at the north end of the east wall in the lowest course is 17 feet 4 inches long, 8 feet high, and 2 feet 8 inches thick. These stones have a draft 5 inches wide and 1½ inches deep; the boss is smoothly dressed with a pick, as are the drafts. The adze-dressing of the Jerusalem Haram is nowhere observable. The stones were kept in place—as can be seen on the north wall near the

'ARÂK EL EMÎR.

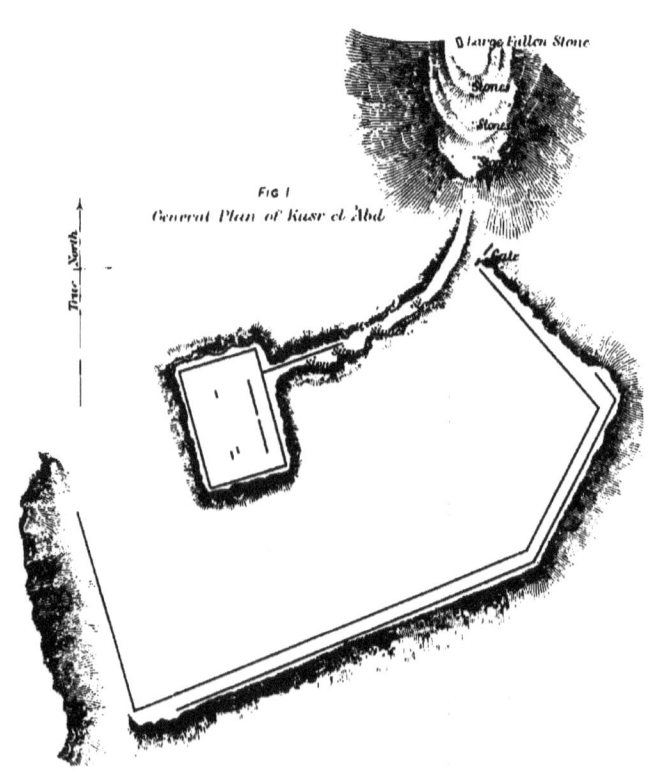

FIG 1
General Plan of Kasr el Abd

# TYRUS

west—by tenons in the upper course fitting into holes in the lower. The average thickness of the wall is 2½ feet to 2 feet 8 inches.

A long stone 2 feet 1 inch high (see profile), with a bold cornice-moulding, may have formed the top of the wall above the sculptured lions, or may have been a lintel-stone over one of the doorways.

The lions are four in number, on four blocks of stone 6½ feet high, and from 7 feet to 10 feet long. The two southern lions face south, and the two northern north. The figures of the end ones have no heads, as the head was no doubt cut on the end stone of the wall, which was formed by the thickness of

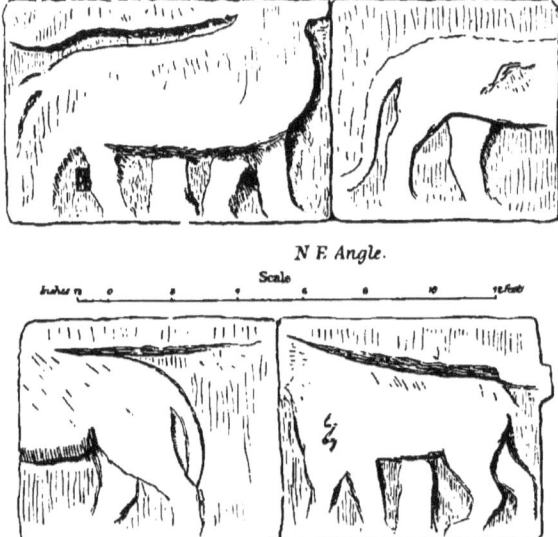

N E Angle.

Scale

S.E. Angle

the course in the south and the north walls respectively. The carving is in high relief, and appears to have been executed after the stones were placed in position in the wall, as the relief surface is flush with the general face of the wall, the depressed part being, in fact, scooped out in the thickness of the wall, as is shown by its not being continued to the top of the stone above the lions (see sketch). Beneath the lions is a simple dentellated string-course. There are traces of a staircase towards

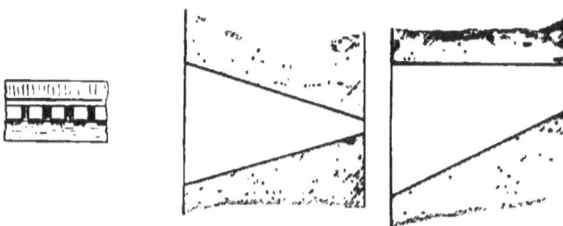

the north part of the east wall on the interior, ascending apparently in two flights, the lower northwards, the upper southwards. There are three small loops or windows in the east wall, which seem to have given light to this staircase. The loop is 8 inches high and 3 inches wide on the outside, 2 feet high and 22 inches wide on the inside.

The southern wall appears to have fallen outwards, as though by a sudden shock—perhaps of earthquake. The stone is a coarse crystalline

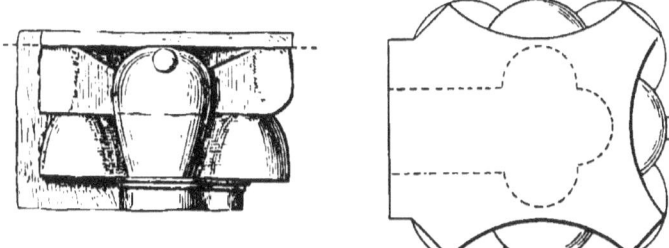

limestone from the cliff close by. The character of the capitals lying inside the building is very peculiar, and approaches perhaps most nearly to Egyptian art. The attached semipillars to which they belonged were 15 inches in diameter on three sides (as is shown above), as though belonging to a porch or colonnade. The north doorway was flanked by semipillars 18 inches in diameter (see p. 82), which rudely approach the Corinthian order. Two fragments of a frieze with triglyphs and guttæ of Ionic character occur; one is on a block 6½ feet long, 2½ feet high, and thus appears to have been originally placed over the gateway on the north. The lintel of the north door is 2½ feet thick, 19 inches high, and

 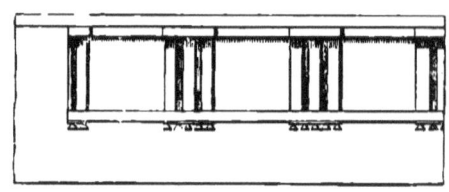

still lies fallen beside it. On the south lies a pillar-shaft 2 feet 3 inches in diameter, and there is another with a fluted shaft. The workmanship of the capitals is generally coarse, and the stone, being of inferior quality, was not fitted for fine tracery-work. The capitals are very much weathered. The bases of two attached semipillars were also measured. All these details present the same rude and imperfect reproduction of Greek art which is observable in the Jewish tombs of Western Palestine dating about the same time.

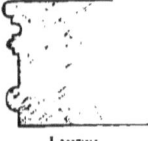  

LINTEL.  SEMIPILLARS.

The restoration given by De Vogüé ('Temple de Jerusalem,' p. 39) of this building seems to show that the demolition or decay of the ruin has continued since about 1860. According to this authority, the north entrance was divided into three, with two central pillars and two semipillars attached to the jambs. The inner wall on this side (still partly traceable) is shown with three entrances, and in the south-west angle De

Vogüé recognised the spring of a vaulted roof to a chamber or cloister on the west wall, the radius of the arch being, according to his calculation, 3·77 metres. He gives the details of the north door correctly, but omits any description of the curious Egyptian-like capitals above described, which, however, may be unfinished.

The gate on the east side of the enclosure is 13 feet wide, and several drafted stones occur in the wall on either side. This wall is 1 foot thick,

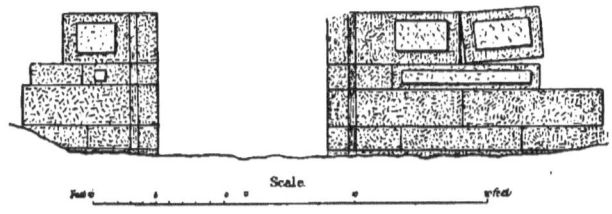

ELEVATION OF GATE.

and five courses remain standing. The masonry is fairly well finished, in alternate high and low courses, varying from 3 feet 8 inches in the top course to 1 foot 8 inches in the lowest but one. The longest stones are 10 feet 4 inches in length. The courses on the two sides of the gate are not of corresponding height. The drafts on the five drafted stones are irregular, and rudely finished. Close by the gate (which faces southwards) on the west is a fragment of cornice, with honey-suckle and other classic details; but this, like most of the Jewish work of the same period, is remarkable on account of the irregularity and want of symmetrical arrangement of the various members. The drawing shows accurately how this irregularity is visible.

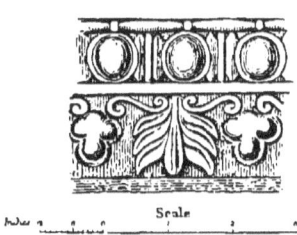

A remarkable feature of the ruin remains to be noticed, namely, the narrow causeway leading to the palace, and the pairs of cippi which are arranged along this causeway, and thence northwards towards the quarry and cliff. The causeway is 6 paces to 10 paces (15 to 25 feet)

INSCRIPTION ON THE ROCK AT ARAK EL EMIR.

*To face page 84.*

broad, and about 15 feet high. The pairs of cippi are arranged at from 20 to 30 paces (50 to 75 feet) between each pair. Four pairs were found on the causeway, and the same arrangement was traced 80 paces (200 feet) north of the gateway just described, in the direction of the west end of the 'Arak or cliff. Here lies fallen on the slope a stone evidently intended for the palace wall, either abandoned when the unfinished palace was left at the death of Hyrcanus, or else discarded as unsound (of which, however, there is no indication). This stone is 8 feet high and 25 feet long, and only 2 feet 3 inches thick.* It lies immediately west of the double line of cippi, and between it and the gateway three pairs of cippi occur. The alignment was traced 200 paces (500 feet) north of this fallen block, nine pairs of cippi being found within that distance. The total distance from the cliff to the palace is 600 yards, but the cippi are only traceable about 400 yards in all. The

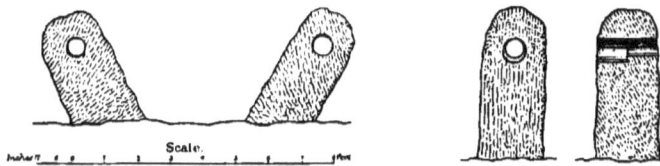

fall from the foot of the cliff to the base of the palace wall was ascertained, by aneroid observations, to be 170 feet. The average gradient is thus one in fifteen, but the fall is not regular.

This double alignment has been supposed, by those who consider the palace to have been an Ammonite temple, to represent a *Via Sacra* from the east; but the width between the two cippi of a pair is only 3 feet, which appears much too narrow for a roadway or avenue. It will be remarked, moreover, that a stone, evidently intended for the palace walls, lies fallen by the alignment, and that the stones of the palace, though of great height and length, are always less than 3 feet in thickness, so that they could, if raised on end in the position they occupy in the walls, pass easily between the cippi.

Each cippus is 4 feet to 4½ feet long, and about 2 feet wide, and the

---

* This is the largest stone on the spot, and its weight must be about 50 tons.

same in thickness. In some places they are not vertical, but lean outwards. Each cippus has a hole, about 9 inches in diameter, near the top; most of the holes are countersunk, as shown in the section of the cippus, the hole on one side being only 7 inches in diameter.

The cippi seem evidently to be connected with the method of bringing the great stones from the quarry to the palace walls. The countersunk holes suggest the use of beams fitted into the cippi, to form a rude tram on which the stones might slide. Wood for this purpose might have been obtained in the neighbouring oak forest, and similar methods were employed by the Egyptians, who moved large blocks on a carriage running on wooden oiled ways.

The distance apart of the pairs of cippi, which averages about 60 feet, seems, however, too great to allow of the supposition that beams or poles could be found long enough to stretch from one pair to another. Perhaps, therefore, the real use of the cippi was to act as a fulcrum or pulley, used by men pulling ropes, possibly passed through the holes; and this might account for the cippi not being vertical, as they may have been pulled out of position in the direction in which the rope was hauled. Whatever be the exact manner in which the cippi were used, there seems little doubt that they were intended to assist in transporting the great stones to the palace.

The ruins on the terrace or plateau, at the foot of the 'Arâk cliff, are apparently those of a small town or village. They may very possibly belong to a period later than that of the building of Hyrcanus' palace. Foundations remain of well-cut masonry, the stones of large size. There are fragments of a simple cornice moulding, and on the south side of the terrace the rocks seem to have been artificially scarped, and in one place possibly formed the base of a small tower. On the east slope of the terrace is a block of rock 13 feet long, with a curious cutting 3 feet wide at the top, beneath which in the east face of the block are seven niches, each 7 inches in measurement in its three dimensions. The object of this cutting is not easily explained.

The stream in the valley (Wâdy es Sir) is fresh, perennial, and abundant. It is surrounded with oleanders which have grown to enormous size, being almost as large as forest trees. The cool shade beneath these thick trees beside the water is extremely refreshing.

The view from the terrace extends southwards over the Moabite ridges, Nebo and Siâghah being visible, with the Minyeh ridge beyond. The natural advantages of this secluded and well-watered nook made it well fitted for the abode of a luxurious tyrant like Hyrcanus the priest.

Explored October 20, 21, 24, 25, 1881.

'Arâk el Hamâm (عراق الحمام, 'the pigeon's cliff' or 'cave').—A cave in a low cliff on the edge of the plain called Merj el Hamâm, south of 'Ammân.

'Arâk Jubr (عراق جبر, 'cliff of Jubr,' p.n. 'hero').—Small cave near a dolmen. See Sûmia.

'Arâk el Mâbarah (عراق المابرة, 'cliff of the quarry').—See el Mâberah. The name here applies to a great cliff north of Shânab. It is omitted from the reduced map as unimportant.

'Arâk el Meghuwul (عراق المغول, 'haunted cliff').—A cliff near Abu Kâûwûkah, east of Umm Kuseir. It is omitted from the reduced map as unimportant, and for want of space.

'Arâk en Nusûry (عراق النسوري, 'cliff of eagles').—A high precipice. See 'Ain en Nusûry. It is the cliff at the spring in question, and is, consequently, omitted from the reduced map.

'Arâk er Rashdân (عراق الرشدان, the root means 'to lead').—A cliff east of the Hâj Road.

'Arâk er Rûâk (عراق الرواق, 'cliff of porches').—This term ' Rûâk' is commonly used east of Jordan for tombs cut in the rock, generally square chambers open in front. See 'Ammân. In the present case the cliff is full of these chambers, and is also quarried in places. It is close to Brikeh.

El 'Areimeh (العريمة, 'the hillock' or 'knoll.'—*Cf.* Sheet VI., ' Western Survey ;' el 'Oreimeh, Name Lists, p. 129.) The ruin stands on a conspicuous knoll, half a mile north of the waterfall in Wâdy el Bahhâth. There are several caves and traces of buildings. The name is omitted for want of space on the reduced map, but the ruins are marked at the foot of the spur.

El 'Arîsh (العريش, 'the hut').—A little knoll in the plain with modern Arab graves of flint stones.

'Arjân (عرجان).—The radical meaning is 'ascent.' These are two ruins on knolls with numerous caves. There are remains of rude walls, and it appears to have been a village like 'Abdûn and others in this vicinity.

'Arkûb el Khelâl (عرقوب الخلال, 'ridge of dells').—This applies well, the ridge being seamed with many narrow ravines.

'Arkûb Serû el 'Abid (عرقوب سرو العبيد, 'ridge of the plateau of 'Abid Arabs').

'Aweilet Nâûr (عويلة ناعور).—The first word is unusual. It is, apparently, the diminutive form of 'Al, 'height.' A large Tell or platform here exists, measuring about 500 feet east and west, by 350 north and south. It commands a view down the valley on the north-west where the ruin Khŭrbet Nâûr, with its houses, is visible. There appears to have been a tower about 120 feet from the west end of the terrace or Tell, 34 feet in interior diameter, with walls circular and 7 feet thick; there are three or four courses of stones 2 feet to 5 feet long, well dressed, and cut in shape to the arc of the circle. The slopes of the terrace on all sides are covered with small rough stones.

'Aweilet et Tubkah (عويلة الطبكة, 'heights of the terraces').—See et Tubkah. This is the name of the cliff, south of the ruin. It is omitted for want of space on the reduced map.

'Aweilet Umm es Semmâk (عويله ام السماق, 'heights of the sumach-trees;' none were, however, seen here).—A Survey cairn was erected here. The ruins are not extensive, but of good masonry. They stand at the edge of the shelf of the plateau. A small double (or corner) pilaster base was found with simple moulding on a block $1\frac{1}{2}$ feet square. Scattered cut stones, 1 foot to 3 feet long, are lying about, and beneath are vaults now choked. On the east, lower down, is a cave 25 feet wide. Some drafted stones were found, one 2 feet by 1 foot 2 inches, the draft $3\frac{1}{4}$ inches wide and $\frac{3}{8}$ inch deep. A stone trough was also measured 2 feet 9 inches by 3 feet 8 inches outside, with 4 inches thickness of the stone sides, and 10 inches deep inside. A small Roman or Byzantine building probably occupied this spot, which commands a fine view, as shown by the lines of the triangulation.

Visited August 24, 1881.

'Ayûn el Ferâwit (عيون الفراويت, 'sweet springs').—A little green patch in the valley bed with a good perennial supply of fresh water.

'Ayûn el Keneiyiseh (عيون الكنيسة, 'springs of the little church' or 'chapel').—These are in Wâdy Jideid. In consequence of the name, they were specially examined by Lieutenant Mantell, but no remains of any chapel or other ruin were found. Near the 'Ain el Jideid, further up the valley, is the lintel-stone with a cross, and ruins which may indicate a chapel. See under the head Hadânieh. The springs in question rise beside the stream in the great ravine, and are surrounded with rushes; there are several of them, and the water is of good quality, with a perennial supply. The stream in the valley was very low when visited in September, and the supply cannot be at all equal to that of 'Ayûn Mûsa and Wâdy Hesbân; but it is called lower down Seil el Hery, which indicates a constant supply; and springs occur along its course, while at 'Ain Sûeimeh (which see) there is plenty of water.

Explored September 27, 1881.

## ASHDOTH PISGAH.

Ayûn Mûsa (عيون موسى, 'springs of Moses').—These are, without doubt, the ancient Ashdoth Pisgah (Deut. iii. 17, אשדת הפסגה, 'streams of Pisgah,' according to Gesenius Lexicon). They appear possibly to be again mentioned in the seventh century A.D., by Antoninus Martyr, who calls them baths—'termæ sunt quæ vocantur Moysi, ubi etiam leprosi mundantur, et ibi est dulcissimus aquæ fons qui bibitur, et multos sanat languores' (*cf.* Reland, vol. ii., p. 978).

There are two springs—the northern in the valley, whence the stream falls over a cliff about 30 feet high; the southern rising at the foot of a cliff, about a hundred yards from the former, and forming a shallow pool 8 feet across, with a pebbly bottom, whence a stream runs to join that from the northern spring. In the pool Canon Tristram found shells of the Neritina and Melanopsis ('Land of Moab,' p. 337). The stream from the springs flows into the Jordan valley, and irrigates the land south of Tell er Râmeh. A modern cottage stands in the cliff, above the southern spring, on a shelf or terrace of the rock; it is used as a store for corn. The Arabs connect these springs with the name of the Hebrew lawgiver, Moses. The water is fresh, and the streams are perennial.

'It is a most picturesque spot. The northern spring, rising in a shallow valley, pours its stream over a cliff some thirty feet high, down which hang long trailing creepers beside the water. The hollow below the fall is full of maidenhair fern, and a large wild fig grows up against the cliff. There are two cascades again lower down, and the rushing brook disappears in a narrow gorge between tall canes and various shrubs. The contrast of this vegetation with the great blocks of limestone in the valley, the tawny hill above, glaring against the blue sky, without a tree or a blade of grass, is very effective. The southern spring, some hundred yards away, issues from a cave at the foot of a cliff, forming a fine clear pool with a pebbly bed, flanked by two aged wild figs, curiously gnarled and twisted, but with rich foliage. The stream breaks down hence in a rapid shoot to join the northern brook in the gorge.'—Conder's 'Heth and Moab,' p. 128.

El Baniyât (البنيّات, 'the buildings ').—This name appears to apply to a number of ruins perched on little spurs on either side of Wâdy Jâwah, an open cultivable valley. They were visited by Captain Conder; but nothing distinguishable was observed beyond scattered stones, and foundations of small houses with ruined cisterns, and quarried rock. With regard to these ruins, and all those in the plateau round 'Ammân, it appears probable that (like the Haurân towns) they belong to the prosperous period from the second to the fifth century A.D., when the settled Christian and Pagan population of this district appears to have been large. The ruined villages are, it is true, much more rudely built than the towns of 'Ammân Jerâsh, etc., but this is no evidence of different date for their erection, and such indications as exist all point to a post-Christian period.

El Bardawil (البردويل, compare 'Western Survey,' Sheet XIV., Burj Bardawil or Baldwin's Castle).—Traces of ruins only remain near ed Deir (which see); but it is curious that the spot is very probably on the route of Baldwin II., who attacked Jerâsh in 1121 A.D. It is in Wâdy es Sir.

El Barrakât (البرقات, probably from برق, 'to glitter').—A clump of canes, with a little water.

El Bassah (البصّة, 'the marsh').—Close to the last. Two ruins, with a ruined mill; only a few walls and stone heaps remain. The valley is swampy.

El Bassah (البصّة, 'the marsh').—Near 'Ain Abu Turfah. A green patch in the valley (see Kalât Ummeh).

Batân el Baghl (بطان البغل, 'mule's girth').—This curious name is given to the valley east of Mâäin. It should be noted that the latter is Baal Meon (Num. xxxii. 38), and that the word 'Baghl' contains all the letters of Baal, though with a different meaning. Possibly the name originates in a corruption of an older term.

## JAZER.

Beit Zerâh (بيت زرعة, 'house of sowing').—This is perhaps the place in Moab called by Josephus Zara (13 Antiq. xv. 4). It might also very probably represent the important site of Jazer, the boundary between Reuben and Gad (Num. xxi. 32; xxxii. 1; Josh. xiii. 25; 1 Macc. v. 8; 12 Antiq. viii. 1). The Targums, it is true, identify Jazer with Machærus (*cf.* Neubauer 'Geog. Tal.,' p. 28); but the position of the latter place is entirely unsuitable, for Jazer was clearly north of Heshbon. The modern Arabic Zerâh contains the three radicals of the Hebrew Jazer (יעזר), though transposed, as in other cases, so as to give a modern meaning to the word. Jeremiah speaks of the 'waters of Jazer' (xlviii. 32), which, if correctly translated, may refer to the stream in Wâdy Hesbân, west of the plateau of Beit Zerâh. Wine-presses have been found not far west of this site, which seems to agree with the mention of the vine in connection with Jazer; but the best argument in favour of the proposed identification consists in the position near Heshbon (Josh. xiii. 25, 26), on the border of Gad. The site of Jazer given by Eusebius and Jerome ('Onom.') appears to be the ruin of Sir or Sar (see Khurbet Sâr), but the 'Onomasticon' is not a safe guide.

The present site is a large one, but the remains are not of great importance. There are foundations, and vaults with barrel-roofs, lintel-stones, pillar shafts, and fragments of cornice, all apparently of the Byzantine period, but too decayed to measure. A rude vase and a stone with a tablet in low relief were noticed. Corn and chaff are stored here. The vicinity is flat, bare, and treeless.

Visited August 23, 1881.

Berdeleh (بردلة).—Only traces of ruins remain here. There is an ancient road on the west from Heshbon. The place was visited by Captain Conder, but foundations only were observed.

Bir Abu Nuklch (بير ابو نكله, 'well of murmuring' water).—This is a large well in a flat valley, with ruins to the south called also Abu Nuklch (see Khurbet Abu Nuklch). It is said to be filled only by the rains, and a sort of channel leads to it; the water is said to be cold and good, and the supply constant; some women were washing clothes beside it. There are many such wells in the vicinity, which the Arabs were clearing out in expectation of the rains. The well is also called Bir Gharîb Muhammed, or 'well of the stranger Muhammed'—possibly from a family settled at the ruins.

Bîr 'Arâd (بير عراد, apparently 'well of barrenness').—A well by the roadside north of Mââin.

Bîr el Haleisîyeh (بير الحليسيه, 'well of verdure').—On a hillside near the old road west of Mââin.

Bîr es Sebîl (بير السبيل, 'the wayside well').

Birket et Trâb (بركة التراب, 'pool of mud').—This is a sort of pond, which is formed by the rains in the flat valley bed north-west of Mâdeba. It was dry when seen in September.

Birket Umm 'Amûd (بركة ام عمود, 'pool of the pillar').—A pool by the main road to es Salt, towards the north edge of the Survey.

Brikeh (بركه).—Perhaps a peculiar pronunciation for Birkeh, as the Arabic letters are the same. There is, however, no doubt as to the name, which was also collected by Sir C. Warren. It is a ruined village built of chert or flint. Ruined walls still remain standing (compare el Baniyât). On the east and west are ruined watchtowers, and on the south tombs (see 'Arâk er Rûâk).

El Bûeib (البويب, 'the little gate').—This name applies to the cutting at the top of the ascent from 'Ain Hesbân to the town (see Hesbân). It may perhaps be the gate of Bath Rabbim (Cant. vii. 4).

El Bûeida (البويضا).—This is probably the Bedawin pronunciation for el Beida (compare el 'Ameireh) 'the white,' which applies to the chalky-white soil of the hill. There are two ruins here near each other, sometimes called Abu Kedeis ('father of the pearl'), from an Arab owning property here. At the eastern ruin, only scattered stones were found; at the western, a pillar stump, a few drafted stones, and some small caves. It is a very insignificant ruin.

Visited September 17, 1881.

El Bureikeh (البريكة, 'the little pool').—This name applies to two ruins, a mile apart, and west of Brikeh. The names of these two places may probably be connected. At the more northerly Bureikeh was found a ruined tower, built of fine rough blocks. It was round, and two jambs of its door, about 5 feet high, were observed to be carefully cut, but not dressed square. Foundations of flint and limestone with caves occur at both ruins, and on the north is a quarry.

Visited October 6, 1881.

Burj es Sahel (برج السهل, 'tower of the plain').—This was not visited, being beyond the 'Adwân boundary.

Butmet Halhûl (بطمة حلحول, 'Prince's terebinth').—In the Jordan Valley. It is said to have been the site of a great Arab battle or skirmish.

Butmet et Terki (بطمة التركي, 'Turk's terebinth').—This is a fine terebinth on the road to Heshbon from Kefrein. On the west is a spring, 'Ain et Terki (which see). The tree is sacred to the Arabs, the Turk having been a holy man. It is curious that a Turkoman prophetess is also revered in the 'Adwân country (see Mâta et Turkômâniyeh).

Sixty-five paces north-west of the tree is a sacred circle, apparently the grave of the Turk. It is 10 paces in diameter, and the circular wall is built up of rough stones 2 feet to 4 feet long. There are ancient graves within, and the circle is filled up with earth nearly to the top of its surrounding wall. There is no lintel-stone or entrance.

Fifty paces further north again is a circle about 20 paces (50 feet) in diameter, built up to a height of 3 feet, with stones about 1 to 2 feet long. In this circle is also a tomb, and three radiating walls about $1\frac{1}{2}$ feet below the top of the circular wall. The ground inside this circle is lower than outside. On the west side is a sort of doorway $2\frac{1}{2}$ feet wide, $2\frac{1}{2}$ feet high, formed by a lintel-stone resting on a sort of jamb one side, and on stones piled up in the wall on the other (compare 'Ain Hesbân). On this lintel were found pieces of metal and a chain as offerings to the dead.

Ploughs and other articles are stored in this circle, together with branches which have fallen from the terebinth, and another tree trunk is said to have stood here about fourteen years since. Several Arab graves occur south of this circle.

Visited September 14, 1881.

Ed Deir (الدير, 'the monastery or hermitage').—This curious rock-cut habitation was visited by one of Sir C. Warren's party ('Quarterly Statement,' 1870, pp. 298, 299). It consists of three stories with wooden floors, and windows and doors all cut in the live rock of the cliff, which appears above the oak wood on the south side of the valley (Wâdy Sir). There are traces of foundations in the valley itself, to which also the name of ed Deir is applied. A fine supply of good water is obtained from the perennial stream in the valley. The rock hermitage is about 200 feet above the stream. On the east is a cave, now destroyed, but which seems to have formed a similar hermitage.

There is a rock-cut courtyard 19½ feet wide by 10 feet to the back in front of the hermitage, now closed in by a masonry wall with a door on the west; the wall may, however, be later work. The lower story is entered by a door 2½ feet wide, and consists of two parallel chambers, without any windows. Each chamber is 10 feet by 24 feet, and the rock wall between is about 2 feet thick; two doorways lead through it. The chamber is 7 feet high, and round the walls are niches arranged in six tiers; the total number was about 740. Each niche is 8 inches high, 7½ inches wide at the base, and 8 inches to the back. They are 11 inches apart from centre to centre.

The second floor was reached with difficulty through a window, and found to resemble the first. The third was inaccessible without a ladder, as the wooden floor of the second story is unsafe. The details of the rock-cut windows are best explained by the elevation.

The object of these niches is not known for certain,* but they would be just large enough to contain one skull each (compare the niches at

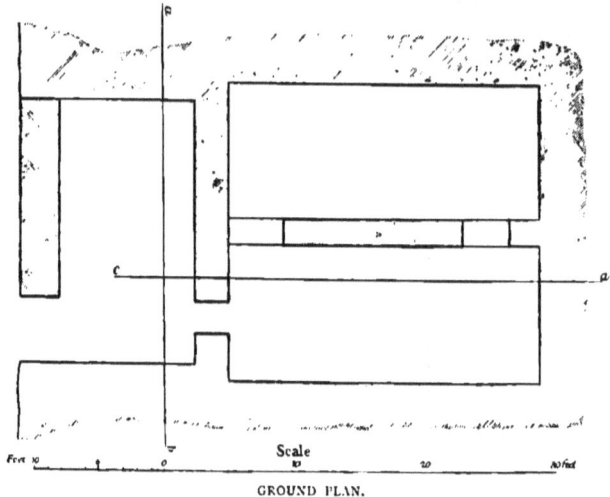

GROUND PLAN.

Sebbeh, 'Memoirs of Western Survey,' vol. iii., pp. 419, 420, which are connected with a hermit's cave and a small chapel, and which it was proposed to recognise as intended for erecting a trophy of skulls.)

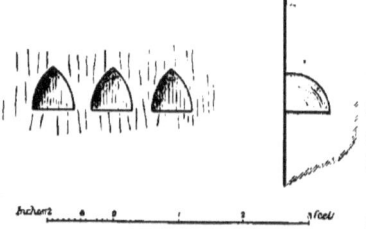

It is well known that the hermits of the middle ages were accustomed to preserve the skulls and skeletons of deceased brethren after this fashion. In Malta, and also at the Mar Sâba monastery, such trophies of skulls may still be seen. It is possible that the monastery itself was in the

---

* Dr. Post ('P.E.F. Quarterly Statement,' October, 1888) suggests that the building is a dove-cot. This should not be hastily dismissed, though it seems improbable that such an excavation in hard rock would be made for such an object. The main objection is the size of the niches, for 8 inches is not a large enough measurement to contain even a small dove.

valley, where are ruins of a small mill by the spring, and that the rock-cut building, called sometimes Muállakat ed Deir, or the 'overhanging place of the monastery,' was the mortuary. The great number

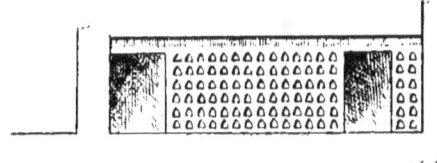

*Section on c d*

of the monks may be judged by the fact that there are niches for 1,600 skulls, and perhaps (if they occur also in the third story) for more than 2,300 heads.

Monastic remains are rare beyond Jordan. The only other hermitage found in 1881 is in Wâdy Hesbân (see Umm el Kenâfid). West of Jordan they are very numerous in the Mar Sâba desert, and in the gorges of Wâdy Serâr, Wâdy Suweinît, and elsewhere. The earliest hermit in Palestine was Hilarion (290-371 A.D.). Jerome speaks of them as very numerous, and the followers of St. Simon Stylites (390-459 A.D.) were spread over Syria in the fifth century.

Explored October 20, 1881.

Deir Ghabâr (دير غبار, 'monastery of dust'?).—This applies to several ruined towers built of flint like that at Khŭrbet Sâr.

Deir Shillîkh (دير شليخ).—Remains of a tower occur here, the north-west corner being *in situ*. It was built of limestone ashlar, the stones 2 feet to 3 feet long, and drafted with a boss rudely dressed. The stones have been piled up by the Arabs to form a rude circle. There is a cave reached by ten rock-cut steps, and with its mouth to the east near the tower. The cave is about 5 paces (12 feet) east and west, by 10 paces (25 feet) north and south. The site is part of Kefeir Abu Bedd.

Visited August 29, 1881.

Ed Deleiyeh (الدليّة, 'the dripping').—This name applies to the hill south of 'Ain ez Zerka, and also to a conspicuous knoll near Siâghah, in Wâdy 'Ayûn Mûsa.

Demen edh Dhabâih (دمن الذبائح, apparently 'dung of the slaughterings' or 'sacrifices').—This name, collected near 'Ain Minyeh, was considered doubtful, and its exact locality was not ascertained.

Ed Denneh (الدنّة, 'the jar' or 'the whispering').—This is applied to a little cave in which water trickles.

Derb el Hajj (درب الحجّ, 'pilgrim road').—This is the road from Damascus to Mecca, which it was proposed to make the east boundary for the Survey.

Ed Dereibeh (الدريبة, apparently 'the path').—A little pool not visited, east of the Dead Sea.

Dhahr Hamâr (ظهر حمار, 'the donkey's back').—This is a flat isolated red hilltop, with a single bush on it. Traditions collected respecting it were: first, that it was the only hill left visible in the Flood, though there are higher mountains near, and that some of the faithful were saved on its summit; secondly, that it was so named by Noah as he floated past in the Ark, and saw it standing above the water. 'See! only the donkey's back shows!' he is said to have exclaimed.

Dhahret Khaû (ظهرة خوّ, 'flat ridge').—This is the ridge with caves, west of Mâdeba. See under that head.

Dhahret Salkhad (ظهرة صلخد, 'lofty ridge').—North of 'Arâk el Emîr.

Dhrâa es Safandi (ذراع الصفندي, 'arm of S').—This is a ridge with cairns.

Diret el Burj (ديرة البرج, 'site of the tower').—A spot where a tower is supposed to exist buried, near Tell el Hammâm on the west. It is omitted for want of space on the reduced map.

Dirs Mesh-hûr (ضرس مشهور, 'the wonderful tooth').—A crag of limestone by the roadside, north of Kefrein. It is a very remarkable natural feature (or, perhaps, partly artificial), and is very like a gigantic tooth some 10 feet high or more.

Dufiânet Abu en Naml (دفيانة ابو النمل, 'burial-place of Abu en Naml,' that is, 'father of ants').—A name which seems to apply to the district. See Rujm Abu en Naml, about a mile away. If a proper name, the person so called is no doubt buried at the Rujm. There is a

curious legend in the Korân of the valley of Ants, to which Solomon
went aided by men, birds, and demons (Sura xxvii., ' the Ant'). This
may, perhaps, be localized here, as the district is full of legends. The
present name applies to the cemetery by Kabr Abu Redeineh. Being
unimportant, the name is omitted from the reduced map.

Ed Dumeineh (الدمينه, ' the little dunghill ').—A small ruin with
heaps of scattered stones.

El Fahes (الفحص).—Scattered stones and a cistern on a mound.

El Gharâbiât (الغرابيات).—A plot of ground. See the next.

El Gharbeh (الغربه, apparently 'the west,' but probably 'the
Gharab shrub'). See the next.

Gharûbet Nimrîn (غروبة نمرين, the Gharab plants of Nimrîn).—
This is a name of a shrub which grows wild in great quantities in the
Ghor, not far from the river. It is mentioned by Sir C. Warren (' Quarterly
Statement,' 1870, p. 285).

El Gharûs (الغروس, ' the plantations ').—This is applied, apparently, to the oak and terebinth woods, north of 'Arâk el Emîr.

Ghôr es Seisebân (غور السيسبان).—This name is applied to
the plains of Shittim opposite Jericho (Num. xxxiii. 49). It is
apparently derived from the name of a tree, Sesbania Ægyptiaca, whence
arrows are made (Lane).

El Habis (الحبيس, ' the cell ').—On the south side of the Zerka
Mâân, just beyond the Survey. It appears to be a hermitage in the
rock.

El Habjeh (الهجبه).—This is probably a mistake for الحجبه, ' the
trysting-place,' a common Bedawîn term. The name applies to a valley
west of Mâân.

Hadânieh (هدانيا, ' sepulture ').— Under this head may be
described the two circles, the cave, and the remains at the spring ('Ain
Jideid) below. There may be some possible connection between the
Hadânieh circle and the great cairn of Rujm el Mekheiyit (' the needle
cairn ') on the hilltop to the east (about in a line of the summer solstitial
rising of the sun). The name Hadânieh is possibly derived from the
small modern tomb circle; the slopes to the south and east are thickly

strewn with dolmens from Kueijiyeh to Wâdy el Jindil (see Wâdy Jideid).

The great Hadânieh oval measures 250 feet in major diameter to the outside of its walls, which are from 41 to 27 feet thick, and about 5 feet high above the inner platform. The position is on a flat spur, with a deep valley to the north and another on the east. On the south the hill rises with a gentle slope; on the west a slope descends to the spring 300 feet below. The walls are made up of undressed stones, measuring about 2 feet across, piled up as a vallum. The Survey camp was pitched inside the circle, which is divided into two irregular portions by a wall 6 feet thick running in the line, 260° true bearing; that is, in the direction approximately of the Rujm el Mekheiyit, on the hilltop about $\frac{3}{4}$ mile away. The Kueijiyeh hilltop, with its curious disc-stone, occupies a somewhat corresponding position about $\frac{1}{2}$ mile towards the south-east. The dividing-wall is so placed as to cut a diameter-line drawn at right angles to its direction at distances of 80 feet and 135 feet from the outside of the circle, the diameter in this direction being 215 feet, the enclosure being an oval.

The modern circle is on the south, and is 19 feet in exterior diameter, with a lintel towards the north-west; a line from the lintel-centre through the middle of this little circle having a true bearing of 133°. This circle was photographed (No. 7, Lieutenant Mantell's series). The lintel is of irregular form, 2 feet long, 1$\frac{1}{4}$ feet wide; the side-stones are 1 foot high and 1$\frac{1}{2}$ feet high respectively, and 1 foot 3 inches apart in the clear. The first is 2 feet thick, the second 2 feet 3 inches. The walls of this *mukâm* are 2 feet high and 1$\frac{1}{2}$ feet thick. On the lintel-stone were flint chips, two knife-blades, two buckles, some bits of iron, fragments of blue and white crockery, a shell, and a sheikh's stick with crutch handle. Inside were stored two swords, with ploughs, coffee-mortars, a metal coffee-jug, and some sticks.

On the hillside north of the circle is a cave or chamber. The door is 2$\frac{1}{2}$ feet wide; the interior is 8 feet wide, 5$\frac{1}{2}$ feet to the back, 3 feet 3 inches high. There is a recess at the end 4 feet square, and a smaller recess 2$\frac{1}{2}$ feet by 1 foot, and 2 feet 3 inches high. This may probably be a tomb.

The great circle commands a view down Wâdy Jideid to the Jordan

Valley. Jericho, Kuruntul, and Jerusalem are visible, and it seems to be a great centre round which rude-stone monuments abound. Neba, with its dolmens, cairn, and circle, is on the north.

The spring called 'Ain Jideid in the ravine below rises in a clear pool under some boulders. There is a gravelly bottom, and the water is fairly good, and found abundant even in the dry autumn, with a temperature of 80° F. in the shade, or less than that of the air. Close to the spring lies a lintel-stone 5 feet long, 1 foot 10 inches high, with a Greek cross in a circle of 1½ feet diameter well carved. On the hill to the south are scattered stones, and it seems probable that a small chapel once stood on the spot. About 30 yards north of the spring is a rock on which an Arab inscription has been rudely scrawled. It is in parts almost illegible, but the words Allah and Ibn Salaadi can be read. It appears to contain an enumeration of names.

An Arab tradition attaches to this spot to the following effect. An Arab girl who was called Ghareisah ('palm') loved a young man named Zeid ('increase'), who was of another tribe hostile to her own. Her relations disapproved of the union; but she hid her lover in a box, which she seems to have placed on a camel, and endeavoured to flee with him. The movements in the box, which she was unable to conceal, excited the suspicions of her relatives, who thus discovered her lover, and in their wrath slew both Ghareisah and Zeid (others say the murderers were of Zeid's tribe). As she fell, her hand rested on the lintel-stone by the spring, and the cross and circle still visible are believed to result from the impress. She is also said to have scrawled the inscription on the rock just before her death to record the names of the murderers. Her death was avenged, some say, by her relations, who, finding the inscription, slew a certain 'Amr of the tribe to which Zeid belonged.

Explored September 21, 1881.

Haddâdeh (حَدَّادَة).—In Arabic this would mean 'the black-smiths,' but it is probably connected with Hadd, a limit. In the ruins is a large fallen menhir (see 'Ammân, stone marked N). It may be a boundary stone. This is a ruined village, of which wall foundations still remain, with caves, two troughs of stone, a ruined tomb, and remains of a small square tower with a vaulted roof of round section. A broken sarco-phagus and a pillar stump were also noted. There are also modern Arab

# WADY JIDEID.

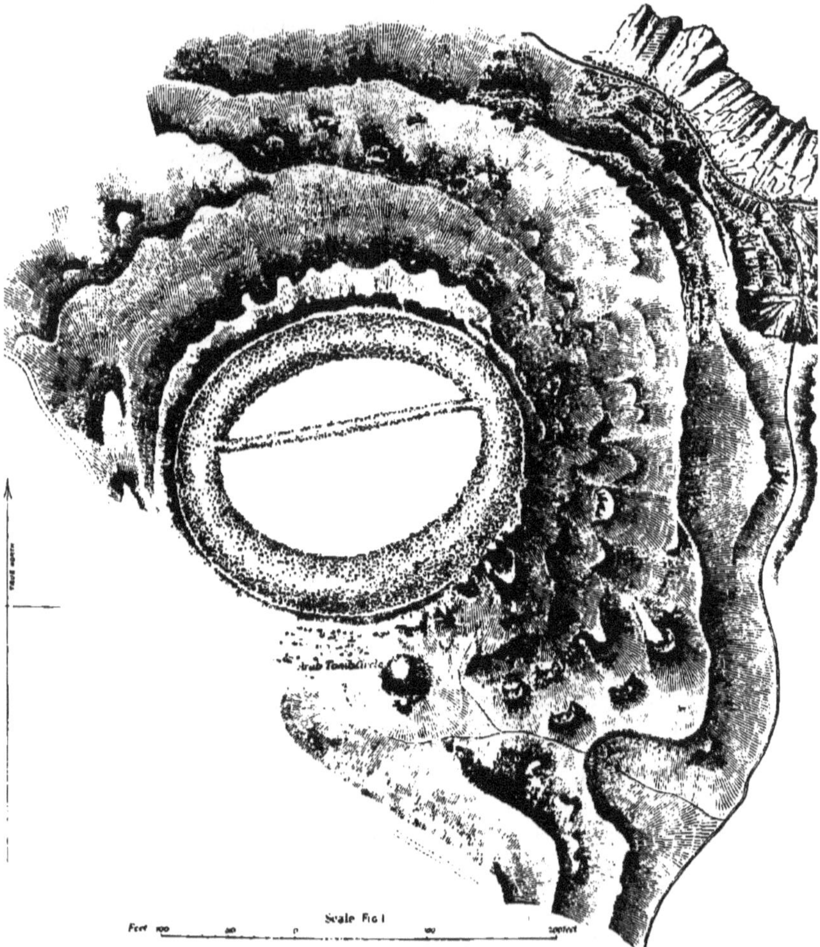


Scale Fig 1

Feet 100 50 0 100 200 feet

Lintel at Ain Jideid.
Fig 2

Scale Fig 2.

Vincent Brooks Day & S

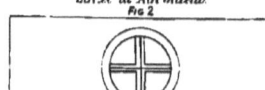

graves, and fragments of a simple cornice-moulding at the tower, and a rock-cut winepress.

Hadîb es Sufa (حديب الصفا, 'shining hump').—This is a long ridge, east of 'Ammân, of white limestone.

El Hadûd (الحدود, 'the bounds').—Half-way between the winter camp of 'Aly Diâb at Nimrîn, and that of Kablân en Nimr at Kefrein. The road here leads through a pass between the rocks of the long spur projecting into the Jordan Valley. This pass may be natural, or may have been cut through in Roman times.

Hajr ed Dûmeinîyeh (حجر الدومينيّة), or Hajr ed Dumîyeh (حجر الدوميّه, 'stone of blood;' explained to mean دم, *i.e.*, blood).—This is a stone by 'Ain Jeriâh, and the legend is that two brothers once fought here, and never struck one another, but only struck the stone. Other details of the fight were not translated by the interpreter, who said they were 'unfit for publication.' The name is omitted from the reduced map, but the spot is marked by the 'Ain Jeriâh.

Hajr el Mansûb (حجر المنصوب, 'the erected stone').—This is described under the head el Mareighât.

Hajr el Mena (حجر المنا, 'stone of desire').—This is a block of stone, 8 feet long, 3 feet high, on the hillside. It is so called because it is a 'wishing-stone,' where the 'Ajermeh Arabs go to wish. This superstition was treated with contempt by Sheikh Kablân.

Hajâr en Nûâblisîyeh (حجار النوابلسيّة, 'stones of the men of Nâblus').—Two men of this city (Shechem) here wandering perished in the snow. Their bodies were found by the Arabs next spring, when they returned from the Jordan Valley to the hills, and were here buried.

El Hammâm (الحمّام, 'the hot bath').—This is a thermal spring in the Jordan Valley, east of Kefrein. It was twice visited. It is a pool of hot sulphurous water, which on each visit was found to register 98° F., and which was covered with a sort of coruscation, as of floating oil. It rises in flat ground, surrounded with rank growth of canes and rushes, with a few tamarisks. The warm water at Kefrein (see under that head) appears to come from this spring.

## CALLIRRHOE.

Hammâm ez Zerka (حمّام الزرقا, 'hot bath of the Zerka valley').—This is the name of the principal hot spring in the gorge of Callirrhoe. The gorge and its springs, and the legend of the demon slave of Solomon, in whose honour sacrifices are here offered by the Arabs, is given in full in 'Heth and Moab,' chap. iv., and also well described by Canon Tristram, 'Land of Moab.' The chief spring registered 143° F., and, like the others, is sulphurous. It issues from the northern crag of the valley, opposite a cliff of black basalt, called Hammet ez Zerka (see next article). It flows over a sort of shelf, formed by the sediment of the water. In about half a mile to the east two other streams, from 130° F. to 110° F., are found. There are many palms in the gorge. The smell of sulphur is very strong. The stream above the hot springs in the bed of the valley registered only 80° F., and was full of fish, surrounded with canes and tamarisks, and flowing over hard rock. The gorge is very desolate. The grackle (Amydrius Tristramii) was seen flying about in it. It was here that Herod the Great was brought from Machærus to bathe (Antiq. xvii. 6, 5; 1 Wars xxxiii. 5).

Pliny also mentions these springs (v. 17). In modern times they had only been visited by Irby and Mangles in 1818, the Duc de Luynes in 1864, and Dr. Chaplin; while in 1872 Canon Tristram descended from the 'Ain Zerka. The Survey party, consisting of Captain Conder, Lieutenant Mantell, and Mr. Armstrong, descended the northern cliff from Umm 'Erneh—a tedious operation. Near the chief spring there are remains of a channel of masonry. This may indicate the site of the baths, which may have existed in Herod's time. Coins were found here by Irby and Mangles. The Arabs place boughs to form a little platform over the steam from the spring, and seated on this platform they take a sort of Turkish bath.

Visited September 30, 1881.

Hammet el Minyeh (حمّة المنية, 'the black or basaltic place of Minyeh').—This is a great outbreak of basalt in the plateau below 'Ain el Minyeh. It is traditionally the city of 'Antâr, and looks in the distance like a large ruin. The legend is given under the head 'Ain el Minyeh.

Haninah (حنينه, 'the reservoir').—These are foundations of rudely-squared stones of moderate size. Rock cisterns with bell-mouths of small size also occur, with a rock sunk tomb, as at Umm el Hanâfish. It appears to be a small ruined village on a flat hill-spur.

Visited September 29, 1881.

Hannûtieh (حنوطيه, perhaps from حنط, 'wheat ').—The name applies to two ruins near each other. Scattered stones and ruined walls exist, and on the north is Birket Umm 'Amûd. It is a small site (compare el Baniyât).

El Hârât (الحارات, 'the quarters').—This applies to a hillside above the Dead Sea, close to 'Ain Sûeimeh.

El Haretein Zabbûd (الحارتين زبّود, 'the two quarters of Zabbûd ').—These are modern ruins, one each side of a shallow valley, with lime-kilns and other remains of rude masonry.

Hasalûlyeh (عصلوليه).—A glade in the oak woods near Mâhas.

El Haud (الحوض, 'the cistern ').—This is the name of a conspicuous peak over the Jordan valley. It has remains of a large cairn on it, but no cistern. The cairn was used as a trigonometrical point in 1881, and originally built by the American surveyors.

El Hawâsiyât (الحواسيات).—Flat ground with strewn flints east of Elealeh. The name is omitted from the reduced map as apparently unimportant.

El Helâly (الهلالي, 'the crescent-shaped ').—A peak on a curving ridge, which consists of white marl, north of Kefrein.

Henu el Kelbeh (حنو الكلبه, 'the corner of the bitch,' also the name of a plant).—This is a valley.

Henu el Merbat (حنو المربط, 'corner of the place of tying up ').— The corner of the great valley, Wâdy el Habis, close to Hesbân. It seems to be so called because animals are here tied up on a halt, as the place is one fitted for concealment.

Henu Tassîn (حنو طسّين, 'the corner of Tassîn '—a valley head) —In these cases, as also in that of el Henu—a bend of Jordan—the term applies to the curve of a valley bed.

## Hesibon.

Hesbân (حسبان. Heb. חשבון).—The remains in the valley are noticed under the head 'Ain Hesbân, the rude-stone monuments west of the city under the heads el Kurmiyeh and el Kalûa; the present subject is confined to the Roman remains on the plateau, including the Tell and the Kalât Hesbân.

The site is that of a comparatively large and important town, but there is little distinguishable amid the heaps of fallen masonry which strew the slopes of the Tell and the flat ridge south-west of it. There is not a tree nor a spring near the city, and the whole aspect of the plateau round it is bare and deserted; to the south is land partly cultivated with maize, to the north-east and west gray downs of chalky limestone. The Tell on the north-east is the highest part of the ruin, and appears to have been the site of a citadel, or a forum. The Survey station (north end of the base) was fixed on the hillock, which is a conspicuous object, especially from the south, for many miles. The Kaláh, or 'castle,' is about ¼ mile south-west, and the whole ground between these two is covered with the remains of houses, some of which appear to have had considerable architectural pretensions.

There are many ruined vaults on the sides of the Tell, and north of this again extends a sort of suburb; and beyond this the rock is quarried, and a row of small caves, with scattered stones, perhaps marks the site of the oldest part of the city. On a low brow on this side are remains of a small square tower, called Kusr el Homrah ('the red tower').* It is 8 paces, or 20 feet, square, and built of well-cut blocks, 3 feet to 4 feet in length, and 1½ feet to 2 feet high. South-east of this, about 25 paces off, the rock is cut down, apparently to form a birkeh, or tank, measuring 18 paces (or 45 feet) by 23 paces (58 feet), with steps cut in the rock-wall on the east side. It is at present 3 feet or 4 feet deep, but is partly filled with accumulated soil. About 40 paces, or 100 feet, north of the tower, is a natural cave 10 paces square and 5½ feet high; and 10 paces south of this a second cave, now closed, and a good-sized bell-mouthed cistern.

\* *Homrah* might be a corruption of Himyarite. There is nothing red about this ruin, but there are several traces of Himyar influence in Moab: for instance, the ruin called Humrâwîyeh; the Kusr en Nûeijis (Nejis being a Sabean word for a king or ruler); the Jineinet Belkis (which see).

ARAB TOMB AT HAIDANIEH.

The ancient road from 'A i n  H e s b â n winds by a steep ascent up the hill, and approaches the town from the north-west. Just below the general level of the plateau it reaches a narrow pass, called e l  B u e i b, ' the little gates,' where the rock appears to have been artificially scarped down some 8 feet or 10 feet. This may have served for defence against those approaching from below, although there are other means of approach further north. The gap formed by the cutting is a conspicuous object on the skyline, as seen from the valley below. It is possibly to this gate that a reference is made in the Song of Songs, when the ' Gate of Bath Rabbim ' ('daughter of great ones') is mentioned as near the pools of Heshbon (Cant. vii. 4).

The plateau south-west of the city is called e l  J â m â l y e h ('of the mosque'), and is also strewn with masonry similar to that in the main part of the site. On the south of the Tell is the flat open valley which leads to the southern plateau, the city being mainly on a saddle dividing this valley head from the true watershed. In the open valley is the great tank to which the name 'A l w â n appears to apply. It measures 191 feet north and south by 139 feet east and west, and is about 10 feet deep. The masonry is well dressed, but the stones are not drafted ; the walls have been apparently shaken by earthquake ; stones were measured 15 inches long by 11 inches high, and 10 inches by 15 inches, representing the average dimensions of the ashlar. In the south-east corner of this tank lies a trough measuring 6 feet 2 inches by 3 feet outside, and 5 feet by 20 inches inside ; the height 18 inches outside and 12 inches inside. It has probably fallen from above, and was no doubt used for watering animals when the tank was full of water.

On the west side of this tank is an Arab graveyard, with a stone circle round one tomb. The southern part of the reservoir is in ruins, and a rude capital with the acanthus-leaf design lies within the tomb-circle.

Towards the south-east part of the ruins of the city (west of the tank) a cave was found with a sarcophagus, and a square pilaster capital having acanthus-leaves carved on two sides.

Returning to the Tell, or citadel, we find the top occupied by a building (plan) measuring $131\frac{1}{2}$ feet east and west by $153\frac{1}{2}$ feet north and south. On the north, south, and west, within those limits, are traces of vaults, now choked and ruined ; those to the north and south about 40 feet wide, that on the west 54½ feet. There are traces also of vaults built against the east side of the enclosure. The court surrounded by these vaults is at a lower level than the mounds which cover them. It was once paved and ornamented by a colonnade, the bases of several pillars remaining, as shown on the plan. The paving - stones measure from 20 by 30 inches to 10 by 20 inches; the bases stand on stools, with a bold moulding, and are 33 inches in diameter where the shaft fitted on (see sketch). The total height of base and stool is 34 inches.

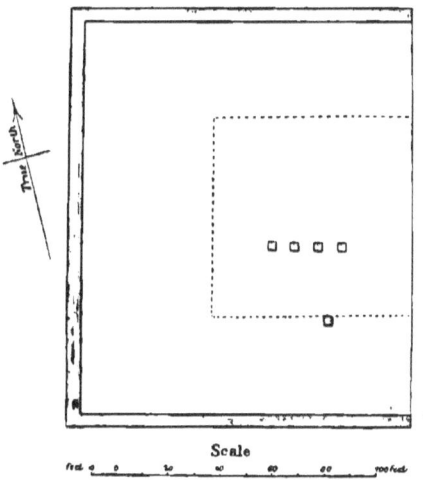

Scale

The outer wall of this building is 5 feet thick ; the masonry is well dressed, but not drafted ; the horizontal joints (as is the case in some of the best Byzantine work west of Jordan) are not continuous. Some of the stones are 6½ feet long, others only 2 feet ; the general height of the course is 1½ feet—a sketch is given, showing the style and arrangement of the joints. On the south side of the building two pillar-shafts are still standing, which may mark an approach or gate, or outer colonnade.

On the north-east slope of the citadel hill a lintel-stone lies among the heaps of fallen masonry ; it is 5 feet long, and appears to have been inscribed—the letters read being as shown on next page.

It should be noted that the square shape of the letters is not that usually found in the Byzantine Greek texts of the fourth to the ninth centuries.

Possibly the word E s b a n, or H e s b a n, is to be here recognised.

The average length of the cut stones in these ruins is only about 2 feet; the stones are sometimes drafted with a boss dressed smoothly. Not far from the citadel, on the south, lies a block with an attached pilaster in low relief; but whether it is a base or a capital is uncertain. Further south-west are other sculptured 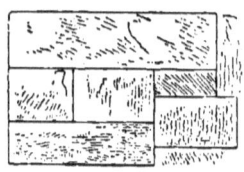 blocks, including a capital, a fragment of cornice, and part of a moulded lintel, 5 feet long (see next page), with a block, apparently an archi-

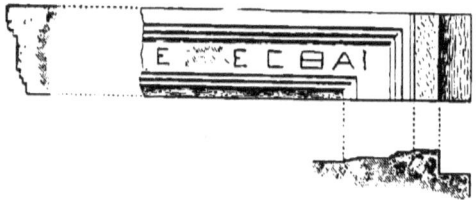

trave, having similar mouldings; also a rude capital with acanthus-leaves. All these were measured and drawn, and may serve to indicate date. It should be noted that the details in the cornice are not symmetrically arranged; but this is very 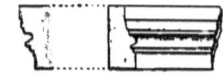 common, not only in Byzantine work in Syria, but also in earlier Roman and Jewish work, and may be due to the employment of native stone-cutters.

The Kaláh, or castle, is also known to the Arabs by the name Hosn Bân; but this may be (as is very common in Western Palestine) a mere play on the name Hesbân. It appears to have been a fine building; the west wall and part of the cross-walls remain, but the building is in part, at least, a reconstruction. The masonry is finely dressed, and the stones of very square proportions, like some of the work at 'Ammân. None of the

14—2

stones appear to be drafted. One was measured 18 inches in length and 2 feet high, which represents the average dimensions of stones in this wall. As in the Tell masonry, so in this, the horizontal joints are not always continuous. The west wall is about 15 feet high, and has a bevelled set-back at the top. Modern hovels are built against its inner side. In the south-east corner stand four shafts of p'llars about 2 feet in diameter, leaning over in various directions. On the south-west of the Kalah the ruins consist of foundations, cisterns, and caves: and here was

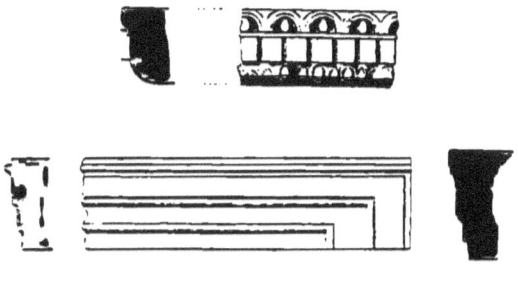

found a rude and massive pillar capital, 2 feet 4 inches high and 2 feet in diameter, perhaps once belonging to one of the shafts in the Kalah.

The ruins on the hill west of Hesbân, separated by a shallow valley head, are known as Harât Hesbân ('the quarters or suburbs of Heshbon'), and also as Khûrbet el Harât, as marked on the map. They consist of small rude caves and foundations without any features of interest.

The date of these remains must be decided by architects with the aid of such details of moulding and ornamentation as it has been possible to recover. But the oldest period to which it seems at all possible to ascribe them is the age of the Antonines (the second century A.D.), comparing them with the early buildings at 'Ammân, Jerâsh, or Baalbek, which are, however, much more important than anything at Heshbon. Many of the details seem to resemble the Byzantine work of Western Palestine, perhaps as late as the fifth century A.D. The caves, cisterns, and rock-cuttings are all that can fairly be supposed to be of great antiquity. Heshbon is spoken of as a city in the time of the Council of

Chalcedon (πόλις 'Εσβούντων; *cf.* Reland's ' Palestine.' p. 720), and was thus not only known in the fourth century (' Onomasticon '), but apparently still inhabited by Christians in the fifth.

Visited August 27 and September 16.

**H i r s h  e l  ʾA m r î y e h** (حرش العمريه, the 'forest of ʾAmriyeh').—This is the only instance of the use of this word on the Survey maps, **H i r s h** being the same as the Hebrew Choresh, חרש, a wood. In the present case the name is applied to a thick wood of good-sized oaks and terebinths extending for about twenty square miles. It is the only large wood south of the Jabbok, and the only large wood on the Survey. The rest of the hills are quite bare, with single trees here and there. West of el Mareighât (at the south limit of the sheet) there are a few scattered terebinths over the hills, but no wood as shown by De Saulcy. In the wood near Zabbûd there is a ruin called Khŭrbet el ʾAmriyeh (which see). This wood is part of the larger one to the north, divided from it by the gorge of Wâdy en Nââûr. In the thickest part of the great wood there are many pines, which are conspicuous on the horizon. A few pines also occur at **e s  S i n o b a r â t**.

**E l  H o w e i j** (الحويج).—A hilltop with some large trees, and a cliff on the north side.

**E l  H u m r â w î y e h** (الحمراويه).—This may only mean 'the red,' but it is one form of the word which is rendered Himyar in English, and it may be connected with the Himyarites, or ancient Arabs of Yemen, who claimed descent from Kahtan (500 to 800 B.C.). Foundations occur here, and remains of a square tower of flint stones.

**J a h a r a h** (جحرة, ' the den ' or ' pit ').—A small ruin with foundations and walls of rude masonry.

**J â w a h** (جاوه).—A large ruin on a prominent knoll beyond the ʾAdwân border. It could not, therefore, be visited.

**J e b e l  ʾA n â z e h** (جبل عنازه, ' mountain of the he-goats ').—The name also applies to the great tribes of the Syrian desert ('Anazeh ), but the hill in question is out of their territory. El ʾA n a z is also the name of a star in the Auriga. The root means ' to descend ' or ' to bend.' The hill is a conspicuous top on the plateau. east of the Dead Sea.

El Jereineh (الجريعة, 'the little trough').—This word *Jurun* is also used in Western Palestine instead of Náder (vulg. Báder) for a threshing floor, and is the Hebrew גֹּרֶן, *Goran*, 'a threshing floor.' This is a little ruin on the low ground in the plateau about a mile south-east, and in view of Kabr 'Abdallah. Scattered stones and cisterns were found, and a few caves. There was also a sacred Arab circle (compare 'Ain Hesbân) with this peculiarity, that the lintel-stone was towards the east. There is a grave within, and ploughs are stored for safety in the circle. Possibly this circle may be oriented with reference to the Kabr 'Abdallah (which see), as it is unusual to have the lintel on the east.

Visited September 16, 1881.

Jineinet Belkis (جنينة بلكيس, 'garden of Belkis').—This name applies to the flat ground on the south side of Wâdy Hesbân, west of Ain el Fudeili (which see). Queen Belkis, in the first century of our era, was one of the Himyaritic line of the Tobba; but in Syria she is identified with the famous Zenobia or Zebba, Queen of Palmyra, who revolted against Rome in 273 A.D., and was defeated and slain. She is to the Arabs a mythical heroine, to whom many great works are attributed, as to Queen Helena among the Syrian Christians. According to the commentators on the Kôran (Sura xxvii.), she was the Queen of Sheba who visited Solomon. The reduced map is too crowded with names here to allow of writing this title.

Jofet Derbâsy (جوفة درباسي, 'hollow of the wild beast').—The word Jôf is applied to recesses where the hills recede in a kind of theatre, the plain running up eastwards between the spurs. On the south side of this recess a 'tomb' is marked on the Survey map. This is a very peculiar monument. A remarkable square block of rock stands isolated, with its sides trimmed vertical. It appears to have been a fallen boulder, and is 12 feet high, with a flat top. Climbing to the top, it is found to be hollowed out to form a tomb. The rock is 15 feet square; at the top the chamber or excavation is 3 feet north and south, by 8 feet east and west, and 4 feet deep. From the east end a little passage leads to a round cistern-like chamber 5 feet in diameter, with a mouth only 2 feet in diameter in its roof, on the level of the floor of the little passage, and rather lower than the other chamber. The whole excavation may have been intended to hold rain-water originally. A skeleton of quite recent times was lying in the round or lower chamber.

Visited October 27, 1881.

Jôfet el Ghazlâniyeh (جوفة الغزلانيّة, 'hollow of the gazelles'). —A recess in the hills.

Jôfet el Mahder (جوفة المحضر). 'hollow of the enclosure.' See el Mahder).—This is north of the ruin.

Jorf Abu ez Zighân (جرف ابو الزيغان, 'bank of the crows,' *i.e.*, the gray or hooded crow).

## JOGBEHAH.

Jubeihât (جبيهات).—This is the collective name (in the plural) of the three ruins representing the site of the ancient Jogbehah, יָגְבְּהָה, a town of Gad (Num. xxxii. 35), famous in the history of Gideon (Judges viii. 11). The Arabic, as recovered, represents the Hebrew, with exception of the loss of the first letter *yod*. The name is sometimes pronounced *Ajbeihah*, which is even closer to the original word, meaning apparently a 'lofty place.' Under the name Jubeihât the Arabs include four ruins about a mile south of Jubeihat es Saghireh, and south of Jubeihat el Kebireh. These mark the remains of a large ancient village; foundations, ruined walls of rough masonry (probably Roman or Byzantine), cisterns and caves occur in all the ruins so named. In the north-eastern of the four was observed a vaulted roof, as at Kefeir el Wusta (which see). The ruins and quarry of el Bureikeh (see under that name) belong to the same site, and the ancient main road from 'Ammân to es Sâlt passes by the place.

Jubeihat el Kebireh (جبيهة الكبيرة, 'great Jogbehah ').—See the last article. This is the most northern of the group of ruined towns so called, and is the most important of them. It is an extensive ruin, standing on high ground west of the road, with a watch-tower at some distance on the north-east. A small building with massive walls and a round-arched vault occurs among the other ruins. There are bases and broken pillar-shafts—Roman or Byzantine—ruined walls, cisterns, and fallen lintel-stones. Sarcophagi also occur, showing that the town belongs to the Roman period; and on the south is a row of cave-tombs, apparently intended to hold one or two bodies, and shaped like sarcophagi. (Compare Umm el Hanâfish.) These are cemented inside, like the eastern tomb at el Kahf, and like some Christian and also perhaps Jewish tombs in Western Palestine (Sheets VII. and X. 'Memoirs.' vol. ii., pp. 141, 362). Though Jogbehah is a Biblical city, the remains found appeared to be probably all later than the Christian era.

Jubeihat es Saghireh· (جبيهة الصغيرة), 'Jogbehah the little '). —A small ruin, probably of the same age as the last. Heaps of stones and foundations of walls only were found.

Jûeidet el Mesheirfeh (جويدة المشيرفه).—The first word in Arabic means 'land which is rained on;' but it is more probably a Bedawîn corrupt pronunciation for *kôd* or *kâid* قود, 'a ridge,' as the Arabs in a great many words pronounce the *koph* or guttural K just like the *jím* (*e.g.*, Jurn for Kurn, Rafîj for Rafîk, etc.). The name applies to the ruins on the pass by which the Roman road from 'Ammân crosses the ridge of Râs el Mesheirfeh to el Kahf. The name probably, therefore, means 'the ridge of the little elevated place.' The ruins are those of a little village of the Roman or Byzantine period. Two watch-towers near the road are traceable, being about 30 feet square, of roughly-dressed stones of medium size. Heaps of cut stones are also found, and on the east by the road a broken Roman milestone. On the west are some small caves and cisterns. The fine tombs to the south belong to the same site, and are described under the head el Kahf.

Visited October 10, 1881.

El Jûeismeh (الجويسمة).—This appears to be the Kawâsimeh of Sir C. Warren ('Quarterly Statement,' 1870, p. 294), and he includes under this name the Kusr es Sebâh in the same vicinity. Possibly Sir C. Warren's pronunciation is the more correct, the Arabs often pronouncing the guttural K as J. In this case the ruin is connected by name with Kâsim, a common Arab name. Four ruins are included under this name, being remains of a small town. Foundations of houses and of small towers, some built of limestone, some of flint, were found with rock-cut cisterns. The remains of 'Arâk Abu 'Âisheh belong probably to the same site, which appears to be of the Roman period. (See also Kusr es Sebâh.)

Visited October 10, 1881.

**Kabr 'Abdallah** (قبر عبدالله, 'grave of Abdallah').—This is a very conspicuous site, in consequence of three masonry tombs having been erected on high ground on the plateau close to the old sacred tomb circle. The original *mukâm* is a rude oval about 10 paces (25 feet) in diameter, with the usual trilithon or little altar on the west side. (*Cf.* 'Ain Hesbân.) The lintel or table stone has in this case fallen down. The person here buried—'Abdallah, 'servant of God'—is said to have been a 'Persian' or 'stranger' (the word having both meanings, viz., *'Ajemy*).

Three masonry tombs stand in a line east and west, end to end, the first or most eastern being nearly north of the circle just described. All three are tombs of chiefs of the Ghaneimât tribe. The most eastern is that of Abu Marzûk ('father of luck'), and on it are shown in relief coffee cups and jug, spoons and mortar; the middle tomb is that of Mustafa, the western of Fadl el Herâwi, who is represented on a horse, while on the south side are designs of coffee-cups, bowl, and spoons. (Compare Kabr Fendi el Fâiz and 'Ain. Hesbân.) Each tomb is about 7 feet high and 10 feet long. Between these and the grave of 'Abdallah is a well, now disused. Immediately north-east of the line of three tombs are two small rude circles of uncut stones, marking the graves of others of the same tribe. The distance between the line of three tombs and the circle of 'Abdallah is about 20 paces, or 50 feet.

Visited September 13, 1881.

**Kabr Abu Redeineh** (قبر ابو ردينه, grave of Abu Redeineh—a proper name, 'father of pleasing,' that is, pleasing to God).—A white tomb, like that at Tell Kefrein or Tell er Râmeh, where an Arab sheikh is buried.

**Kabr Dâhis** (قبر داحس, 'grave of Dâhis,' p.n.).—This name, meaning 'discord,' was that of a famous horse for which two Arab tribes fought for twenty-four years. It does not appear whether this story applies to the tomb in question, which is a conspicuous white Arab tomb on the top of Tell er Râmeh.

**Kabr Fendi el Fâiz** (قبر فندي الفايز, grave of Fendi el Fâiz). —He was a famous chief of the Fâiz family of the Beni Sakhr tribe, and was the leader of the whole tribe. He died apparently in 1877, or at all events not earlier, and was on his way back from Nâblus to his own country on the plateau near Mâdeba. He is thus buried in the 'Adwân country at the junction of Wâdy Râmeh and Wâdy el Kefrein. The

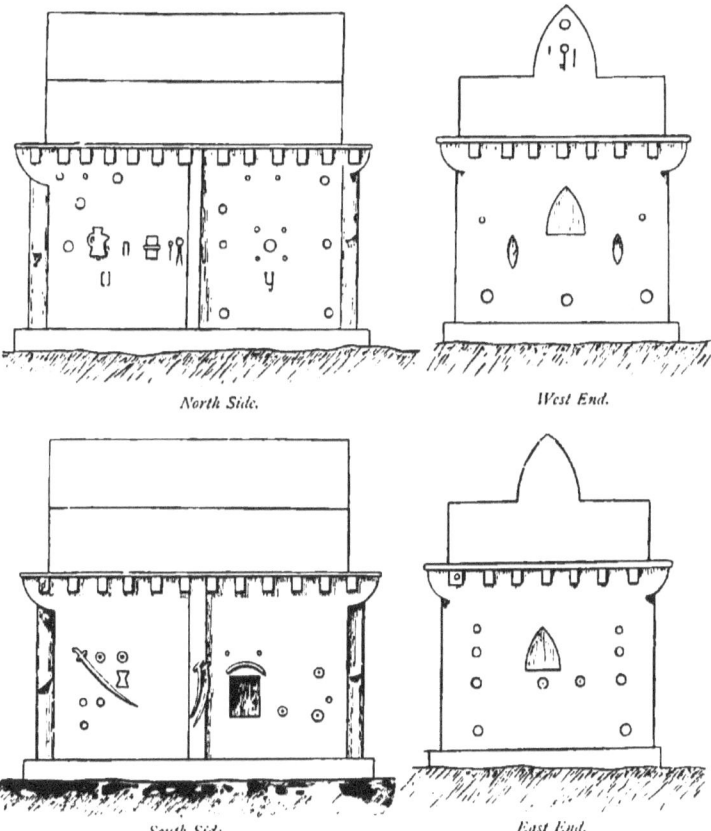

TOMB OF FENDI EL FAIZ.

tomb is very conspicuous, and was carefully measured and drawn by Lieutenant Mantell, R.E., being a fine specimen of the tombs now erected by the Bedawin for famous heroes, which seem to be rough reproductions of the Roman freestanding sarcophagi such as occur near 'Ammân. The tomb is 10 feet long, 6½ feet wide, and the height of the ridge of its roof is 10 feet from the ground. It is probably solid, with a grave in the earth beneath, and is built of masonry cemented over, and the plaster whitewashed. As the Arabs cannot write, there is no inscription; but at the west end the tribe-mark of the Fâiz family occurs, being a variation of the Mihmasah, or 'spoon,' which is the tribe-mark of the Beni Sakhr. The two cross strokes are the family 'difference,' and the mark thus modified is known as the *Tuweikeh*, or 'little necklace.' This is the Himyarite letter ᛒ (see elevation of west end of tomb).

The crutch-headed sticks hung on the south side of the tomb are probably those carried by Fendi el Fâiz when alive. Such sticks (exactly resembling one of the sceptres of Osiris) are commonly carried by sheikhs as signs of authority, and are also offered at all sacred places. On the same side of the monument a sword, coffee-cups, and a coffee-pot are represented in relief, and on the north side the coffee-mill, coffee-jug, tongs, and spoon, with cups, are also represented. These are indications of the prowess and liberality of the chief here buried.

In the side and ends of the monument are niches where offerings may be placed. Other ornamental designs occur, which, together with the other features, cause this tomb to be regarded as a great work of art by the Arabs. The tomb lies, as all Moslem tombs in Syria must, with the length east and west, so that the corpse, lying on its right side, has its face to Mecca. There is an enclosure round the tomb, quadrangular with the corners rounded off. It measured 7 paces (17 feet) east and west, 6 paces (15 feet) north and south. The wall is about 1½ feet high, and consists of uncut stones set in mud. On the west is a kind of trilithon (compare 'Ain Hesbân, etc.) about 2 feet to the top surface of the lintel, which has in it a little cup-hollow, as on Moslem tombs. Round this grave are ten or twelve ordinary Arab graves, one of which is said to be that of the grandfather of Fendi el Fâiz. This monument is carefully kept in repair, and visible at a great distance from the hills, being whitewashed.

Visited October 27, 1881.

**Kabr Habib** (قبر حبيب, grave of Habib, a proper name signifying ' friend ').—This is one of the four Kabûr el Hasâsineh (which see).

**Kabr Mujâhed** (قبر مجاهد, ' champion's grave ').—See Kefrein. This is a grave like that of Fendi el Fâiz, on the top of Tell Kefrein.

**Kabr Jerwân** (قبر جروان, grave of Jerwân, a proper name signifying ' daring ').—This is one of the Kabûr el Hasâsineh (which see).

**Kabr Sâid** (قبر سعيد, grave of Sâid, a proper name signifying ' fortunate ').—It is beside el Khudr, south-east of Tell er Râmeh.

**Kabr Sâideh** (قبر سعيده, see last).—This is one of the Kabûr el Hasâsineh (which see).

**Kabr Sâlim el Muslim** (قبر سالم المسلم, grave of Sâlim the Moslem).—This is one of the Kabûr el Hasâsineh (which see).

**El Kabu** (الكبو, ' the vault ').—A little ruin by the road west of Butmet et Terki. A small vault, probably modern, perhaps intended for storing corn.

**Kabûr el Amârah** (قبور الاماره, ' graves of the Emirs,' or princes).—A small ruin by the main north road north of Khurbet Sâr.

**Kabûr el Hasâsineh** (قبور الحساسنه, graves of the Hasâsineh, namely, of (1) Habib, (2) Jerwân, (3) Sâideh, (4) Sâlim el Muslim, as above given. These are near Khûrbet Kefrein. Nos. 2 and 4 are north of the ruin, No. 2 (Jerwân) being on the north-west of No. 4. Nos. 1 and 3 are west of the ruin, Habib (No. 1) being east of Sâideh (No. 3). They are four modern Arab graves.

**El Kahf** (الكهف, ' the cave,' a word generally implying a larger cavern than is understood by the ordinary word Mughârah).—This site is that of a Roman cemetery of the early Christian period. The large eastern tomb was explored by Sir C. Warren (' Quarterly Statement,' 1870, p. 295), but the western tomb is not noticed in his report. A Roman road from 'Ammân passes close by on the south. The town itself is east of the tombs, and above the road ; the ruins are of the ordinary type, like those of Mâdeba, but the place appears to have been a small one.

The eastern tomb faces south, and has in front of it two olive-trees and a good-sized terebinth, which are conspicuous objects from a great distance on the south. There are also foundations of a mosque or shrine in front of the tomb by the trees, and a tower once stood on the rock

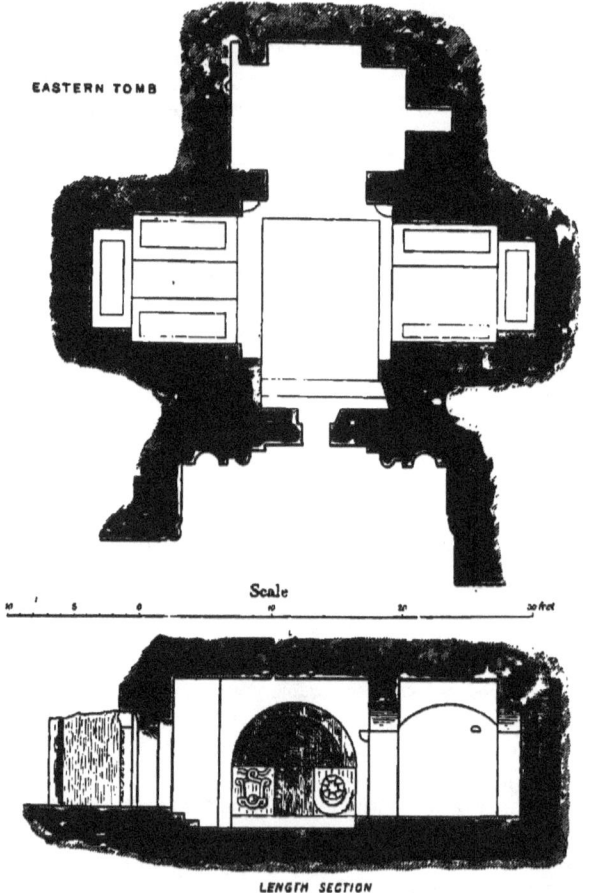

above. The mosque is about 20 paces (50 feet) square, and has a mihrab in the south wall. The tower above measured 33 feet east and west, and

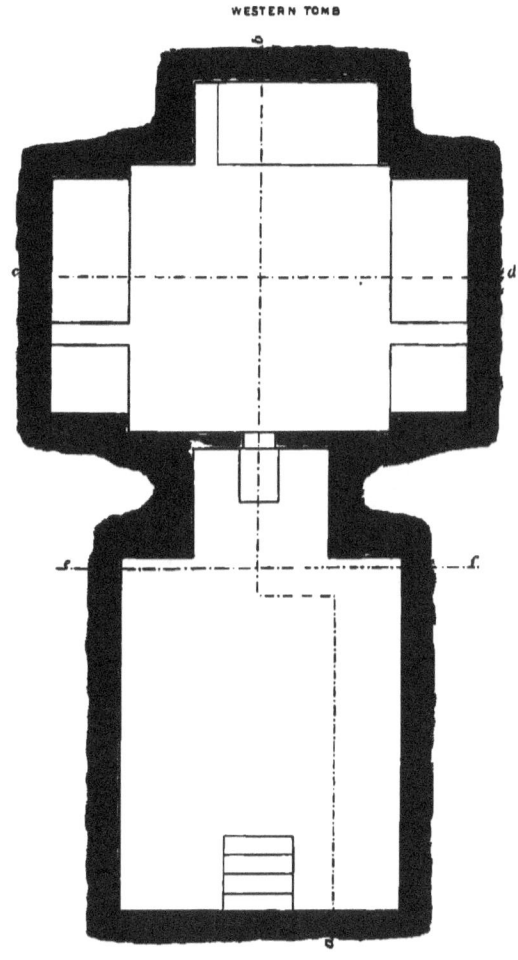

31½ feet north and south. Only the foundations remain, consisting of stones 2 or 3 feet long. A photograph of the façade was taken by Lieutenant Mantell, but there was not enough light to allow of its being successful. The drawing (Fig. 3) of the façade is prepared partly from the photograph and partly from a measured sketch made on the spot. The entrance will be seen to be flanked by two rock-cut semipillars, and two flat pilasters, with capitals of the Corinthian order. The peculiar shape and finish of the capitals is, however, clearly Byzantine, and they are probably to be attributed to the fifth century at earliest. Over the door is a rock-cut panel or sculptured frieze, with five medallions. The

central medallion has a Greek cross in a circle plainly traceable, though partly defaced, probably by intention. This design seems clearly to be as old as the original execution of the façade, and shows the tomb to belong to the Christian period.

The two alcoves, one each side of the pillars of the porch (as shown on the plan), have each a scallop-shell pattern to their domical roofs. The total breadth of the courtyard, all cut in rock, is 20 feet, and rough pillars are cut so as to chamfer off the corners of the rock scarp, which is 6 or 7 feet high at the sides of the court.

The tomb within is reached through the door under the frieze, an entrance only 3 feet 2 inches wide, and 5 feet 9 inches high. There are three steps leading down to the floor of the chamber, which measures 11½ feet square, and is 11 feet high, with a flat roof. A bench or step 11 inches high and about 1 foot wide runs round the three sides, and to the right and left two large arched recesses, or *arcosolia*, run back, having in each case a pair of sarcophagi parallel to each other, with a passage between. In each case also there is a third sarcophagus (making six in all) placed across the further ends of the parallel sarcophagi, and having over it an *arcosolium* rather lower than the roof of the recess. These details will be clearly understood from the plan and section.

The ends of the sarcophagi abutting on the chamber are sculptured. Those to the left have on the northern a wreath and a rosette, on the southern a kind of ribbon with a small rosette. On the right or east the southern sarcophagus is ornamented by two interlaced squares, very irregularly cut. The sarcophagi are 6½ feet long, 2 feet wide, 3½ feet deep.

At the corners of the back wall of the central chamber are two brackets, about 6 feet from the floor. They were, perhaps, intended to hold lamps or urns, and, like all the rest of the tomb, they are rock-cut.

In the back wall of the chamber opens an archway 7 feet 9 inches in  span, with 2 feet 2 inches rise. This segmental arch is 2 feet thick, and on the southern face a moulding, with classic details, runs all round the arch and down the jambs of the archway, which are 6 feet 2 inches high. This archway leads to an inner or more northern chamber, 1 foot above the level of the former, and measuring 7 feet 9 inches square. It has an arched recess 3 feet deep on the west and east walls, and a similar one 1 foot 8 inches deep on the northern. A sort of *koka* runs in from the end of the eastern recess 3½ feet long, 21 inches wide. This inner chamber seems probably to be unfinished, and perhaps the general arrangement was intended to be similar to that of the outer (as may be judged by the plan). The details of sculpture in the tomb are in many places incomplete, giving the impression that the monument was never finished.

The tomb has been twice cemented inside, the later coating of cement covering up the details on the sarcophagi. This would probably have been done in Moslem times, as at Jerusalem and elsewhere. The original plaster covering the walls of the inner chamber shows traces of neat arabesque designs, and this chamber was probably painted. The colour used is a brown, similar to that used in the painted tomb at 'Abúd. (See 'Memoirs,' vol. ii., p. 362.) Both Jewish and Christian tombs are found thus painted in Palestine (compare 'Memoirs,' vol. i., p. 346; vol. ii., p. 142), though rarely.

There are a great many Arab tribe-marks scratched on the cement of the walls, but they are evidently recent. On the older cement, however, occur other marks, painted in black and red, which may be thought to be of earlier and of Christian origin.

This tomb has been used for burial by the Bedawin at a late period.

Leaving this tomb, and proceeding westwards about 100 yards, a sarcophagus is found lying by the side of the ancient road. It is much worn and broken down. The side appears to have been adorned with wreaths. The total measurement outside is 8 feet by 3 feet 2 inches, the height 2 feet 4 inches. Inside it is 6 feet 8 inches by 1 foot 8 inches, and 1 foot 8 inches deep. It has a pillow or raised stone support for the head, 8 inches wide, cut at one end. The latter half only of the inscription remains, and was read . . . KATAINA.

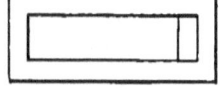

EL KAHF.

Near the sarcophagus is a *loculus* cut in the face of the cliff, under an *arcosolium*, on the east side of the spur. The rock is much quarried in the neighbourhood. Another tomb rather further west has a porch, supported on two rudely-cut piers of stone. It is 20 feet square, and the piers about 6 feet high. This resembles many examples in Western Palestine (compare 'Memoirs,' vol. iii., p. 355), which generally belong to rather a late period.

The western tomb is interesting for comparison. Its façade was photographed by Lieutenant Mantell (Photo. No. 9 of his series). It is about 200 yards from the eastern tomb, and was carefully planned by Lieutenant Mantell. It might easily be passed unseen, as it is entered from a sunk court about 6 feet deep, and is invisible to anyone who passes by it lower down the hill. It was shown to Captain Conder by Sheikh Kablân en Nimr.

The courtyard is $21\frac{1}{2}$ feet across, and 26 feet long; it has a flight of steps on the south opposite the façade of the tomb 5 feet broad, $5\frac{1}{2}$ feet long, with five risers in a height of $5\frac{1}{2}$ feet. The rock face at the back of the court (owing to the slope of the hill) is $13\frac{1}{2}$ feet high, and in this is cut an arched recess $10\frac{1}{2}$ feet wide, 8 feet to the back, and 9 feet high in the middle. It has a niche at the back 2 feet 10 inches high, 16 inches deep, 2 feet 2 inches wide, with a rounded roof. Over the niche is a simple cornice, and on the cornice a bust in low relief, much defaced. In spite of the shade in the recess, these details are well seen in the photograph.

The arched recess is flanked by two rock-cut Ionic pillars, which support a pediment with a low pitch. In the pediment is another defaced bust in low relief, with arabesque tracery either side. The total width of the pediment is 20 feet, and the apex is very near the top of the rock scarp.

As regards the busts, it should be noted that such busts occur over the tombs of Sûk Wâdy Barada (Abila) with Greek inscriptions, which are not earlier than the fifth century. At es Sâlt there is also a rude tomb with two such busts inside it, and this appears to be connected with a Christian ruined chapel not far off. The general style of the tomb now under consideration does not seem to forbid us to consider it as of the same date with the Christian tomb just described on the east, viz., the fifth century, when a large Christian population appears to have inhabited all Moab.

On the façade of the arched recess there are a great many tribe-marks, including the 'hook' of the Ajermeh, the cross of the Jibbûr, and other

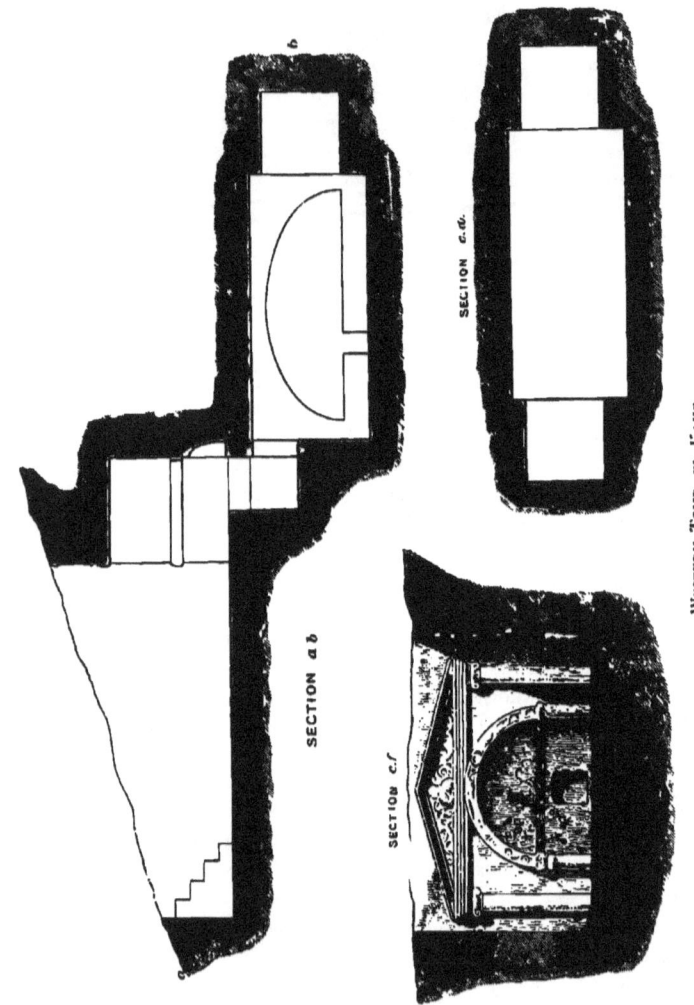

WESTERN TOMB, EL KAHF.

signs of the 'Anazeh and Sakhûr clans. These might be mistaken for inscriptions, and such marks have greatly puzzled De Saulcy and other travellers, though there is no mystery as to their origin.

The arrangement of the tomb to which this ornamental façade belongs is peculiar, and may be compared with that of the tombs at Umm el Hanafîsh and Umm el Buruk (which see). A shaft exists in the floor of the recess 5½ feet deep, 4 feet 8 inches wide, 4 feet long. It was originally closed by a slab fitting into a counter-sunk rim. The mouth was only 3 feet 2 inches wide. This shaft gave access to the real tomb-door right under the centre of the façade. The door was only 3 feet 4 inches high, and its sill is on the level of the bottom of the shaft. The width was 2 feet 10 inches, and a slab which closed this door, 2½ feet broad, 3 feet 9 inches high, 7 inches thick, fitted originally into a counter-sunk fitting, and is now lying in the shaft. The tomb chamber, reached by the little entrance, is 20 feet square, and 9 feet high, there being a drop of 5 feet 8 inches (according to Lieutenant Mantell's section) from the sill of the door to the floor of the chamber. The roof is flat, and there are three *arcosolia*, one on each side wall, one on the wall opposite the door. They are 6 feet high, and under each is a pair of raised rock benches, on which, perhaps, sarcophagi were placed, or which may have been intended to be sculptured later into rock sarcophagi. It should be noted that a sarcophagus could not be brought down the shaft, and that there are no traces of any having been cut in the tomb. Shelf tombs are not uncommon in Western Palestine, but were generally intended either to be finished or to support sarcophagi on the benches (compare 'Memoirs,' vol. i., p. 346, etc.). The tomb was, perhaps, like that on the east, never finished. As there are no traces of Christian work, it is of course possible to suppose that it is earlier than the eastern tomb; but as the later Jews (100 B.C.), the Romans, and the Byzantines, down to the sixth century, all used the *loculus*, the *arcosolium*, and some kind of classic style of façade, it is not easy to give a definite date in the present instance. It is clear, however, from the eastern tomb, that important sepulchres were cut in the Byzantine period at el Kahf.

Explored October 6 and 8, 1881.

Kalât Hesbân (قلعة حسبان).—See Hesbân.

Kalât Ummeh, or Kalât Ummet Abu el Hosein (قلعة أمة ابو الحصين), 'castle of the people of the father of the fortress,' which means 'fox-tribe castle ').—This name applies to the crags and caves of the spur between Wâdy Hesbân on the north and Wâdy Abu Turfah on the south. The cliffs are here of sandstone, and the place is hardly accessible save on the east, where it is reached by a descent down a narrow winding tract on the ridge among fragments of sandstone. It was explored by Captain Conder, with one guide. The cliff has four caves on the north side, and on the south is seen, about 300 feet beneath, a marshy spring with caves (called el Bassah, 'the swamp') in Wâdy Abu Turfah ('valley of tamarisks'), while an equally steep slope falls to Wâdy Hesbân on the north. The most eastern cave measures 7 paces (18 feet) by 10 paces (25 feet) to the back; the second, 10 paces by 20 paces to the back (25 feet by 50 feet); the third, 10 paces by 15 to the back; the fourth, 10 paces by 18 to the back. The height is 8 to 10 feet in all four. They are close together. Remains of beds made of *retem* broom, and manure of goats and bats cover the floors. These caves are hiding-places and stables for sheep in snowtime. The *Ausâm*, or tribe-marks, of the Ajermeh and the Dâja ('Adwân), of the Jibbûr (Beni Sakhr), and of the Khadir (Beni Sakhr), occur on the walls, showing that all these tribes have used the stables. Other marks were not determined (see Appendix on tribe-marks).

ᒆ ᑕᒪ + ᓇ ᑎ ⸝⸍

Visited September 12, 1881.

El Kaleilât (الكليلات, 'the hilltops').—Compare Kullet below.

### Dolmens North of Sûmia.

El Kalûa (الكلوح, 'the castles').—This is a very remarkable group of crags, a natural but unusual feature of the landscape, on the north side of Wâdy Hesbân, near Sûmia. It was photographed by Lieutenant Mantell (No. 6 of his series), and the Survey party examined a large group of dolmens existing on the slopes of the ridge west and south of the crags.

The crags are some 20 to 30 feet high, of a gray colour, with streaks of rusty brown. In the distance they have all the appearance of castles. They are inaccessible above, but approached over flat open ground below. On the south side of the group is a fallen block in which is an excavation 5 feet square and 3 feet high. It has two entrances 1 foot wide, at 3½ feet from the ground, and the floor of the excavation inside is 3 feet from the ground level outside. The block of rock in which this occurs is 12 feet high. On the west, close by, is a second similar cave, now much broken, also excavated in a detached boulder, and lower down the hill on the south is a third chamber in a boulder.

On the east slopes of a spur which runs out south from the main ridge west of el Kalûa a group of dolmens was found. This spur commands a view eastwards to the Kurmiyeh mountain, where the great dolmen-centre of Heshbon was found. There are about eighteen dolmens in all, two having fallen. These were all sketched and described, as below :

No. 1.—A rude trilithon, the table-stone measuring 7½ feet by 4 feet. The supporting stones are on the east and west, the former being appar-

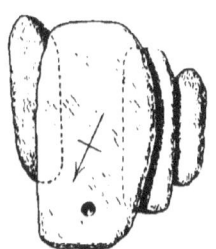

Nº 1 Dolmen Kalûa group    Plan of Nº 1

ently kept in place by a stone leaning against it outside. The clear height under the table is 3 feet. A hollow occurs in the capstone. This is one of the most easterly of the group.

No. 2.—A tiny dolmen, 30 paces (75 feet) east of the last. The capstone measures 4½ feet by 4 feet. The clear space beneath is only 1½ feet.

No. 3.—Higher up the hill than No. 1, on the north. The capstone is 6 feet long, but only raised a foot from the ground. It has two sidestones and an endstone.

Nº 2 Dolmen Kalúà Group.

Nº 3 Dolmen Kalúà group.

No. 4.—In this case a stratum of the rock has been prized up (compare el Kurmiyeh, No. 25), and is supported on the south by a stone on end, 3 feet high. The table thus formed is 8 feet north and south, by 4½ feet.

No. 5.—A topstone 8½ feet by 4 feet, supported partly by two stones, partly on the ground. The clear height beneath is 2½ feet at the down-hill end.

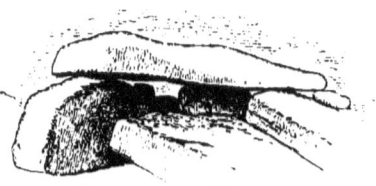

Nº 4 Dolmen Kalúà group.

No. 6.—One of the sidestones seems to have fallen. The table-stone measures 6 feet by 5 feet. This is on a flat spur west of a little valley-head.

No. 7.—Resembles some of the French and English 'rocking-stones.' The table is 6 feet by 4 feet, and 1½ feet thick. The upper surface is about 3 feet from the ground. The supports are small stones. There is an artificial hollow in the upper surface of the tablestone. This is some 200 yards north of No. 6, and higher on

Nº 5 Dolmen Kalúà group.

the hill. Two medium-sized fallen dolmens occur to the east of it, and on the higher part of the hill here (as at Neba and el Kurmiyeh) there are Meshâhed, or little modern stone piles of the Arabs.

No. 8.—This is a fallen trilithon, interesting because the cup-hollows are well marked, and cut with evident care. They are, perhaps, more

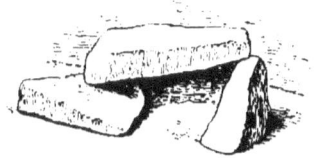

No. 6 Dolmen Kaliá group.

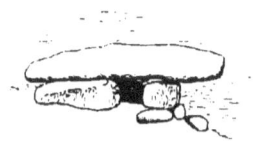

No. 7 Dolmen Kaliá group.

clearly artificial in this case than in any other observed in Moab. The table-stone is only 4½ feet by 4 feet, but it has six hollows, the largest at one end, the smallest at the other. They are respectively 10, 9, 4, 3, 2, and 2 inches in diameter, varying from 2 inches to about half an inch in depth, and quite round. The clear height under the table appears to have been 3 feet, and the two sidestones lie close by.

No. 8 Dolmen Kaliá group.

No. 9.—This has been partly overturned. The table measures 5½ feet by 6 feet, and there were two sidestones.

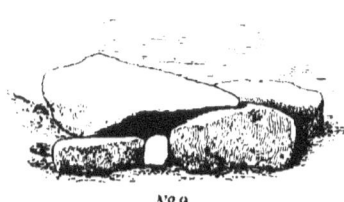

No. 9.

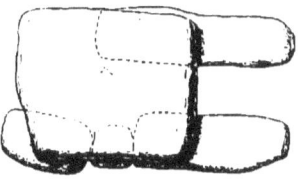

Plan of No. 9.

No. 10.—North of the last; has a capstone 4½ feet by 5½ feet, with two cubical blocks as supports, and a clear height of 3 feet and width of 2 feet 3 inches under the table. There is a hollow in the flat rock on the east side of this specimen.

No. 11.—A topstone 6 feet by 4½ feet, supported on irregular sidestones. The clear height beneath is 3 feet 8 inches, with a width 2½ feet. This is close to the last, on the north-east.

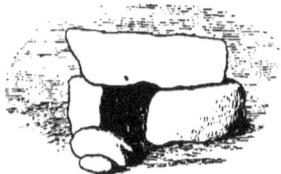
Nº 10 from the South.

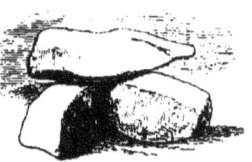
Nº 10 from the North.

No. 12.—A very low specimen east of the last, on a flat plateau. The capstone measures 4 feet by 3½ feet, and one sidestone is 4 feet long, 2 feet high, and 1½ feet thick.

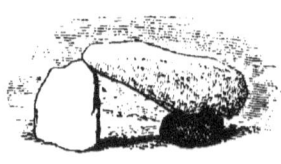
Nº 11.

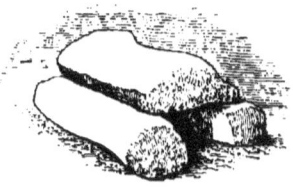
Nº 12.

No. 13 is a small specimen, about 100 yards east of the last, and higher up the hill than No. 1.

Nº 13.

Nº 14.

No. 14 is about 100 yards west of the Kalûá crags. It is a box-formed dolmen, but the cover-stone was not identified. The sidestone was 5 feet long, and about 2 feet high. Perhaps this was an unfinished example.

No. 15, about 50 yards west of No. 13, is a demi-dolmen. The flatstone is 5 feet long, supported at one end to a height of about 2 feet.

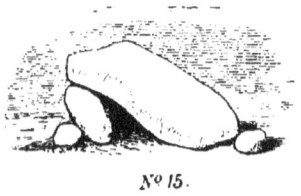

No. 15.

No. 16, near the last, but fallen, appears to have been a large trilithon. The capstone is $8\frac{1}{2}$ feet by $6\frac{1}{2}$ feet, and has upon it three hollows, two being joined together, with a diameter of 7 inches and a depth of 3 inches; and the third, about 6 inches away, is 8 inches in diameter, and 4 inches deep. The sidestones are $6\frac{1}{2}$ feet by $3\frac{1}{2}$ feet each.

Near No. 4 there are some fallen blocks of rock 20 feet long. About 50 yards further south on the spur are remains of a drystone structure, which might have been an altar or the base of a watch-tower. It is 20 feet square, and the stones are 2 feet to 3 feet long. East of No. 4 there are remains, possibly of another very small dolmen, the clear height under the capstone of which would have been about 1 foot.

About 100 yards south-west of Nos. 5 and 6, on the west slope of the spur, is a detached block of rock, with a small excavated chamber. The rock is 5 feet high, and 6 feet wide by 8 feet to the back; the chamber is $3\frac{1}{2}$ feet wide, 5 feet to the back, and 3 feet high. The door is 2 feet high and $1\frac{1}{2}$ feet wide. This small chamber resembles those at el Kurmiyeh, el Mareighât, etc., and one example of a somewhat similar kind was found west of Jordan (see Kulât el Ghûleh, 'Memoirs Western Palestine Survey,' vol. iii., p. 131). If they were intended for tombs, the body must have been buried in a cramped position. They occur generally in connection with dolmen groups.

East of this, by the side of a little ravine-head, is another fallen block of rock, in the west side of which is a niche or chamber 1 foot 9 inches wide, $1\frac{1}{2}$ feet to the back, $2\frac{1}{2}$ feet high. East again, and lower down in the ravine, is a large block with a chamber opening on the east measuring 3 feet square and 3 feet high. This excavation is not on the ground level, as the other two are, but has its floor 4 feet above the bottom of the rock. About 50 paces (125 feet) north-west again from the last is a fourth excavation in a detached block 3½ feet wide, 5 feet to the back, 3 feet high, the floor on the same level with the ground. There were some remains of bones in this chamber, but whether human or not was not clear.

The second day's exploration of this centre brought to light other examples, which were measured and described by Lieutenant Mantell.

About a quarter of a mile south of the crags of el Kalûâ, in the open ground not far from the stream of Wâdy Hesbân, is another detached rock boulder, with a niche 1 foot high, 1½ feet broad, and 1 foot to the back (see Sûmia); and about 130 yards south of the Kalûâ crags is a similar block of rock with a *koka* or chamber 8 feet 3 inches long, 3 feet 9 inches high, and 5 feet wide. The door is 3 feet high and 2½ feet wide, so that the excavation is much larger than those previously described (see others below).

No. 17, about 20 yards south of the last-mentioned dolmen, is a trilithon which has fallen. The topstone is about 4 feet square; the sidestone is 3 feet high, and 7¼ feet long. This stands on a flat terrace of rock.

No. 18, another fallen dolmen westwards from el Kalûâ on the plateau, had a table-stone fallen to the west, measuring 4 feet by 2 feet 9 inches, and 1 foot thick. The southern sidestone was 4 feet high, 3½ feet long, 1 foot thick. There were three other smaller stones on the east.

Nº 17.

Nº 18.

No. 19, about a quarter of a mile south-east of the Kalûâ crags, close to a tomb in a rock, and south-east of No. 18, is another trilithon, which, being on a slope, very nearly approaches the demi-dolmen class. The capstone is 5 feet square, and has a ridge in the middle, where it is 1 foot 9 inches thick, being 1 foot thick at the sides. This table-stone is unusually square in shape. The mean height under the table is only 1 foot.

N° 19.        Plan of N° 19.

No. 20 is east of the last, with an unusually thick table-stone 5 feet square, 1 foot 9 inches thick, with a clear height under the stone of 2 feet 9 inches.

In connection with this south-eastern group occur several other examples of the chambers in boulders above described. One of these is

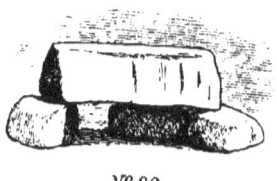 

N° 20.        Plan of N° 20.

north of No. 17, not far from the crags of the Kalûâ. It is 5 feet long, 4 feet high, 4½ feet wide, with an entrance 2 feet 3 inches high, and 1½ feet wide. Close by in a flat rock is a hollow 1 foot 9 inches in diameter.

The next example (the ninth of the chambers in and round the Kalûâ described under the present head) is about a quarter of a mile from the crags, and south-east of No. 18 dolmen. It is 11 feet wide, and 4 feet to the back, and varies in height from 2½ feet to 4 feet. The door is, at one end, 2 feet wide, and rudely shaped. No. 19 dolmen is about 10 feet from the door of this chamber on the south-west.

South of the Kalûâ two other chambers, each in a block of rock, were found. The first, 6 feet long, 4½ feet wide, 3 feet high, with a door near the right end 2 feet wide, 1 foot high; the second was 6 feet long, 3½ feet wide, 3 feet high, with a door 21 inches square at the end. In the same block with the first was cut a niche 19 inches wide, 22 inches high, and 10 inches to the back.

Passing along eastwards from this plateau to the rocks on the hill north of 'Ain Fudeili, which rises some 300 yards or so to the south, a detached rock is found 6 feet wide, 8 feet high, having in the middle an entrance 3 feet high, 3 feet 9 inches wide. This is only a niche or half-finished chamber, measuring 2 feet to the back. Another block of rock has been apparently overturned by earthquake. It is 7 feet long and 5 feet high, with a chamber 3 feet square, and 5 feet to the back. There is also not far off a broken *koka* in the rock 5 feet long and 1 foot wide.

Comparing this article with those on el Kurmiyeh, el Kalûâ, and Sûmia it will be seen that in Wâdy Hesbân some fifty dolmens in all have been described, and about twenty of the curious chambers, generally in detached blocks, and, as a rule, not long enough to allow of a body being laid flat in them. The rock is not too hard to forbid the supposition that the chambers may have been cut with a flint tool, and though none such were found in the chambers, worked flakes were recognised on the ground near the 'Ain Hesbân. The constant occurrence of the chambers near dolmens suggests that they may belong to the same period, and it may not be impossibly found credible that they represent the tombs of the dolmen-builders, excavated near the sacred stream of Heshbon, and generally intended to contain a kneeling or sitting corpse —the attitude most commonly found in Europe in sepulchres of the stone age.

Visited September 13, 16, 19, 1881.

Kareiât Mansûr (قريعة منصور, ‘Mansûr's skull ').—A sacred tree and traces of ruins. Probably a legend exists concerning this place.

Katât Mismâr (قطط مسمار, ‘chip of the nail ').—This name is applied to the slopes of the Kurmiyeh hill, which are quarried and covered with dolmens. The name may have some connection with the curious pointed menhirs which occur all over the hill.

El Kateitîr (الكطيطير, the root means ‘to drip ').—A small spring in the ravine north of Minyeh.

**Kefeir Abu Bedd or el Gharby** (كثير ابو بدّ الغربي, 'the little village of the millstone,' or 'the western little village').—A small site on the flat plateau close to the western slopes, remarkable for the large disc stone standing up in the midst—a conspicuous object from a great distance. North of the ruin is a modern circle enclosing a grave in the usual manner, with a trilithon on the west (compare 'Ain Hesbân and el 'Âl), but peculiar in this respect, that the wall of the circle is built entirely of cut stones from the ruin. Ploughs are placed within. With respect to this and other circles of small size, the 'Adwân Arabs stated that they constructed them to mark the graves of sacred persons. They also saw a resemblance (which was not suggested to them) between the trilithon and the larger dolmens of the country, but as to the latter they do not know when they were erected.

Near these graves the rock is much quarried. The ruins extend over some 50 yards north and south, including rock-cut cisterns and foundations of houses with vaults below, like those described at Kefeir el Wusta.

The great disc-stone is called *bedd*, or 'millstone,' by the Arabs, but has no hole pierced through the centre, as millstones usually have, and is, moreover, much larger than ordinary millstones, which in Palestine average about a yard in diameter. The stone at Kefeir Abu Bedd is $9\frac{1}{2}$ feet in diameter, and 1 foot 4 inches thick. It stands upright, with the flat faces on north and south, and is partly sunk in the ground, measuring 6 feet 3 inches to the highest part. Part of what may have been a socket for a shaft lies on the ground on the north-west. This stone is to be compared with **Mensef Abu Zeid** and the great disc-stone of el Kueijîyeh.

South of the disc-stone are foundations of a tower of well-cut stones 1 foot to 3 feet long, drafted as usual with a flat boss; three courses only remain. On the south-east is a rock-cut cistern, with a pillar-shaft near it. Further south again is a group of ruined houses of unsquared stones, the foundations only remaining.

Visited September 20, 1881.

**Kefeir Abu Sarbût** (كثير ابو سربوط, 'little village of the shaft').
—The last word is peculiar; it comes from a root meaning 'to be long and thin,' and is applied to pillar-shafts and milestones by the Arabs

## KEFEIR ABU SARBUT

(compare Seràbit el Mushukkar). In the present instance the title is derived from the peculiar pillar or menhir in the ruins.

The site in question is a ruined village, with a square fort on the north-east. This and the column are the most conspicuous objects. The pillar stands in the middle of the east side of a building which appears to have had an open court with vaults to the south, the north, and the west. The total outer measurement of the structure is about 90 feet north and south by 63 feet east and west, the court being about 50 feet square. The pillar is on a bank raised a couple of feet or more above the courtyard on the east. It is possible that the peculiar appearance is due only to weather action, but there are no traces of any capital or base. The shaft is a monolith 8 feet high, and 5 feet 9 inches in circumference at the bottom.

On the north side of the courtyard a pillar-stump about 1½ feet in diameter exists, but there are no other traces of pillars, capitals, or bases visible. The vaulting of the chambers round the little court is of the usual Byzantine type—barrel roofs of well-cut stones, as at Kefeir el Wusta, and no doubt of about the same age. These roofs have fallen in in places, and the interiors are choked up to a level higher than that of the

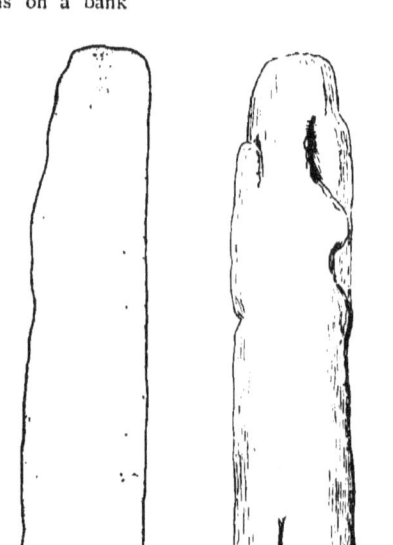

*Pillar at a.*

courtyard. On the north, south, and west respectively, a door with a flat lintel-stone leads from the court to the vaulted chambers.

South of this building with its peculiar and conspicuous monolith are many caves, cisterns, and foundations of rudely-dressed stones, many of which are drafted. Two broken sarcophagi have been used up in the walls of one building, indicating a late construction.

There are also remains of an arch, the entrados of which is carved with mouldings in low relief (like the arch inside the Prophet's Gate at Jerusalem, probably dating from the sixth century). On the west of the site are remains of what seems to have been a small chapel, but the plan

 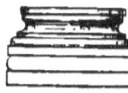  

is not distinguishable. The building seems, however, to have measured about 30 paces (75 feet) east and west by 20 paces (50 feet) north and south. The masonry consists of well-squared stones averaging about 2 feet in length by 1½ feet in height, and some of the foundation-stones are drafted. Several pillar-shafts about 20 inches in diameter are lying about.

A base and a Corinthian capital were measured and sketched. The capital is that of a square corner pilaster, the two sculptured sides being similar to each other. The shaft must have been about 1½ feet square.

North of the S a r b û t or pillar already described as the peculiar feature of this ruin, and about 50 yards from it, are remains of the tower,

which is also a conspicuous object at this site. It measures outside about 20 paces (50 feet) north and south, by 25 paces (67 feet) east and west.

## KEFEIR ABU SARBUT

It was well built originally, with vertical walls, but onto these a sloping scarp of rougher masonry has been built, but is not bonded in. On the north side is a door, with a fallen lintel in front of it. The lintel and the door-jambs are of well-cut and squared masonry; the rest of the walls are built of stones more rudely finished. On the door are *ausám*, or tribe-marks, of the 'Adwân and Beni Sakhr Arabs, including the cross, which is said to be used as a tribe-mark not only by the Christian men of es Salt when living as nomads, but also by the Jibbûr, a division of the Beni Sakhr (this same tribe also uses the 'raven's foot' as a tribe-mark). The first mark is the 'Adwân Mutluk, but the rest are Beni Sahkr marks.

| + ౭ B

These correspond to the Himyaritic letters ڡ ظ, and to the Himyarite numeral I.

There are several pillar-shafts lying near this tower, and on the west is a well, the mouth of which has been stopped with such a shaft.

Inside the tower a capital of the Corinthian order 17 inches in diameter, and a very simple base 20 inches in diameter of shaft, were measured and drawn. The tower walls are standing to a height of about 10 feet. The interior is much filled with accumulated rubbish. The sloping scarp has fallen down on the north side, showing the face of the vertical wall. This tower somewhat resembles the Jâmiâ el Arbâin at Shiloh (see 'Memoirs Western Palestine,' vol. ii., p. 369).

Caves, with masonry additions at the entrances, and rock-cut passages leading down, also occur west of the tower (compare Khûrbet 'Aziz, 'Survey Western Palestine Memoirs,' vol. iii., p. 348). These caves are found in many Byzantine ruins in the south of Palestine.

A building was also found west of the tower, of which only foundations remain, with fallen pillar-shafts and ruined vaults, while on the ground close by lies a lintel-stone, broken at one end. It is 1 foot 9 inches high, and the present length is 4 feet 8 inches. A curious cross is incised upon it 2 feet broad and 1½ feet high, with the ends furcated, as shown in the sketch on p. 137.*

We have thus evidence that Kefeir Abu Sarbût is a Christian ruin, and, with the other sites near it, it is probably to be ascribed to the fourth century at earliest, as all the buildings existing at this site are of one style and character.

Visited September 16, 1881.

Kefeir esh Sherky (كفير الشرقي), 'the little village on the east') is the most eastern of the group of four sites all called Kefeir, and all apparently having lost their old names. It is situated at the east end of the ridge, some 200 feet above Wâdy Habis. Foundations, caves, and scattered stones were observed. On the east are Arab graves, but nothing distinctive was noticed, though the site was carefully examined.

It appears to have been a Byzantine village, like the other three, but probably the smallest and least important of the group.

Visited September 16, 1881.

Kefeir el Wusta, or Abu Khân (كفير الوسطى ابو خان), 'the little village in the middle' or 'of the Khân,' *i.e.*, 'inn').—This ruin is immediately south of the knoll with Arab graves which marks the south end of the base-line of the English Survey. The ruins are those of a Byzantine village. Towards the north-west, close to the Survey station, is a vault broken open at either end, but covered with a well-shaped barrel-vaulting of round cross-section 20 feet span. The voussoirs are graduated from a narrow keystone to the broad haunch-stones. The vault is about 67 feet long and 12 feet high. On the south of this was found a lintel-stone 7 feet long, 1½ feet high, having a Maltese cross in a circle upon it (see p. 139). In the roof of the vault another stone is built in with a cross in a circle of very peculiar form (see p. 139). South-east of these remains, which are clearly Christian, were found foundations of a tower about 50 feet square; and west of the Survey station are caves. The stones in these ruins are fairly well dressed, and average about 2 feet in length; many are drafted with an irregular draft, and a roughly-dressed boss. One measured 14

---

* This furcated cross may be compared with one found by Sir Charles Fellows in 1838, at Aphrodisias, in Caria.—Fellows' 'Asia Minor,' p. 253.

inches square, the draft being 2½ inches wide, and the projection of the boss 1 inch.

About 150 yards east of the Survey station is another vault, of which a plan was made. The entrance is on the east through a cave and a hole

in the wall, and the length of the cellar is north and south, with a kind of apse at the north end. The building measures 21 feet 6 inches along the west wall, not counting the apse, and is divided by piers into a western part 14 feet wide, and a side-chamber 6 feet wide. The apse measures 8 feet to the back. The roof of the western part was supported on ribs running east and west, of good masonry, on the arches of which flat stones were laid. The arches are about 2 feet thick each, and the stones very

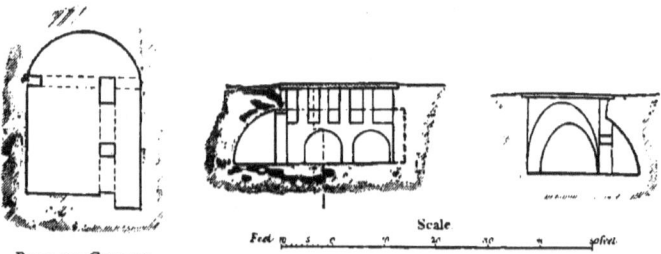

PLAN OF CISTERN.

well cut. The sides of the vault are of rock cemented. This building, although called a Kenisch, or 'church,' by the Arabs—probably because of the rounded end—seems to have been only a large reservoir. No entrance originally existed save through the roof, where was a place for a water-wheel; the sides appear to have been cemented throughout to hold water.

West of this last is a vault 25 yards long and 8 yards broad, with a well-built barrel-roof. There is a descent in the southern part of this vault, now much clogged with rubbish, which may lead to one now covered up. A stone with a kind of willow-leaf pattern on it is built into the east wall near the floor. On the floor lay a drafted stone 4 feet 3 inches long, by 2 feet 3 inches, by 1 foot 8 inches high; the draft is 4 inches to 8 inches broad, with a rustic boss projecting 4 inches. This draft occurs on two faces of the stone (the length and the end). The north end of the vault is open, the southern closed, with a recess 5 feet square and 5 feet high with a flat roof. An inscription is said to have existed here, but it was destroyed by the Arabs. There are several other vaults of the same kind in the ruin.

South of the ruins on the road to Hanina is a fine birkeh, or tank, measuring 60 feet east and west by 80 feet north and south, and 25 feet in depth. The masonry is of moderate size, and of square proportions; the joints are packed with smaller stones. A trough has fallen into the tank (*cf.* el 'Alwân at Hesbân). West of this tank there are two rock-sunk tombs resembling those described at Umm Hanâfish.

The various indications thus obtained, the crosses, and rock-sunk tombs, and the character of the masonry, all indicate that Kefeir el Wusta, like the other three village ruins called Kefeir, belongs to the early Christian period, probably about the fifth century A.D., when it is clear that a considerable Christian population must have existed in towns occupying the whole of the Mishor, or plateau of Moab.

Visited August 29 and 31, and September 26, 1881.

Kefrein (كفرين 'the two hamlets').—A few hovels of small masonry and reeds on the north bank of the stream, where Sheikh Kablân en Nimr pitched his camp in winter. The stream is about 10 feet wide at the most, and generally only 3 or 4 feet. The temperature of the water was 98° F. on two occasions. It is a branch of Wâdy Kefrein, which is deflected for purposes of irrigation. There are fine groves of the zizyphus, or *sidr*, and among them, south of the stream, stands Khŭrbet Kefrein (see under that head). On the north is the knoll of rock artificially shaped into a Tell, called Tell Kefrein, on the summit of which is a modern white Arab tomb, which is called Sheikh el Mujâhed (شيخ المجاهد), 'the champion chief'). He is said to have been the father, or others said an uncle, of Kablân, and was here buried by his own

TEMPLE AT KHARBBET ES SŪK.

*To face page* 140.

command. The Tell is about 140 feet high above the general level of the plain. The tomb is similar to the Kabr Fendi el Fâiz. The view hence is very extensive, the three ridges of S i â g h a h M a s l u b î y e h and M i n y e h being specially conspicuous against the sky on the southeast, with the lower hump of M e n s h a l a h on the plateau below Minyeh. The tree of Shânab and the Zabûd ridge are prominent on the east, while below these are seen Tell el Hammam, Tell esh Shaghûr, Tell Iktanû, Tell er Râmeh; the tree at the M e n s e f A b u Z e i d is also seen, and on the north the most conspicuous points are the peaks of el H e l â l y and el H a u d. West of the river appears the similar peak, 'O s h e l G h u r â b, with K u r n S a r t a b a, the monasteries of el Y e h û d and K u s r H a j l a h, and beyond these 'A i n e s S u l t â n, 'A i n D û k, and E r î h a. Higher up over K o r u n t u l appear T e l l e l F û l and N e b y S a m w i l, while T e l l 'A s û r, Olivet, J e b e l E k t e i f, el M u n t â r (or the Scapegoat Mountain), Herodium Bethlehem, T a i y i b e h, are all conspicuous on or near the sky-line. This point, in short, gives the best and most characteristic view of the plains of Shittim and of Jericho with the surrounding hills.

The Tell is of natural rock, and various rude caves are scooped in the west side, which may be old graves. The limestone is soft, and the caves are very roughly excavated. One measured 9 feet by 6 feet, and was 6 feet high; a second was 9 feet by 5 feet, and 3 feet high; a third only 3 feet by 4 feet; another had three rude *loculi* on the three sides, each about 3 feet by 3 feet; another is 6 feet by 4 feet, and 3 feet high. There are perhaps twenty or thirty in all, and the Arabs use them for storing corn and straw.

Close by is a little rocky peak (on the west), which is flatter than the preceding. This is also full of similar small caves. It is called e n N a s l e h, which see.

The 'Oshîr plant (*Calotropis Procera*), or ' apple of Sodom,' allied to the Indian family of Asclepiadaceæ, was found here in profusion.

August 17 and October 25 and 27, 1881.

E l K e m u k k a h (الكمكة, pronounced Gemuggah).—This name applies to a group of three small ruins west of 'Ammân, on the main Roman road west to 'Arak el Emir. Heaps of flint stones and foundations of rough walls remain. The buildings are probably not older than the second century A.D.

El Kereik (الكريك).—This may be a mistake for كريك, a word commonly used, and applying to small fortresses. In Syriac the latter word means 'fortress' (cf. Sheet VI. of the 'Western Survey,' Kerak or Tarichea). The same name applies to the great fortress east of the Dead Sea, south of the Survey. The ruin in question is on the plateau north of Máâin. It might perhaps be the Biblical Karkor (Judg. viii. 10), the name of which signifies 'flat ground,' which applies to this plateau very well. Walls, cisterns, and a rough rock-sunk tomb, probably of the Christian period, were found here.

El Khalfeh (الخلفة).—The name is from a root meaning 'to follow.' In Hebrew it is the name of a Galilean town, Heleph (Josh. xix. 33), (see also 'Ain el Khalfeh). The name applies to a plot of ground with dolmens south of el Kalûâ, and the spring may be the object whence the place is named. 'Ain el Khalfeh is written on the map to note the spot.

Khareibet es Sûk (خريبة السوق, 'little ruin of the market').— The ruins (also noticed by Sir C. Warren, 'Quarterly Statement,' 1870, p. 291) include a building which seems to have been a temple (Lieutenant Mantell's photos, Nos. 20, 21, and Sir C. Warren's photo, No. 304); a tomb tower further east (Lieutenant Mantell's photos No. 22, Sir C. Warren's, No. 305); a tomb tower to the north; and a large reservoir near it. The plan of the temple has been obscured by later additions and alterations. It consisted originally of three walks, with pillars of the Ionic order, 2 feet 10 inches in diameter, 15 feet 9 inches high from the present ground level. The bases are, however, hidden. There are three to

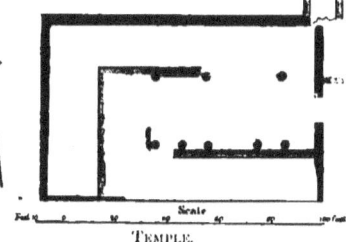

TEMPLE.

the north and five to the south of the central walk, which is 22 feet wide in the clear; the inter-columniation is 6½ feet. The total length of the building outside was originally 111 feet, and the breadth 62 feet. The remains of an entrance on the east are still clearly visible. The reconstruction was effected by walls built just outside the central arcade to

Capital in Temple.

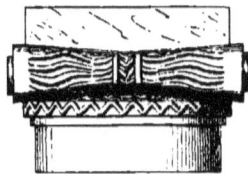 

north and south, while on the west the building was shortened by 23½ feet. In this cross wall some column shafts are built in horizontally. The true bearing of the building is 97°. The stones in the walls are of moderate size, and without any draft. The walls are 4 feet thick.

The mausoleum or tomb-tower to the east measured 39½ feet north and south, 41 feet 9 inches east and west, with a true bearing of 104°. This building is some 300 yards from the temple. The foundations remain, showing a plinth or podium at the base of the wall, and a cornice of which the profile (as given below) was taken. The wall is 8 feet high; the cornice at the top is 9 inches high, and projects 9 inches. On the west side of this building an arch (A) is built against the wall, but not bonded in. It consists of nine voussoirs of equal width, and is 6½ feet in span and 3 feet 9 inches in rise (including haunch stones). A bold moulding (see Section) is carried round this arch. The walls of the building are in some parts fallen, and only 4 feet high. There are no remains of any roof; the walls appear to average about 3½ feet thick; the interior is filled with stones and rubbish. There are two sarcophagi outside on the west, without any covers; one was

Eastern Tomb.

Detail of Eastern Tomb.

Section of Arch A.   Section of Cornice

8 feet long, 3 feet 4 inches broad. North-west of this building is a rock-cut tank, 31 feet east and west, 26 feet north and south, with a masonry roof. Captain Conder descended into it to measure the details. Two piers of masonry are built to support the roof; they stand north and south, and have arches from which the barrel-vaults spring. The arches are of different span, round with a narrow keystone; the arch from the north pier to the west wall has been supported later by a pier under its crown. The tank is 15 feet deep; the walls are covered with flat pieces of stone aid in mortar, and over these the cement was spread. Close by the tank are the foundations of a tomb, measuring 27 feet by 36 feet. There is a podium, or sculptured plinth, at the base of the wall, and on the platform so formed are placed sarcophagi, two to the west, two to the north, one to the south. There are remains of pillars on the east, as though the building were originally *in antis*, or had some sort of porch. Fragments of sculpture were also observed, representing a vine-leaf and bunch of grapes.

TANK.

NORTHERN TOMB.

The principal ruins of the site (which was a large and important town), occupy two tops of a spur north and south of the supposed temple; but the buildings described are the only ones of which any distinguishable plan could be made out. On the west are several caves.

Visited October 11 and 17, 1881.

K h a s h m  J â w â n (جعوان خشم, 'snub-nose').—This is the name of the spur west of el Maslûbîyeh, probably from its appearance as a short projecting headland.

K h a z e i k â t  e n  N a s â b a h (خزيقات النصابة, 'the upright stakes'). —This term is applied to the peaks of the plateau above the Dead Sea, west of Hammet Minyeh.

E l  K h e i m e h (الخيمة, 'the tent').—This word is not generally used of Bedawin tents, though applied to travellers' tents. It seems to apply to a slope on the north side of Wâdy Sîr, but is rather a doubtful name.

E l  K h u d r (الخضر, 'the green').—This name applies to two shrines, one being at the northern edge of the Survey, close to Mâhas in the oak wood, north of 'Arâk el Emîr; the second in the Jordan valley, by Kabr

NORTHERN TOMB AT KHAREIBET ES SUK.

*To face page 144*

Sáid, south of Tell er Rámeh. The latter is omitted from the reduced map for want of space. In both cases the shrine stands in the midst of luxuriant natural growth. West of Jordan there are many shrines of el Khudr. On Carmel he is identified with Elijah. At Ascalon, and in other Crusading sites, he becomes St. George. At Banias he replaces Pan, having his shrine at the source of the river. (See also Sheets III., IX., XII., XV., XVI., XVII., 'Memoirs of the Survey of Western Palestine'). In the Kor'ân this personage is mentioned in connection with a non-Biblical story concerning Moses, who is supposed to search for him. He is there called the vizier of D h u e l K a r n e i n, 'the lord of two horns,' who is the mythical Alexander or Ammon, who had drank the fountain of immortality (Sura xviii., 50-82). There is no doubt that the 'green old man,' el Khudr, is the personification of fertility, as represented (especially in the desert) by greenness. His shrines are generally in fertile spots, and the sacred green colour of the Moslems is connected with the same idea. His original prototype was probably the Asshur of Assyria, who, with Ashtoreth, was universally worshipped in Arabia by the pre-Islamite Arabs. The first place so named near Mahas is a square masonry tomb, near which is a rock-cut tomb with three *loculi* under *arcosolia*.

K h û r b e t A b u N u k l e h, named from the well (see Bîr Abu Nukleh).—The ruin is south of the well, and is small and unimportant. Scattered stones and small caves were found, and the place was inhabited by an Arab family. On the south, and separated by the flat open valley, is another, similar ruin. A few courses of stones undressed and of no great size were standing in the ruined walls.

Ptolemy, speaking of Moabite towns (see Reland's 'Palestine,' i., p. 464), mentions Necla (Νέκλα) with Heshbon, Ziza, etc. This (as is suggested by Rev. Selah Merrill) might be connected with the Khurbet Abu Nukleh. Ptolemy's latitudes and longitudes are not of any exact value (as an examination of them proves); but in this case the latitude is south of Heshbon and the longitude west, which does not agree with the identification. Some place south of the Dead Sea seems more probably intended.

K h û r b e t A b u S h e r i â h ( خربة ابو شريعه, 'ruin of the drinking'). —A little ruin with walls which appear to belong to a sheepfold.

Khŭrbet 'Ain el Beida (خربة عين البيضا, 'ruin of the white spring ').—A small ruin with walls and heaps of stones near 'Ain el Beida, at the north edge of the Survey.

Khŭrbet el 'Âisheh.—See 'Arâk Abu 'Âisheh.

Khŭrbet el 'Amriyeh (خربة العمريه, 'ruin of the perpetual one'). This ruin is in the outskirts of the Hirsh el 'Amriyeh, the oak-wood north-west of Heshbon, and it is beside a road leading north-east towards 'Ammân. About 200 yards to the north-east there is a very fine terebinth. The ruin was visited and described by Lieutenant Mantell, R.E., and found to extend over about 150 yards north and south by 80 yards east and west. Foundations remain of rudely squared stones, and there is one standing on end—a small menhir apparently, $4\frac{1}{2}$ feet high, $1\frac{1}{2}$ feet thick, 3 feet wide at the base, $1\frac{1}{2}$ feet at the top. Forty yards north of the terebinth there is a rock-cut winepress, consisting of two chambers, one 10 feet by $5\frac{1}{2}$ feet, and 3 feet deep ; the other a small round cutting 3 feet in diameter, deeper still, with a connecting cut.

WINEPRESS.

About a quarter-mile south of the ruin among the oak-trees there is a circle of stones. They are from 2 feet to 4 feet in length by $1\frac{1}{2}$ to 2 feet. No lintel doorway belongs to this circle, and there is no central grave. The Arabs say it is not a sacred place, but only an old *kasr* or tower.

Visited September 12, 1881.

Khŭrbet Bahhar (خربة بحر), perhaps named from some pool (Baheirah) not now existing. The name applies to a pair of ruins south-west of 'Ammân. Foundations, heaps of stones, rude caves, and rock-cut cisterns were observed.

Khŭrbet Beddîh (خربة بديح, probably from بدح, 'a court'—Freytag Lex.).—Foundations and scattered stones only remain. It is a small ruin of no importance.

Khŭrbet Belâl (خربة بلال, in Arabic, 'ruin of damp').—A ruin in the oak-woods north of 'Arâk el Emir, overgrown with large oak-trees. Great heaps of stones remain here on a hill-top. Belâl Ibn Rubâh was the Muedhdhen of Muhammed, but there is nothing to show any connection with his name.

Khŭrbet Belâth (خربة بلعت).—This does not appear to be an Arabic word. It might be a corruption of בעלת (Baalath), which is rendered more probable by the vicinity of the sacred tree at Rujm Belâth. At the ruin is a sort of Tell about 300 yards by 100 yards, with remains of a square building at the north-west end. It is 16 paces (40 feet) side, with a bearing 310°. The stones in the walls are 2½ feet to 5½ feet long, and 1½ feet to 2 feet high. Most of them have rude bosses projecting some 6 inches, the draft being 3 inches to 12 inches wide, but averaging 6 inches. The walls are standing, from 4 feet to 8 feet high. Thence for about 100 yards south-west are remains of house foundations built of small stones rudely squared. One of the stones in the tower has two bosses on one side and one on the end. The stone is 5 feet 8 inches long, 1 foot 8 inches high, and 2 feet 3 inches wide. The bosses project 3 inches and are dressed; the drafts are 12 inches, 7 inches, 6 inches, 5 inches, and 4 inches wide. This seems to be Byzantine work, or Roman of the second or third century. About 30 yards north-west of the tower is a natural cave, 12 yards by 10 yards, and 4 feet high. There is a well in the ruin. The sacred tree is a conspicuous object to the north-west.

The name of this ruin—evidently once a place of some importance—is very closely similar to that of Bela, the earlier name of Zoar (Gen. xiv. 2 and 8); but the situation on the plateau does not seem to agree with the situation of Zoar. Eusebius speaks of a Balá as inhabited in his own time (fourth century), and as having a Roman garrison. He describes it as in the east limits of Judæa above the Dead Sea, apparently east of Jordan. Jerome also states it to be the place called Zoora by the Syrians, which might be thought to agree with the vicinity of Rujm Sáàùr, about a mile to the west. It is curious also that a place called 'Amriyeh (the proper equivalent of Gomorrah or Amorah) exists not far west. It is possible that these names are survivals of an ecclesiastical tradition of the fourth century, but they cannot be considered the real Biblical sites (see Reland's 'Palestine,' vol. ii., pp. 622, 1065; see also Tell esh Shâghùr).

Visited September 13, 1881.

Khŭrbet ed Deir (خربة الدير, 'ruin of the monastery').—Two cisterns, and a few foundations of roughly squared stones.

Khŭrbet edh Dhràâ (خربة الذراع, 'ruin of the cubit, or forearm').

—This is evidently an ancient Edrei אדרעי, a name signifying a 'strong place' (Josh. xiii. 31, and xix. 36). Two cities so called existed, one in Bashan (now edh Dhrâ), one in Galilee, probably the present Yâter. The present ruin appears not to be historically known at all. It consists of foundations and heaps of stones on the ridge east of 'Arâk el Emir.

K h ū r b e t  e d  D u b b e h (خربة الدبة, 'ruin of the she-bear,' or 'of the pack animal,' most probably the former, as the Mughâret ed Dubbeh, or 'bears' cave,' exists close by. No bears are, however, now found in this district). The ruin is south of the last. Foundations and heaps of stones, cut rudely, or quite undressed, occur on the hill. To the north, about 200 yards away, there are several Arab graves. Three of these are surrounded with circular walls of stone (compare 'Ain Hesbân, etc.); these also are modern.

K h ū r b e t  F e r â w î t, see 'Ayûn Ferâwit.—It is a small ruin, consisting of rough foundations, near the springs.

K h ū r b e t  e l  G h a r b e h (خربة الغربة, 'west ruin').—An insignificant ruin, apparently. It was not actually visited, but seen at a little distance, and said to be unimportant by the guide.

K h ū r b e t  e l  H a m â m (خربة الحمام, 'ruin of the pigeon'), see 'Arâk el Hamâm.—It consists of heaps of small stones only. It was visited by Captain Conder, but found to be quite insignificant.

K h ū r b e t  H a m z e h.—See Umm el Hanafish.

K h ū r b e t  e l  H â r â t (خربة الحارات, 'ruin of the quarters,' or Hârât Hesbân).—See Hesbân.

K h ū r b e t  e l  H â w i y e h (خربة الحاوية, 'ruin of the circle').—This is on the plateau north of el 'Al. There are three natural caves, the largest 12 paces by 10 paces (30 by 25 feet), and 8 feet high. Three cisterns also occur, and a fragment of a torus-moulding on a stone 5 feet long, 2 feet high, 15 inches broad at the top, 8 inches at the bottom, the torus projecting 7 inches in a height of 13 inches. A pillar shaft, 19 inches in diameter and 18 inches long, was found; and a second, lying on the ground, 5½ feet long, and of the same diameter. The ruin is extensive, and occupies the west slope of the flat hill. There are many foundations without any distinguishable plan. A few of the stones are large and well cut: one was 5 feet long, 21 inches high, 19 inches thick;

another was only 23 inches by 20 inches. The ruin was visited and described by Lieutenant Mantell, September 13, 1881.

Khûrbet Jezzûâ (خربة جزوع). Perhaps from جزع, 'high land ').—This was beyond the border of the 'Adwân, and, consequently, could not be visited under the arrangement made.

Khûrbet el Kefrein (خربة الكفرين, ' ruin of the two villages ').—This is a large mound with graves, nearly a mile south-west of the Tell Kefrein. On the mound stands the sacred circle of ez Zâby, to the north and west are the Kabûr el Hasâsineh, and on the west is Sâlhah, another grave and shrine. The spot is thus a centre of Arab graves, and a sacred place. The site is an open space, about 100 yards across, in the midst of the thickets of *sidr* and other trees. A few scattered stones, and one modern Arab hut remain, and the place does not seem to be an ancient site.

Khûrbet Kerâdeh (خربة قرادة, ' ruin of camel-ticks ').—It seems possible that this is another plural, instead of Kerûd, meaning ' goblins.' It is a small ruin, presenting only heaps of roughly cut stones, extending for some 20 or 30 yards. It is north-west of 'Arâk el Emir, and is a favourite camping-ground of the Arabs. This may account for its name, if it really means ' camel-ticks.'

Khûrbet Khardubbeh (خربة خردبة. This is probably a corruption of some older name).—It is a small square watch-tower, in the open valley north-east of 'Ammân. The plain near is called Sahlet Khardubbeh.

Khûrbet Kheshrûm (خربة خشروم), north of Bir Abu Nukleh, seems to be an old site of some importance. It resembles Umm el Kindib in general character. Ruined cottages were observed, with cisterns, but no very distinctive objects were found.

Visited September 17, 1881.

Khûrbet Khuldeh (خربة خلدة).—This is an interesting name, applying to several places in Western Palestine also. The radical meaning of the word is ' enduring,' but in Syrian dialect the Khuld is the mole rat Spalax Typhlus, the Hebrew Kholed, rendered ' weasel' in the Bible. It is possibly from the ancient Baal Haldim, or ' Lord of Eternity,' that these places are named. The present ruin is quite small, consisting of foundations and heaps of stones on a spur at the north edge of the Survey. Near it is the Kusr Khuldeh, which is the real ruin. (See under that name.) The hilltop above is a very prominent feature—a trigonometrical station, with a large tree to the east. This may very probably have been a sacred place.

K h û r b e t  e l  K u r s i  (خربة الكرسي, 'ruin of the throne' or 'chair').—A small ruined tower, with a large tree, east of Rabahiyeh.

K h û r b e t  M â s û h  (خربة ماسوح).—The root سبح means 'flowing,' and is applied to surface water; but Wády Mâsûh is quite dry, and the site is supplied by cisterns. The ruin is that of an important place on the plain east of Heshbon. The town stood at the foot of a flat slope ascending northwards, on a low mound about 200 yards across. Foundations of houses remain, built of rudely-dressed drafted stones, 2 feet to 3 feet in length. A lintel stone 7 feet long was measured. Under the houses are caves (as at Dhibân, Mââin, and at Khûrbet 'Azîz, and other sites on Sheet XXI. of the 'Western Survey'). The caves are reached by passages cut in the rock, with steps leading down from the surface of the ground. One passage is 7 feet long and 3 feet wide. The caves are about 10 paces (25 feet) square. A wall remains of well-squared ashlar, looking like Roman work; but the masonry is either not *in situ*, or, for some other reason, very irregularly built. The horizontal joints of the courses are not continuous (a feature often observable in Byzantine ruins). This wall runs north and south, and is in the north-west part of the ruin. There are many rock-cut cisterns at the site, and a fine arch stands up alone, consisting of 14 voussoirs of squared stone. It is 12 feet in span, 5 feet rise, and 28 inches thick. This appears to be Roman work. On the south-east there are modern Arab graves, and also remains of a building with pillars of great size. There are remains of three shafts 3 feet in diameter, one being 9 feet long; another shaft, 1½ feet in diameter, was measured, and three massive bases, about 20 inches high and 50 inches square, one supporting the pillars 3 feet in diameter, but now overthrown. These are probably remains of a temple like that on the citadel hill at 'Ammân; but the ruins are in part, at least, attributable to the fourth or fifth century A.D.

Visited September 16, 1881.

## KHURBET MESHUKKAR

**Khûrbet el Meisah** (خربة الميسة, 'ruin of the Meis tree, Cordia Myxa').—Heaps of stones and a few foundations near Dhahr Hamâr, on the east.

**Khûrbet Merj el Hamâm** (خربة مرج الحمام, 'ruin of the meadow of the pigeon').—This is an insignificant ruin—a few stones on a hill.

**Khûrbet el Merussus** (خربة المرصّص, 'ruin of pebbles').—A small ruin consisting only of a great heap of stones, with a few foundations. It is south of Dhahr Hamâr, and named, perhaps, from 'Ain el Merussus to the west.

**Khûrbet el Meshukkar** (خربة المشقّر).—This is the name of a district or ridge west of Heshbon. The root means 'dark red,' which does not apply to the colour of the ground. The **Shakkâra** is the anemone flower, and the ridge may be named from these plants, which are plentiful in spring. The ruin in question is the site of a small town on high ground. An ancient road passes beneath the hilltop on the east. A high flat mound, about 50 yards in diameter, is covered with foundations, built of rude masonry of moderate proportions. On the north, rather lower, are modern huts of some fugitive Fellahin here settled. They cultivate a little corn and tobacco. There are caves on this side, and a few drafted stones. A simple pillar base was also observed, but nothing very remarkable was found. Half a mile east of this ruin, on the crest of the hill, looking down towards 'Ain Fudeili, there

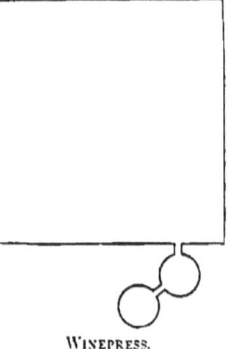

WINEPRESS.

is a very fine rock-cut wine-press, showing that the vine was once cultivated in the vicinity of Heshbon. The chief chamber is 18 feet square and 1 foot deep. On the west a little channel leads to a circular well 1½ feet deep and 3 feet in diameter, and another channel from this again, on the west side, communicates with a third well 2 feet deep, 3 feet in diameter.

Visited September 13 and 16, 1881.

**Khŭrbet Nâàûr**, named from the spring, see 'Ain Nâàûr.—This site is immediately west of the spring on the south slope of the valley and above the waterfall. There are half a dozen modern houses where corn is stored, and a little enclosed vegetable garden east of the spring is the property of Sheikh 'Aly Diâb, under the care of a fugitive Arab from the Nejed.

**Khŭrbet Nineh** (خربة نينه).—This is the same word as Nein, generally rendered 'colony.' It is a small ruin, with foundations of rough stones, east of the springs called 'Ayûn Nineh.

**Khŭrbet er Ramleh** (خربة الرملة, 'sandy ruin').—A small ruin ; a few foundations and ruined walls with a tree. It is named from the sandstone which appears in these great gorges. It is on the east side of Wâdy esh Shita.

**Khŭrbet er Raseifeh** (خربة الرصيفة, see 'Ain er Raseifeh), north-east of 'Ammân.—Foundations extending over some 50 yards, with a central tower 16 paces (40 feet) square and 10 feet high. It is on a ridge nearly 4 miles west of the springs.

**Khŭrbet er Rijjâhah** (خربة الرجاحة. In Arabic this means 'ruin of the swing ').—It is quite a small ruin on the hill, east of 'Arâk el Emir.

**Khŭrbet er Rônak** (خربة الرونق, 'ruin of shining,' of the sun, etc.), near Khŭrbet Sâr on the east. There is a *kusr*, or tower, at this site, built of flint stones ; it is 50 feet in diameter and round (compare the tower at el Bureikeh). This may have been a beacon station, as the situation is very elevated. The remaining ruins are foundations and scattered stones.

**Khŭrbet er Rûâk** (خربة الرواق, 'ruin of porches ').—This is the word applied to certain cave tombs (*cf.* 'Arâk er Rûâk). The ruin is a mile to the north of the 'Arâk er Rûâk, and consists of walls of large stones with a rock-cut cistern. Other cisterns and a ruined watch-tower occur on the hill farther north.

**Khŭrbet es Safrah** (خربة الصفرة, 'yellow ruin ').—Foundations of houses built of small rough stones. It is on the high ridge called Hadib es Sufa, east of 'Ammân, and is named, no doubt, from the tawny colour of this barren ridge.

**Khŭrbet es Sahel** (خربة السهل, 'ruin of the plain').—Was not visited, being beyond the 'Adwan border.

**Khŭrbet Sâr** (خربة سار, see 'Arâk el Emîr).—This is the ruin of an ancient place of some importance. The site is large, extending some 500 yards in either direction. The ancient west road from 'Ammân passes by it, and on the north by the roadside six sarcophagi were found lying in a square enclosure. There is a large pool or Birkeh in the ruins, and in the north-west angle of the site are remains of a fine tower, which is a conspicuous object in the landscape from every side. It is 21 paces or 53 feet square, and is built of great blocks of chert or flint, taken from the bands which run through the rock (a soft white chalk). These blocks are 5 feet to 7 feet long, and 1 foot to 2 feet thick. The use of flint is common all over this plateau, and also in the Beersheba Desert, where the same formation occurs.

East of the tower are remains of a building with two parallel rows of arches running east and west, 22 feet apart. Probably the rubbish is here of great depth, and the piers beneath the arches are covered up. There are four arches in each row, 4 feet 9 inches span, and round in shape, with voussoirs 2 feet deep. The arcade is 30 feet long, and the arches 6 feet thick north and south. The face of each arch is ornamented with mouldings (as in the structural tombs of 'Ammân). There seem thus to have been two rows of vaults which may have been tombs. Among the ruins was found a pillar shaft 3 feet 3 inches in diameter. Not far from the arcade some large bases were also noted, and masonry of Roman appearance. This, with the presence of the sarcophagi, seems to indicate the date of the ruin, which is a large and important site.

It is probably to this ruin of Sâr that Eusebius refers (s.v. Azor in the 'Onomasticon') as being 10 Roman miles west of Philadelphia ('Ammân), and 15 Roman miles north of Heshbon. Jerome mentions a great stream as flowing thence to Jordan (*cf.* Jer. xlviii. 32). The ruin of Sireh and the spring 'Ain es Sir are in the valley below Khŭrbet Sâr. It is probably to the stream which flows thence to Jordan that Jerome refers. The names in question come, however, from the root צוּר (see under the head 'Arâk el Emîr), and these words have no connection with the name

Jazer, from the root עזר (see under the head Beit Zerâh), only the R being common to the two names.

Visited October 20, 1881.

### PISGAH.

Khŭrbet Siâghah (خربة صياغة).—This ruin probably takes its name from the Aramaic Seath (סיעת), which is called in the Targum of Onkelos (on Num. xxxii. 3), 'the house of the burial of Moses.' The Aramaic and the Arabic are as close as possible, the important guttural

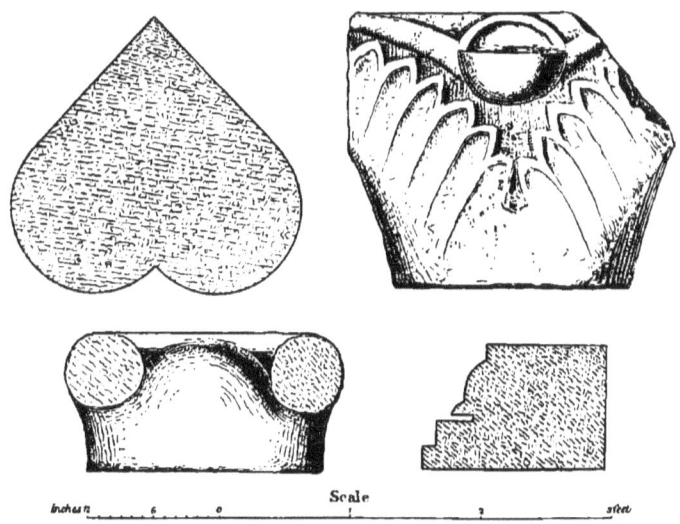

being retained. The ruin is a conspicuous mound of broken masonry, on the ridge of Pisgah (Râs Siâghah), west of the summit of Nebo. It seems most probably to have been a Byzantine settlement, with a church towards the east of the site, which measures (according to Sir C. Warren) 300 yards east and west, by 100 yards north and south. Towards the south lie about a dozen pillar shafts, 2 feet in diameter, and six rude Ionic capitals, which resemble those found at Tantûrah ('Memoirs of Western

Palestine,' vol. ii., p. 8) and elsewhere. In the Christian buildings of the Hauran (second to fourth century) similar Ionic capitals are common. Another capital has a rude foliage, somewhat like the work of the Basilica of Justinian in the Aksa mosque.

A double column was also found, resembling those of the Galilean synagogues. Each of the two shafts was 1 foot 6 inches in diameter. These double columns are also found at Tyre (perhaps relics of the old Temple of Melcarth), at Khŭrbet Belât ('Memoirs,' vol. i., p. 171), and at Jerâsh; they were certainly therefore used by Jews and Romans in the second century of our era.

The principal building at Siâghah—whether church or temple—lay east and west. The plan is not easily distinguishable. Sir C. Warren makes the length 70 feet. Captain Conder paced it as 24 paces (about 60 feet); the breadth was not certain, and there are no apses (cf. Mâdeba). There appears to have been a nave and two aisles. The moulding of a cornice which belonged to this building was measured. The masonry in this and other parts of the ruin is very well cut; the stones being about 2 feet by 1 foot by 1 foot on an average. On the south are cisterns, one of which is of considerable size. On the west is a vault, explored by Sir C. Warren and Captain Conder: the roof is supported on ribs over round arches of good masonry, the voussoirs 2½ feet deep, the span 10 feet, the pier 2½ feet thick. Across these ribs a flat roofing of flags is placed—an arrangement found sometimes in Byzantine work (cf. Deir 'Arâby, 'Memoirs,' vol. ii., p. 313). A few fragments of a skeleton and rags of clothing were found in this vault, and there were traces of cement on the walls, showing that (as in other ruins) it was probably once used as a rain-water tank underground.

Immediately north-west of the vault is another vault of rudely squared stones, the joints of the masonry packed with smaller stones; this is also a peculiarity of Byzantine work, as at Bidieh ('Memoirs,' vol. ii., p. 306), or in the Birket Isrâil at Jerusalem. This tank measures 8 paces north and south, by 6 paces east and west. In it lies a pillar shaft, which is chiefly remarkable for the exaggerated bellying at the centre, the two ends having a smaller diameter.

The indications of date thus obtained, though not very definite, seem all to point to the early Christian period, or to that of the Antonines, as the time when this small town of Siâghah was built. As no crosses or inscriptions were found, it is not possible to say certainly whether the principal building is Christian or Pagan; but this ridge was known to Jerome (*cf.* Neba) as the site of Nebo, and also, apparently, of Peor. It seems, therefore, not improbable that a church may have been built on the supposed site of the spot whence Moses viewed the Promised Land, in or about the fourth century.

The large cairn on Râs Siâghah, south-west of the present ruin, is said to have been originally constructed by the American Survey party in 1873. It was used as a trigonometrical station, also, by the English Surveyors.

Visited August 20, and September 7, 1881.

**Khûrbet es Sireh** (خربة السيرة), 'ruin of the sheep-fold,' in Wâdy es Sîr; *cf.* 'Arâk el Emîr).—This is the ruin immediately west of 'Ain es Sîr, but presents only heaps of stones among the oak-trees.

**Khûrbet Sûeimeh** (خربة سويمة).—This is the Hebrew Beth Jeshimoth (ביתישימות, 'house of solitudes') mentioned in Numb. xxxiii. 49; Josh. xii. 3, xiii. 20; Ezek. xxv. 9. It was known to Eusebius as being 10 miles from Jericho, near the Dead Sea. There is a small sandy mound, or Tell, here, covered with chips of pottery and glass, and some modern Arab graves. Also a spring. (See 'Ain Sûeimeh).

**Khûrbet es Sûr** (خربة السور, 'ruin of the wall ').—The pronunciation of the Bedawin was very indistinct, and the scribe was doubtful as to the S, which may be a Sâd. The name is no doubt derived from the ancient צור, or Tyrus (see 'Arâk el Emîr), and the Sin and Sâd in Syrian mouths are often indistinguishable, as also in dictionary Arabic (see Lane and Freytag on the words صرق and سرق). The ruin is conspicuous, occupying the flat top of a ridge west of 'Arâk el Emîr. Heaps of rudely-cut stone and numerous foundations occupy two knolls, lying north and south, and about a quarter of a mile apart. These sites were explored by Lieutenant Mantell, but nothing of interest was found.

**Khûrbet Umm el 'Akâk** (خربة ام العكاك).—This is also known as Muntâr el Mushukkar, on the flat ground, east of an ancient road. The latter term, however, applies, properly, to a ruin rather further south, on the west side of the same road. Foundations of a small house remain at

Umm el 'Akâk, at the top of the rapid descent leading down to 'Ain el Fudeili. There is a rock-cut cistern, and a rock-cut wine-press, also a modern circle, no doubt surrounding a grave. It is 12 paces (30 feet) in diameter, the wall built up of small unhewn stones without any trilithon or other entrance.

Khŭrbet Umm Hadawîyeh (خربة أم هدويّه, apparently ' ruin of the gift,' on the pass immediately west of the Survey Camp, near 'Ain Hesbân').—There are strewn stones here, some of which are rudely squared, others not dressed at all; they are from 1½ feet by 1 foot, to 3 feet by 1½ feet in size. There are also a few walls showing the remains of a rough hamlet, which perhaps dates from the time when Muhammed 'Aly commanded the Arabs to reside in houses. The ruins extend over about 40 paces (100 feet) east and west, by 50 paces (125 feet) north and south. On the south of the ruin, some 30 paces (80 feet) away, is a rock-cut wine-press with one chamber measuring 8½ feet by 7½ feet, whence two channels lead, one to a chamber 4 feet by 2 feet 10 inches, and 20 inches deep, the other to a separate chamber 1 foot deep, and 1 foot by 1½ feet in area. These remains were measured and described by Lieutenant Mantell, R.E.

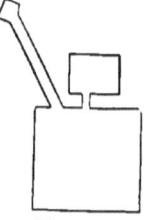

WINE-PRESS.

Visited September 12, 1881.

Khŭrbet Umm Rummâneh (خربة أم رمّانه, ' ruin mother of the pomegranate ').—This may be an ancient Rimmon. The name is common in Western Palestine. No pomegranates exist at it. A small ruin on high ground of no special features, resembling the others on the plateau (see Umm el Kindîb), with heaps of masonry, cisterns, and foundations of rough stones, probably of the Byzantine period. (See Sir C. Warren's remarks on this subject. ' Quarterly Statement,' 1870, p. 290: ' We now arrived in a very remarkable piece of country. . . . . A great portion of the masonry is no doubt Roman.')

Kissârah (كسّاره, the root means ' to break ').—Apparently a ruined village or pilgrim station, on the Hâj Road, east of 'Amman.

Kôm Yâjûz (كوم ياجوز, ' heap of Yâjûz ').—At the northern edge of the Survey. This is an irregular circle on a hilltop about 200 feet in diameter (compare el Hadânich). It has a stone breastwork or wall with sloping sides, heaped up as at Hadânich. This encloses other ruined walls. Similar circles were found in the same district at Râs el Merkeb.

El Kûeijiyeh الكويجية, the word فوج means 'an ornament' for a woman's head-dress).—This is a prominent isolated hill crowned with ruins. On all sides near the foot of the hill, but especially on the south slope, there are numerous dolmens which are specially described with others under the head Wâdy Jideid. On the top of the hill are remains of a small village, consisting of cottages built of unsquared stone, and having a modern appearance. It may have been built up at the time when Muhammed 'Aly endeavoured to compel the Arabs to live in houses. There is a large Arab graveyard here and two modern sacred circles (see 'Ain Hesbân), each with its trilithon on the west. Inside were laid crutch-headed sticks about 2 feet long, such as mark the dignity of Sheikh. They were adorned with strips of red and green cloth. Ploughs, coffee-mills, etc., were stored in the circles, and on the lintels were small offerings, including a few small modern coins.

On the south were graves, two of which were honoured by strings of hair. A stick was placed upright at each end of the grave, and a string tied between these stakes; from the string depended the plaits of hair, from a foot to 18 inches in length, carefully plaited as is the hair of married women among the Arabs, and bleached by exposure to sun, wind, and rain. Over one of the graves forty-five of these plaits were hanging, and over the other thirty-three plaits. This is more than is usual, though such offerings are frequently found (as at Mââîn, Rujm el Meseik, etc.).

In the middle of the ruins there is a remarkable disc stone standing upright. It must be compared with the Mensef, Abu Zeid, and the stone of Kefeir Abu Bedd. (See under those heads.) It is 6 feet in diameter, and has no hole in the middle, being likewise too large for an ordinary millstone.

The Arabs store corn in *metamîr*, or underground silos, at this place—no doubt because it is a sacred spot.

Visited September 27, 1881.

**Kullet es Sekûriyeh** (كلّة الصئوريه, apparently 'the collection of falcons ').—This applies to the plateau east of Neba. It may, perhaps, be a mis-pronunciation for قلّ, 'hilltop.'

**El Kureinein** (الكُرينين, 'the two little horns' or 'peaks').—This appears to be a ruined village. Rough walls remain, and a cistern was noted. On the north-east there is a ruined cistern. It may perhaps be an old site named from Ashtoreth Karnaim, or from the Arab Dhu el Karnein. The whole district is full of ruins of the same class.

**Kuriet el Hammâm** (قرية الحمّام, 'village of the bath ').— Applies to the ruins on the top of Tell el Hammâm.

### HESHBON DOLMENS.

**El Kurmîyeh** (الكُرميّه, probably from قرم, meaning 'hard rock.' as this is a very rugged spur).—This name applies to the long spur running out west of Hesbân, and having 'Ain Fudeili at its feet. It is one of the great centres of rude stone monuments, which also occur further west along the course of Wâdy Hesbân. (See Sûmia and el Kalûâ.)

The ridge runs out at first on the level of the Mishor plateau, north of the Tell at Hesbân, and then falls with a steep slope to the terrace, or spur, to which the name Kurmîyeh appears specially to apply, some 400 feet above 'Ain Fudeili. At the west end of this spur, which is partly arable ground, is a knoll, on which stands a large ruined cairn, with remains of a circular enclosure of small stones. The steep slopes on the south-west, west, and north are covered with dolmens down almost to the bottom of the valley, and the

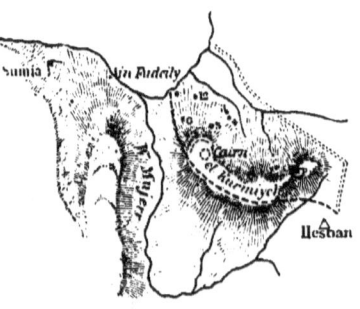

total number of rude-stone monuments on the hill is at least twenty-six. They do not appear to have any orientation or systematic arrangement, but were constructed probably wherever fallen blocks and fragments of the limestone strata were found lying at hand on the slopes. From the cairn a good view is obtained down the course of Wâdy Hesbân, including the vicinity of the Kalûâ rocks.

The cairn above-mentioned has been destroyed almost to its foundations, and measures 6 paces (15 feet) across the foundation ; the stones are unhewn, and of no great size. There seems to have been once a circle of 15 paces (40 feet) diameter round this centre, consisting of rough stones, about 2 feet high. Lower down the west slope there are remains which seem to indicate a larger double circle traceable for some distance round the contour of the hill. The diameter (measuring from the cairn as a centre) would have been about 200 yards, and the two rows of stones are 8 feet apart. Most of the stones have been set on end, and they stand in places touching each other, some having a curious pointed form ; they appear to be unhewn blocks, averaging about 2 feet in height, probably selected on account of their pointed, or tapering, shape. On the flat rock, near the central cairn on the knoll at the end of the spur, or terrace, there are a good many round holes, 1 foot to 2 feet in diameter, and 6 inches to 1 foot in depth. These resemble the cup-hollows in the dolmens at this and other sites (see No. 3).

The dolmens are found mainly on the west and north, outside the double circle above described. There is a fine single specimen, however, standing quite alone at the foot of the upper slope, in the north-east corner of the terrace. It bears 79° true bearing from the central cairn, while the top of the hill, or centre of the upper spur, bears 97° from the same cairn : this example is No. 1 of the enumeration below, and was called B e i t  e l  G h û l, 'the Ghoul's house,' a title which was, however, found to apply to dolmens generally among the more ignorant Arabs of the district. The lower slopes of the hill are known as Katât Mismâr (see under this head). The dolmens on the Kurmiych ridge may be divided into four groups. The northern, near the foot of the slope, including Nos. 3 and 4 ; the western, lying west and north-west of No. 6, on the steeper part of the slope, low down the spur : the third (above the first), on the south, extending south from No. 2, on the south-west slope, which is gentle, and down which an ancient road from Heshbon descends towards 'Ain Fudeili. The fourth group is further north, near No. 5 dolmen, above the first group.

The monuments highest up the hill appear, as a rule, to be smaller than the fine examples found near the foot.

No. 1 dolmen, already mentioned as standing alone on the north-east, is a very fine trilithon, which was photographed and sketched. The table-stone measures 6 feet along the south face, and 5 feet 3 inches along the west face. The sidestones are on east and west, the eastern standing nearly upright, measuring 6 feet in width and height, and 1½ feet in average thickness. The western has, perhaps, subsided from its original position, and is 5½ feet high, 4 feet long, 1½ feet thick. These two

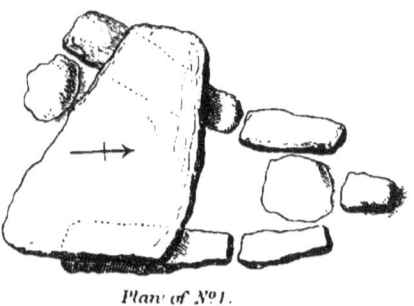

Plan of Nº 1.

Scale of Feet.

supports are 6 feet apart. The capstone is tilted up eastwards, and averages 1 foot to 1½ feet in thickness. It may originally have been

No. 1 from South.

horizontal. On the north side are two other sidestones, and an end stone, as though intended to support a second table-stone, which would make the original length of the monument north and south 10 feet 6 inches.

21

On the south side of the monument is a small stone adjoining the western sidestone, and forming a step. The clear height inside the dolmen is 6½ feet in the middle, and a man standing on the stepstone, which is about 2 feet high, can place his hands conveniently on the top of the table-stone. Three other stones on this side seem to form a little enclosure (as in other examples), dividing off the interior of the trilithon. The great blocks thus piled up are of heavy hard limestone. They are not dressed, but may have been rudely trimmed for their purpose.*

No. 2 From East.

No. 2 dolmen stands on the hill due west of the central cairn on the flatter part of the slope outside the double circle, or enclosure; it was discovered by Lieutenant Mantell, half a mile west of No. 1. It was photographed by him (photo No. 5 of his list). The table-stone is only raised 3 feet (clear beneath the stone) above the ground; it measures 6 feet north and south, and 4½ feet along its northern face; it is about 1 foot 3 inches thick, and supported by a stone on the north (4 feet by 2 feet, and 3 feet high), and by another at the south-east corner (4½ feet by 3½ feet). There is also a long stone on the west, which may have been intended to support the table-stone; but the latter has either been moved or was never placed in its intended position, as it now only touches this sidestone, which measures 7 feet north and south, by 2½ feet east and west, by 3 feet in height. This is a remarkable specimen of a very distinct dolmen, which is, nevertheless, much lower than the average of such monuments.

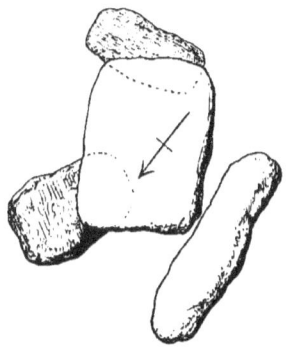

Plan of No. 2.

* The scale, ₁/₆, on last page is that of all the figures of rude-stone monuments in this volume.

No. 3, together with the next, is on the north slope of the hill, quite low down. It is, perhaps, the finest specimen east of Jordan, and was discovered, measured and photographed by Lieutenant Mantell (photo No. 2 of his series). It is a trilithon with a floor stone, and the blocks which form the supports are so well shaped, that it seems necessary

No. 3 From the West

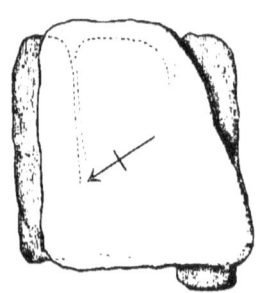

Plan of No. 3

to suppose that they were trimmed to shape by human art—perhaps with a stone or flint axe. The table, or capstone, is very flat, from 1 foot to 2 feet thick, and measuring 8 feet by 9 feet along two sides. The supporting stones are in a line directed at 119° true bearing (the view through the monument being thus south of west). The southern sidestone is 9 feet long, 5 feet 3 inches high, and 1 foot 6 inches thick, of very regular shape. The northern stone is 8 feet long, 2 feet thick, 5½ feet high; the capstone rests irregularly on these; the floorstone is 6 feet long, 4 feet wide. In the upper surface of the capstone are six or seven holes, varying from 1 foot to 18 inches in diameter.

No. 4 is some 20 yards north of No. 3, lower down the slope. It was discovered at the same time by Lieutenant Mantell and photographed (No. 3 photo of his series). This is also a fine specimen, with a capstone intended to rest on three supports, and having a curiously pointed ridge on the upper surface. The sidestones are towards the north and south (according to the contour of the hill), and there is a cross or endstone towards the west. The capstone is 2 feet thick in the centre and 1 foot thick at the sides ; it measures 4½ feet by 4½ feet, but at one end is only 3 feet broad. The northern sidestone is 8 feet long, 1½ feet thick, 3½ feet high ; the southern is 13 feet long, but broken, and 3 feet 9 inches high and 1½ feet thick. The cross stone is 3 feet high and 1 foot 3 inches thick ; the space between the sidestones is 3½ feet wide north and south, and the mean height under the capstone is 3½ feet. The four dolmens thus described are the finest specimens on the Kurmiyeh hill. About 100 yards north-east of Nos. 3 and 4 was observed a niche cut in a low cliff about 1 foot wide, 1½ feet

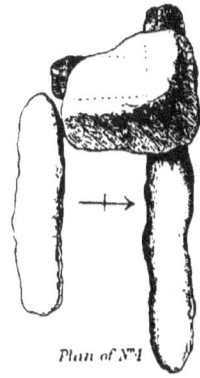

Plan of Nº 4

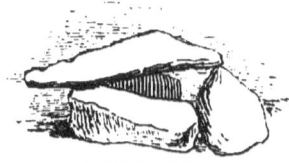

Nº 5 West Side.

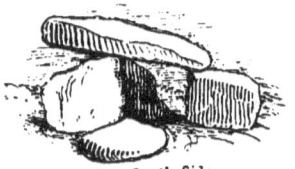

Nº 5 South Side.

high, and 9 inches to the back, and rather further east there are two

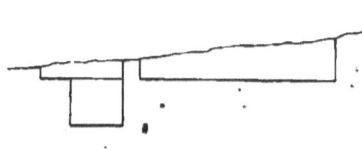

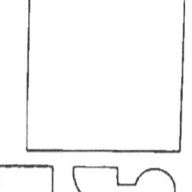

chambers, or *kokim*, cut in the rock (*cf.* el Kahûâ). These chambers were found in several other instances (*cf.* el Mareighât) in connection with dolmens. There is a fallen dolmen west of No. 3, the topstone of which measures 4½ feet by 8 feet.

No. 5 is south-west of No. 3, in a line bearing 119° true bearing, and 48 paces, or 120 feet, distant, higher up the hill; it has been partly destroyed, but the capstone is still supported by three stones (photo No. 4 of Lieutenant Mantell's series). The clear space under the table

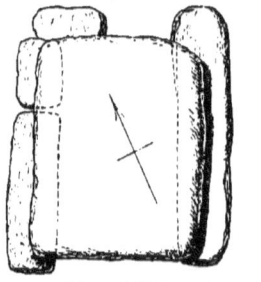

Plan of Nº 6.

Nº 6 From North

is only 2½ feet; the capstone is 5 feet by 7 feet in measurement. North-east of this specimen was found a rock-cut winepress, the larger chamber 12 feet square, with three smaller chambers about 3 feet wide, varying from 2 feet to 4 feet in depth.

No. 6 is a dolmen close to No. 5, which has subsided somewhat from its proper position. The capstone (2 feet thick) is rectangular, measuring 6 feet by 8 feet. The sidestone towards the west lies in a direction 22° true bearing along the length, and is 9 feet long, and 4½ feet high, and 2 feet thick. The western side of the table is supported by two stones only 3 feet high, and measuring together 6 feet in length.

Nº 7.

There is also an endstone on the north, 2 feet long, 1½ feet thick, and about 3 feet high.

No. 7 is 50 yards south-west of the last, and is a peculiar monument, perhaps fallen, though by comparison with other examples, and judging from the horizontality of the table-stone, it seems more probable that it stands as originally constructed—a flat table, 5 feet by 4 feet, being supported on the down-hill side by two large blocks, but resting on the upper side on the ground. The slope is here so steep that the height from table to rock on the down-hill side is 6 feet.

Nº 8

No. 8, west of No. 6, is a yet ruder structure, two small flat stones lying one on the other, evidently not a natural feature.

No. 9 is a dolmen which has fallen over or has been destroyed; with the next two it forms a group about 200 yards west of No. 6, near the foot of the spur east of the junction of Wâdy Hesbân and the ravine

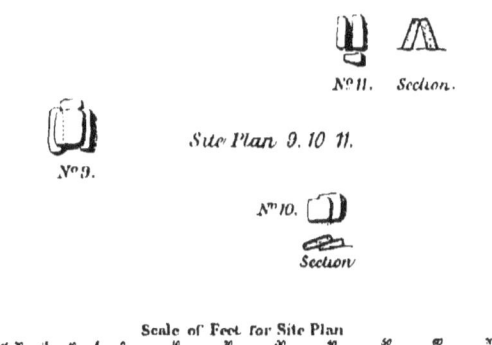

south of the Kurmiyeh hill. The table-stone of No. 9 measures 4½ feet by 6 feet, and was once raised on three supports, one each side and one at the end.

No. 10 is 20 paces (50 feet) south-west of the last, and consists, like No. 8, of two small flat stones placed one over the other.

No. 11, about 10 paces (25 feet) north of the last, consists of one end and two side stones, but the table-stone has disappeared.

No. 12 is north-west of No. 6, and it is the most northerly of the group (including Nos. 6 to 15), on the extreme west part of the spur. It is merely a great heap of stones, perhaps marking a fallen dolmen.

No. 13 is a single menhir standing south of the last, and rather higher up the hill; it is 5 feet high, 6 feet wide at the base, 1 foot thick, and has

a pointed or tapering shape towards the top. It appears to be unhewn—a natural stone raised up vertically.*

No. 14 is east of the last, and may perhaps be a fallen dolmen. It is

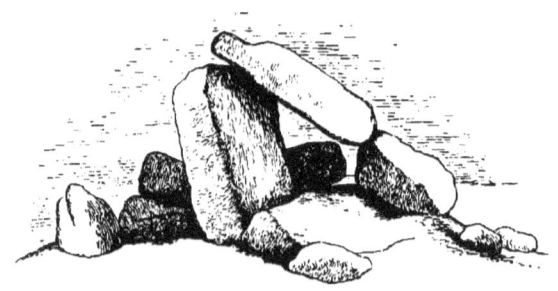

north-west of No. 6. One stone, apparently the western sidestone, is 4 feet high and 6 feet long. The table-stone was about 5 feet square.

No. 15 is a little structure which would be easily overlooked if found alone, though it is evidently artificial, and resembles others found near 'Ammân. It is immediately north-west

---

* The pointed form of this menhir, as well as of those at 'Ammân and el Mareighât (though in other cases the top is carefully rounded), is worthy of special notice. It is clear that it cannot be accidental that so many menhirs should have this pointed form, and especially as the menhirs of Brittany and of the Dekhân in India are also generally pointed at the top. The appearance of the menhir circle at el Kurmiyeh and of the menhirs at el Mareighât is very similar to that of the Carnac menhirs—a row of points bristling one above another, as the stones are arranged in lines gradually increasing in height.

of No. 6. It consists merely of a stone 3 feet long, resting on a little stone at one end.

No. 16 appears to be a structure still existing as originally built

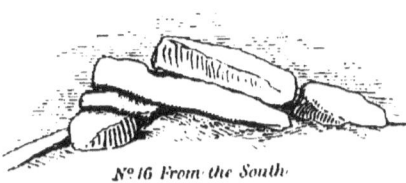
N° 16 From the South.

rather than a fallen dolmen, and is a larger example of No. 15. It is high up on the slope of the spur, about 20 paces east of the wine-press already described, on the north slope. A stone measuring 5 feet by 6 feet is supported on the down-hill or north-west side by two smaller stones, which, together, are 3 feet high ; the other end rests on the ground—as in a demi-dolmen—and on this flat stone is placed another of almost equal size, 2 feet thick, and 5 feet by 4½ feet on the

N° 17 From North.

upper surface. Another stone is placed nearly touching this last, which is not quite horizontal, but slightly tilted. It is clear that this structure is more probably intended for a table or altar than for a grave.

No. 17, high up on the hill, south of No. 5, and thus west of the central cairn, is a ruder example of the same class with the last. Three flat stones are piled one on the other with a slight tilt, and the top stone is 8 feet by 4 feet.

No. 18, west of No. 2, on the flatter part of the west slope of the hill,

N° 18 From South.

N° 18 From North West.

may perhaps have fallen. The arrangement is peculiar—a flat stone being apparently (if in its proper position) balanced on one much smaller, and steadied by another resting against it. The flat stone measures 4 feet by 6½ feet, and is 2 feet thick ; the one resting against it is of the same size.

No. 19 is, perhaps, a fallen dolmen, though the position of the stones might, perhaps, equally indicate intention. A flat stone, 5 feet by 4½ feet, by 15 inches in thickness, lies on a small stone, and is balanced by a stone 5½ feet by 6 feet, by 15 inches thick; which is again held in place by another block, 6 feet by 3 feet, by 1½ feet, and scotched beneath by small pebbles.

Nº 19 From North.

The whole structure is thus very infirm, and might be thought to have fallen but for the position of the last-mentioned stone.

No. 20.—This is a rude pile, apparently standing as originally erected, and clearly built up to support the top table-stone, which is some 5 feet square. The structure lies 15 paces south-east of No. 2, on the flatter western part of the spur.

Nº 20.

No. 21 lies 20 paces (50 feet) south of No. 2, on the west of the central cairn, and is a variety of the same class with the last—a single flat stone resting on two flat stones.

Nº 21.

Nº 22.

No. 22 is towards the south, 100 yards from No. 2. In this case, also, the table-stone is supported, not on stones placed vertically, but on slabs lying flat; it measures 5½ feet by 6 feet.

No. 23, on the south-west slope of the hill, further east than the last, resembles No. 19. In this case four slabs have been placed one over the other. There do not seem to be any other remains south-east of this example.

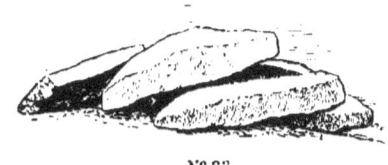

N₀. 23.

No. 24, about 20 paces (50 feet) north of the last, is quite small, resembling No. 15. One stone is supported on another, laid across beneath one end.

No. 25 is, perhaps, the most remarkable and instructive of all. A thin stratum of rock has here been prized up, and a stone placed under the downhill side. The table

N₀. 24.    N₀. 25.    N₀. 26.

so formed is about 3 feet square. This is found 30 paces (75 feet) north of No. 24.

No. 26.—The last distinct example noted is north of the last, on about the same level. It may, perhaps, have fallen, or it may be rudely piled ; the topstone is only 3 feet 4 inches long, and 2 feet (at the upper surface) above the ground.

Such is the detailed account of the examples measured, photographed, and sketched, presenting almost every variety found in the district. At least half the number are well-defined dolmens, and in no instance could the stones have been so piled save by human agency. The menhirs are all small, but well defined, with peculiar pointed forms. The tables supported on flat slabs are specially interesting for comparison with the trilithons, seeming to show that in both (as also in the demi-dolmens), the main object was to obtain a table flat or slightly tilted, the method of arranging the supports being optional.

No orientation or speciality of position could be discovered, but the supporting stones of the trilithons are usually parallel to the contour, which would allow of the capstones being easily fitted by sliding them downhill over supports, on to the uphill leg of the dolmen table, and thence pushing the slab on to the taller downhill stone. In the cases of Nos. 3 and 4, the capstone was seemingly not pushed quite far enough, only resting partly on the north support in No. 3, while in No. 4 it never reached it at all. Nos. 16, 19, 23 may perhaps be thought to be stones intended for trilithons, but never placed in position. It is, however, equally possible that they are monuments requiring less time and work than the finer specimens, and more hastily erected.

There are no dolmens on the flat terrace, for No. 1 stands on the rock close to the foot of the higher slope above the terrace. Most of the examples are founded on naked rock, and none save No. 3 appear to have any floorstone. No runes, or flint chips, or implements were found, though carefully sought.

The builders seem to have had little power of transporting the blocks, and to have only prized up strata, or used scattered blocks of rock, piling them up wherever they happened to occur. The little specimens, like Nos. 15 and 24, are interesting as showing that, for whatever use designed, a surface of about a yard square, raised only 1 foot to 2 feet from the ground, was sufficient. Round holes (as in No. 3) were found on the hill in some cases, beside the monuments, as also in other cases near 'Ammân.

The view from the hilltop is not extensive : the Jordan Valley, and the groves at Kefrein can be seen, and Tell 'Asûr is conspicuous on the western Palestine horizon. On the south side of the spur, by the old road descending to the spring, are M e s h â h e d, or little stone piles of the modern Arabs, such as are erected on roads in sight of Neby Mûsa (cf. Neba); but this shrine (west of Jordan) is not visible from the piles, which may have some relation (as at Neba, also) to superstitions connected with the dolmens. The small rock chambers are also worthy of notice, being elsewhere also connected with dolmen centres. These centres are also, as in this case, generally found near springs and streams.

Explored September 9 and 10, 1881.

K u r n K e b s h (كرن كبش, ' ram's horn ').—A ruin on a prominent spur, which is, perhaps, so named from its curving ridge. It is also called Abu en Naml, ' father of the ant.' See Rujm Abu en Nâml. Heaps of small undressed stones lie on the ground, and Arab graves occur at the end of the ridge, which is steep and narrow. An ancient road is traceable northwards from the ruin to Khŭrbet el Mushukkar, beside which are two ruined watch-towers and a rock-cut wine-press, which, including that at Khŭrbet el Mushukkar, that at Rujm Abu Naml, the one at Khŭrbet Umm Hadawiyeh, and one east of Sûmia, makes a total of four fine examples in the Heshbon district. (See Sûmia.)

Visited September 13, 1881.

Kusr el 'Abd (قصر العبد, 'the black slave's palace;' cf. 'Arâk el Emîr).—This is the Palace of Hyrcanus.

Kusr Homrah (قصر حمرة, 'red palace,' or 'bitumen palace').— See Hesbân.

Kusr Khuldeh (قصر خلدة; see Khŭrbet Khuldeh).—An enclosure, 150 feet by 100 feet, with a wall 10 feet high of very large rough stones, much weather-beaten. The Kusr, or tower, itself is 75 feet by 60 feet outside. Its walls are 6 feet thick. No mortar appears to have been used. Cisterns and caves occur at the ruin, which resembles that at el Bureikeh (which see). There is no certain indication of date, but it may probably be a Roman fortress like Khŭrbet Sâr.

Kusr en Nûeijis (قصر النويجس, probably from نجس, used also in Himyaritic and Æthiopic to mean a 'ruler'—i.e., 'Palace of the Princes').—This is a fine specimen of the mausolea, or tomb-towers, of the district (cf. 'Ammân, Khareibet es Sûk, and Kusr es Sebâh). It is a square of 40 feet side, with a small chamber in each corner, and a large masonry recess

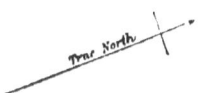

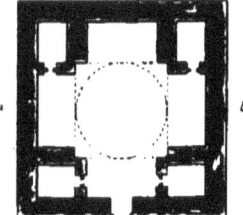

*Section on a.b.*

under an arch on each wall; the entrance is on the east; the roof in the centre is a dome rising from pendentives between the side-arches, and

## KUSR EN NUEIJIS

supporting the little vase on the crown. A parapet 3½ feet high, 3 feet thick, runs round the flat part of the roof. The outer wall is adorned with corner pilasters 2 feet wide, projecting ¾ inch, with capitals of Ionic

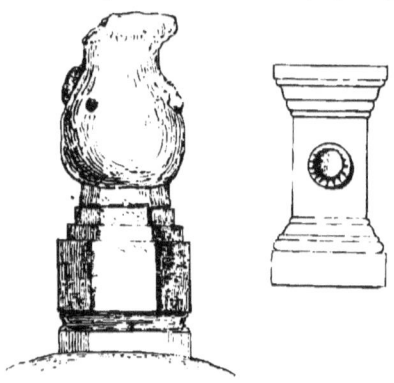

type. These support a regular entablature, the total height of which is 10 feet 2 inches. The total height of the building, to the top of the parapet, is 2 feet 7 inches, including the podium on which the pilasters stand, which is 1½ feet high, and the bases 1 foot high, and capitals 16 inches high. There are two intermediate pilasters on each wall. There are marks at the four corners of the parapet where iron cramps appear to have been used, and these, no doubt, supported four pedestals, of which one is still lying on the roof.

The fluted frieze shown in the drawing is superseded on the east side by a sculptured frieze with scroll patterns and mutilated figures, once representing animals. The walls of the tower are of finely-dressed masonry, not drafted. The stones are 2 or 3 feet long. The masonry of the arches, pendentives, and dome is also very good, and the details of the capitals and frieze are boldly cut. This building was discovered by Mr. T. Black, and photographed by Lieutenant Mantell (No. 15 of his series). It was also visited by Captain Conder. The vase on the dome is 2 feet 8 inches high, and stands on an octagonal pedestal, the total height being 5 feet from the dome. The corner pedestal, ornamented with a wreath in bold relief, is 3 feet 3 inches high, and 21 inches square at the base.

There can be little hesitation in ascribing this building to the second century A.D., and it probably once contained sarcophagi. The ruin of the east wall seems more probably intentional than due to earthquake or dilapidation.

Visited October 15, 1881.

K u s r  e s  S e b â h (قصر السبع, 'house of the lion,' probably from some sculptured figure, now no longer to be found).—This is a fine tomb-

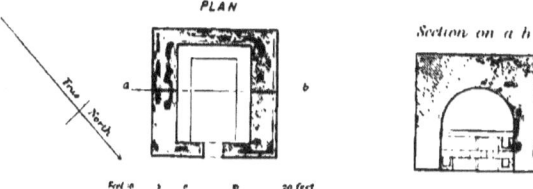

tower,* containing sarcophagi. It was photographed by Lieutenant Mantell (No. 19 of his series), and the measurements of the plan and elevation are his. There are a good many scattered sarcophagi on the hillside, both north-east and south of the building. One to the north-east was measured, 8 feet by 4 feet by 3 feet high, 1½ feet wide inside, with a lid once carved, but too weather-worn to represent. The Kusr measures 23 feet north and south, and 23½ feet east and west, the true

---

* The Greek funerary inscriptions of Asia Minor, collected by Sir C. Fellows, furnish us with very clear ideas as to the appropriation of such tombs. They were built for family use, and the burial of any person not designated by the builder was forbidden under pain of a curse and of a fine to the State. As an instance: 'Epagathos, son of Crateros, has built this monument for himself, and his wife, and his children, and the children born of them; but none shall be allowed to bury, or put into this monument, except when I shall permit it myself. But if any shall violate this, he shall pay to the people of the Cadyandeans a thousand denaria.'—Fellows' 'Inscriptions,' No. 121 (on a tomb).

bearing being 43°. Inside it is 18 feet north and south, 14 feet across. The door is on the north, 4 feet wide. The height of the building is 20 feet outside, and the roof is a fine barrel-vault with a narrow keystone; the voussoirs are all very well cut. The sarcophagi are placed in two tiers, against all the walls but the north one. On the south wall there are two tiers of two each, opposite the door, each 6½ feet long, and each covered with slabs, two in some cases to each sarcophagus. The west wall had also four sarcophagi, two above two : the east wall had only two in the lower row, of which one was short, measuring 4 feet 9 inches only, and probably intended for a child. There are thus ten sarcophagi in all. The short sarcophagus is ornamented on one side with a wreath, on which is a design of a circle with eight rays. This looks like a cross, but is not of necessity Christian. Another sarcophagus in the upper row to the right, in the south wall, has also an ornamented lid.

The arch of the roof is semicircular, and forms a tunnel-vault running north and south; it starts from a simple cornice, projecting 6 inches from the

wall of the chamber, and running all round. The stones in the outer walls of the building are drafted with a bold rustic boss. They are 2 feet to 4 feet long, and 1½ feet high; the bosses are 4 inches to 6 inches wide, and the projection is 2 inches to 4 inches. On the interior of the walls, the stones of the four lower courses are also drafted, but the bosses do not project so much. The dressing is very much like that in Byzantine masonry, the draft being dressed with an adze, and the face picked over roughly.

This building should be compared with Kusr en Nûeijîs, and with the towers at Khareibet es Sûk, and at 'Ammân. It might be as early as the second century A.D. or possibly as late as the third, but is most probably of the Antonine age (second century A.D.).

Visited October 6 and 8, 1881.

Kusr el Werd (قصر الورد, 'tower of the rose') is possibly named from some sculptured fragment representing a rose. The name applies to ruins on the hill immediately north-east of Mââin; but nothing appears now to exist save ruined walls and a cistern in the middle of the ruin.

## Baal Meon.

Mââin (ماعين, the Hebrew מעון, or 'place of springs').—This is an important site, very conspicuous as a high dark Tell, or mound, on the plateau, visible from all sides. The situation is, however, peculiar in this respect, that the plateau rises on the west so as to shut out from the top of the Tell any view of the trans-Jordanic ranges. Thus, while on the east, north and south the view is extensive, extending to Heshbon and to Dibon, it is restricted on the west to within a distance of about a mile, although just the top of the Maslûbîyeh ridge can be seen. This is important, as entirely precluding the identification of the place with the Bamoth Baal, which is probably to be placed at el Maslûbîyeh. The ruin marks the site of the ancient Baal Meon of Reuben (Num. xxxii. 38; 1 Chron. v. 8), called also Beth Baal Meon (Josh. xiii. 17). It was known to Eusebius and Jerome as 9 miles from Heshbon (which is very nearly the right distance), and as near Baaru of Arabia, which, as Reland has carefully made out, is the site of Machærus (see Reland, 'Pal. Illustr.,' pp. 487, 611, 881). The latter name is the Aramaic, בירה, or 'palace' (*i.e.*, of Herod the Great), now called Mekaûr, and situate south-east of Mââin, beyond the bounds of the Survey.

On the Moabite Stone (line 9) this city is mentioned with Kirjathaim (now Kureiyât, south of the limits of the Survey), as fortified by Mesa, King of Moab, when Omri was in possession of Madeba. It is called Beth Baal Meon on the same monument (line 30). The name was probably derived from the fine springs in the Zerka Mâin Valley on the south.

The ruins are very extensive, covering the whole Tell, and extending over the lower ground to the west. The head of the valley, which runs down southwards from the west side of the Tell (Wâdy Jiâma, or Kiâma, *i.e.*, 'of ascent'), is occupied by a large ruined birkeh, or pool. North of this, on the flat ground, are numerous cisterns cut in rock. There is no

KUSR ES SEFAH

*To face page 176.*

## BAAL MEON

water at the place and no trees. The ground is a soft chalk rock with open arable lands in the valleys. The Tell is about 250 yards in diameter, and the ruins are like those of Hesbân, consisting of the foundations and walls of private houses of the Roman or Byzantine period, with caves beneath and many cisterns. The stones are mostly not squared, but some few have a rough draft round them. Under the houses there are vaults of good masonry with round-arched tunnels, 7 feet or 8 feet in diameter, of Roman or Byzantine masonry, having the narrow keystone and voussoirs of graduated width, the haunch stones being broad.

On the hill to the west are rough shepherds' caves in the soft rock. Ancient roads lead to the city from the west and north. On the top of

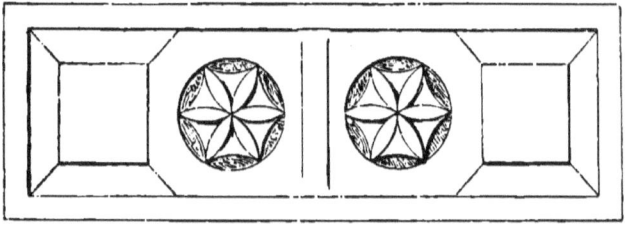

the Tell towards the east is an Arab graveyard—some of the graves hung with plaits of hair (see el Kûeijiyeh). Below the Tell on the west is a well with two pillar-stumps beside it. There are several carved fragments lying about, of cornices with feeble mouldings, probably Byzantine. A lintel-stone, 4 feet 9 inches long by 1½ feet, was also found, having a very Byzantine appearance. Another slab, 1 foot square, has a cross cut in relief, and the remains seem clearly, for the most part, to be those of the Byzantine city known to Jerome and Eusebius. Inscriptions were carefully sought, but none were found on the surface.

Visited September 22, 1881.

El Mâberah (المبعرة, 'the quarry').—On the south side of Wâdy Kefrein, near the low cliff to which this name applies, is the monument marked Altar. It is at the west end of a spur on the highest point. On the north, south, and west are many dolmens of moderate size. A circle of blackish limestone, rudely shaped and about 12 feet in diameter, is built of blocks 2 to 3 feet broad and high, and about 1½ feet thick. In the centre of this circle is a stone 2½ feet by 1½ feet, by 2½ feet high, of the same material as the rest, but rudely squared. Its length is directed north and south. The monument resembles those found at 'Ain Minyeh, and described under that head.

Visited by Lieutenant Mantell, R.E., October 26, 1881.

## MEDEBA.

Mâdeba (مادبا, Hebrew מירבה, Medeba).—This is perhaps the most important site on the Mishor plateau. It was an episcopal city in the fifth century, and is said to have been an important place in the time of the Council of Chalcedon—a city of the Nabatheans (*cf.* Reland's 'Palestine,' vol. ii., p. 893). The Christian remains at the site agree with these notices, as showing Mâdeba to have been a very important place in the Byzantine age.

Canon Tristram in 1872 found at Mâdeba a Greek inscription in five lines, a Latin inscription illegible, and another in Phœnician characters (or some cognate character) on the south ('Land of Moab,' p. 311); but so eagerly have inscriptions been sought in this district that the stones in question had all been removed or destroyed before 1881. In the Latin Patriarchate at Jerusalem four inscribed stones are now preserved, all said to have been sent from Mâdeba or its vicinity by the Jesuit missionaries. These were copied by the kind permission of the Patriarch.*

The ruins at Mâdeba occupy a low mound, surrounded with downs, or hills, rather higher, the whole site being very open. On the west are the remains of the cathedral; on the south the great reservoir; on the north-east is a gateway and street of columns. The Tell and the flat ground,

* These four inscriptions in the Latin Patriarchate at Jerusalem, said to have been found by the Jesuits at Mâdeba, were submitted to Dr. Euting, who regards them as forgeries. They are therefore not noticed in this work.

especially north of it, are covered with heaps of stones, as at Heshbon. The few remains of distinguishable detail seem nearly all to be Byzantine.

The church on the west is remarkable for the pair of pillars with one block across them, which once formed part of the porch in front of the west door. These are called Mishneket Abu er Rôk, 'gallows of Abu er Rôk,' or possibly 'gallows of the porch.' Abu Rôk is now said to have been a powerful chief, who in old times did justice at this spot, and hung offenders between the pillars. The pillars are about 18 feet high and 5½ apart; the shafts bulge considerably in the middle, and are not monoliths, but consist of two drums, the capital being a third block. They are 7 feet in circumference at the middle, and about 5½ feet at the bottom; the bases were not visible. The capitals, much worn, were apparently not intended for the shafts, being much too small. The southern is Ionic; the northern is a rude Byzantine copy of Corinthian style. Probably the shafts were derived from an older building, and the capitals either badly adapted, or also taken from another building. The erection can hardly be supposed earlier than the fourth or fifth century of our era.

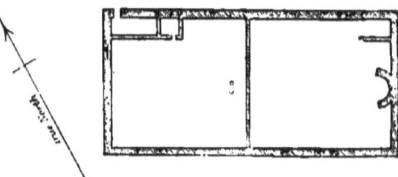

PLAN OF CHURCH.

The basilica east of these pillars was 119 feet long and 106 feet wide. It had a central apse 21 feet in diameter. On the west an atrium existed, with surrounding chambers, of the same width as the basilica, and 105 feet long. The outer walls, of which only the bottom courses remain, were 6½ feet thick. Towards the north-east part of the atrium are remains of a well. The masonry is of squared stones, and some of those on the outer face of the walls are drafted. One was measured, and found to be 2½ feet long, 1 foot 7 inches high, with a draft 2½ inches wide, the boss, dressed flat, projecting 1 inch. The tooling of this stone was a rough picking diagonally, but not like the Crusading tooling. The church is 200 yards west of the Tell, or central hill of the city, round which the ruins extend for nearly half a mile either way. East and west of the church are many caves, now inhabited by Christians from Kerak, who have been converted from the Greek to the Latin rite by the Jesuit missionaries, and were settled at Mâdeba, under the leadership of these priests, in the spring of 1881. Some were yet in tents in the autumn of the same year, but were repairing cisterns, and preparing to build. They had constructed a sort of fort on the mound, called e d D e i r, 'the monastery,' measuring about 80 paces (or 200 feet) square, and including graves, apparently of Arabs. The walls are drystone, carefully packed, and no doubt intended for protection.

The general impression obtained in exploring Mâdeba was that a Byzantine town had been built partly out of the remains of an earlier Roman city, perhaps dating as early as the second century A.D. The best built structures are to the north of the Tell, on flat ground. Furthest north was found a building, which appears to have been a small quadrangle of well-dressed masonry, the stones very square in proportions, and not drafted. They do not appear, however, to be *in situ*, and may have been re-used. Five stumps of pillar-shafts, about 1 foot 8 inches in diameter and 3 feet high, are planted, touching one another, in a line, north and south, on the west of the chamber; these, no doubt, have been removed from their original position. Inside lie some bases with feeble mouldings, and a lintel-stone broken, but, when joined up, measuring 9 feet in length by 13 inches in height. On this is a design, including three crosses in circles, which was

carefully measured and copied. Beneath the chamber there seems to be a cistern, with a mouth now choked, and there are remains of a small channel leading to it. The plan of the chamber is not very clearly traceable, but it appears to have been about 20 feet square.

South of this chamber are remains apparently of private houses, built of good masonry, but with older material used up, including cornices, pillar-bases, etc., built into the walls. Towards the east in this northern part of the city are remains of another building, which seems to have been of importance. It had two doors, one to the south, the other on the north, each spanned by pieces of a cornice, the profile of which was measured. The cornice blocks are each 11 feet 9 inches long. There are pillar-stumps at the corners of this building, but nothing appears to be *in situ* Beneath the north door there is a vault, now ruined.

Further east, again, is a curious circular chamber with a polygonal addition to the east. The foundation courses alone exist. The circle was 31 feet in diameter; the west entrance is flanked by two pillar-stumps. This may have been a little shrine, or small temple or tomb.

Yet further east are remains apparently of a city gate, with part of the wall of the city. The gate faced towards the south-east, and was apparently flanked by two towers, measuring 16 feet by $18\frac{1}{2}$ feet, and $26\frac{1}{2}$ feet apart. The gateway itself was $13\frac{1}{2}$ feet wide, and a street of columns, 26 feet wide, led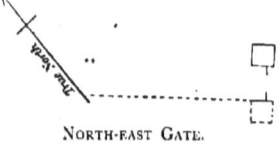

NORTH-EAST GATE.

north-west, in continuation of the inner line of the towers. The pillars were $2\frac{1}{4}$ feet in diameter, with an inter-columniation of 5 feet. The bases of five pillars remain *in situ* on the north side of the street. The foundations of the northern tower are intact, and those of the southern just traceable. A sort of podium with a simple moulding ran round the four sides of this building. The jambs of the gateway also presented a profile, which was measured and drawn. In the tower walls were well-wrought stones, of which three were

MOULDINGS.

measured, being respectively $3\frac{1}{2}$ feet long by $2\frac{1}{2}$ feet high, 2 feet 8 inches by 2 feet 5 inches, and 7 feet 3 inches by 1 foot 4 inches. At the four corners of the two towers were pilasters standing on the podium, being each 2 feet wide, and projecting only 1 inch. In the general character of masonry and detail this gateway resembles some of the tomb-towers found at 'Ammân, Khurbet es Sûk, and elsewhere, and it seems probably to have belonged to the Roman city of perhaps the second century A.D., rather than to the later Byzantine town. The Arabs said that Mâdeba had once twenty gates, but were unable to show the sites of any others.

South of the gateway are remains of a large tank, or *birkeh*, east of the Tell already mentioned. It is much choked, and in ruins. On this side there are many foundations of houses and ruined vaults with round barrel-roofs. Cisterns are said to exist beneath these ruins.

Returning westwards, at the foot of the Tell, on its north side, a lintel-stone was measured and drawn. It is now placed over an oven (*furn*),

and much blackened with smoke; it is 5 feet 2 inches long, and 1 foot 7 inches high. The two medallions appear to have been adorned with crosses, which have been purposely defaced.

On the south side of the Tell there are other remains of ruined houses, vaults, lintel-stones (without sculpture), and fragments of pillars and cornices, built in among roughly-squared stones, probably of the later period. On the south-west of the Tell, and south-east of the church first described, is a fine tank, or *birkeh*, formed by damming the flat valley. Its southern and eastern walls are about 12 feet thick; the other two are retaining

LARGE RESERVOIR.

walls. The tank measures 308 feet north and south, by 395 feet east and west inside, and its depth is 10 feet. The east wall is 13 feet 6 inches thick at the top, and strengthened inside by twelve buttresses, each 10 feet wide, 10 feet apart, and projecting 1 foot. Outside, the wall is stepped back each course from the bottom (6 or 8 inches), giving a thickness of about 20 feet at the bottom. The south wall is 20 feet high, and 12 feet thick at the top, its sides being vertical without buttresses or sets-back. All this walling is of good masonry, the stones not drafted; two which represent the average size were measured, one 2 feet 4 inches long by 1 foot high, the second 1 foot long, 1 foot 3 inches high; the joints are very fine, and no packing with small stones or chips is observable. At the north-east corner of the pool is a tower, 30 feet by 25 feet, and two flights of steps lead down just inside the east wall, one from the north, the other from the south. The steps are 1 foot 5 inches tread, and 10 inches rise ; the breadth of the flight is 23 feet. The lintel-stone of the tower-door lay on the ground west of the foundations of that building, and was 6 feet long and 2 feet high, with a design as shown. It seems to be probably Byzantine.

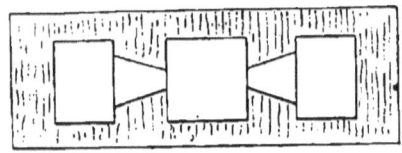

The ruins of Mâdeba are being much injured by the new Christian settlers, who remove the stones to build walls before their caves.

Explored September 27, 1881.

El Madowerah (المدورة, 'the round place').—A hilltop, with cairns on north side of the Zerka Mâin, south of Mââin.

Madowerat el 'Âl (مدورة العال, 'the round place of Elealah'). —South of the ruined city el 'Âl. A low round natural hillock, on which is a cairn and two *kehâkîr*, or stone pillars, made by piling small stones one on the other ; both cairn and pillars are between 3 feet and 4 feet in height, and are very conspicuous objects in the plain. It is a sacred place, probably a tomb. Round the cairn are foundations as of a small square tower or building of some kind. On the north-east, at the bottom of the hill, there is a cliff with cuttings, as though large blocks had been quarried thence. This is probably the quarry whence Elealah was built. In the cliff there is also a small chamber, 6 feet high and 6 feet square, with an entrance 2½ feet wide. Round three of the walls runs a bench 1 foot wide. This is probably a tomb of the Roman period, intended to hold sarcophagi. (See 'Ammân, Kabr es Sultân, and Kûsr es Sebâh.)

Mâhas (ماحص).—At the north edge of the work north of 'Arâk el Emîr. Foundations, walls, broken pillar-shafts occur here. There is a large cave, and a fine spring gushes out of a crevice in the rock. A rock-cut tomb occurs near, by el Khudr (see under that head). The site is important, and probably that of a Roman town.

El Mahder (المحضر, 'the enclosed place').—This is radically the same word as הָצֵר, Hazor. It is a conspicuous Tell, with a great number of stones strewn on the top, and in the middle an open circular space about 45 feet in diameter. It thus appears to be one of the class of stone circles found at Hadânieh, Neba, Râs Merkeb, Kom Yâjûz, etc. The name is evidently derived from this circle.

El Mâilik (المعيليق; the root means to 'hang,' or be suspended).— This name applies to cliffs on the south side of the great ravine of Wâdy Nâaûr. It is omitted from the reduced map as unimportant.

El Makâbelein (المقابلين, 'the two places opposite each other'). —This applies to ruins or knolls west of Taihin. There are two ruins, each on a knoll, and south of these a goat-fold. Foundations and small caves only were noted.

Mâkker ed Derbâsy (معثر الدرباسي, 'the place of slaying the lion,' or 'wild beast').—This is a cairn, apparently modern. Derbâsy may be an Arab's name.

Mâkker el Jerba el Jedhûr (معثر الجربة الجذور, 'the place where the Jerba Arab slew the camels,' as explained locally).

Maksar el Bakarah (مكسر البكرة, 'the place of the death of the cow').—Ruins of a few foundations near Hajâr en Nûâblisiyeh.

Maksar el Hisân (مكسر الحصان, 'the place where the horse died'). —A hilltop south of Minyeh. (See next.)

Mamât el Kheil (ممات الخيل, 'the death-place of the horses').— A hilltop east of el Helâly, west of Wâdy Mebna Beit el Maghanyeh. It is omitted from the reduced map for want of room. In this case, and also in the former, it appears that the name is due to the killing of horses in an Arab skirmish, which is always an important incident in Bedawin life.

El Mareighât (المريغات, 'the things smeared,' with oil, or blood, or other thick liquid).—The name is no doubt connected with the title Umm Zûeitineh (ام زويتينه), which applies to the whole site, the former name applying to the menhirs. The latter seems to be a corrupt word, meaning 'mother of little olive-trees ;' and the Arabs stated that there had once been an oil manufactory at this place. They pointed out the rock-cut press to the east as evidence, and evidently regarded the menhirs as stone posts of oil-presses, such as are common west of

Jordan. This is, however, quite an erroneous idea ; the press is certainly a wine-press, and quite unfitted for oil manufacture, and the menhirs are neither of the shape nor size, nor do they possess the grooves and holes, of the stone posts of olive-presses. It seems far more probable that the name 'smeared' is a tradition of the smearing of these menhirs, either with blood or with oil ; the former being a custom of the pre-Islamite Arabs, and the latter a very ancient practice in connection with menhirs.

The site of el Mareighât includes rude-stone monuments extending over an area of about a mile east and west, and half a mile north and south, on the ground at the top of the steep bank north of the 'Ain ez Zerka. These include a large series of menhirs, surrounded on west, north, and east by dolmens, a single menhir further east called Hajr el Mansûb ('the erected stone'), and a wine-press east again; while other dolmens occur north of the 'erected stone,' and hollow chambers in the cliff, north of the principal menhir centre.

Commencing the description of the site from the east, a flat plateau occurs, which is crossed by the main south road from Mââin, descending into the valley to 'Ain Mâlt. On this stands the Hajr el Mansûb, and east of this, about 300 yards from the stone, on the slope of a low rocky spur, is the wine-press. The large chamber is to the east, 16½ feet north and south, by 15 feet east and west, 3 feet deep on the east, and owing to the slope of the rock, only 15 inches deep on the west. There are two smaller chambers communicating with this on the west. The southern is 3 feet square, and only 10 inches deep. The northern is 3 feet 11 inches square, and 3½ feet deep, without any outlet.

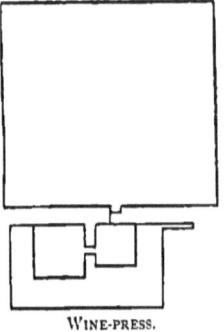

WINE-PRESS.

The single menhir, Hajr el Mansûb, or 'the erected stone,' is the most evidently artificial of all the rude-stone monuments found as yet east of Jordan. Its rounded top, and the groove cut in one side, show, as does its rectangular cross-section, the handiwork of man. It is 8 feet high, 4½ feet wide at the base, and varies in thickness from 23 inches to 15 inches. The groove is 3 feet 9 inches from the ground, 9 inches wide, and 1½ deep. The bearing along one side of the stone is 48°, or about north-east. There are several tribe-marks on the stone, two on the south-east face, above the groove, being those of the 'Abbâd ('Adwân) and of the Khadir ('Anazeh), while the 'raven's foot,' or 'trident' of the Jibbûr (Beni Sakhr), also occurs with others. These might be easily mistaken for some kind of letter or rune, but there is no doubt as to their meaning and origin, while close inspection shows the marks to be recent.

HAJR EL MANSÛB.

West of the Hajr el Mansûb there are two low knolls at the top of the bank, which falls to the spring 1,000 feet beneath; from them, and from the Hajr, the spring can be seen. These knolls extend westwards about half a mile, and are covered with dolmens. On the south and west sides of the western knoll, and all round the eastern, these occur, and some are very fine examples. There are none on the north of the west knoll; the total number was counted to be about seventy.

Immediately west of the west knoll there is a sort of little plateau about a quarter of a mile square, and rather lower than the plateau of the Hajr el Mansûb. It is surrounded by a sort of amphitheatre of low spurs, on all sides but the south, where it reaches the brink of the great slope or bank of the ravine. In the middle of this little theatre rises another small and very rocky knoll, and its summit is crowned by a group of very conspicuous menhirs, while round the foot of the knoll runs a circle of smaller menhirs about 300 yards in diameter. The boundary of the plateau on the east is marked by a line of menhirs running approximately north and south, and there are traces of another line running westwards from this, along the brink of the valley bank at the south edge of the little plateau. East of the group on the knoll

EL MAREIGHÂT.—PRINCIPAL GROUP OF MENHIRS.

there are three or more alignments of menhirs running parallel, approximately north and south. The plateau on the south side of the knoll is strewn with other small menhirs without any order, and on the northwest side of the 300 yards circle, close to the menhirs, there is a dolmen standing alone. The hill spurs to the north, and to the west of the plateau, are also strewn with dolmens, and it was calculated that, including the seventy on the two knolls west of the Hajr el Mansûb, and those north of it, there are at least 150 dolmens at this site.

The menhir groups, as above described, thus form a circle 300 yards diameter, and a square about 500 yards side, or more. Those on the top of the knoll are about 5 feet high, the tallest being 6 feet. They seem to

Menhirs at el Mareighât

have been arranged in a little circle 15 paces (40 feet) in diameter. The three alignments to the east are 12 paces apart, and 20 paces long north and south, and are about 50 yards from the group on the Mareighât knoll.

The row on the south side of the plateau is traceable about 30 yards, the stones often touching each other. The tallest is 6 feet, and the average about 3 feet.

North of the circle, in the side of the hill, is a little cliff pierced with three chambers well cut. The western was 3 feet wide, 4 feet to the back, the central one 6 feet by 7 feet, the eastern 2 feet by 3 feet. These resemble the chambers found elsewhere with dolmens. (See el Kurmîyeh, and el Kalûâ.) This spur has about 40 dolmens on its west side, and 20 on the east, which are included in the former total estimate of 150 dolmens. There are, beside the dolmen adjoining the circle on the north-west, two hollows in the flat rock, each 1½ feet in diameter, and 9 inches deep.

Circumstances did not allow of an exhaustive examination of the

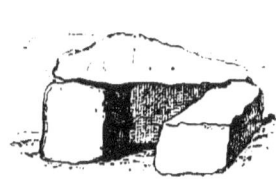

Nº 1 el Mareighât.

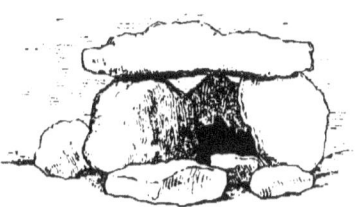

Nº 2 el Mareighât.

dolmens, which are much like those of Wâdy Jideid; but five of the finest specimens were measured and sketched. The first, on the west side of the hill north of the menhir circle, had four stones; the cap measuring 9 feet by 6½ feet, the sidestones 7 feet long, 2½ feet thick, 3½ feet high, and 3 feet 4 inches apart, with an endstone. The second, on the east slope of the same hill, has a capstone 8½ feet by 6½ feet, and a sidestone 8 feet long,

Nº 3 Mareighât

4½ feet high. The clear interior space is 4 feet high, 3 feet 9 inches wide.

The third dolmen sketched was in the saddle between the two knolls west of Hajr el Mansûb, and is of medium size. The fourth,

*N° 4 el Mareighât.*

on the north-west slope of the knoll just west of Hajr el Mansûb, is a demi-dolmen with a very large capstone, 13 feet by 8 feet. The fifth and last, on the north-east side of the last-mentioned hill, is the only example found in Moab as yet, which is closed at both ends. Including the floorstone, it consists of six stones. The capstone is 9 feet by 8 feet, and has a peculiar channel in it 4 feet long, 1 foot wide.

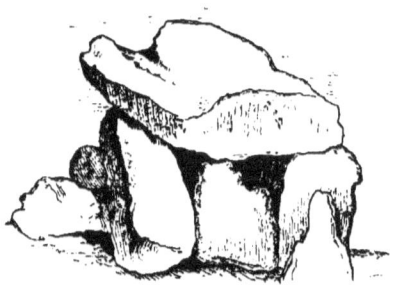

*N° 5 el Mareighât.*

This very remarkable group of monuments is briefly noticed by Irby and Mangles in 1820 A.D. (p. 465). The Hajr el Mansûb has also been described by Herr Schick. The Mareighât group is perhaps the most extraordinary and suggestive monument yet described in Moab.

Explored October 3, 1881.

Marma Mansûr (مرما منصور, 'the stone-heap of Mansûr').—A cairn over a dead Arab.

El Mâsieh (الماسيه, 'the inaccessible').—A high crag with trees at the northern limit of the Survey.

El Maslûbiyeh (المصلوبية, 'the place of crucifixion').—The origin of this curious name was not ascertained. It applies to the ridge south of Mount Nebo, the north slopes of which have an extraordinary number of dolmens (see Wâdy Jideid). This, with the Minyeh ridge to the south, forms one of the main mountain features. It seems probable that the Maslûbiyeh ridge is that of Bamoth Baal, and the Minyeh ridge that of Baal Peor. The arguments are given in full in 'Heth and Moab' (chap. iv.), depending mainly on relative position and the view westwards obtained from these ridges. The ruins on the Maslûbiyeh ridge are not important. On the highest point is a cairn (apparently built by the American surveyors), and east of the cairn there are ruined foundations; further east are rude-stone enclosures occupying about 80 yards either way; about 70 paces (175 feet) further west are remains of a wall in a circular form. There seems, however, no reason to suppose any town to have stood here, the enclosures being probably intended for the defence of cattle. They may be of any age.

The view from the hilltop extends up the Jordan Valley to Kaukab el Hawa and the Safed hills; but on the south it is bounded by the Minyeh ridge, and on the east by the watershed west of Maâin.

Mâta et Turkomânîyeh (ماطا التركمانيّة, 'the print of the Turcoman woman').—An erosion in a flat piece of rock venerated by the 'Adwân and other tribes of the vicinity as the footprint of a prophetess, who here alighted from her camel while on pilgrimage to or from Mecca, the tradition being that the Hâj road once passed this spot (cf. Serâbît el Meshukkar). It was shown also to Sir C. Warren, and is on the west side of the main road on high ground. The original print is about 20 inches long, and rudely resembles a human footprint of a person walking northwards. On the east the Arabs have cut an artificial duplicate, rather smaller in size, representing presumably the right foot. They, however, allow that only the original is genuine and sacred. The flat piece of rock shows above ground for about 3 feet north and south. On the north and on the south sides two little cairns are erected to mark the spot. They are of small pebbles about a foot high. The Arabs consider it a pious act to clear the earth and dust off this print. The nationality of the prophetess is curious, and has some connection probably with the adoration of the Turkish saint at Butmet et Terki (which see). Sacred footprints are adored by Moslems at Hebron, at Mecca, at Jerusalem, at Baalbek, and elsewhere.

Visited September 20, 1881.

El Mâterdeh (المعترده, 'the hard land').—A district of the Jordan Valley north-west of Tell er Râmeh.

Mefret Sukr (مفرط صقر, 'desert place of the falcon').—Applies to a plot above the cliff at 'Arâk el Emîr. It is omitted from the reduced map.

Mehatt el Menâkh (محطّ المناخ, 'camping-ground of the place where camels lie down').—A flat plateau west of Serâbit el Meshukkar. It is omitted from the reduced map as being of no importance.

El Mehterjeh (apparently should be el Mehterkeh, المحترقه, 'the place burnt with fire').—This name applies to the desert plateau east of Tell el Jorfeh (cf. Wâdy el Mehterkeh).

Mejmâ el Benât (مجمع البنات, 'the gathering-place of maidens').—This is a spot marked by a small cairn on the border between the country of the 'Adwân and that of the Beni Sakhr.

Mekerr Subeihah (مكرّ صبيحه, 'the flat ground of Sheikh Subeih').—See under Sheikh Subeih. It is omitted from the reduced map as not being important.

El Mekheiyit (المخيّط, 'the little needle').—This is named from the Rujm el Mekheiyit, a great cairn on the south side of the valley. On the east slope of the hill, which has several round knolls, are a few ruins of houses not apparently of great antiquity, and of rough materials. Some heaps of hewn stone also occur, with a large rude rock-cut cistern. North of these ruins, at the head of the valley called ez Zerânik, a tomb is marked. It was the only tomb with *kokim* found south of 'Ammân in the district surveyed. The chamber, or cave, is 49 feet north and south by 27 feet east and west. On the west is a recess 5 feet by 6 feet; on the north and east are ten radiating *kokim*, each about 5½ feet long by 2¼ feet wide. The cave is 6 feet to 7 feet high. West of this, again, are five rock-cut tombs in a low cliff, but with the doors blocked with stones. They are used as graves by the Arabs, and plaits of women's hair were hung on sticks and strings in front of the door. They were, therefore, not dis-

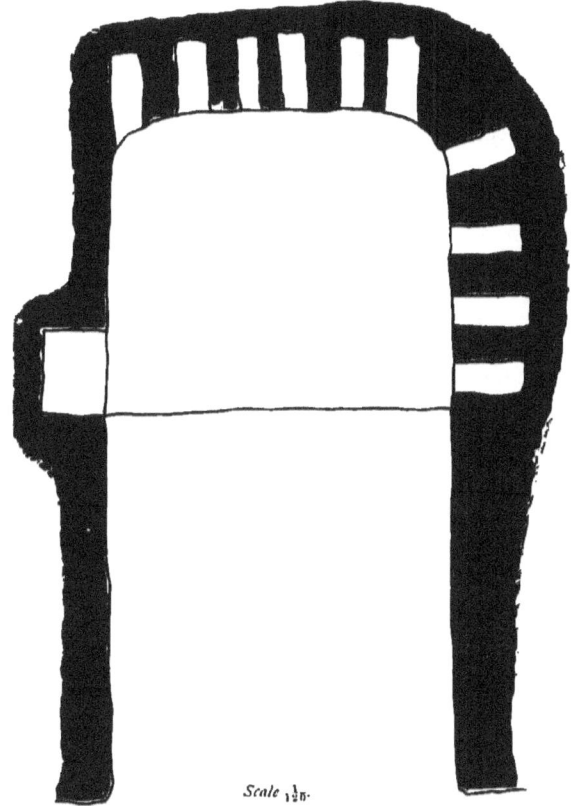

Scale 1/120.

PLAN OF TOMB.

turbed. On the hill west of the tombs were remains of an old road with watchtowers of the usual kind in ruins.

Visited September 26, 1881.

El Melfûf (الملفوف, 'the cabbages').—This name, probably a corruption of an earlier name, applies to scattered ruins along the Roman road leading westwards from 'Ammân. There are six ruins in all, including several watchtowers, two of which are round, like that at el Bureikeh. Foundations and ruins of walls also exist, and west of the *Kusr*, or tower, marked on the road, there are two rock-cut tombs, one a simple *loculus*, the other a small square chamber. These ruins are probably of Roman origin.

Mensef Abu Zeid (منسف ابو زيد, 'the dish of Abu Zeid').—An immense disc of stone lying flat in the plain beside a thorn-tree (*Sidr*). The tradition is that Abu Zeid, when about to leave the district, here feasted the local tribe, placing a whole camel on the stone and piling it up with rice. The melted butter (*Semn*) is said to have run down into the hole which pierces the centre of the stone. Abu Zeid ('father of abundance') is a famous mythical hero of the Arabs. He is said to have been black, and his other name was Barakât (see el Barakât). He belonged to the Beni Helâl, or 'sons of the crescent,' and was son of Rizk ('provision'), and of Khadra ('greenness'). His history is given by Lane ('Modern Egyptians,' vol. ii., p. 105, *seq.*).

Disc stones somewhat similar were found at Kefeir Abu Bedd, and at el Kueijîyeh. (See under those heads.)

In the present instance the stone is 11 feet 4 inches in diameter, $3\frac{1}{2}$ feet high. The hole in the centre is 2 feet in diameter. The whole is cut in a single block of limestone, which must have been conveyed from a considerable distance. The weight cannot be less than about 19 tons. The origin of these disc stones cannot easily be explained; they are evidently not millstones, although in the case of Kefeir abu Bedd the stone is called a millstone (*Bedd*).

Visited October 27, 1881.

Menshalah (منشله, a word meaning 'tongs').—A very conspicuous top at the edge of the plateau, east of the Dead Sea. A spring occurs here, with a few palms and ruined foundations in the valley-head. Remains of an ancient road, probably from Machærus to Lybias, cross the plateau immediately east of this place.

El Mereijmeh (المريجمه, 'the place of the little cairn ').—This word is used in the Bible to define the stone-heap of Hermes (Prov. xxvi. 8). Cisterns, caves, and foundations of rude walls occur here close to the south-east corner of the Survey.

Merj Abu 'Âisheh (مرج ابو عايشه, 'meadow of Aisha ').—The open ground near Zabbûd (cf. 'Arâk 'Âisheh, further north).

Merj Abu Nukhleh (مرج ابو نخله, 'meadow of the palm ').—South of Sûmia.

Merj el Bawâti.—See 'Ain el Bawâti. It is the ground by the spring. The name is omitted from the reduced map.

Merj el Emir (مرج الامير, 'prince's meadow ').—West of 'Arâk el Emir. An open plateau, with oak-trees at the edge of the great wood, south of Arkûb Seru el 'Abid. It is omitted from the reduced map.

Merj el Hamâm (مرج الحمام, 'meadow of the dove').—Near 'Arâk el Hamâm.

Merj el Hareithiyeh (مرج الحريثيه, 'tilled meadow ').—The plateau west of 'Ain Hesbân. It is omitted from the reduced map.

Merj Jubeil (مرج جبيل, 'meadow of the little mountain ').—A low shed forming the east border of the 'Adwân country east of Heshbon.

Merj Umm Khureiribeh (مرج أمّ خريربه, 'meadow of the little carob-trees,' Ceratonia Siliqua).—At the south extremity of the Survey, near el Habis. The hills are here dotted with a few small trees. The name is omitted from the reduced map. It applies between Mekerr el Faras and el Madowerah.

Merkeb ed Dufiâneh (مرقب الدفيانه, 'the outlook place of the cemetery ').—A small ruined watch-tower, on a hill north of 'Ayûn Mûsa.

Merkeb Juwar Subeihah (مرقب جور صبيحه, 'outlook place of the hollows of Subeih ').—See Sheikh Subeih.

Merkeh (مركه).—Foundations occur here extending over an area about 40 yards across.

El Mesh-hed (المشهد, 'the monument ').—Foundations of a small tower overlooking the 'Ayûn Mûsa.

El Mesheiyidah (المشيّدة, 'the whitewashed ').—This name was understood to apply to a district south of Kefrein. It may have some connection with the whitewashed tomb at Tell er Râmeh.

El Mesterâh (المستراح, 'the grazing-place ').—A small ruin west of Hesbân. Only stones strewn on the hilltop remain.

Misdâr 'Âisheh (مصدار عايشه, 'the track of Aisha,' named from 'Arâk 'Âisheh).—The first word is used of all the broad roads leading down to 'Ammân, and comes from a root meaning 'to return.' It is omitted from the reduced map, and applies only to the roads by Khurbet 'Âisheh.

Misdâr el Mâdhneh (مصدار الماذنه, 'track of the minaret ').—A road leading down the valley southwards towards the minaret of the 'Ammân mosque.

Misdâr Umm Suweiwineh (مصدار ام صويوينه, 'track of the mother of little flints').

Mishneket Abu er Rôk (مشنقة ابو الروق, 'gallows of Abu er Rôk,' or, ' of the porch ').—See under Mâdeba.

Mishrâ 'Abeid (مشرع عبيد, 'drinking-place of 'Abeid '). — A stream west of Tell el Hammâm. The name is omitted from the reduced map as unimportant.

Mishrâ el Hasâsineh (مشرع الحساسنه, 'the watering-place of the Hasâsineh') is named from the vicinity of the Kabûr el Hasâsineh (which see). It is omitted from the reduced map.

Muâllakat ed Deir (معلّقة الدير, 'the overhanging place of the monastery').—See ed Deir.* It is marked R on the reduced map, south of ed Deir.

Muâllakat Umm el Kenâfid (معلّقة ام الكنافد, 'the overhanging place of Umm el Kenâfid ').—See under that head. This is close to the 'Ain marked west of Umm el Kenâfid on the reduced map ; on southeast side (left) of valley.

El Mûeiniyeh (المويّنه, probably 'the little store ').—The ruin is a small one south of Wâdy es Sir, east of 'Arâk el Emir. A few foundations of

* This word Mu'allakah is generally used of cliffs.

old walls and heaps of stones exist here, and further east there are rock-cut tombs. It is north of Abu Lôzeh.

Mughâir el 'Adeisiyeh (مغاير العديسية, 'caves of lentils').—Six rock-cut tombs occur here. The first is $5\frac{1}{2}$ feet long, 1 foot 10 inches broad, and $2\frac{1}{2}$ feet high, roughly hewn inside. The second (see Plan and Section) is $7\frac{1}{2}$ feet long, $3\frac{1}{2}$ feet broad and high. The door is 3 feet high and 2 feet wide. The four others resemble this one. There are also niches in the rock facing northwards (see drawing), one of which as measured, and found to be 2 feet 8 inches high, 21 inches wide at the bottom, and 10 inches deep to the back. On the hill above are remains of a cairn, with traces of masonry and steps on the hillside.

The site was explored by Lieutenant Mantell.

Mughâret ed Dubbeh (مغارة الدبة, 'cave of the she-bear').—See Khŭrbet ed Dubbeh. It is close to the ruin, and the name is, consequently, not written on the reduced map.

Mughr Talât es Sufa (مغر طلعة الصفا, 'caves of the white ascent').—In this name is preserved the Hebrew Zophim (see under Neba). The caves are small, and apparently natural. The name is omitted from the reduced map for want of space.

Mukerr el Faras (مكرّ الفرس, 'plain of the mare') applies to flat ground north of the Zerka Mââin Valley.

Muntâr Abu Nukhleh (منطار ابو نخله, 'watch-tower of the palm'). —Close to 'Abd el Jûwâd—a large cairn. It is omitted from the reduced map for want of space.

Muntâr el Fudeili (منطار الفضيلي, 'watch-tower of the Fudeili spring').—A little ruined watch-tower near 'Ain Fudeili. It is omitted from the reduced map.

Muntâr el Khelâl (منطار الخلال, 'watch-tower of the dells').— A large cairn of good-sized stones on the ridge called 'Arkûb el Khelâl. It may be a ruined watch-tower.

Visited October 22, 1881.

Muntâr el Meshukkar (منطار المشقّر, 'the watch-tower of Meshukkar;' cf. Khŭrbet Meshukkar).—This name is sometimes applied to Khŭrbet Umm el 'Akâk, but seems properly to indicate remains beside the Roman road rather further south on the same ridge. Two well-shaped stones, each 4 or 5 feet long, are placed, one upright, one leaning against it, as though originally belonging to an altar or dolmen. No third stone was visible. On the north-east

*Monument at Muntaret el Meshukkar.*

are two or three rock-cut wine-presses (compare Sûmia), and the side-stones of the ancient road here resemble those on Roman roads in Western Palestine. The *Muntâr*, or watch-tower, itself is further north again, and west of the road. Only the foundations remain of a square tower, 8 paces (20 feet) side. It has a view westwards. There are other ruined towers near, all three being probably remains of vine-yard towers, for the numerous wine-presses on this ridge seem to prove the existence at a former period of large vineyards.

Visited September 7, 1881.

Muntâr Umm Medeisis (منطار أم مديسيس, 'watch-tower of the hiding-place').—Ruined foundations on the road from Kefrein to Hesbân. The valley to the north is Wâdy el Medeisesât, which is marked on the reduced map.

Mureijib Beni 'Atiyeh (مريجب بني عطيه, apparently 'the holy place of the Beni 'Atiyeh').—It is a very high ridge with ruins. The word رجمه refers to worship of the Arab period before Islam, and رجميه is a 'victim' of the pre-Islamite times. The ruins appear to be those of a small fort. Due west of this hill on the plateau is an ancient stone-circle, perhaps connected with it.

Muturrâh el Hejâya (مطرّح المجايا, 'the place of giving up the riddles').—This curious name, probably due to a tradition not collected, applies to a ruin north of Wâdy Nâaûr among trees on the hilltop. The remains are insignificant.

El Mutkh (المطخ, perhaps مخ, 'débris').—This name applies to a hilltop.

El Mutull (المطلّ, 'the heap' or 'Tell').—This is an eminence near Kh. Sûcimeh.

Mutull el Hisân (مطلّ الحصان, 'place of rising of the horse').— From a legend (see 'Arâk el Emîr). It is omitted from the reduced map from want of space.

Nâifeh (نايفة, 'humped').—A hilltop east of Mââin.

Nakib er Raml (نقيب الرمل, 'the little mountain road or pass of sand').—The name appears to apply to a ridge on the north side of Wâdy Hesbân, and it is no doubt derived from the Nubian sandstone visible in this gorge.

En Nasleh (النصلة, 'the spear-head').—This name may be a mistake for نسلة, 'a settlement,' but was carefully ascertained. It applies to the little rocky point west of Tell Kefrein, described under the head Kefrein, which is close to Goblân's huts at his winter settlement. Another derivation of the name may be from the Arab practice of setting up the Sheikh's spear to indicate the position of a new encampment. The name is omitted from the reduced map for want of space.

## Nebo.

Neba (نبا).—This name is applied by the Arabs (according to several statements carefully obtained from independent sources, and after much questioning) to the flat top with a cairn, from which the ridge south of the 'Ayûn Mûsa runs out west. The ridge receives the names Neba and Siâghah indifferently, but the name Râs Siâghah applies to the end of the spur south-west of the ruin of Siâghah. The name Talât es Sufa (طلعة الصفا) applies to the northern slope above the 'Ayûn Mûsa and the Talât el Heisah (or Heith), to the valley descending southwards from Siâghah. These names appear to represent Nebo, Seath (see Khŭrbet Siâghah), the field of Zophim (see Mughr Talât es Sufa), and the ascent of Luhith (see Talât Heisah).

It is now generally admitted that the Arabic Neba ('swell') represents the Hebrew Nebo (נבו), which appears to have received its name from the Semitic divinity Nebo—the planet Mercury (see Num. xxxii. 38, where the name is evidently regarded as Pagan). The name Pisgah

(פסגה) was evidently applied to the same ridge (Deut. xxxiv. 1), but does not seem to have survived in the modern nomenclature.

The view from Mount Nebo is important, as being that of Moses. The points visible were carefully noted on the spot. The height of the trigonometrical station of Neba is 2,643·8 feet above the Mediterranean. The ridge to the east is 2,731·6 feet at the Kabr 'Abdallah, and is thus nearly 100 feet higher than Nebo.

The ridge of Mount Nebo has been often described, and some have claimed to know the very spot on which Moses stood. Yet we were able to make one or two additions to previous discoveries, and as the view is of the highest interest and importance, a new description may not be considered unnecessary. The ridge runs out west from the plateau, sinking gradually; at first a broad brown field of arable land, then a flat top, crowned by a ruined cairn, then a narrower ridge, ending in the summit called Siâghah, whence the slopes fall steeply on all sides. The name Nebo, or Neba ('the knob,' or 'tumulus') applies to the flat top with the cairn, and the name Tal'at es Sufa to the ascent leading up to the ridge from the north. Thus we have here three names which connect the ridge with that whence Moses is related to have viewed the Promised Land, namely, first, Nebo, which is identically the same word as the modern Neba; secondly, Siâghah, which is radically identical with the Aramaic Se'ath, which is the word standing instead of Nebo in the Targum of Onkelos (Num. xxxii. 3), where it is called 'the burial-place of Moses'; thirdly (and this was a new discovery of the Survey party), *Tal'at es Sufa*, is radically identical with the Hebrew Zuph, whence Mizpeh and Zophim; it is the modern representative of the old 'Field of Zophim' (or of views), in the form 'Ascent of Zuph.' The field of Zophim is, no doubt, the field close to the cairn of Nebo, and there are, indeed, few places in Palestine as well fixed as is this interesting ridge, whence Moses took his last look of the land he was not to enter. The name Pisgah is not now known, but the discovery of Zophim (*cf.* Num. xxiii. 14) confirms the view generally held, that it is but another title of the Nebo ridge.

The view is much the same from Neba and from Siâghah, and I have thrice carefully noted it on separate occasions, although the autumn haze unfortunately always obscured some distant features of the view which are clear enough in the spring-time. Standing on the ruins of Siâghah (which are Byzantine and of no great interest) one sees down into the Jordan Valley better than on the cairn of Neba, and the latter has the disappointing peculiarity that it commands no view at all to the east. The top is actually lower than the level of the great shed or western brink of the Belka plateau, and this ridge shuts out entirely the eastern view towards Mâdeba and sites further east. On this side the view only extends, therefore, a couple of miles, and on the south only four or five, for here another parallel ridge of equal height runs out from the summit called el Maslûbiyeh, although the peak of el Mureijib and the top of Tell M'ain can be seen above.

On the north-east, the site of Heshbon appears on the edge of the Mishor plateau, with Elealah behind, and on the north the ridge of Neby Osh'a bounds the picture, entirely concealing Hermon and the Sea of Galilee. The view is therefore only extensive towards the western half of the circle, and the chief places were observed through our theodolites from both Neba and Siâghah. The northern half of the Dead Sea is visible, but the Lisân is concealed by the eastern ridges south of Nebo. On the west rises the watershed of Judea and Samaria, while Bethlehem and Jerusalem and the molehill of Herodium can be clearly made out. The 'nest of the Kenite' appears on the south-west (Num. xxiv. 21), and thence the ridge runs by Beni N'aim—whence Abraham saw the smoke of Sodom rising in the deep gorge—on to Olivet and Mizpeh (Neby Samwîl), while the cone of Taiyibeh (Ophrah) and the ridge of Tell 'Asûr (Baal Hazor) with its great oak-trees—remnants of an old 'enclosure' of Baal—are prominent objects. North of these again are Gerizim and Ebal, with the cleft between, indicating Shechem, and on the right Hazkin, the lofty summit of 'Ezekiel's' mountain, and on the slope lies Bezek, where Saul numbered Israel gathered for the relief of Jabesh Gilead—a good deed which brought its own reward, since the men whose eyes he saved were those who rescued his body and that of his son from shameful exposure on the wall of Bethshan.

Tabor and the castle of Belvoir (Kaukab el Hawa) are said to be visible with the chain of Gilboa in clear weather, but as Carmel is only 1,700 feet high, and the ridge of Hazkîn 2,400 on an average, a very simple calculation shows that, even neglecting curvature, it would be necessary that Neba should be 1,200 feet higher than Carmel, or over 3,000 feet above the Mediterranean, to allow of the place of Elijah's sacrifice being seen at all. The actual height of Nebo, as now ascertained, is only 2,643·8 feet at the cairn.

Returning south, the eye travels along the line of the lower hills and the Jordan Valley. The mosque of Neby Mûsa (ignorantly supposed to be the site of Moses' tomb) is visible, as is the cliff of the Quarantania, with the dark groves round Jericho. The Sartabah peak towers above the Far'ah Valley, and the black snaky line of this affluent (bearing to Jordan perhaps the waters of Ænon) is clearly marked. The Jordan itself winds like a great dusky dragon through the white valley, and the streams from the Jericho plain creep down to meet those which dash from the hills of Moab. The little island of Rujm el Bahr (the Cairn in the Sea) is visible off the north shore of the Salt Lake, whose calm oily waters sleep shining under the sun. This island is perhaps an old jetty, raised when the Crusaders or some other enterprising race sought to realize Ezekiel's vision of a Dead Sea made alive by traffic. The new Russian hospice at Eriha (Crusading Jericho) shines white in the valley, and the old brown fortress monasteries of Beth Hoglah and St. John on Jordan are now partly rebuilt, and entirely spoiled, by Russian money and monkish vandalism.

At our feet on this side Jordan we see the waters of Nimrim, flanked by tamarisks and oleanders, running by the mound whence they are named. Further south, the Seisaban plain expands, the Moab ridges receding to form a basin corresponding to the plain of Jericho. This is the old Abel Shittim, or 'Meadow of Acacias,' where the black tents of Israel were an offence to the sight of Balak standing where we now stand. The plain is yet covered with its thickets of the thorny sidr, or lotus, and with the scattered 'oshir, or 'apple of Sodom.' Just below us is the dusty mound of Râmeh, with bushes all round it, which look black rather than green. This is the old Beth Haran, and behind it is Kefrein, Goblân's winter home, with its hillock crowned by the tombs of his ancestors. Zoar, at our feet, is not distinguishable, but the tomb of Fendi el Faiz, the great chief of the Sakhûr, shines new and white. Coming from Nâblus he fell sick, and died within the territory of his enemies, the 'Adwan; yet, through the courtesy which Arabs never fail to show, he here lies peacefully in an honoured grave in Abel Shittim, the land of his foes.

Another tomb should also be noticed, namely, the Kabr Abdallah, shining on the skyline to our north-east. Some have sought to connect this 'Servant of God' with Moses whose sepulchre no man knoweth unto this day; but the idea is fanciful at best, for the tomb in question is apparently that of a Persian derwish, and has three more conspicuous monuments of the Ghaneimât Arabs beside it.

The general effect of the scene thus described is bare and colourless in the extreme. The distant gray ridge is hazy and tame in outline; the Jordan Valley is white, with black serpent streams; the foreground is yet more barren. But we are looking on the scene, not, as probably Moses did, in early spring, when the hills were newly bathed, the sky blue, the luxuriant valley green, and we must not be led to express too unfavourable a judgment on the Land of Promise as he saw it from afar. The long reflections in the Dead Sea, the white marl hillocks round Jordan's course, the drab-coloured mountains, with shadows blue and black, are, however, the features which rise to the memory in recalling an autumn day on Nebo.

And now, having detailed the features of the landscape visible from Neba or from Siâghah, it remains to compare them with the Old Testament account of the scene visible to Moses, or to Balaam when he would have cursed Israel had he dared.

When we turn to the account of the death of Moses (Deut. xxxiv. 1-3), we find a description which answers well to that above given, with only two exceptions. The land of Naphtali (extending to Tabor) can be seen, and the mountains of Gilead: the land of Ephraim and of Manasseh, of Judah, with the Negeb (the dry or south country), is seen for more than a hundred miles. Jericho, the city of palm-trees, and its plain, is at our feet unto Zoar, which lies at the foot of the Moab chain. If we make the simple change of reading 'towards' instead of 'unto' in the cases of Dan and 'the western sea '—a change not forbidden by the meaning of the Hebrew particle—the whole account reads as correctly as that of an eye-witness; but it is certain that Dan (if the site near Bâniâs be intended), and the utmost, or 'hinder,' or most western sea, cannot be visible from Nebo to any mortal eye. It is a physical impossibility to see either, because the Palestine watershed hides the Mediterranean, and the ridge of Mount Gilead bars out the view of Hermon. The reader, then, must choose either to accept the very small modification of translation here suggested, or to attribute to Moses a superhuman power of vision.

Scarcely less interesting are the indications to be derived from the poetic vision of Balaam; but these may be better considered in connection with Baal Peor—for, in strict accordance with the Biblical account, we find that Israel, only partly visible from Nebo, would be better seen from Bamoth Baal and Peor.

We have not, however, yet finished with the subject of Pisgah and the Field of Zophim, for close beside the knoll of Neba we found, to our great delight, an ancient monument which seems to have escaped the attention of other explorers, namely, a dolmen, standing perfect and unshaken. Subsequent research proved that others are to be found on the southern slopes of the mountain, a little below the Field of Zophim, and another specimen, which has been overturned, occurs to the west of the cairn of Nebo. A great rude-stone circle was also found on the southern slope, and the extensive dolmen centre of the Maslûbiyeh is only just the other side of the gorge. Clearly we are in the presence of an old centre either of burial or of worship, and in another chapter will be given in detail the reasons for supposing that these monuments are altars rather than tombs. How strikingly, then, not only at Nebo, but also at Bamoth Baal and Peor, do these words recur to our minds, 'Build me here seven altars, and prepare me here seven oxen and seven rams!' (Num. xxiii. 1).—Conder's 'Heth and Moab,' pp. 129-136, 1st edition.

The flat field of red ploughed soil immediately east of the cairn at Neba is called Merj Neba, 'the meadow of Nebo,' and probably represents the old field of Zophim (see Mughr Talât es Sufa). The ancient road which seems to have passed down north of the cairn is marked by sidestones—as in Western Palestine—and may be of Roman origin. Beside it on the north is the foundation of a small watch-tower, which is called Kusr en Neba; it is square, and includes a cistern, which was fed by a channel from the east. The masonry is of moderate size, and resembles that used in the Roman and Byzantine structures of the country.

The cairn on Neba is very flat, and has apparently been partly destroyed. The stones are of no great size, and are unhewn. There are a good many stone pillars (Meshâhed) erected by the Arabs on this hilltop, and beside the road where Neby Mûsa, west of Jordan, becomes visible.

On the southern slope of Neba, some 500 yards south-west from the cairn on the summit, there is a circle of undressed stones piled up to form a kind of vallum. The diameter is 100 paces, or 250 feet, and the wall

View of Nº 1 from the West.

12 feet thick. It was discovered by Lieutenant Mantell, R.E., and resembles the Hadânieh circle (see under that head). There is also at least one dolmen on this slope, about a quarter of a mile south-west of the circle. There are four dolmens on the flatter part of the hill, north-west of the cairn, and probably others may yet remain to be found. Old quarryings and square wine-press chambers were also observed on the hill.

Of the dolmens on the north-west, the first and most distinct is the furthest east. It was photographed by Lieutenant Mantell. The top stone measures 3 feet 9 inches and 5 feet 6 inches at the two ends, and 7½ feet and 4 feet at the two sides. It is supported by two stones on the west, and by a small one on the east, the greatest height under the capstone being 3 feet 3 inches, and the highest point on the upper surface about 5½ feet. This dolmen is about 30 paces south of the ancient road with watch-tower, and rather higher on the flat knoll than the road. Not far off, on the north-west side of the hill, is a small cave, and by it four stones, arranged in a square measuring 7 feet by 5 feet: these seem to be supports of a dolmen (No. 2) whose capstone is gone. About 100 yards west of the first example is the third, which, though in ruins, seems clearly to have been a dolmen. The fourth, further south, has also been overthrown; the side stones are small, and the table must have been low, but the supposed capstone now stands on end by its supports, and measures 6 feet by 8 feet. It would thus seem probable that the stony knoll of Neba was once surrounded with dolmens

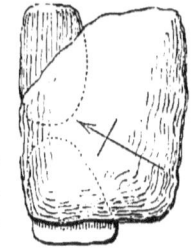

*Plan of N°1 Dolmen.*

*Elevation N°1 Dolmen M! Nebo*

*N°2 M! Nebo*

on the south-west and north, if not on the east, and the cairn seems to form the centre round which they were grouped, but at some time unknown the cairn was ruined, and most of the dolmen tables overturned.

Visited August 20, and September 7 and 27, 1881.

En Nettâfah (النطافه, the root means 'to drip').—This is a large cave-reservoir west of Mâdeba. It is about 30 paces (75 feet) in diameter, and is 40 feet deep. On the south side the rock-walls drip with water, filtrating through the strata—whence the name. There is a regular descent from the east side. The water is good and drinkable.

En Nûeijis.—See Kusr en Nûeijis. The name applies to ruins near the Kusr, consisting of rude walls, cisterns, etc., marking the site of a former village, or small town, probably of the Byzantine period.

Nukb ez Zâgh (نقب الزاغ, 'the hollow way of the crow').—This name applies to a road from Nââûr to the 'Ain el Jâmûs. It is omitted from the reduced map as unimportant.

Rabâhiyeh (رباحيه. The word رباح means an 'ape').—This is probably a corruption of some older name. The ruin consists only of heaps of stones in the wood.

Râfâ (رافع, 'lofty').—This applies to a cliff north of 'Ain Minyeh.

Rajijet es Sidreh (رجيجة الصدره).—In ordinary Arabic would mean 'quaking of the breast.' It applies to a district in the wood. Sidr, however, among the Arabs, means a broad path (cf. Misdâr 'Âisheh, etc.), and Rajijeh is no doubt a Bedawin mispronunciation for Rakikah (رقيقه, 'narrow'). The name thus really means 'the narrowing of the broad road,' which applies very well.

Er Ramleh (الرمله, 'the sandy').—A heap of stones above Wâdy er Ramleh. The Nubian sandstone shows in this valley at the north edge of the Survey.

Râs Abu en Naml (راس ابو النمل, 'hilltop of the ant').—See Rujm Abu en Naml. The possible origin of the name is noticed under Wâdy Abu en Naml. The name applies to the hill by the Rujm, and is omitted from the reduced map.

Râs Kuseib (راس قصيب, 'the amputated head').—Applies to a hilltop with a quarry, 'Arâk el Mâberah, on its north side.

Râs el Merkeb (راس المرقب, 'hilltop of the observatory').—This is a conspicuous hill, with a large terebinth-tree west of the highest point. It is east of 'Ammân, and was used as a trigonometrical station.

Close to the terebinth, on the east, is a rude-stone circle. A second exists about a quarter of a mile further east. Both are about 25 paces (63 feet) in diameter, with walls about 2 feet high, made of uncut stones 1 foot to 1½ feet long. Near each of these circles there are remains of three or four smaller circles of about half the diameter.

Visited by Lieutenant Mantell, October 13, 1883.

Râs el Meshcirfeh (راس المشيرفه, 'hilltop of the little high place').—Hilltop with Survey cairn and trigonometrical station.

Râs Siâghah (راس صياغه).—A hilltop with a large cairn made by the Americans, and used by the English surveyors as a trigonometrical station (see Khŭrbet Siâghah).

Rasfet Nimrîn (رصفة نمرين, 'the stony, or hard ground of Nimrîn,' from the character of the soil).

Er Rekiâiyeh (الرقيعيه).—The meaning is uncertain, as the root includes the meanings 'to sew,' 'to deceive,' with nouns, 'a husband,' 'a kind of tree,' and 'the seventh heaven.' It is an insignificant ruin near Mââin.

Rimeh (ريم).—In modern Arabic the Rîm is the fallow-deer; in Hebrew and Assyrian it is the wild-ox—now extinct. The name applies to the foundations of a small tower, which is marked R on the map east of Arkûb el Khelâl, at the north edge of the Survey.

Rujm Abu 'Alandah (رجم ابو علندة, 'cairn of Abu 'Alandah '— a proper name).—A large cairn east of the Hâj road.

Rujm Abu Hashireh (رجم ابو هشيره, 'cairn of Abu Hashireh ' —a proper name).—In the Jordan Valley.

Rujm Abu en Naml (رجم ابو النمل, 'cairn of the father of the ant ;' cf. Wâdy Abu en Naml).—A cairn with a rock-cut winepress to the east. It is marked R. south-west of Kurn Kebsh on the reduced map.

Rujm Abu Zeitûn (رجم ابو زيتون, 'cairn of Abu Zeitûn.' Probably a proper name. It means 'father of olives ').—He appears to have been a robber shot and buried here.

Rujm 'Ameish (رجم عميش, cairn of 'Ameish. Probably a proper name. It means 'weak-sighted ').—Foundations and ruined walls form two small ruins here.

Rujm Belâth (cf. Khŭrbet Belâth).—The spot is conspicuous on account of a large sacred tree, by which are foundations apparently belonging to a small tower.

Rujm el Benât (رجم البنات, 'cairn of the girls').—This is immediately east of the Serabit el Meshukkar. Probably women were buried at it.

Rujm Dhaheiret Jemân (رجم ظهيرة جمعى, 'cairn of the little ridge or back of Jemân').—This is a ridge east of Elealah with a great many cairns on it.

Rujm el Fahûd (رجم الفهود, 'cairn of lynxes').—Fahed is also an Arab proper name. It is apparently a ruined tower.

Rujm el Fureidiyeh (رجم الفريديّة. The root means to be separate or distinct.)—Ruined folds for cattle, and a rough sarcophagus exist here near Brikeh.

Rujm el Haiyeh (رجم الحيّة, 'cairn of the snake').

Rujm Hâmi Kursch (رجم حامي قرصه, 'cairn of the defender of the disc' or 'loaf').—This curious title occurs also in Galilee, applied to a Tell (see 'Name Lists of Western Survey,' p. 55). The meaning is unknown. The translation (as given by Palmer) is also not very certain.

Rujm el Jâzel (رجم الجازل, 'the large cairn').—Foundations of a watch-tower beside the road.

Rujm el Madowerah (رجم المدوّرة, 'the round cairn').

Rujm Mehâwish (رجم مهاوش, 'mingled cairn').

Rujm el Mekheiyit (رجم المخيّط, 'cairn of the needle').—A great cairn, perhaps 20 feet high, on a conspicuous top (see Hadânieh).

Rujm el Meruffa (رجم المرفّع, 'the high-built cairn').

Rujm el Mesâhem (رجم الساهم, 'cairn of the place of the arrow,' or, perhaps, 'arrow-like').

Rujm el Meseiyik, or Meseik (رجم المسيّك).—A cairn on a low flat top, beneath which two recently-buried bodies were lying. On the south are other Arab graves, some of which were adorned with plaits of women's hair (see el Kŭeijiyeh) hung on strings tied to sticks above the grave. About 100 yards north-east of the cairn a circular trough, 2 feet deep, 31 inches in diameter, is excavated—perhaps an Arab powder-mill. East of the cairn there is a rock-cut cistern with a manhole 4 feet in diameter in its roof. South of the cairn another trough, 21 inches in diameter, 1½ feet deep, was seen. A Survey station was established at the cairn.

Visited September 22, 1881.

**Rujm el Meselhy** (رجم المصلحي). The root means 'good' or 'wholesome.'

**Rujm el Misdâr** (رجم المصدار), 'cairn of the broad road').

**Rujm el 'Oshîr** (رجم العشير), 'cairn of the oshir-plant,' Asclepias Procera, or 'vine of Sodom').

**Rujm 'Oteiyik** (رجم عتيق), 'the ancient cairn').—This is on the hill east of Hesbân. The name is omitted from the reduced map as being of little value.

**Rujm er Rûâk** (رجم الرواق), 'cairn of porches').—The hill is here covered with remains of old enclosures, made of chert or flint ; north of the cairn there are remains of a watch-tower, also of flint, called Muntaret er Rûâk. These are apparently signs of former cultivation, as are the cairns of Rujm Dhaheiret Jemân also. The hill was divided into orchards, probably belonging to the town of Umm el Kindib.

Visited September 17, 1881.

**Rujm Sââûr** (رجم ساعور, 'cairn of light').—This is a sacred tree and tomb, and the name is of special interest, for the pre-Islamite Arabs had a stone idol, called Sâir—according to the early Arab poets. The thorn tree (Samûr, or Spina Ægyptiaca) was adored by the Beni Ghatafân and the Nabatheans, as the habitation of the goddess Allat, or of Bel. In Assyria the shining tree was sacred to the moon and to Asshur. Thus at the present site we find in the 'tree of light' (or 'flame') a sacred place among the modern Arabs, preserving the name and idea of one of the early Pagan Arab divinities closely connected with an Assyrian or Babylonian original.

The tree is a Zârûr, or Nebk (the Nebk is the jujube, or Zizyphus Spina Christi : Tristram, 'Nat. Hist. Bible,' p. 429). On the north side is the sacred circle enclosing the grave of Sheikh Kâsim ; it has the usual trilithon on the west side of the circle (see 'Ain Hesbân). On this were laid three axe-heads, two gun-locks, and some pottery chips; ploughs and wooden coffee-mortars were stored inside; the grave in the centre is rudely covered with stones. A basket was hung up in the sacred tree.

On the south are two rock-cut cisterns, and foundations of a building forming the *Rujm*, or stone-heap, 10 yards in diameter, of rudely-hewn stones, 1 foot to 3 feet long. Some of the stones have rude drafts and rustic bosses.

Visited August 24, 1881.

Rujm Serârah (رجم صرارة, 'cairn of boulders').—This is an enclosure made of stones which must have been brought from some distance. It measures 16 paces (40 feet) east and west by 12 paces (30 feet) north and south. The majority of the stones are not squared. They are all about the same size. One was 3 feet 9 inches by 2 feet 2 inches; another 5 feet by 3 feet. Only one or two courses are standing, except on the east, where there are three. The corner-stones at the south-east corner are rudely squared and have rough drafts. On the south is a well, now choked up. Probably this was built as a cattle enclosure, perhaps in the Byzantine period. Near the well, on the south, there are several scattered stones. The enclosure is on the plain south of Heshbon.

Rujm Sirr edh Dhiâbeh (رجم صر الذياب, 'the cairn of pebbles of Dhiâb').—A cairn east of the Hâj road.

Rujm es Sûwâniyeh (رجم الصوانية, 'cairn of flints').—A heap of flints on the hill south of Heshbon.

Rujm Taihin (رجم طيحين, 'cairn of Taihin').—This is a very conspicuous ruin, and was used as a trigonometrical station. It appears to be a ruined tower near Taihin.

Rujm Tassin (رجم طسين, 'cairn of Tassin').—Foundations of a square tower.

Rujm Umm edh Dhaheb (رجم ام الذهب, 'cairn of gold').— The name Umm edh Dhaheb appears to apply to the plateau round this cairn, which, with two others, one on the north and one on the south, is east of el 'Âl. The cairns are only little heaps of flint-stones.

Rujm Weled Shahwân (رجم ولد شهوان, 'cairn of that fellow Shahwân').—The word Weled, 'child,' is used in a contemptuous manner often of grown persons. The cairn in question covers the body of a thief who was shot in the camp in the valley below and here found dead next morning.

Rujm el Wust (رجم الوسط, 'cairn of the middle').—South of 'Abdûn; a ruined tower.

Rujûm Mubrakat Nâket en Neby (رجوم مبركة ناقة النبي, 'cairns of the place of kneeling of the prophet's she-camel').—This is probably a tradition of the Hâj, as the place is near the Hâj road. They are two large cairns about a quarter of a mile apart.

Rujûm Rafiâh (رجوم رفيعه, probably named from Wâdy Rafi'ah, which see). There are several cairns 8 or 10 feet in diameter, with some traces of ruins included under this name. Three groups of Roman milestones were also found in the valley at distances of a Roman mile apart. The most easterly group included five pillars, of which four stood on square bases. One was measured, the shaft being $1\frac{1}{2}$ feet in diameter and the stone $2\frac{1}{2}$ feet high, including a base 2 feet by $1\frac{1}{2}$ feet, by 11 inches in height.

The fifth was a fragment of a shaft, 21 inches in diameter and 2 feet high, bearing an inscription in seven lines, broken off on the right. This text, discovered and copied by Lieutenant Mantell, R.E., reads thus:

```
IMP CA · · S MARC · · ·
AVRELVS SEV · · · · · · ·
ANTONINVS · · · · · · · ·
   FELIX AVGPI · · · · ·
       VS MAXIMUS · · · ·
       TANICVS MAS · · ·
       INT MA · · · · · · · ·
```

On this inscription the names of Marcus Aurelius (161-180 A.D.) and of Antoninus Pius (138-161 A.D.) are clearly legible, with perhaps that of Severus (193-211 A.D.). The milestone was evidently erected in the second or early in the third century, and the name of Antoninus Pius (at Jerâsh and at Baalbek, etc.) is that found most frequently on the finest temples of Syria. The Roman road to which these milestones belong was probably made at the time when the Roman buildings in and round 'Ammân were erected.

Explored October 12, 1881.

Es Sâdûny (السعدوني, 'the fortunate').—A sacred place on the north of Wâdy Kuscib, east of Tell Hebbeseh. It is omitted from the reduced map for want of room.

Es Safrah (الصفرة, 'the yellow').

Sahel Ghabneh (سهل غبنة, 'deceitful plain').—Near Mâ'ain.

Sahel el Jâmiâiych (سهل الجامعية, 'plain of the mosque or meeting-place').—It is omitted from the reduced map (see Hesbân).

Sahel Khardubbeh.—See Kh. Khardubbeh.

Sahel Musheirfeh.—See Jûeidet el Musheirfeh.

Sahel en Nûeijis.—See Kusr en Nûeijis. This is omitted from the reduced map.

Sahlet el Menakh (سهلة المناخ, 'plain of the place where camels lie down').—Omitted as valueless from the reduced map.

Sahlet Merkeh.—See Merkeh.

Sakarah (صقرة, 'falcons').—Three small ruins consisting of walls of flint on the hill west of 'Ammân.

Es Saleib (الصليب, 'the cross').—A spur south of 'Arâk el Emir. It is omitted as of no special value from the reduced map.

Sâlhah (صالحة, 'good').—This is a shrine west of Tell er Râmeh, probably consecrated to some Sheikh Sâleh.

Salûkâ ez Zabbûd (سلوقع الزبود, 'the rough ground of Zabbûd'). —This is the name of a conspicuous ridge north-west of Heshbon. The name Zebed, or Zabbud, is not uncommon topographically (see Kefr Zibâd, Sheet XI., 'Western Survey').

Es Sâmik (السامك).—This may perhaps represent the Samega which Josephus mentions in connection with Medeba (13 Ant. ix. i.). It is a conspicuous cairn marking the boundary between the 'Adwân and the Beni Sakhr tribes, on the highest part of a flat ridge commanding an excellent view of the Mishor, or Belka plateau. Among the chief places visible are Mashitta, Ziza, Mââin, el Kahf, Jelûl, el 'Âl, and Hesbân.

The cairn consists of unhewn stones, 2 feet to 4 feet long, piled up over the remains of Arabs slain on the spot. At least one recent interment was distinguishable by the smell, of a Beni Sakhr Arab killed by the 'Adwân.

There appears to have been originally a square tower, 15 paces (40 feet) side. On the hill to the south are some curious blocks, looking somewhat like dolmens, but when visited they appeared to be only natural blocks of chert. All round the tower and cairn there are Arab graves. On the north is an enclosure, apparently a cattle-fold, built up of blocks of limestone and flint; and immediately north of this is a rock-cut wine-press. There are many tribe-marks on the tower-stones, including several of the Beni Sakhr, and also the Mehjan, or 'crook,' of the Ajermeh.

ⵙ   ψ   ⲛ   ℞   ⁊⁄   ⲛ⁄

(See note on Arab tribe-marks.) These include the marks of the 'Ajermeh, Fâiz, Khadîr, Jibbûr, and Khurshân.

Visited August 23 and 30, and September 1, 1881.

S e i l   e l   H e r y (سيل الهري, apparently 'the stream struck'—with a staff or stick).—This is the name of the lower part of Wâdy Jideid. The legend of the enchanted spring at 'Ain Minyeh, which was produced by being struck with the spear of 'Aly, should be compared with this title.

S e k k e h (سكّة, 'the path.' Compare the Hebrew סככה, Secacah, as a town name in Josh. xv. 61, applying to a place west of Jordan).—The ruin consists of foundations, ruined walls, cisterns, and caves, west of Merj el Hamâm.

E s   S e l e i t y (السليتي, 'the peeled,' or 'shaved').—Applies to a slope on the south side of Wâdy Jideid. It is omitted from the reduced map.

S e n â i n   H a m â r a h (سنايى حمارة).—Cliffs near the Dead Sea. The root of the first word means 'to be elevated.' The second comes from Hamâr, a donkey, apparently the feminine form, but the root means 'to be red.'

Serâbit el Mushukkar (مرأبيط المشكَّر).—The first word means 'pillar-shafts' (cf. Kefeir Abu Sarbût), the second applies to the whole ridge, and may be from Shakkâra, 'the anemone,' so called from its deep red colour. The root means 'dark red,' which would not apply to the colour of the ridge, but the anemone grows all over these hills.

Under this head may be described two groups of monuments, though the name is confined generally to the eastern group, the western being generally called Serâbit el Mehattah, 'pillars of the unloading place' (of a caravan). The two are about a mile apart, and the name is applied on the map to the western group near the Rujm el Benât, or

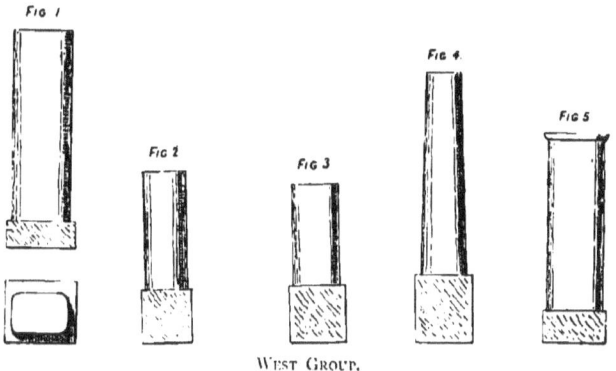

WEST GROUP.

'cairn of maidens.' The local Arabs assert that the Hâj, or pilgrimage to Mecca used formerly to pass by these pillars, and hence the name Mehattah, marking a halt on the journey. Thence, on the south, the pilgrims, according to this account, went to the Mâta et Turkomâniyeh (which see). The story was obtained from independent witnesses, and, although there is no good road from the north in this direction, still water is much more abundant than further east, where the Hâj road now exists. It is thus not impossible that fear of the 'Anazeh tribes may, at some former period, have compelled the pilgrims to choose a route not visible from the plateau above.

The western group, or Serâbit el Mehattah, consists of 12 monoliths.

The most westerly pillar is of oval shape, 19 inches by 22 inches along
the two axes, and it is 5 feet 8 inches high, not including a base 10 inches
high, and measuring 22 inches by 26 inches on plan. The base and shaft
are all in one. The second pillar is 9 paces (22 feet) south-east, and is 16
inches in diameter, and 3½ feet high. Nine others lie fallen in a line
without any particular order, in a north-east direction (230° true bearing)
over a distance of 46 paces (115 feet), and about 12 paces (30 feet) south-
west of the second column. The ground on which they are strewn has a
gentle slope southwards. There are no traces of any ancient road near.
Four other columns in the alignment were measured, each with a cubical
base in one block with the pillar itself. One was 16 inches in diameter,

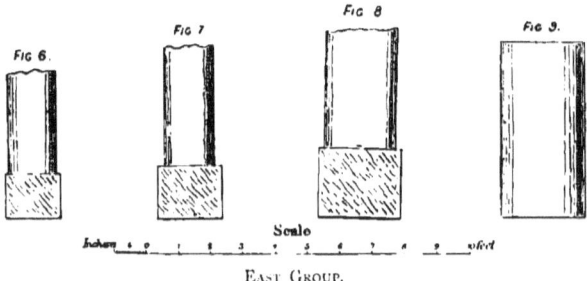

East Group.

3½ feet high, the base 19 inches square and high; another was 13 inches
in diameter at the top, 18 inches at the bottom, 6 feet in height, the base
2 feet high, and 21 inches by 19 inches across. A third has a simple fillet
at the top, 21 inches in diameter, 5 feet 3 inches high, not including the
base 11 inches high, and 23 inches square. This is a well-cut specimen.
A fourth is 18 inches in diameter, 3 feet high, exclusive of a base 20
inches high, and 21 inches square. One of these pillars is thus of tapering
form, and in some others it was noted that the shaft bulged out in the
centre. (*Cf.* pillar at Sûmia.) About 200 yards north of this group are
foundations of a square building on an undulation of the hill spur. This
measured 7 paces (18 feet) either way, and was surrounded with scattered
stones. A lintel and a pillar like those already noted (making the twelfth)
were built in. This may have been a watch-tower.

In the eastern group, a mile further up the spur, there appear to have been twenty-four of these pillars. They lie irregularly scattered over a space 20 yards square on the west slope of the hill. Four were measured; the first, apparently broken or unfinished at the top, is 18 inches in diameter and 3 feet high, not including the square base, 16 inches high and 20 inches square. The second is 18 inches in diameter, 3½ feet high, not including a base 19 inches high, 20 inches by 24 inches on plan. A third is 23 inches in diameter, 3½ feet high, not including a base 25 inches high, 27 inches in diameter. The fourth is 27 inches in diameter, 5 feet 2 inches high, and has no base.

The object of these *stelæ*, or *hermæ*, is not by any means easy to discover. They are too short to have been pillars, and there are apparently no remains of *epistylia* or of other members of the pillar-shaft. They are more like the Roman milestones, yet differ from these in other respects. None are inscribed, yet all are dressed to shape, and none have the pointed top often found on the Roman milestones west of Jordan. There are no traces of any ancient road near either group, though tradition says the Hâj once passed by them. On the north below them is the Hajr el Mena, or 'stone of desire,' which is a wishing-stone. On the south is the modern grave of Abu Redeineh. A good road (though showing no signs of antiquity) ascends the spur not far from the western group leading from Tell er Râmeh (ancient Lybias) to Nebo. The ridge commands a fine view westwards across Jordan.

It is, of course, not certain that these monuments remain in their original position, and they may, after all, be only milestones; but it is also not impossible that they were sacred stelæ. The Arabs do not seem to have any tradition concerning them, and they may have existed before the present tribes entered Moab. On the other hand, the ancient Pagan Arabs adored two chief deities, Allah and Allât: the first, male, and symbolized by an upright stone; the second, female, and denoted by a cubical block (see Lenormant, 'Lettres Assyriologiques,' vol. ii.), and the present kind of monument might, perhaps (like the Indian Lingams), denote this pair of divinities. The suggestion is here hazarded, as worthy of consideration, since menhirs are so common in the district, and also because M e n a, or M e n a t, was one of the names of the great goddess Allât, and is found at the present site still lingering at the Hajr el Mena (which see). The Serâbit may be relics of early Arab Paganism, and should be compared with the pillars at Kefeir Abu Sarbût, or at el 'Al, and with the Hajr el Mansûb and the menhirs round 'Ammân.

It is also possible that the stones may have been erected by pilgrims, either as memorials, or as tombstones, at the time when the Haj took this route. In this case they are of the same class with the modern *kehákir*, or stone piles, erected by pilgrims on roads, only carefully hewn instead of rudely piled up.

It is possible that the following passage, in which Pausanias describes pillars near Helos, in Greece, may throw some light on the question :

'Not far from thence there are seven pillars raised in memorial of this affair (the oath of the suitors of Helen), after the manner of the ancients, as it appears to me, and which they say are images of the seven planets.' (Pausanias' ' Description of Greece,' iii., chap. xx.)

It should be noted that somewhat similar monuments stand over tombs in Phœnicia. There are three at 'Amrit, one having a pillar 14 feet high on a base 6 feet high and 16 feet square, while another has a cylinder with a conical top on a base 15 feet square and 10 feet high, the total height being 33 feet. These monuments, which are only larger examples of the same kind, are held by Lenormant to be phallic emblems.

Visited September 19, 1881.

S h â n a b (شَنَب, 'curved' [of horns, etc.], perhaps on account of the curving ridge).—The ruin occupies the western part of a natural knoll, which measures about 200 paces (500 feet) east and west, by 80 paces (200 feet) north and south. There are foundations of houses built of stones 1½ feet to 4 feet long, rudely squared, and in no instance drafted or well-dressed. A lintel-stone with rude mouldings was observed. On the south the rock has been quarried, and there is a natural cave 12 feet by 4 feet. In a flat rock on this side there is a hollow 11 inches in diameter and 10 inches deep (perhaps an Arab mortar for making powder, as in other instances). On the top of the knoll is a cave filled up with cut stones— perhaps used as a grave. There is also a cistern, which is choked. On the south slope of the knoll there are also ruins. There is a small spring (see 'Ain el Meiyiteh) on the west, and on the knoll is a tree, which is a very conspicuous object from the Jordan valley. There are Arab threshing-floors at the site.

Visited September 14, 1881.

Sheikh el 'Ajemy (شيخ العجمي, 'the Persian chief'). — The Belâd el 'Ajem is originally all the world excepting Arab-speaking countries, but in common use it applies to Persia. There are some fine trees here, and a few ruined walls, also Metâmir for storing corn.

Sheikh Kâsim (شيخ قاسم, proper name).—See Rujm Sââûr.

Sheikh Nasir (شيخ نصير, p.n.).—In the Korân the title Nasr is applied to the Medina converts ('Sura,' lxi. 14). A sacred circle, with trees, and Metâmir to store corn, east of 'Arak el Emir.

Sheikh Shehâb el Fuliyeh (شيخ شهاب الفليّح, 'Sheikh Shehab, the splitter ').—This is the principal tomb with sculptures at 'Ain Hesbân (which see).

Sheikh Subeih (شيخ صبيح, proper name, ' ruddy ').—This is due west of Mount Nebo. There are two sacred Arab circles at this place, one having, as usual, a lintel, on two jambs on the west side of the circle. The upper surface is only 2 feet from the ground, and the wall of the circle is not more than 6 inches above the present surface of the ground. There are remains also of a small watch-tower, and a grave with a stone at the head and another at the foot.

Sheikh Sûeileh (شيخ صويلح, proper name).—A sacred place near the dolmens at Tell el Matâbâ. Omitted from the reduced map from want of room to write it.

Esh Shemsâni (الشمسانه, 'the Samsonian ').—This is no doubt an old centre of Sun-worship, taking its name from Shamash, the Sun. Ruined towers of flint remain here, but the position is principally remarkable for its naturally commanding site on the plateau. Sir C. Warren ('Quarterly Statement,' 1870, p. 296) used the hill as a trigonometrical station, and speaks of the extensive view which the hill affords. No legends were, however, obtained in connection with the spot, although inquiries were made on the subject.

Shûnet edh Dhiâbeh (شونة الذياب, 'barn of Dhiâb ').—A small fort built on the hillside west of the stream of Wâdy Hesbân. It measures 35 paces (87½ feet) square outside, with a courtyard on the south, measuring 150 feet by 100 feet. This contains a well, and the south wall has a row of loopholes. West of the building there is a ruined tank, or Birkeh. The building belongs to 'Aly Diâb, chief of the 'Adwân tribe, and it is said that helmets and coats of mail belonging to this tribe are here stored. The masonry is fairly good, but mostly modern. Over the south door of the tower (leading to its central court) there is an inscription fairly well cut in Arabic:

بسم الله الرحمن الرحيم لا اله الا الله محمد
رسول الله بنا هذه القلعة الشيخ اديات
العدوان بي مندر حسبان سنة ١١٩١ وكان
منتهاه في شهر ربيع اوال ثم في شهر رمضان

'In the name of God, the merciful, the compassionate. There is no God but God; Muhammed is the messenger of God. Built this castle the Sheikh Adhiâb the 'Adwân, at the barn* of Heshbon in the year 1191 (of the Hejirah), and it was done in the month Robiâ el Awal; then in the month Ramadân.'

The account given by the Arabs to Sir C. Warren with regard to this and to the Shûnet Sukr was that they were erected when Ibrahim Pasha (in 1840) commanded the 'Adwân to live in houses; but the date thus obtained would represent 1773 A.D., and, if correct, makes the Shûnet edh Dhiâbeh considerably older. The Shûnet Sukr and the Shûnet Makbil en Nimr are said to be also of the same date, and to have been erected in the time of the great grandfather of Kablân en Nimr, which agrees very well with the date obtained, allowing thirty years to each generation.

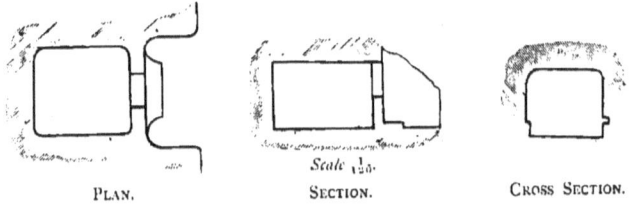

PLAN.     Scale 1/120.     SECTION.     CROSS SECTION.

On the east slope of the hill below the Shûnet edh Dhiâbeh is a small tomb, or *koka*, in the rock. It is 7½ feet long, 6 feet wide,

* The word نادر is used in Western Palestine for a threshing-floor, and the explanation was obtained on the spot (*cf.* Endor).

and 5 feet high, with a ledge 4 inches wide on one side and a groove 4 inches deep on the other, as though for a slab fitted 1 foot 3 inches above the floor. The entrance is only 2½ feet high and wide, with a rock step in front. The face of the rock is cut back on either side of this door, forming recesses about 2½ feet across and 3 feet high. The sill of the door is 2½ feet above the floor inside, and on the left side (entering) are remains of bolt-holes of the door, with a hinge socket at the top on the right. Below this on the east is a small cave, now partly closed by a dry-stone wall of ancient materials, with an old lintel-stone placed over its entrance. Between the tomb and the cave are ruined foundations of rudely-cut and uncut stones. These are called Khŭrbet esh Shûneh, 'ruin of the barn,' from the Shûnet edh Dhiâbeh. The rock has been quarried, and a little trough a foot square is cut in one place. A rude tomb with three rough *arcosolia*, or recesses, was also observed.

About a quarter of a mile north-east of the Shûneh is a group of broken tombs, or *kokim*, like the last. One appears to have been originally 7 feet long and 4 feet broad. These tombs face east and north. Near them is a curious cutting in the rock—perhaps the remains of a shaft-tomb (as at Tyre)—subsequently destroyed in quarrying. The shaft is 6 feet 6 inches high to the top of the scarp, and 1 foot 6 inches wide, and cut back also 1 foot 6 inches in the face of the rock. The recesses on either side at the ground level (the foot of the scarp) are 2½ feet square, and cut back 1½ feet. In the stream below is a curious boulder pitted full of holes, some 6 inches in diameter, in rows like the cup hollows in dolmens.

Shûnet Sukr (شونه صقر, 'barn of the falcon'—proper name).—This is a ruined hamlet east of the stream, near Shûnet edh Dhiâbeh, having a small modern mill still working, fed by a masonry lade from the Hesbân stream. There are remains of modern-looking stone cottages, with a little tower and stores for corn, and a ruinous wall surrounds the site. The lade forms a sort of fosse on the west side of the ruins, which appear to have been erected in recent times of old materials; perhaps, as stated to Sir C. Warren by the 'Adwân, in the days of Ibrahim Pasha.

About 300 yards north of the tower, or granary, which is conspicuous at the above site, there are two sarcophagi cut in detached boulders (see Sûmich). One was measured and found to be 5 feet 9 inches long, and

## SHUNET SUKR

1½ feet wide and deep, with a flat rim for the cover-stone 6 inches wide. The rock, or boulder, measured about 7 feet by 3 feet in length and width. The second sarcophagus measured 5 feet 9 inches by 2 feet, and 1 foot 9 inches in depth. It has a raised rim 1 foot high and 4 inches thick to prevent the entrance of rain.

The Shûnet Sukr itself is the building with the tower in the hamlet; the masonry is modern, and the south door has a pointed arch. The

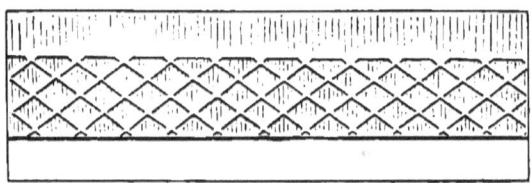

outer walls at the site are loopholed in places. The tower measures 32 feet north and south by 47 feet east and west. Over the doors of several of the cottages ancient lintel-stones with designs have been built in. They appear to be of Byzantine origin, perhaps brought from the ruins of Heshbon on the hill above. One is 4 feet long by 1 foot 3 inches high, with a diaper pattern. A second, 1 foot high by 1 foot 4 inches

 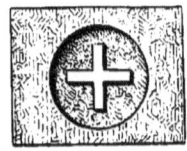

long, has a Greek cross in relief in a sunk circle. A third has a similar design, flanked by two sunk discs. A fourth, 3 feet 2 inches long by 1 foot 2 inches high, has a central design with six rays, and on the left a cross with four crosslets. The lintels have been daubed with henna in places in dots, as in the shrines of Western Palestine.

It is remarkable that in this case, as at 'Ain 'Ammân and 'Ain

Hesbân, the cross appears to be used as though of good omen by the Arabs. They, however, always refused to acknowledge that these were crosses at all.

Visited August 18 and September 16.

Shûnet Makbil en Nimr.—See Sûmieh.

Shûnet Nimrin.—See Tell Nimrin.

Sidd Bareiz (سدّ بَريز, 'cliff of the bare land').—The words Sidd and Sâdeh are used by the Bedawin of a cliff or bank. This was observed also in the Jordan valley west of the river, and in Assyrian Sâdeh means 'a hill.' This is a cliff west of 'Arâk el Emir. The name is not on the reduced map.

Sidd ed Daghamah (سدّ الدغمه, 'dark cliff').—This is a cliff of dark sandstone on the north side of Wâdy Nââûr.

Sidd Khuweilid (سدّ خُوَيلد, probably 'cliff of mole-rats'—Khuld being the Syrian form* of Khulnud, the Spalax Typhlus).—This is a cliff north of Wâdy Ayûn edh Dhib.

Es Sinôbarât (الصنوبرات, 'the firs').—A conspicuous group of fir-trees on the high ground, which is otherwise bare of trees. It probably indicates that the great wood called Hirsh Amriyeh has been thinned considerably, leaving these few trees. Firs are found in many places on the ridges of Jebel 'Ajlun, and in the great wood north of 'Arâk el Emir.

Es Sûeifiyeh (الصويفيّه, 'the woolly,' probably an old Zuph or Mizpeh).—Foundations, ruined walls, and cisterns remain here, on the plateau west of 'Ammân. It seems not impossible that this may be the Mizpeh of Moab (1 Sam. xxii. 3), to which the parents of David were sent; but another equally possible site for that town would be Sûfa, east of Tell Mââin, which is, perhaps, more probable.

Sufr Jeriâh (صفر جريعه, 'the yellowness of Jeriâh').—Applies to a ridge with yellow rocks on the west of Wady Jeriâh.

* Here, as usual, the Syrian form is archaic, being the Hebrew חלד, rendered 'weasel.'

## SIBMAH.

Sûmia (سومیا, or سومیه, probably 'towering').—This ruined site seems possibly to be that mentioned in the Bible under the names Sibmah and Shibmah * (Num. xxxii. 38; Josh. xiii. 19; Jer. xlviii. 32; cf. Isaiah xvi. 8-9). Jerome, commenting on the passage in Isaiah, speaks of Sabama as hardly 500 paces from Heshbon. The present site is two English miles from Heshbon, but Jerome's knowledge of Peræa was not very exact, and no other similar name is found in the district. Shebam of

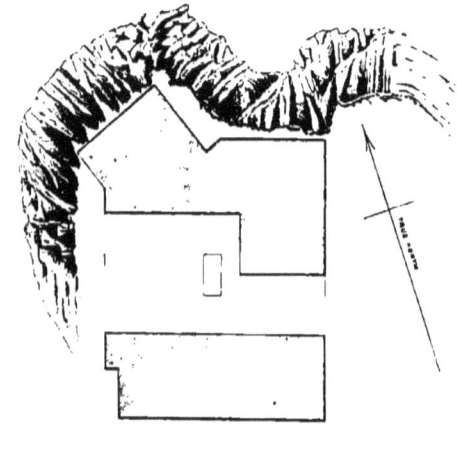

Reuben (Num. xxxii. 3) is presumably the same, and in all the passages mentioned this town is classed with those of the Mishor, or Belka Plateau. The mention of the Vine of Sibmah may be illustrated by the discovery of rock-cut wine-presses in the hills south-east of Sûmia—near Muntâr el Mushukkar, and Umm el Hadawîyeh, and at Kurn Kebsh.

The existing ruins are south of the stream of Wâdy Hesbân, consisting

* שבמה supposes the *Beth* of the Hebrew to become the Arabic *Wau*. The confusion of these letters is very common in the Samaritan dialect.

of a small ruined building—apparently a monastery—with a modern water-mill, fed by a lade from 'Ain Sûmieh, the stream from which flows into Wâdy Hesbân from the south. There are ruined houses beneath the fort or monastery, and rock-cut sarcophagi further down on the north-east, beside the stream of Wâdy Hesbân. There is also a dolmen on the hill to the south-west. Each of these ruins must be described in detail.

The fort or monastery is on a cliff, with a sheer face on the north 40 or 50 feet in height.

The building measures 120 feet along its east wall, and 80 feet along the south wall. The bearing of the former is 18°. There is a projecting portion in the north-west angle, as though to give flank defence. The modern name of the building is Shûnet Makbil en Nimr, 'the barn of Makbil of the Nimr family,' after a chief who lived three generations ago—a brother, apparently, of Kablan I. It seems probable, however, that he only repaired an older building, the general plan of which is distinguishable amid the more modern chambers constructed within the walls. There was a courtyard, with a vault or cistern beneath, and with chambers to the north and south. On the east was an entrance-gate, approached by a narrow path on the face of a very steep slope. The cistern is of good masonry of Roman appearance, like that found in Byzantine towns, and the roof is a round-arched barrel vault, cemented. West of the cistern are remains of an arcade of round arches, with the narrow keystone, graduated voussoirs, and broad haunch-stones—as in so many Byzantine buildings. These seem to have formed part of old vaulted foundations beneath the courtyard. The eastern wall of the enclosure is partly built of drafted masonry, the stones rudely dressed

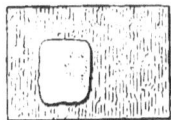  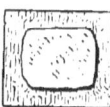

with an adze. Three stones were measured in the outer or east face of this wall. The first is 2½ feet long, by 1 foot 8 inches high, the draft very irregular, 6 inches at the top, 3 inches at the bottom, 6 inches to the left, 1 foot 3 inches to the right; the boss projects 4 inches, and is irregularly shaped. The second stone is 1 foot 5 inches high, 1 foot 8 inches long; the draft is 3 inches wide all round, and projects 5 inches. The third stone is 1 foot 7 inches high, and 1 foot 4 inches long; the draft is as in the preceding, the boss projecting 8 inches. It is doubtful whether these stones are in their original situation.

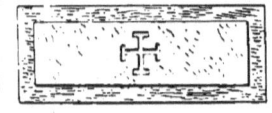

Within the fort is a doorway near the east, with a lintel above it. The lintel-stone is 3 feet 10 inches long, and 1 foot 5 inches high, with an even draft of 3 inches width on all four sides. In the middle of the raised face—which is well dressed—is a cross potent (the Jerusalem cross), 7 inches square, incised, and well cut. Near this is another stone, broken, measuring 1 foot 8 inches in height, 1 foot 9 inches long, with a draft between 3 and 4 inches wide on three sides (the end being broken off); and a geometrical design of a hexagon, with radiating leaves in a circle 8 inches in diameter, is irregularly placed in a corner of the raised face. Near it is a kind of bracket, or voussoir, with two curious cones projecting 3 inches. There is another gateway in the west wall of the fort, the original jambs of which remain, possibly *in situ*, in the foundation course. The gate was

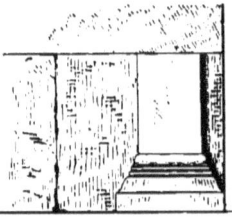
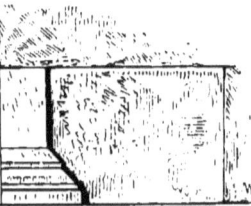

Scale

1 foot 9 inches wide, and the jambs are carved with bases of pilasters rudely executed in low relief.

The pilaster-shafts were about a foot wide, but the details are almost too much worn to measure. The two pilasters differ, and one seems to have been cut off on the side. They may have belonged to an earlier building. The lintel above is not *in situ*, but placed on the Arab masonry of the latest restoration. It has a rude design of cubes, with diagonal lines joining them, and a border with a rough dog-toothed pattern.

The dog-tooth moulding on this stone has considerable interest for purposes of comparison (see 'Ammân, Arab period), because we here find in use, at least as early as the sixth century, exactly the same moulding observed at 'Ammân (perhaps in the ninth). It differs from the dog-tooth moulding in relief used by the Crusaders.

It is also interesting to find here and at Shûnet Sukr the Jerusalem Cross and the cross with four crosslets, which are generally known as becoming the arms of the Crusading kingdom of Jerusalem in the twelfth century, but which, in Moab, occur with remains evidently not later than the beginning of the seventh century.

The building thus described seems evidently to have been a Roman, or, more probably, Byzantine structure, re-used by the Arabs about a century or rather more ago. The position is commanding, though the hill rises higher behind, and the stream from the spring 'A i n S û m i a, on the west, some 50 yards off, is picturesque. There are two stunted palms and some small wild figs beside it, and the lade leading to the little modern mill is fringed with canes and brambles. The water is clear and the supply fresh and perennial.

Between the spring and the fort are the fallen ruins of a small town. The masonry is well cut, and the stones are of proportions similar to those above noticed. These seem to be remains of houses rather than of any public buildings.

East of the fort, and rather higher up the hill, some 40 or 50 paces from the east wall of the fort, as above described, are remains of a tower foundation; on the south-east the rock has been scarped down, and a flat platform is thus formed. The faces towards the north-west are of masonry. The building measured 20 paces along the north-west face, and 14 paces along the south-west. A stone was measured in this wall 5 feet 3 inches long, 2 feet high, with a draft 4 inches wide and the same in depth. It appears probable that stones have been taken from this tower to build the walls of the fort. North of the tower, rather lower down, are three rock-

## SIBMAH

cut tanks close together. They each measure about 3 paces north and south, by 2 paces east and west, and are in one line, east and west (a pace of 2½ feet).

The remains near the stream of Wâdy Hesbân, north-east of Sùmieh, are, perhaps, older than anything on the cliff: they include a remarkable tablet and some tombs and sarcophagi. The tablet is cut in the north face of a large fallen block of limestone close beside the brook. It is sunk back some 6 inches into the face of the stone, and is 7 feet 3 inches high and 8 feet wide. It was carefully examined, but no traces of any inscription were detected. Immediately east of this, on the north brink of the stream, is a sarcophagus about 6 feet long, and further east a pier of modern-looking masonry, as though a bridge had spanned the stream. There are remains of walls for mill-lades all along the valley between Sùmieh and Shûnet edh Dhiâbeh, but only two mills are now working, namely, that at Shûnet Sukr and that at Sùmieh, both belonging to the 'Adwân chiefs.

On the south bank of the stream, just east of the great tablet, are other fallen boulders, having small chambers cut in them. One of these was found to measure 2 feet in height, 1 foot 9 inches in width, and the same to the back. The entrance, 1½ feet high, was rounded, as was the roof of the chamber, and the floor sunk 6 inches lower. This is in the east face

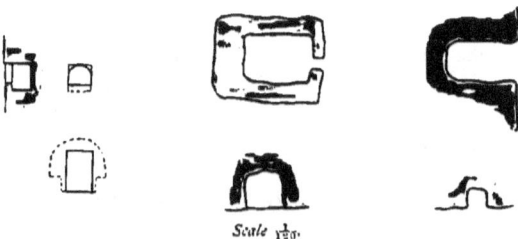

Scale ¹⁄₁₂₀.

of a large rock, which seems possibly to have been moved by earthquake, or by some other cause, after the niche, or chamber, was cut, as the floor of the latter is not now horizontal. East of this another boulder had a chamber measuring 4 feet by 3 feet, having a well-cut door 1 foot 9 inches wide and 2½ feet high. There are remains of the sidestones of an ancient road close by. A little lower down the slope is a boulder, in the upper surface of which a double sarcophagus is cut. The boulder measures 6 feet wide by 8 feet long; each sarcophagus is 5 foot 10 inches long, north and south, and 1 foot 7 inches wide, with a partition between

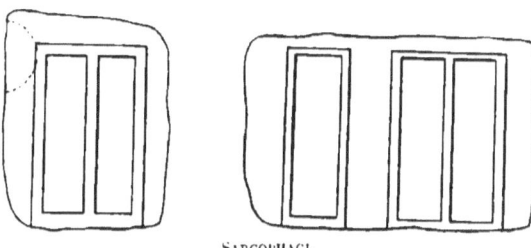

SARCOPHAGI.

5 inches thick, and a sunk rim of the same dimension all round. On the east side of the block, 2 feet from the ground, is a recess 2 feet 8 inches wide, 1 foot 2 inches to the back. The rock is 3 feet high; the sarcophagi are 1 foot 6 inches deep. West of this is another rock, with three

 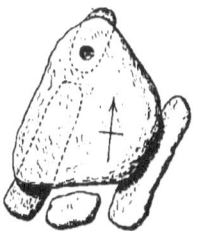

Dolmen W. of Sûmia. View from South.    Plan of Dolmen W of Sûmia

sarcophagi, or graves, sunk in it; they are 6 feet long, 1 foot 9 inches wide, and 1 foot 6 inches deep, with a sunken margin for the lids. The rock is 7 feet by 11 feet. These sarcophagi are about 200 yards north-east of the fort at the bottom of the hill.

On the plateau opposite Sûmieh, on the north, are the dolmens of el Kalûà (see under that head), but a single dolmen was found on the hill to the south-west of this site. The covering-stone measured 5 feet by

7 feet, and was about a foot thick; it was supported on three stones, and a small endstone was found on one side, as though to stand on. A hole 6 inches in diameter and 2 inches deep (a cup-hollow) occurs in the upper face of the covering-stone. The clear height under this stone is 2 feet 10 inches. Near the dolmen is a cave, called 'Arâk Jubr, 'cave of the hero.'

As regards the small chambers in the boulders, others were found near el Kalûâ and at el Mareighât; and there are others on Jebel Oshâ, possibly of the same character. If they were intended for sepulture, the corpse must—in many cases, at least—have been placed in a crouching attitude. The entrances are often well cut, but the limestone is not very hard. It seems possible that they might have been excavated by flint implements, and in each case they occur with rude-stone monuments, belonging, probably, to the later stone or bronze age. It was the early practice of this prehistoric period to bury in a crouching posture (according to Sir J. Lubbock), and it seems not impossible that these are very early tomb chambers. There is a somewhat similar chamber at the Kulât el Ghûleh (Sheet XVII., 'Memoirs of Western Survey,' vol. iii., p. 131), but no other example has been found west of Jordan.

The rock-cut sarcophagi somewhat resemble those at Seffûrieh ('Western Survey,' Sheet V., vol. i., of Memoirs, p. 330); they belong, no doubt, to the Roman period between the second and the seventh centuries. It is remarkable that no traces were found of the cover-stones, which may, however, as at Seffûrieh, have been very rough.

It appears, on the whole, probable that in this ruin we may recognise a town still standing under the name Sabama in the fourth century A.D.

Canon Tristram ('Land of Moab,' p. 346) speaks of several tablets like the one above mentioned, but without inscription. In the course of three visits the surveyors, however, could only find one. Sir C. Warren ('Quarterly Statement,' 1869, p. 287) speaks of only one, and makes the boulder 30 or 40 feet high. The ancient road mentioned above appears to lead down to the Ghor.

Visited August 20, and September 12, 1881.

S u t î h a h (سطيحة, 'the plain ').—A few ruins of rough walls with a cistern. It is on the plateau south-east of Mââîn.

Tâhûnet Dhiâb (طاحونه ذياب, 'the mill of Dhiâb').—See Shûnet edh Dhiâbeh. The mill is on the east side of Wâdy Hesbân, and flour is ground at it.

Tâhûnet Jôdeh (طاحونة جوده, 'mill of Jôdeh ').—Jôdeh is said to have been one of an older tribe dispossessed by the 'Adwân. There are two mills named from him, one in Wâdy Kefrein, one near Tell Iktanu.

Taihin (طيهين).—Ruins north of the Rujm Taihin; they appear to be the remains of houses of the Roman or Byzantine period. The foundations are of well-cut stones of large size, but the site is a small one.

Talâ el 'Aly (طلع العلي, 'the lofty ascent ').

Talât el Benât (طلعة البنات, 'ascent of maidens ').—A conspicuous knoll east of 'Ain Minyeh, used as a trigonometrical point.

Talât Heisah, or el Heithah (طلعة هيسه).—This is the valley with a path leading up on the south side of Mount Nebo. It may, perhaps, be a corruption of the Hebrew Luhith. The ascent of Luhith (Is. xv. 5; Jer. xlviii. 5) might very well be that leading to the plateau near Nebo.

Talât el Makharrakât (طلعة المخرقات, apparently 'ascent of flat places'; from خرق).—See Freytag's Lexicon.

Talât Reiyeh (طلعة ريه, 'well-watered ascent ').—Omitted as doubtful.

Tassin (طسين).—A ruined village with foundations of houses and small ruined watch-towers on a flat ridge. It was explored, but nothing of interest was observed.

Et Teim (التيم, 'the desert;' cf. Lane and Freytag).—This is a large ruin—a Byzantine town on two sides of a flat valley north-east of Ma'ain. Foundations and walls of houses, caves, cisterns, remains of rough masonry, and cairns of stone remain. Burckhardt suggested its identity with Kiriathaim (Jer. xlviii. 1; Ezek. xxv. 9), which is, however, now fixed at Kureiyât, further south.

Teleil Muslim (تليل مسلم, 'the little mound of Muslim ').—Is said to be the grave of a warrior.

Teleilât el Beid (تليلات البيض, ' the little white mounds ').

Et Tell (التلّ, 'the mound ').—A conspicuous knoll north-east and close to esh Shemsâni. There is an old sheep-fold on the top.

Tell Abu Kurr (تلّ ابو قرّ, ' mound of the flat ground ').—A mound, possibly natural, close to the stream of Wâdy Kefrein.

Tell Bileibil (تلّ بليبل, ' mound of the bulbuls ').—This is a hill-spur, with sides artificially scarped, and with a flat top. It is of very large size.

Tell Dcheileh (تلّ دحيله, ' hollow mound ').—This name appears to apply to a hill-spur east of Kefrein.

Tell Dufiânet esh Shânab (تلّ دفيانة الشعنب, ' mound of the cemetery of Shânab ').—Arab graves near Shânab.

Tell Ghassûl (تلّ غسّول, ' mound of the water used for washing '). —There are several little hillocks of sand here strewn with pottery and glass.

Tell el Hammâm (تلّ الحمّام, ' mound of the hot bath ').—This takes its name from the thermal spring to the west called el Hammâm, (see under that heading). The ruin on the mound is called Kuriet el Hammâm, but the real name is probably lost. The ruin is not important. The Tell is a flat natural hillock. Foundations and heaps of small stones remain. This Tell 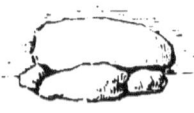 marks approximately the northern limit of the great dolmen field, which extends southwards to the vicinity of Tell el Matâbà (which see). There

 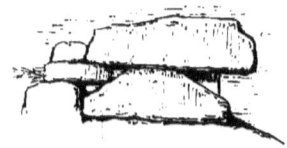

are some twenty or thirty dolmens at least on the spurs near el Mâberah, and others again to the north-east, near 'Ain el Meheiyineh. Under the head el Mâberah, a curious monument of this class is described. The dolmens near it and above Tell el Hammâm on the east are small, and are roughly constructed of brown crystalline limestone. They are,

however, very well-preserved specimens. Five of them were here sketched by Captain Conder, one having a capstone 7 feet long, supported about 4 feet from the ground. The others consist of three, four, or five stones, and are about the same size.

Tell Hebbesch (تل حبش, perhaps named from 'Ain Hebbesch, which see).—A natural hillock of limestone at the foot of the hills. On the south are ruins about 20 to 30 yards across, consisting of rough stones of the peculiar dark brown limestone of the district. Many dolmens exist round it.

Tell Iktanu (تل اكتنو).—A natural hillock of dark limestone and basalt, about 100 feet high and 40 yards in diameter. On the top there are many heaps of limestone blocks, but no walls standing. It has been proposed to identify this spot with Zoar (see Tell esh Shaghûr), on the supposition that its name means 'little'; but the pronunciation was very carefully ascertained, and the K is a *Caf*, not a *Koph*, as would be necessary if it were connected with the root קטן, while the T is a *Tau*, and not a *Teth*. The suggestion can therefore hardly be maintained.

Tell el Jorfeh (تل الجرفه, 'mound of the bank').—A little hillock, on which lay two pillar-stumps. It seems to be perhaps an old site.

Tell Kefrein.—See Kefrein.

Tell el Mahder.—See el Mahder. The name applies to a small mound west of the principal ruin in the valley. It is omitted from the reduced map as unimportant.

## JORDAN VALLEY DOLMENS.

Tell el Matâbá (تل المطابع, 'sealed mound').—From this Tell the rude-stone monuments occur along the low spurs just above the plain in great numbers, as far north as Wâdy el Kefrein—a distance of 2¼ miles. It was estimated that in this distance at least 200 to 300 monuments must exist, but they are generally smaller and ruder than the fine examples described under the heads el Maslûbiyeh and el Kurmîyeh. They are all of hard crystalline limestone blocks. Some of the more northern specimens are described under the heads Tell el Hammâm and el Mâberah. The group was, however, not so carefully examined as were those above mentioned, in consequence of want of time. The Arabs know of no other group of such remains between those at Kefrein here noticed, and the group discovered in 1820 by Irby and Mangles, beside the road from the Dâmieh to es Sâlt, south of the Zerka or Jabbok, and—as in the present instance—close to the east edge of the Jordan plain.

Close to the Tell is a stone circle, possibly modern, 30 paces (45 feet) in diameter, and beside the road. The wall is higher than usual on the south-west, where it stands 4 feet high, being about 2 feet in other parts. The stones are rudely heaped together, and not regularly arranged.

The Tell itself is a large natural hillock, on which five monuments stand in a rude circle—or, rather, arc of a circle—which measures 70 paces or 60 yards in all, from the most north-eastern to the example furthest south-west. This group appears to be the one mentioned by Canon Tristram ('Land of Moab'). The dolmens were measured and described by Lieutenant Mantell.

No. 1 is a very peculiar monument, unlike any other observed in Moab, but not unlike some of the cists found in tumuli in England (see Fergusson's 'Rude-stone Monuments,' pp. 142, 158). Three stones, 6 feet, 3½ feet, and 12 feet respectively in length, are placed end to end in a line bearing 347°, or nearly north and south. The first, or northern stone, is 4½ feet high, 2 feet 3 inches thick, and has a curious slit in its upper face 1½ feet long, 5 inches broad, 1 foot deep. The middle stone is 3 feet high and 21 inches thick. The third, or southern stone, is only 14 inches thick, but is 5 feet high. On the inner or west side of this line of stones three stones project at right angles, forming compartments. The southern of these three stones is 6 feet long, 3 feet high, 1½ feet thick. The middle stone is 4 feet 9 inches long, 4 feet high, 15 inches thick, and has through it a hole measuring 2 feet 10 inches either way.* The third stone is 5 feet long, 3 feet high, and 10 inches thick.

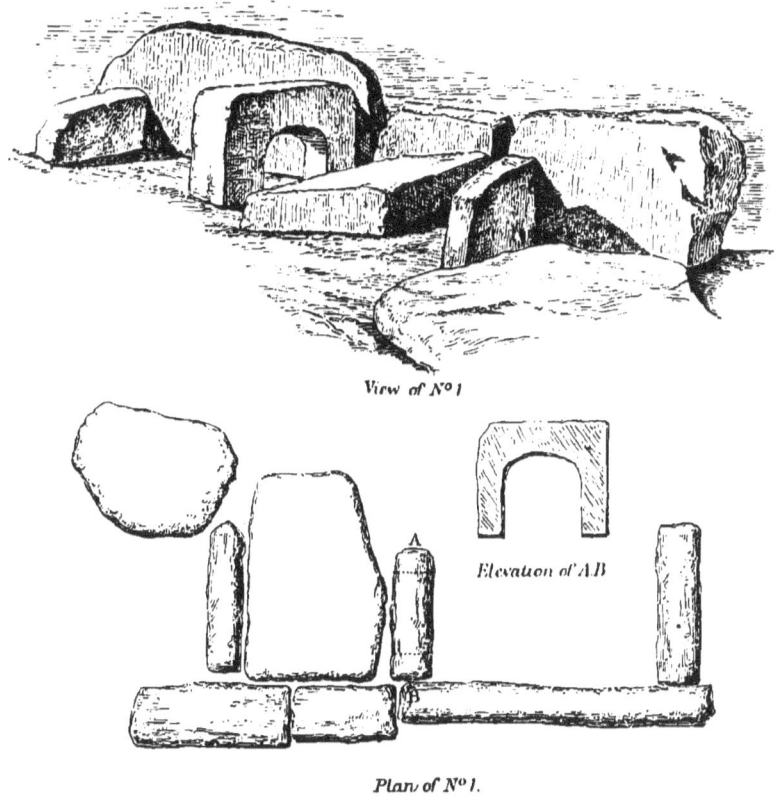

View of Nº 1

Elevation of AB

Plan of Nº 1.

Scale of Feet

In addition to the stones so arranged there are two other blocks. One

* Holes in menhirs are well known in Cornwall, in Scotland, etc. They are often connected with the superstitious custom of 'passing through'—*e.g.*, crawling through a menhir or under a dolmen. Perhaps this holed stone had such an original use.

has fallen within the middle compartment, and measures 6 feet by 7½ feet, and about 1½ to 2 feet in thickness. The second stone, fallen west of the northern compartment, is 7 feet square and 2 feet thick. This monument is towards the north-east side of the Tell, and is surrounded by a sort of platform, or flat mound, of undressed stones measuring about 20 yards in diameter. Possibly a grave may exist beneath this mound. The arrangement of the stones is most like that of the contiguous dolmens at el Maslûbîyeh. The monument does not seem to have been covered with any cairn or mound in either case.

No. 2 is 14 paces (35 feet) west of the preceding, on the flat surface of the Tell. In this case a single stone, perhaps a fallen menhir, is surrounded by a circle 9 paces (22 feet) in diameter. Traces of smaller stones were observed west of the large one, and within the circle. The large stone (cf. the menhirs L N O at 'Ammân)

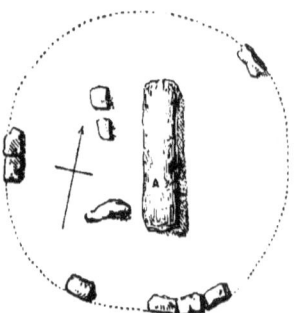

ELEVATION OF A IN NO. 2.   SKETCH PLAN OF NO. 2.

lies in a line 350° true bearing, and is 11 feet long and 5 feet high at the south end, tapering towards the other. It is 1½ feet thick, and on one side (the eastern) there is, near the southern end (which is, perhaps, the base), a hollow 1½ feet long, 8 inches wide, and sunk 6 inches. The stones composing the circle are flush with the present surface of the Tell, which has, no doubt, gradually risen since the monument was erected.

No. 3, 23 paces (57 feet) west-south-west of the last, has two side-stones placed approximately in the same line with the last stone (350° true bearing). These are 4½ feet apart; one of them measures 16 feet in length, 5 feet in height, 1 foot in thickness; the other is 10½ feet long, 1 foot thick, and 2½ feet high. There is a small endstone only 6 inches high, and a floorstone 8 feet by 4½ feet, but no traces were found of any capstone.

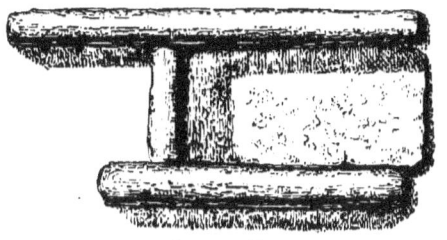

PLAN OF No. 3.

The remains of a circle surrounding this monument were observed. About a third of the circumference is visible, and the dolmen is not quite in the middle of this enclosure. The circle, or platform, was about 10 paces (25 feet) in diameter. Similar circles of small stones occur also round the dolmens near Tell el Kâdy and at el Kurmîyeh, and in the Jaulân examples.*

No. 4 is 9 paces south of the last, and is a small menhir standing erect all alone; it is 4 feet high, 3½ feet wide at the base, and 9 inches thick. The broad sides (as in the Hajr el Mansûb; cf. el Mareighât) are on the north and south. This menhir is towards the west side of the Tell.

No. 4.
Tell el Matâba.

No. 5 is 24 paces east of the curious monument which has been called No. 1. It is a somewhat similar structure, and, as in Nos. 1 and 3, there

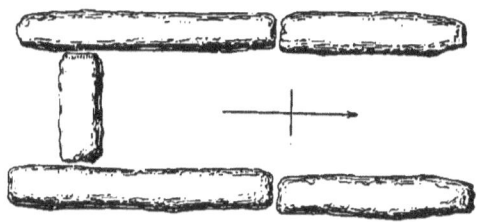

Nº 5 Tell el Matâba

Herr Schumacher ('Across the Jordan,' pp. 63, 64, 70, 152) gives drawings of two or three dolmens at 'Ain Dakkâr and Tisîl in the Jaulân. He says that the dolmens in the former group are always built on terraces, and shows one surrounded by a quadrangular enclosure. He also refers (p. 67) to circular openings in the stones, such as Irby and Mangles noticed at the Jabbok in the group they visited.

is no trace of any covering or table stone. No. 5 consists of five stones, two placed end to end, north and south; two others parallel to these and 4½ feet from them (clear internal measure); while the fifth is an endstone on the south. The two southern stones are 10 feet long each; the western of the two is 1 foot thick, 3 feet high; the eastern is 1½ feet thick and 3½ feet high. The two northern stones are respectively 7 feet and 7½ feet long; the first, or western, of these is 1½ feet thick and 2 feet high, the eastern 1½ feet thick, 3 feet 3 inches high. The endstone is 4½ feet long, 1½ feet thick, 4 feet high. The south-eastern stone has, in its south-east angle, a niche 1 foot long, 8 inches high, 4 inches deep (compare No. 2). This monument appears to have been surrounded by a platform, which was about 20 yards in diameter, and covered with small stones heaped up to the very foot of the dolmen.

N° 6 Tell el Mataba.

In addition to this remarkable group, five other examples were recorded by Lieutenant Mantell. The first (No. 6) is a dolmen some 300 yards east of the Tell, and near the road. The capstone is 7 feet square and 15 inches thick. It is supported on three stones, one each side, one at the end. The sidestones are 3 feet apart in the clear. One is 6 feet high, 4½ feet long, 8 inches thick. The other is only 2 feet high, 5 feet long, 1 foot thick, but a smaller stone is here placed above the sidestone, to support the cap in the required position. The second example (No. 7) is a single stone (like that described as No. 2). It is 6 feet long, 10 inches thick, and 1½ feet wide or high. Probably it has fallen down on its side. It was surrounded by a rude platform of stones, about 5 paces (12 feet) in diameter.

These platforms and circles resemble those on, or within, which the dolmens found in Algeria sometimes stand (*cf.* Fergusson's 'Rude-stone Monuments,' pp. 398, 401).

Near some of the dolmens of this group—within a radius of 10 yards—a great many small stones, measuring about 6 inches to a foot across, are piled up, but these are not sufficiently numerous to indicate any cairn covering the dolmen. They were observed also in some cases at the Kurmiyeh group, and elsewhere, and they seem possibly to have been there placed by the shepherds as propitiatory offerings to the ghouls supposed commonly to inhabit the dolmens. The practice of erecting such little cairns, as memorials of individual visits, is, however, common to many early races, as, for instance, to the Celts of Scotland. It is also a Jewish custom at Jerusalem and elsewhere.

The examples further north were not so large, and were rudely formed without either platforms or circles surrounding them. They were explored by Captain Conder, who measured five examples (see Tell el Hammâm). Close to the menhir No. 7 Lieutenant Mantell measured subsequently three other dolmens. The first was 18 paces south of the menhir, and had a capstone 10 feet by 5 feet, and $2\frac{1}{2}$ feet thick. The sidestones were 2 feet 3 inches high, and one 3 feet 8 inches long, 1 foot 2 inches thick, the other 4 feet 3 inches long, $2\frac{1}{2}$ feet thick. The next example, 13 paces south-west of the last, has a capstone 8 feet by 4 feet, and 1 foot thick. The sidestones are 4 feet 3 inches high, and 8 feet long, and 3 feet apart in the clear. The third example is only 4 paces west of the last. The topstone has disappeared. One sidestone is 6 feet long, 2 feet 9 inches high, and $1\frac{1}{2}$ feet thick. The other sidestone is $5\frac{1}{2}$ feet long, 1 foot only in height, and $1\frac{1}{2}$ feet thick.

These examples are fairly representative of the remains in this group, including menhirs, dolmens, circles, etc., all together at one site. The extraordinary stone called Mensef Abu Zeid is in the plain not far west of the dolmens.

It should be observed that Wâdy Hesbân appears to be a great centre of the dolmen builders, and it is very remarkable that careful exploration did not lead to the discovery of a single example north of Wâdy Kefrein, although the stream of Nimrin seems an equally likely site for such remains.

Explored October 26 and 27, 1881.*

* The following is a list of dolmen centres at present known in Syria :

600 to 700 explored in 1881.
1. Maslûbiyeh, 150 specimens.
2. Mareighât, 150 specimens.
3. Kurmiyeh and el Kalû'a, 50 specimens.
4. Ghor es Seisaban (Tell Matâb'a), 300 specimens.
5. 'Ammân, 20 specimens.

Tell el Meselhah (تل المسلحة, 'mound of the place of weapons'). —Near Tell er Râmeh on the north. There are some half-dozen underground dwellings in the Tell, said to be ancient; they have entrances built of masonry, and are inhabited by the Ghawarneh, who are serfs of the 'Adwân. These are apparently regarded as storehouses for arms.

Tell el Mustâh (تل المسطاح, 'flat mound').—Traces of ruins on a flat mound east of Tell Bileibil.

## NIMRIM.

Tell Nimrin (تل نمرين, 'mound of Nimrin').—The Hebrew Beth Nimrim, or Beth Nimrah, meaning 'house of abundant waters' (*cf.* Josh. xiii. 27; Num. xxxii. 3; Is. xv. 6; Jer. xlviii. 34). 'The waters of Nimrim,' mentioned by the prophets, are the perennial streams of good drinkable fresh water in Wâdy Nimrîn. The stream bathes the north foot of the Tell, and is surrounded with canes and shrubs. It flows as a brook, even in autumn, in the deep Wâdy Shâib, where its course is hidden by canes resembling Wâdy Kelt. The stream is fed by springs in the mountains north of the Survey, and the head-waters are found in the magnificent 'Ain Jeidûr at es Sâlt. This site was known to Eusebius and Jerome (see Reland's 'Palestine,' ii., p. 650) as being five Roman miles north of Lybias (Tell er Râmeh). It is called Βηθναβραν and Βηθντμρα. The confusion of the B and M was probably due either to a

---

6. South of the Jabbok (Irby and Mangles).
7. Sûf and northwards (Finn, etc.).
8. Wâdy Wâleh (two menhirs, Irby and Mangles).
9. Near Baniâs (Tell el Kady). Discovered by Conder in 1882.
10. Galilee (Upper and Lower). Five dolmens and a circle.
11. South of Sidon. A quadrangle of menhirs.
12. Bashan. (See Herr Schumacher's report.)

The following are the ancient circles discovered by the Survey party. Others occur south of the Zerka Mâ'ain.

| Hadânieh. | Kôm Yâjûz. |
| Neba. | El Mahder. |
| Râs el Merkeb. | El Mâberah. |
| Umm Huwatt. | |

See descriptions under those heads.

clerical error or to local pronunciation, as in the cases of Jamnia = Jabnia, etc., etc.

The Tell is a conspicuous object in the plain, being very white and lofty, and surrounded with dark groves of the *sidr*, or lotus-tree. It resembles Tell Kefrein, but is flatter. On the top there are three masonry tombs like the Kabr Fendi el Faiz, which are graves of the chiefs of the elder, or Diâb branch, of the 'Adwân. Smaller graves surround them, and with exception of scattered stones there are no other remains on the mound. The water in the stream to the north was found to have a temperature of 75° F., and this with an air temperature of about 95° in the shade. East of the Tell is a small modern *shûneh*, or 'barn' tower, and remains of a mill lade.

Tell Nimrin was visited by Sir C. Warren ('Quarterly Statement,' 1870, p. 285). He speaks of a sculpture on one of the tombs which escaped the observation of Captain Conder. It resembles that on the tomb at 'Ain Hesbân, described under that heading, 'a man on horseback with a sword hanging in the air in front of the horse's head.'* A capital was also found by Sir C. Warren lying on the mound.

## Beth Haran.

Tell er Râmeh (تل الرامه).—This is the ancient Beth Haran (Num. xxxii. 36; a town of Gad, Josh. xiii. 27). In the Talmud it is called Beth Ramtha, בית רמתה ('Tal Jer Shebiith,' ix. 2), and to Eusebius and Jerome it was also known as Beth Ramtha ('Onomasticon'). Jerome informs us that Herod named this town Livias, after the wife of Augustus. Josephus speaks also of Libyas (Antiq., xiv. 1, 4) east of Jordan, probably the same place. Reland, however, seems to confuse this place with Julias, or Betharamphtha (Antiq., xviii. 2, 1), which seems to be Bethsaida, and in this he is followed by Neubauer and others (*cf.* Reland, vol. i., p. 496; vol. ii., pp. 642, 869).

The mound of er Râmeh is the most conspicuous feature of the Seisebân plain, and with Kefrein, Nimrin and Tell esh Shaghûr, certainly marks the site of an ancient town of importance. The Tell is 22 paces (55 feet) across at the top, and 70 feet high. The white tomb of Dâhis

---

* See 'Ain Hesbân. The account exactly applies to the carving at the latter place.

occupies the summit resembling the Kabr Fendi el Fâiz, or the Kabr Mujâhed on Tell Kefrein. There are also six or eight Arab graves round this monument, and on the south-east is the sacred place of el Khudr and the Kabr Sàid (see under those headings). The Tell is very white, and contrasts with the dark groves of lotus which surround it. There are remains of foundations on the top and on the slopes, just visible above the surface. The stream of Wâdy Hesbân on the north gives a fine perennial supply of fresh water.

## ZOAR.

Tell esh Shâghûr (تلّ الشاغور).—The word has no meaning in vernacular Arabic, but it may possibly be a corruption of the Hebrew צער, or Zoar, 'little,' a word which in Arabic becomes Saghir, صغير. Exception may, perhaps, be taken to the change of the Tzadi to Shin; but it is certain that Sâd and Sîn are interchanged in Bedawîn dialects (as in Sûk, etc.), and that Sîn and Shîn are also interchanged (as in Sejerah for Shejerah, etc.). It is thus quite possible that in course of time the change may have occurred from Zoar to Saghîr, and from Saghîr to Shâghûr. The identification was first suggested by the Rev. W. F. Birch, in the 'Quarterly Statement' of the Palestine Exploration Fund.

The situation of Tell esh Shâghûr fits well the requirements of Zoar. It is on the border of Moab (Jer. xlviii. 34) and of the Jordan plain (Deut. xxxiv. 3). In the lowlands (Gen. xix. 19), and not far from the vicinity of the Cities of the Plain with which it is enumerated (Gen. xiv. 2) in the Vale of Siddim, 'which is the Salt Sea.'

As regards the traditional site of Zoar in the fourth century little need be said, as the authority is of so small a value. A place named Zoar was the station of the Equites Sagittarii Indigenæ (Notitia Imperii Romani), and the see of a bishop of Palestina Tertia in the fifth century (see Reland, 'Palest. Illustr.,' i., pp. 217, 230). It was south of Beth Nimrim ('Onomasticon,' s.v.; Reland, 'Palest. Illustr.,' p. 1066), and Eusebius (under the name Βαλα) says it was above the Dead Sea, and was in his own time a Roman garrison (Reland, p. 622). The remarks on these traditions, which will be found under the heading Khŭrbet Belâth, should be compared.

Antoninus Martyr (*circa* 570-600 A.D.), one of the few monkish travellers who have left us any notice of the sites beyond Jordan, says:

'De Jordani usque ad locum illum in quo Moyses de corpore exivit sunt millia octo et exinde non multum longe ad Segor, in quibus locis sunt multi eremiti.'

He thus seems to place Zoar in the hills—perhaps at Khŭrbet Belâth. The remains of the cells of hermits, such as those to which he alludes, are found at ed Deir and Muállakat Umm el Kenáfid. By the place of Moses' death he evidently means Mount Nebo, and it is not impossible that his Segor is really Siâghah on that ridge. This may also be the Bela and Zoora of the 'Onomasticon' (see Khŭrbet Belâth), in which case Canon Tristram has revived the early Christian tradition in placing Zoar at Siâghah (which he calls Ziara), but there can be little doubt as to the approximate site of the real Zoar.

The site of Tell esh Shâghûr is a whitish hillock of hard limestone, with a rounded rocky surface. It measures 170 paces (530 feet) north and south, by 55 paces (140 feet) east and west, and is highest to the south, where it is about 40 feet above the general surface of the plain. On the north it slopes gradually into the plain. On the east the rock has been quarried. On the north-west is a little hollow about 6 inches across, whence issues a small spring, which flows a few yards even in autumn. On the east again, some 15 yards away on the Tell, there is another larger spring surrounded with rushes and grass, the water from which flows down the Tell. Some 300 to 400 yards west of the Tell there are a few foundations of small stones, 1 foot to 1½ feet long, which are quite rough. This ruin is about 50 yards across, and appears to have been that of a little hamlet.

Visited October 27, 1881.

Thoghret el Beida (ثغرة البيضا, 'the white pass').—A mountain-pass with road.

Thoghret el Ghazlâniyeh (ثغرة الغزلانيّه, 'pass of the gazelles').—A road here crosses the ridge.

Thoghret es Sâjûr (ثغرة الساجور, 'pass of trees').—This is a common corruption for Shejerât 'trees,' and is interesting as bearing on what is said under the head Tell esh Shâghûr. The pass in question is covered with fine oaks. The name is not written on the reduced map, but applies close to 'Ain eth Thoghrah, and Sheikh el 'Ajemy.

Tòr Sebeit (طور سبيت, 'the bare hilltop;' from سبتا, 'bare').

Tor Zebneh (طور زبنه, 'the erect rock;' for زابنه=اكمه; *cf.* 'Lane's Lexicon').

Et Tûâfir (الطوافير, 'the leapings').—A plot of ground near 'Ain Fudeili. It is probably named from the cascades in the stream. This name is omitted from the reduced map.

Et Tubkah (الطبقه, 'the plateau' or 'terrace').—A small ruin with foundations and ruined walls.

Tubkat el Musheirfeh (طبقة المشيرفه, 'the terrace of the little high place').—Near Râs el Musheirfeh. A rocky top with foundations, and a rude-stone circle. A large tree occurs here with a cairn beneath.

Tuweiyil el 'Azzâm (طويل العزّام, 'the peak of the lion').—This is a knoll near 'Ain Minyeh.

Tuweiyil el Ghorbân (طويل الغربان, 'the peak of the ravens').

Umm 'Abharah (ام عبهره, 'mother of the Styrax Officinalis,' or 'mock orange'—a shrub common here).—A small ruin of walls and foundations.

Umm 'Areijât (ام عريجات, 'mother of ascents'). — A few walls.

Umm el 'Asâfir (ام العصافير, 'mother of sparrows').—The hill west of 'Ain Hesbân. The name is not on the reduced map.

Umm Askak (ام اسكك, 'mother of paths').—A plateau covered with many camel-tracks east of el 'Al.

Umm 'Ashireh (ام عشيره, 'mother of the tribe').—A hill-spur on the south side of Wâdy 'Ayûn edh Dhib.

Umm el Buruk (أم البرك, 'mother of tanks').—A ruin in a flat open valley, named from the rock-cut tanks here existing. The ruined site lies north of the principal tank, which is cut in a flat layer of rock, and has steps leading down in the south-west corner along the west wall. This tank is 40 feet wide east and west, by 37 north and south; the stair consists of eight risers, each step about 2 feet broad and 1 foot high. A thin partition of rock (10 inches broad) is left on the east of the flight, and a lintel-stone is placed at the end of this partition (which is 21 feet long), resting on the ground on the west side of the tank and on the partition; this stone is 7 feet 4 inches long by 3 feet, by 1½ feet thick. The tank is 8 feet deep on the south, all of rock; on the north the rock reaches up 5 feet, and a wall of two courses of stone, each 1½ feet high, makes the depth equal to 8 feet.

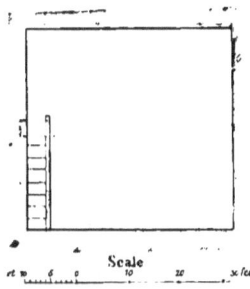

Scale

South of this tank there are two tombs cut in the face of a cliff, about 10 feet high, which faces north. They are of the kind described as 'rock-sunk' in the 'Memoirs of the Western Survey,' and were found in Western Palestine in Byzantine ruins (vol. ii., p. 320), and also in Crusading ruins (vol. i., p. 385; vol. ii., p. 322), and at Jerusalem, on Olivet, where they seem to be of Crusading date, but may be as early as the fourth century. The tombs at present under consideration have an alcove covering the shaft above ground, which is not found in the other cases mentioned; but this is probably due to their position in the cliff instead of being on flat ground. The alcove is 2 feet 8 inches high, and as wide as the shaft under it; the shaft is 4 feet 4 inches deep to the bottom, 6 feet long, 1 foot 8 inches wide, not including the flat rim for a cover-stone, which is 3 inches wide at the ends, and 9 inches at the sides. The two graves at the bottom of the shaft, under *arcosolia*, are 6 feet long, 2 feet wide, and the arch rises 1 foot 10 inches from the floor. These two tombs—alike in plan—have their alcoves facing north-east (Fig. 2, next page).

About 100 yards west of this pair of tombs is another in the same cliff of different character; it is a square chamber, 11 feet 2 inches east and

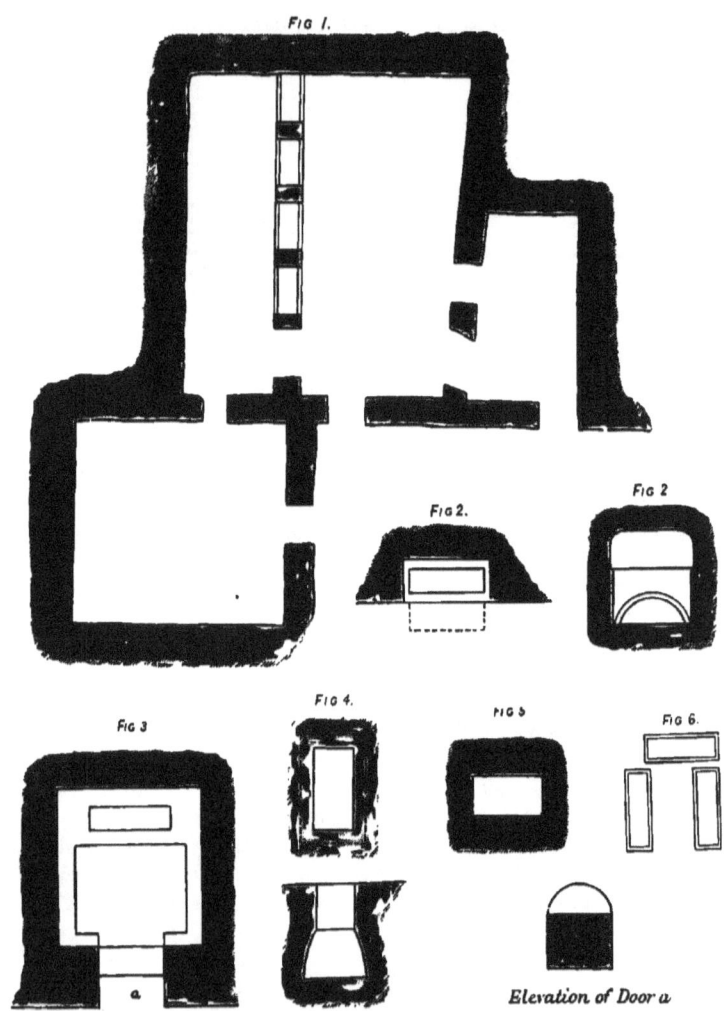

Fig. 1.—Umm el Buruk (Plan of Rock-cut Stable). Figs. 2, 3.—Umm el Buruk (Rock-cut Tombs). Figs. 4, 5, 6.—Umm el Hanáfish (Rock-cut Tombs).

west, 11 feet 9 inches north and south. It is 5 feet from floor to roof, with a door on the north 5 feet 2 inches wide, and 4 feet in height, with a flat top and a false arch or recess rising 2 feet 4 inches; a couple of steps lead down inwards in the passage, 4½ feet long, leading to the door from the face of the cliff (Fig. 3, preceding page).

Round the chamber runs a bench 14 inches high, and 15 inches wide except at the back, where it is 4½ feet wide. On this side a grave is sunk in the bench, 6 feet 4 inches long, 1 foot 10 inches wide.

Beyond this tomb further west is another tank, with side-chambers or troughs. It measures 17 feet east and west, by 21 feet north and south, and the depth varies from 2½ feet to 15 inches. It seems too large to have been a wine-press, though this is the possible use of the excavation. North of this tank is a small cistern 2 feet 8 inches square and 4 feet deep, with a square covering-stone having a hole in the middle 8 inches in diameter. There is a cliff further west again, with another tomb in it.

The ruined town or village immediately north of the remains just described shows foundations of houses supported on round-arched barrel vaults. The whole site only occupies some 50 yards east and west. Towards the west was found lying a lintel 3 feet long, and 1 foot 1 inch high, having a mutilated Greek inscription on a winged tablet :

ΑΝΤΩΝΙΟΣ ΡΟΥΦΟΣ ΕΑΥΤ
ΩΕΠΟΗΣΕ - - - - - ΗΜΕ
ΟΝΕ - - - - - - ΙΩΝ

This records the building of something at his own expense by Antonius Rufus. The limestone block is so much weathered as to be barely decipherable in part. There is another lintel-stone, 2 feet 5 inches long, 1 foot 1 inch high, lying near, also with a winged tablet in very low relief, but, if ever inscribed, it is now too weather-worn to show any trace of lettering. It lies north-east of the former.

Much of the material used in the house-walls is flint. The barrel vaulting of the cellars is of good ashlar. There are fragments of cornice with egg pattern much defaced. Cisterns cut in rock also occur, and there is a stone on which a rude Arab inscription has been scrawled. A cave entered by a well-mouth was examined, but the only other interesting feature of the site was a subterranean rock-cut stable towards the east side of the ruin, of which a plan was made. It consists of four chambers entered from the south. The central chamber is 13 feet wide, by 18 feet to the back ; that to the east about 7 feet by 14 feet, with a door on the south now blocked with stones ; and a door, and south of it a sort of window, communicating on the west with the central chamber. The flat rock-roof of the latter is $8\frac{1}{2}$ feet from the floor ; the east chamber is 6 feet high. The third chamber, west of the central one, is 7 feet wide east and west, and 18 feet long. The partition of rock between it and the central chamber is pierced by a door towards the south, and by four openings, under which are troughs or mangers 8 inches deep, and $3\frac{1}{2}$ feet from the floor at the top (2 feet 10 inches at bottom) ; they are 3 feet 5 inches long, 2 feet 2 inches wide, and the rock-sides 3 inches thick. The pillars between measure 16 inches by 26 inches, and support the roof. The end pier by the door is 1 foot by 26 inches.

The fourth chamber, reached by a door in the south wall of the last, is about 15 feet square, and had a door, now choked, on the east. Nothing has yet been found exactly like this supposed stable in the course of the Western Survey (Fig. 1, p. 243).

The general impression obtained from the character of the masonry, and from the form of the letters E Σ and Ω in the inscription, is that the ruins at this site are of the early Christian period—fourth to seventh centuries of our era.

Visited August 23, 1881.

Umm ed Dubâá (أمّ الضباع, 'mother of hyenas ').—A heap of stones and some small ruined flint towers near esh Shemsâni.

Umm 'Erneh (أمّ عرنه, 'mother of the nose ').—A sharp-pointed knoll with a heap of stones, on the brink of the descent to the Hammâm ez Zerka.

Umm Haleilîfeh (أمّ حليليفه, apparently 'mother of confederates ').—These ruins are south of the conspicuous tree east of Jubeihah, which was the most northerly trigonometrical station of the Survey. The ruins resemble those of Jubeihah, with a small watch-tower in the middle. Walls, heaps of stones, and caves were found among the trees, but nothing of distinctive character. The site may have been an ancient Heleph, as the name occurs west of Jordan in the Heleph of Naphtali.

Umm el Hanâfish (أم الصنافيش, 'mother of vipers').—A small Byzantine town, with an ancient road on the north, situated in a flat valley. On the east is the little hillock of Khŭrbet Hamzeh, which may be best described under the present head.

On the road north-west of the ruin lies a broken sarcophagus of the ordinary size, with its lid beside it. Heaps of pottery-chips, and other fragments, piled on and beside it, seem to show that the spot is held sacred by the Arabs. Near this, on the west, the rock has been quarried. The town occupies a sort of low mound, and on the lower part of this, towards the north-west, a 'rock-sunk' tomb was measured, like those found west of Jordan (cf. Umm el Buruk). The shaft in the present instance is 7 feet deep, 6 feet long, 3 feet wide, but under-cut below, making a tomb about 6 feet by 9 feet (Fig. 4, p. 243). North of this is an attached, or rock-cut, sarcophagus without a lid.

The city mound is about 200 yards across, with ruins of houses and vaults of rude masonry, and occasional pillar-stumps. The stones are from 1 foot to 3 feet in length, and, as a rule, are not squared. The vaults have the usual barrel form, with well-cut voussoirs, graduated from a narrow keystone to broad haunch-stones. Towards the east, by a fallen pillar stump, was found a fragment of ornamental lintel with a honeysuckle pattern. The stone measured 3 feet by 2 feet. The ornamentation is evidently Roman of a low type.

At the bottom of the mound, on the east, are fallen pillar-shafts, perhaps marking the site of a chapel.

The most conspicuous building is the Kŭsr, or tower, which is a small fort at the foot of the hill on the south-west. It measures 41 feet 10 inches along the north wall outside, and 34 feet along the east wall; the bearing of the former is 75°; the walls are 4 feet thick. The west wall is standing to a height of 15 feet, and has three loopholes. The north and east walls are standing about 8 feet high; the south wall is entirely destroyed, and the tower was perhaps once breached and taken from this side. The stones in these walls are from 18 inches to 40 inches in length, and the height of the course is about 1 foot. The outer stones are drafted, but not those on the inside of the wall. The draft is generally 2 inches wide, and the face within projects 1 inch; both boss and draft have been rudely dressed.

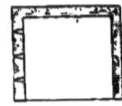

North-west of this tower, on the south side of the Tell or mound, is a modern sacred circle of the usual type, with a lintel on the south-west side of unusual height, the clear space under the stone being 3 feet. As usual (cf. 'Ain Hesbân, etc.), the ploughs and other property of the Arabs are stored within.

The knoll east of this town supports the Khŭrbet Hamzeh, where a small church or temple seems to have stood close to the town, with a cemetery on the slopes below. On the top of the knoll were found pillar-shafts, some standing, some fallen, but no regular plan could be made out. They are 1 foot 9 inches in diameter, and stand about

 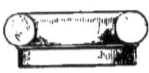 

3 feet high. A base was also found, 1 foot high and 1 foot 7 inches in diameter at the shaft. This base and the top of some of the shafts were pitted with holes, evidently made by shepherds for playing the Mankaleh game; and in one case the pebbles used in this game remained in the holes.

Below this group of pillars, on the east, is an alcove cut in rock facing eastwards, 9 feet wide, 5 feet high in the middle, 4 feet deep to the back, with an arched shape, like an *arcosolium*. It is probably the entrance to a tomb, the door or shaft of which is hid beneath the surface (cf. Umm el Buruk). Large coarse tesserae were strewn on the hill, and stones once composing the walls of the building, which are generally well dressed. South of the pillar-shafts was found an Ionic capital (cf. Siâghah, el 'Âl, etc.), 1 foot 10 inches in diameter of shaft. Some rock-cut cisterns were also found on or west of the knoll. The cemetery is on the south-west slope, and consisted of rock-sunk tombs and rock sarcophagi. In some cases the tomb shaft was covered with a lid like that of a sarcophagus. The most western example had a shaft 4½ feet long, with an *arcosolium* about 6 feet long each side at the bottom (Fig. 5, p. 243). There are two others like it, and further east is a group of three sarcophagi arranged in the flat rock, two parallel, one across at the end, each about 6 feet by 2 feet. In each case the heavy stone lid had been pushed on one side a little way, and this, no doubt, was done in order to rifle the tomb (Fig. 6, p. 243).

Graves of this class are very rare in Western Palestine, but occur at Seffûrieh ('Memoirs,' vol. i., p. 330).

The probable date of these ruins would be about the fourth century A.D.

Visited September 17, 1881.

Umm Huwatt (أمّ حوط). The root means 'to wall in ').—There are remains of old stone circles here resembling that at Hadânieh, whence the name. It is deep down in Wâdy Kefrein. The name is omitted from the reduced map, as the site was not exactly fixed. It is east of Abu Safa.

Umm Jereisât (أمّ جريسات, 'mother of bells ').—There are foundations here, and dolmens, which are described under the head Wâdy Jideid.

Umm el Kehâkir (أمّ الكهاقير, 'mother of stone-piles ').—A ruin on a knoll east of Kefrein. The road here crosses the Thoghret el Ghazlâniyeh, and comes in view of the sacred tombs at Tell Râmeh and Tell Kefrein. The Arabs consequently erect on the knoll Kehâkir, or small stone-piles—called also Meshâhed—such as are common in Syria. Neby Mûsa is also visible.

Umm el Kenâfid (أمّ الكنافد, 'mother of hedgehogs ').—A good-sized ruin at the top of Wâdy Hesbân, just below the plateau of the Belka. There are half a dozen modern houses on the Tell, and enclosures with drystone walls. Ruins of walls of rude masonry occur on the slopes and terraces of the Tell, which has a flat top about 150 yards across.

About a quarter of a mile to the south-east, where a cave and cistern are marked on the map, stands a pillar on the rock, 2 feet 8 inches high and 2 feet thick; one side has been cut flat. There is a cistern partly of rock, partly of masonry above the rock, close to the pillar; it has the usual 'bell-mouth,' and near it are remains of a rock-cut wine-press; there is also a cave, and foundations remain of a building about 90 feet east and west, by 50 feet north and south. A few rudely-dressed stones are scattered near.

In the valley below the Tell is the 'Ain Umm el Kenâfid on the south-west, and the valley here becomes narrow and deep. A little further down in a cliff, on the east side, is seen high up the entrance to a hermit's cave called Muállakat ('the overhanging' or 'precipitous place') Umm el Kenâfid; it is now used as a granary by the Arabs. Passing down further, the valley is found clothed with terebinths, and on the path is a great boulder in which a tomb is cut; it is 8 feet 8 inches long, and 4 feet in width, and 4 feet high; the door is 3 feet high, 2 feet wide. A slab seems to have been placed on a setback of 9 inches in the chamber, 14 inches from the floor. The boulder is 12 feet square, the door on the south. A second, which has fallen on one side, with a similar chamber, was found near.

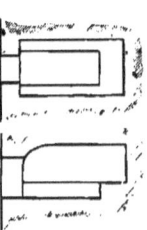

Visited August 23, 1881.

Umm el Kindib (ام الكندب, probably an error for جندب. The word is pronounced Chindib or Jindib, and with the Jim is a well-known word. It is, therefore, to be rendered 'mother of the locusts').—The ruin is that of a former village, or small town, on a spur; but it does not appear to be very ancient. The rock is extensively quarried on the south, and beside the road, on the hill, lies a rock-cut drinking-trough. The Arabs were busy cleaning the mud out of wells on the south-west of the mound, supporting the ruined houses, and thus preparing for the rains. Water is stored in the old wells and cisterns in all parts of this district where no springs exist. Caves, cisterns, foundations of un-squared stones, mostly of chert or the flinty rock which runs in bands through the chalk, are numerous at this spot.

On the hill to the west there is a quadrangular enclosure about 100 yards north and south, by 40 yards east and west, built of one course of unshaped flint-blocks. The guide called it a *Kenîseh*, or 'church,' but it is more probably only a garden. North of it a rock-cut cistern was found, having a little pan cut in the rock beside it about 10 feet square. The rain ran from the pan into a little round well or filter 1 or 2 feet deep and 3 feet in diameter, where the water settled, the clean water flowing over it into the cistern. The ancient enclosures north of this site are described under the heading Rujm er Rûâk.

Umm el Kutifeh (ام الكطيفه, 'mother of the St. John's wort').— A long ridge by which the road ascends from Kefrein to 'Arâk el Emir. Wild-flowers are plentiful here in spring.

Umm Kuseir (ام قصير, 'mother of the little house or tower').— Professor Palmer renders Kusr 'palace;' but it is not generally used in this sense in Palestine, meaning usually a square tower or house. It is a small ruin, with scattered stones and foundations of houses.

Umm el Lôz (ام اللوز, 'mother of almonds').—This is a hilltop south-west of 'Arâk el Emir.

Umm el Medâris (ام المدارس, 'mother of threshing-floors').—This is a hill close to 'Arak el Emir.

Umm Râsein (ام راسين, 'mother of two heads').—A hill with two tops south of Maâin.

Umm Resûm (ام رسوم, 'mother of traces,' *i.e.*, of ruins or of Arab camping-grounds, etc.).—It is a place south of 'Ain Minyeh, without any ruins of importance.

Umm er Rumam (ام الرمم, 'mother of heights').—Possibly this name may be connected with the Hebrew ארמונית (Amos i. 14), rendered 'palaces,' but meaning fortifications, or high places. They were connected with Rabbath Ammon, and the present ruin is close to that city on the south. Only a few foundations now remain on a high spur with a cliff beneath; but the situation is appropriate for a citadel guarding the town on this side, as the ridge is higher than that of the fortress of 'Ammân.

Umm es Semmâk (ام السماق, 'mother of sumach-trees'—there are, however, no trees now).—See 'Aweilet Umm es Semmâk. The ruin is extensive, being that of a Roman or Byzantine town. Pillar-shafts and capitals, with pedestals and pilasters, occur fallen among the foundations of public buildings and houses. The plans of the buildings could not be made out.

**Umm esh Shûâmir** (ام الشوامر), 'mother of hemlocks').—A hill-top south of Mââîn.

**Umm Suweiwineh** (ام صوّيوينه, 'mother of little flints').—Remains of a small town; the houses all built of chert or flint, which is rudely chipped into blocks of convenient size. There are some small towers or square houses in the ruin, which are conspicuous from a distance. The place stands on flat ground, with a precipice and a deep valley to the west. There are many of these flint villages in ruins on the 'Ammân plateau, at 'Abdûn, Khûrbet Sâr, and elsewhere, which are very conspicuous on account of the dark colour of the flint. They may probably be erections of the early Christian period, resembling the flint towns near Beersheba (at Tell Sâweh, etc.), which are found in a similar district where the bands of chert run through the soft chalk.

Visited October 10, 1881.

**Umm Zueitineh.**—See el Mareighât.

**Wâdy Adamah** (وادي ادمه, 'valley of Adam,' or of ' red earth').

**Wâdy el 'Adeimeh** (وادي العضيمه, 'valley of the streak ').—See el 'Adeimeh.

**Wâdy Abu en Naml** (وادي ابو النمل, 'valley of ants').—There is also a plot of ground further north called Abu en Naml, and there is a Wâdy en Naml west of Jordan. These names may perhaps be derived from the legend which is to be found in the Korân (Sura xxvii. 18, called en Namleh) of the visit which Solomon paid to the valley of ants accompanied by his troops and by the genii. The localization of such legends in Syria is common, *e.g.*, the Tannûr, the 'city of the grove,' the place where Saleh's camel was killed, all which are shown by the Syrian Moslems, not in Arabia, but in Palestine.

**Wâdy Abu Nukleh.**—See Bir Abu Nukleh.

**Wâdy Abu Redeineh.**—See Abu Redeineh.

Wâdy Abu Reghif.—See Abu Raghif. This name is not on the reduced map.

Wâdy Abu Turfah.—See 'Ain Abu Turfah.

Wâdy 'Ajeirmân.—See 'Ain 'Ajeirmân.

Wâdy 'Ammân.—See 'Ammân.

Wâdy 'Amr· (وادي عمر).—This names signifies 'ancient,' but it is somewhat remarkable that it occurs close to the Dead Sea, in the vicinity of the most probable site of Gomorrah (עֲמֹרָה), as the Arabic is radically the same with the Hebrew. It would, however, be unwise to lay stress on this coincidence, because the name is so common in Palestine both as a proper name and as a topographical term. Professor Palmer suggested a connection of the names 'Amr, 'Amriyeh, etc., with the Amorites, but it should be noted that the name of this tribe (אמרי) is spelt with *Aleph*.

Wâdy 'Anâzeh.—See Jebel 'Anâzeh.

Wâdy 'Areik er Raml (وادي عريق الرمل), 'valley of the little sandy cliff').—Omitted, as of little value, from the reduced map.

Wâdy el 'Atab (وادي العطب), 'valley of soft ground ').

Wâdy 'Ayûn edh Dhib (وادي عيون الذيب), 'valley of the springs of the wolf ').—There is a perennial supply of water in the valley-bed from the springs of this name. It is, however, not so copious as are the streams in valleys to the north and south.

Wâdy 'Ayûn Mûsa.—See 'Ayûn Mûsa.

Wâdy el Bahhâth.—See 'Ain el Bahhâth.

Wâdy Bareiz.—See Sidd Bareiz.

Wâdy Barrâkât.—See el Barrâkât.

Wâdy el Beidah (وادي البيضه, 'the white valley ').—Omitted from the reduced map.

Wâdy Belâl.—See Khŭrbet Belâl.

Wâdy el Butm (وادي البطم), 'valley of terebinths ').—There do not appear to be any trees here now.

Wâdy ed Dâlieh (وادي الداليه), 'valley of the vine ').—Near Tell el Matâba. Omitted from the reduced map for want of space.

Wâdy Derbâsy.—See Jôfet ed Derbâsy.

Wâdy Dindy (وادي دندي).—This is omitted as doubtful.

Wâdy el Fâlij (وادي الثالج, 'the valley of the gutter').—Omitted as of little value.

Wâdy el Gharbeh.—See el Gharbeh. Omitted from the reduced map as of no value.

Wâdy Ghûeir (وادي غوير, 'valley of the little hollow or chasm'). —This is the lower part of Wâdy Jideid, issuing near 'Ain Sûeimeh. Several ancient roads ascend by this valley to Medeba, or to Beth Meon. The name is, in meaning, equivalent to the Hebrew חור, a hollow or cavern, and comes from an allied root. 'The ascent of Horonaim' (Jer. xviii. 5 and 34; Isaiah xv. 5) might very probably have led from the Jordan Valley, and seems identified, perhaps, with the ascent of Luhith. This would exactly agree with the situation of Wâdy Ghûeir, and of the Talât Heisah (which see). Josephus speaks of Oronas as a town of Moab (13 Ant. xv. 4).

Wâdy el Habis.—See el Habis.

Wâdy Haddâdeh.—See Haddâdeh.

Wâdy Haleilifeh.—See Umm Haleilifeh.

Wâdy Hamârah.—See 'Amûd el Inkliziyeh.

Wâdy el Hammâm.—See el Hammâm.

Wâdy el Haud.—See el Haud.

Wâdy Hawârah (وادي حواره, 'the valley of marl').

Wâdy el Hekr.—See 'Ain el Hekr.

Wâdy Hesbân.—See Hesbân.

Wâdy Jâwah.—See Jâwah.

Wâdy el Jebârah (وادي الجباره, 'valley of the bracelet').

Wâdy Jemn (وادي جمن).

Wâdy Jemmâlah.—See 'Ain Jemmâlah.

Wâdy el Jerbah (وادي الجربه, 'valley of the plantation').

Wâdy Jeriâh.—See 'Ain Jeriâh.

Wâdy el Jiâma (وادي الجياما, 'valley of ascents').—This is an Arab mispronunciation for قبالة.

### DOLMENS.

Wâdy Jideid (وادي جديد).—Under this head may be described the rude-stone monuments which extend westwards from the watershed all along the south slope of the valley, including those near el Kueijiyeh, and those north of el Maslûbiyeh.* This district, surrounding the great Hadânieh circle (which see), was very carefully explored, and in an area of about two square miles no less than 162 dolmens were measured, examined, and sketched.

The first group is on the hillside, immediately south of the Hadânieh circle, commencing low down towards the west, at the edge of the steepest part of the slope, those following being on flat slopes.

No. 1 was a fallen specimen of three good-sized blocks.

No. 2 was 5 feet south of the last, and also fallen; the capstone was 7 feet square.

No. 3, some 20 yards south of the last, is almost indistinguishable.

No. 4, about 25 yards east of the last, has a capstone of irregular shape, measuring 10 feet by 8½ feet, having two hollows in the upper

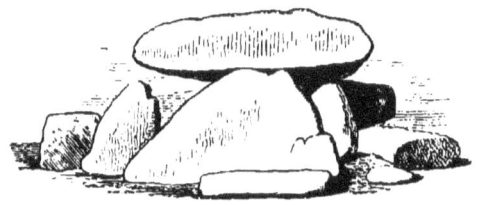

Nº 4.

surface 10 inches by 14 inches, by 6 inches deep. The clear height beneath is 3 feet, the sidestones are irregular, and an endstone 3 feet

* The reasons for considering this Maslûbiyeh to be Bamoth Baal are given in 'Heth and Moab,' chap. iv.

square exists; the sidestones, 4 feet apart, are 8 feet by 3 feet, and $9\frac{1}{2}$ feet by $5\frac{1}{2}$ feet, respectively, and each about $1\frac{1}{2}$ feet thick.

No. 5 is 6 yards east of the last; it has two sidestones 3 feet 8 inches apart. One is 5 feet 10 inches long, the other 7 feet 6 inches, and both $3\frac{1}{2}$ feet high. The capstone has fallen, but measured $8\frac{1}{2}$ feet by $5\frac{1}{2}$ feet.

No. 6 almost touches the last on the south; originally, they were about 2 paces apart, but have fallen against each other. These are on the edge of the steep north-east slope of the spur. The capstone of No. 6 is 9 feet by 8 feet; the sidestones $8\frac{1}{2}$ feet long, 4 feet high; the endstone is $3\frac{1}{2}$ feet by 4 feet, and there was a floorstone 5 feet long by 2 feet 8 inches wide beneath. The cap has fallen, but this monument was originally a well-shaped specimen.

No. 7, close to the last on the south-east, has fallen in a downhill direction. Nos. 4, 5, 6, and 7 thus form a line along the edge of the steep slope, as close together as they could be placed, in the direction of the contour of the hill. The topstone of No. 7 is $8\frac{1}{2}$ feet by 6 feet, the clear height was 3 feet 3 inches, the sidestones 7 feet by 2 feet thick; the endstone on the south is 18 inches broad; the distance between the sidestones is $2\frac{1}{2}$ feet.

No. 8 is about 30 paces west of the last, rather higher up, and south of No. 4. It has a capstone $7\frac{1}{2}$ feet by $9\frac{1}{2}$ feet, and 22 inches thick, two sidestones 4 feet long by $3\frac{1}{2}$ feet high each, and 21 inches thick, and an endstone 3 feet wide on the west.

No. 9, near the last, is in ruins; the capstone was $8\frac{1}{2}$ feet by 6 feet.

No. 10, about 15 yards east of No. 8, has a topstone $6\frac{1}{2}$ feet by 8 feet, and $1\frac{1}{2}$ feet thick. It has an endstone on the east 3 feet square. The sidestones are $7\frac{1}{2}$ feet long. The clear height, beneath the cap, is 3 feet.

No. 11 is 3 yards south of the last, and has fallen downhill northwards. The topstone is 7 feet by 9 feet, and 27 inches thick; the clear height was $3\frac{1}{2}$ feet, the sidestones 9 feet long. It was thus a very large low monument.

No. 12 is 15 paces south-east of No. 10, and is scattered. It was a very small one, the capstones only $4\frac{1}{2}$ feet long by 15 inches thick, by 2 feet 8 inches wide.

No. 13 is 4 paces south of the last; it has fallen downhill. The topstone was 8½ feet by 7 feet; the clear height 3½ feet; the clear width inside 3 feet; the sidestones 8½ feet long, 3½ feet high, 26 inches thick.

No. 14 is a very large well-made example. It is 6 paces from No. 13, and looks north-east, standing at the edge of a steep descent. The capstone is 8½ feet by 8 feet, with a rounded upper surface, and a curious boss 2 feet in diameter, and some 6 inches high — perhaps natural. The south sidestone is 8½ feet long, 3½ feet high, 21 inches thick. On the north are two sidestones, 3 feet long by 5 feet high,

No. 14.

and 5 feet long by 7 feet high, each 2 feet thick. The clear width is 3 feet, and the mean height 5 feet, beneath the table-stone. There are several smaller stones lying round, which may have formed some sort of enclosure.

No. 15 is fallen some 4 paces south-east of the last, and the contour of the hill is, in fact, here lined with dolmens, including Nos. 11 to 16. In

No. 16.

the present case only the sidestones were found, measuring 5 feet by 2½ feet, and 2 feet 3 inches apart.

No. 16 is 4 paces south-east of the last, and leans over, as though about to fall. The general impression was that these lines of dolmens had been shaken by earthquake, and had fallen downhill over the lower sidestone in some instances. The present example, seen from the south-east (see sketch), looks like a demi-dolmen; the capstone is 11 feet by 9½ feet, the lower sidestone 10½ feet long, 5½ feet high, while the other is quite a small stone.

No. 17 belongs to another group, and is some 15 yards west of the last, higher on the hill. It is interesting for comparison with some on the

No. 17.

Kurmiyeh hill (see Nos. 7, 8, 16, 17, 20 of that group). The view from the west shows a flat block supported on others, and measuring 8½ feet by 6 feet, the top surface being 2 feet from the ground. It did not appear to be a fallen dolmen.

No. 18, rather lower down, and some 12 paces north of the last, is west of No. 14. The topstone was 6 feet by 3½ feet. The sidestones were 4½ feet by 3 feet 4 inches, and 5½ feet by 3 feet, both 18 inches thick. There was in this case a floorstone 4 feet by 2 feet 9 inches in measurement.

No. 19 is about 15 paces west of the last, and consisted of large blocks fallen down.

No. 20 is a well-preserved specimen 17 paces south-west of No. 17. It has a capstone of triangular shape (roughly speaking), the base and height of the triangle being about 5½ feet. The two sidestones are each 7½ feet long, one being 2½ feet high and 18 inches thick, the other 5½ feet high by 2½ feet thick. There is also an endstone, but, as is usually the case, the capstone does not rest upon it. The sidestones are not parallel, but converge to suit the shape of the capstone.

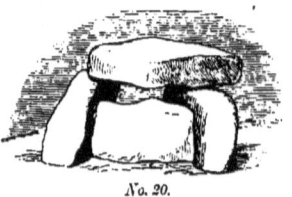
No. 20.

No. 21 is 45 paces west of the last. It seems to have been shaken, and the sides are built up with several stones. The cap is 8 feet long by 5½ feet wide, and the clear height at one end is 5 feet.

No. 21.

No. 22 is remarkable for the great size of the capstone as compared with its low supports. It stands only 6 paces south-west of No. 21, and the capstone measures 10 feet by 8 feet. The clear height beneath is 2½ feet, and the sidestones are only 3½ feet apart. The western, or downhill, sidestone is 9 feet long, 3½ feet high. The topstone is pierced with a hole, which may be natural or artificial.

No. 23 is about 20 paces west of the last, and has fallen down; the capstone measures 8½ feet by 5 feet, and is 2 feet thick. One sidestone was 9 feet long, 4½ feet high, 15 inches thick; the other was 7 feet long, 18 inches high, and 2 feet thick.

No. 24, about 20 paces south-west of the last, has also fallen down-hill northwards. The topstone is very large and heavy, 9 feet by 7 feet,

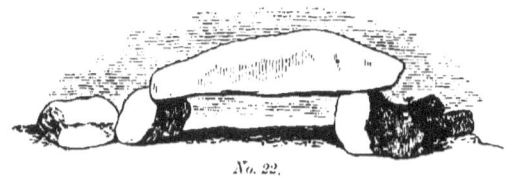

No. 22.

by 2 feet 3 inches in measurement. The sidestones were 9 feet long, 3½ feet high, 4 feet apart. Several blocks lie round, as though forming part of an enclosure, or perhaps another dolmen.

No. 25 is 6 paces south of the last; it had a small topstone 5 feet square, 1 foot thick, with a rounded upper surface.

No. 26, about 7 paces south-west of No. 23, had no apparent capstone. One sidestone was 8 feet long, 5½ feet high, and 2½ feet thick; a second, to the west, 2½ feet by 3 feet. It may be an unfinished example.

No. 27.—This is close to the next, 50 yards south of Nos. 23 and 24, and higher up the hill. It is only a pace north of No. 28, and the two

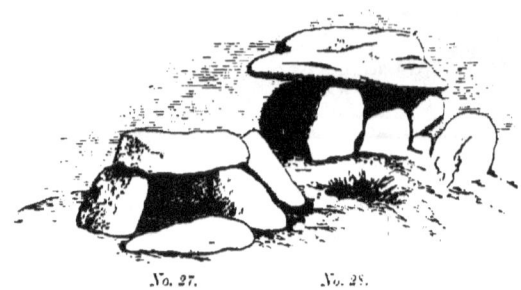

*No. 27.*      *No. 28.*

together, viewed from the north-west, form one group—No. 27 to the left, No. 28 to the right, and higher up. They are very distinct specimens. No. 27 has a capstone $7\frac{1}{2}$ feet long, $4\frac{1}{2}$ feet wide, 1 foot thick. The sidestone measured was $5\frac{1}{2}$ feet by $3\frac{1}{2}$ feet. by 1 foot thick; the clear height under the cap is about 3 feet, and the sidestones $4\frac{1}{2}$ feet apart. It will be seen in the sketch that another stone lies against one side, as if for extra support.

No. 28 is immediately south of the last, and is a very well-shaped specimen. The capstone is of great length, 12 feet by 8 feet, by $1\frac{1}{2}$ feet in thickness.

*No. 28 from North.*

One of the sidestones is $7\frac{1}{2}$ feet long, $3\frac{1}{2}$ feet high, 2 feet thick. The other is 18 inches thick, and the same as the preceding in length and height. They are 3 feet apart. There is a depression in the capstone, which may, however, be natural.

No. 29 is 50 yards west of the last group of two; it has no capstone

33—2

left, and may have been unfinished. The sidestones are 5 and 5½ feet long, 4 feet high, 2 feet apart, 1 foot thick.

No. 30, close to the last, has a capstone 8 feet by 5½ feet, and 2 feet thick, and sidestones 3 feet by 3½ feet, and 1½ feet thick, the clear height under the table is 3½ feet, and the width 2 feet. The top stone is broken, and there is an endstone.

No. 31, about 30 paces south of No. 28, at the top of the slope, with a flat plateau south of it, has fallen over. The capstone was 11 feet by 5½ feet, and 1½ feet thick.

No. 32 is 16 paces south of No. 28, and thus north of the last. It is very low, and has fallen over. The topstone measured 8 feet by 3 feet.

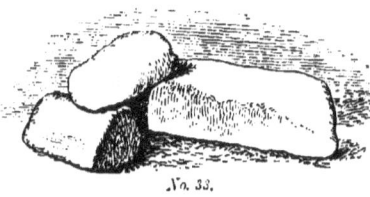

No. 33.

No. 33, adjoining the last on the south-east, is an irregular monument, the topstone of which appears to be broken. The sidestones are 7 feet 4 inches and 4½ feet long, 2½ feet high, and 2½ feet apart.

No. 34 is 15 paces south-east of the last, and has fallen down. One of the sidestones was 9 feet long, 5 feet high (unless, indeed, this be the capstone).

No. 40.

Nos. 35 to 38, inclusive, are fallen specimens within 15 paces of the last. No. 39 is also fallen some 30 paces further south-east.

No. 40.—This is the first of another group on the same hill, but further south-east than those as yet enumerated, 100 paces south east of No. 32. They are on the slope, and lower down than the next group.

No. 40 presents a flat stone 10 feet by 8 feet, and 2½ feet thick, supported by several stones piled at the sides.

No. 41, about 50 yards from the last eastwards, and No. 42, close beside it, are fallen in ruins.

No. 43, higher up the slope, some 80 yards above No. 40, is very interesting, as compared with the example at el Kurmiyeh (see No. 20 under that head). The flat stone is 8½ feet square, supported on various flat slabs.

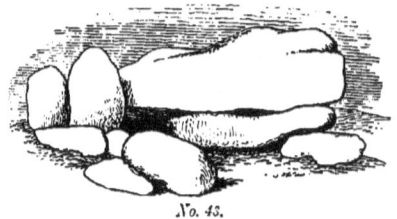

No. 43.

No. 44.—This belongs to another group of two, about 300 yards from the last on the south. It is a fine example, with two sidestones and an endstone. The capstone is 11 feet by 9 feet, the sidestone 7 feet long, 4½ feet high. There are several blocks round it.

No. 45, close by, 5 paces to the north-west, is fallen.

No. 44.

No. 46.—This is about 100 yards west of the last on the flat plateau which commands a fine view of the Ghor and Nebo, and of the western watershed, including Neby Samwil on the south, and Jebel Hazkin, north of Nablus, on the north. This example is fallen, but appears to have been of medium size.

No. 47 belongs to another fine group on flat ground, at the top of a flat slope, falling eastwards into Wâdy Jideid. It is about 200 yards south-east from No. 44, and is also fallen, but of average size.

No. 48, about 150 yards north-east of the last, and 100 yards west of the next, has a capstone 11 feet square broken in two, and supported on sidestones 10½ feet long, 4½ feet high. The average interior height is 3 feet 9 inches, and the width 4 feet. This has no good western view.

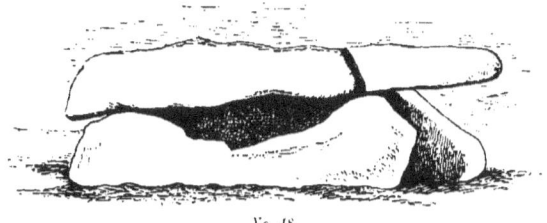

No. 48.

No. 49 is a fallen example, 20 paces north of the next.
No. 50 is one of the best built examples of the group. The capstone is large, being 12 feet by 8 feet. The clear space beneath is 4 feet high and 3½ feet wide. The sidestone is 8½ feet long, and there is also a floorstone. This is at the edge of the flat ground, near a steep descent.

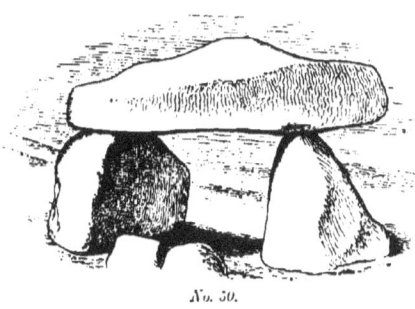

No. 50.

No. 51, about 10 paces west of the last, is a fallen example of medium size. Between this and the preceding are some fallen stones 4 or 5 feet long, which may indicate another dolmen of medium size.

No. 52, near No. 50, on the south-east, approaches the demi-dolmen type. The capstone is 10 feet by 8 feet; the downhill sidestone is 8 feet long, 6 feet high, and there is also an endstone.

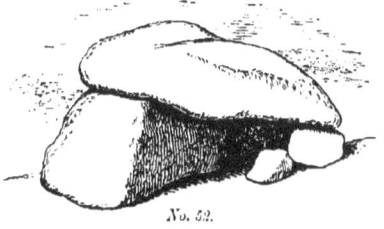

No. 52.

No. 53, close beside the last, on the east, is a fallen mass.

No. 54, about 20 yards west of No. 52, is well preserved, but smaller. The capstone is 6 feet by 5½ feet; the sidestone 4 feet high, 5½ feet long, and the clear height, under the table, 2 feet 9 inches, with a width of 3 feet. Near this is a rude cave or chamber, 6 feet by 5 feet.

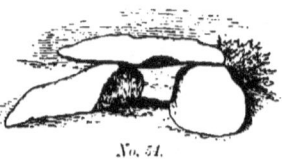

No. 54.

No. 55 belongs to a group 100 yards south of the last. It is, perhaps, the best built and preserved of all on the hill, with floorstone and endstone. The stones seem possibly to have been rudely hewn. The capstone is 5 feet by 6 feet; one sidestone

No. 55.

No. 56.

7 feet long, 6 feet high, 2½ feet thick. The endstone is 3 feet wide, 5 feet high, but the capstone does not rest on it. The other sidestone is 7 feet long, 6 feet high. Thus a tall man can stand up inside this fine dolmen.

No. 56 is 30 paces west of the last (see sketch), and is a well-shaped example. The clear space beneath the cap is 4½ feet high, 2½ feet wide.

Nos. 57, 58, 59 are fallen close together, north of No. 56, and north-west of No. 55.

No. 60 is 20 paces south-east of No. 55. The capstone (see sketch) is 8 feet square, the sides are 4 feet apart, the clear interior height is 3 feet.

No. 61 is a smaller example, 15 paces to the south-west of the last. The topstone is broken, but its upper surface was only 4 feet from the ground.

No. 62, east of the last, is fallen, and was of medium size.

No. 63, at the south end of the plateau, 250 yards south of No. 56, is fallen. About 200 yards south of No. 56 are two or three very small

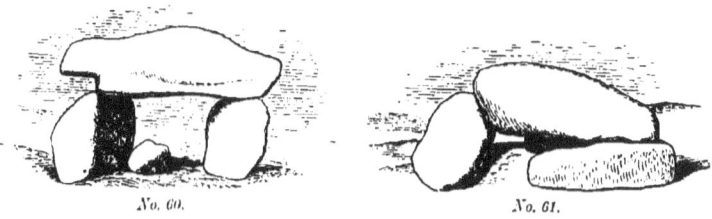

No. 60.    No. 61.

structures, flat stones 5 or 6 feet long, raised up on a single stone beneath; they are 100 yards apart.

Nos. 64 and 65, 200 yards south of No. 63, and higher up on the east slope of the spur, are ruined dolmens of moderate size.

No. 66, about a quarter of a mile from No. 63, and, perhaps, 700 yards from No. 56, is also ruined or destroyed, and of medium size.

No. 67 is a small one, 20 paces south of the last, with fallen topstone.

No. 68, about 200 yards north-east of No. 67, is a very low one of small size.

Looking northwards at the plateau, on which Nos. 50, 55, 56, 60, 66, are the most conspicuous objects, one sees the ridge of Jebel Oshà appearing between Siâghah and Nebo.

The examples noted thus far belong to the north and east slopes of the spur, which runs out northwards from the Maslûbiyeh ridge to the Hadânieh circle; but there are other dolmens further west on the north-west slopes of the same spur, which were next visited. South of them all, the top of the spur is crowned with a ruined cairn (see el Maslûbiyeh).

No. 69 is north of the cairn, and 100 yards distant down the slope. It is higher up, however, on the spur than the former dolmens, which are to the east. This is a fallen example of medium size.

No. 70, lower down the hill, is a well-defined trilithon, apparently shaken by earthquakes. The capstone measures 10 feet by 7 feet, the sidestone is 11 feet long and $4\frac{1}{2}$ feet high, and the clear width between the sidestones is 4 feet.

## WADY JIDEID

No. 71, close to the last, is fallen, but was about the same size.

Nos. 72 to 78, within 100 yards east of No. 71, are small ruined specimens.

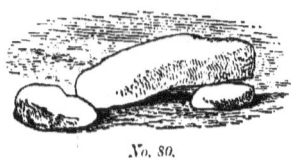

No. 79 is a very small one, 100 yards north-east of No. 70.

No. 80, about 300 yards east of No. 70, on the upper part of the highest

*No. 70.*  *No. 80.*

slope of the hill (see sketch), is a small low example. The capstone is 6 feet long, and its upper surface only 3 feet from the ground.

Nos. 81 and 82 are little examples, lower down the slope than the last.

No. 83 is beside the road which comes from el Maslûbîyeh to 'Ain Jideid, on flat ground near the foot of the highest slope. This specimen is built of five stones, including floor and end stones. The sidestone is 4½ feet high, 6½ feet long, and the clear space is 4½ feet wide.

No. 84 is a fallen specimen 100 yards east of the last.

No. 85 is a small one 20 paces north-east of the last.

No. 86 is a small specimen on the same roadside with, and about 30 paces north of, No. 83.

Nos. 87 to 90 stand in a line on the west of the same road, north and south, and about 10 paces apart. They are fallen, but the capstone in the two first is 8 feet long, and 5 feet long in the second two.

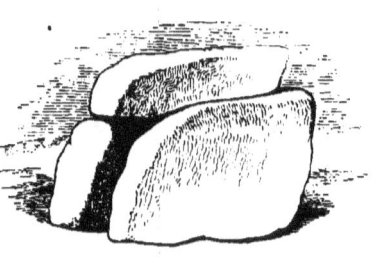

*No. 91.*

No. 91 (see sketch) is north of the last group, and south-west of No. 56, and about 200 yards north of No. 83. It is a well-preserved specimen, having two sidestones, instead of one, on one side. The

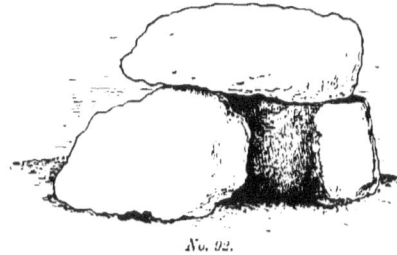
*No. 92.*

capstone is about 7 feet square, and the clear height beneath it is 5 feet.

No. 92, some 70 yards west of the last, is also well-preserved. The sidestones are 8 feet long, the clear interior height is 4 feet.

No. 93, east of the last, has a capstone only 4 feet long and small sidestones, the clear interior height being only 3 feet at the highest point. This, if not overturned, was a sort of demi-dolmen, or rocking-stone.

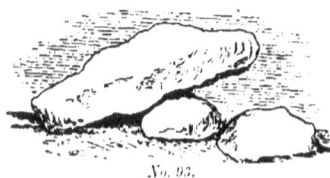
*No. 93.*

Nos. 94, 95, 96 are small fallen specimens, north of the last, about 200 yards distant.

Nos. 97, 98, 99, on the west side of the road above-mentioned—west of Nos. 26 and 27, and about 100 yards distant—are small fallen specimens. On and near the road are also some pointed stones, 3 or 4 feet high, and a fallen block with a chamber about 4 feet long in it.

*No. 100.*

The next group is further south along the road to el Maslúbîyeh, and east of the cairn on the top of the spur already noticed. The first of the group (No. 100) is the furthest south-west, and about half a mile from No. 83. It is a remarkably fine specimen, and the blocks appear to have been hewn. The table-stone is not horizontal, and measures 13 feet by 10 feet, being 1½ feet thick. The larger sidestone is 10 feet long and 7 feet high. The average clear space is 5½ feet under the topstone, and the width 4 feet. There is an endstone about 4½ feet high. There are also hollows in the upper surface of the capstone. There are tribe-marks on the endstone, which might be mistaken for letters.

No. 101 is about 100 yards north of the last, and the cap is 9 feet by

No. 101.   No. 102.

7 feet, and 2½ feet thick. It has an endstone, and the mean height under the capstone is 4 feet 3 inches.

No. 102 is 60 yards east of the last, and is something like a demi-dolmen; being constructed on a slope. The capstone is 10 feet by 8 feet; the mean breadth is 3 feet 3 inches, with a clear height of 4 feet in the middle under the capstone.

Nos. 103, 104, 105, close together, south-east of the last, are fallen specimens of medium size.

No. 106, about 250 yards north-east of No. 102, resembles it closely.

No. 107, beside the road, south of the last, about 80 yards distant, is a smaller specimen, the topstone 7 feet by 6 feet, the clear height beneath 3 feet, and the clear width 3 feet 3 inches. It has an endstone.

No. 108 is a fallen specimen just east of the last.

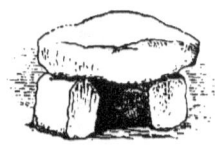

No. 107.

No. 109, about 50 yards north of No. 107, on the road, is about the size of No. 106.

Nos. 110 and 111 are fallen specimens of medium size between No. 109 and the next.

No. 112 is a remarkably well-shaped specimen, suggestive of having

34—2

been built with hewn blocks. This is the furthest north of the present group of 13 (Nos. 100 to 112), including several magnificent specimens.

No. 112.

The capstone is 9 feet by 10 feet, and 1 foot thick. One sidestone is 10 feet long, 6½ feet high, but not vertical; the clear space beneath is 3½ feet wide, 6 feet high. There is an endstone of these same dimensions, and a floor-stone, which has been broken at some time or other, but which rests on rock only beneath; this reduces the height of the clear space. There are roughly-excavated holes in the upper surface of the capstone, probably artificial, though possibly natural.

No. 113.

The next group, placed together with the preceding because belonging to the same system, is found on the slopes south and east of the hill of Kûeijiyeh, and east of the Hadânieh circle. It includes fifty examples, some of which are very large and well-formed dolmens.

Plan of No. 113.

No. 113.—This is a very fine specimen, standing alone, and furthest east of all, on the edge of the plateau of the Belka, at the head of Wâdy Jideid, west of Rujm Jâzel, and north of Umm Jereisât (see map). The topstone measured 8½ feet by 5½ feet, and the clear height beneath is 3½ feet, with a width of 3 feet. The downhill sidestone is 5 feet high and 9 feet long; the uphill 3½ feet high and 8 feet long. There is also and enstone, and several smaller blocks lie round the dolmen. The topstone (see plan) is pitted all over with small hollows, no less than forty in all being counted. The largest, on the lowest part of the stone (which has a slight cant), is 10 inches in diameter and 9 inches deep. Five of the larger hollows are in one line, with a channel communicating between them (*cf.* 'Ammân), the others are round the outer edges of the stone.

No. 114, north-west of the last, and on the spur east of the Kûeijîyeh knoll, is also a fine specimen. The capstone is 10 feet by 8 feet, and one of the sidestones is 10 feet by 4 feet 3 inches, by 2½ feet thick. The clear space is 3 feet 9 inches high, and 5 feet wide. There are four holes in the upper surface of the capstone, about 7 inches in diameter and 3 inches deep.

*No. 114.*

and a yet larger hollow or basin 1½ feet in diameter and nearly a foot deep near the middle.

No. 115, about 50 yards further north, is a fallen specimen.

No. 116, close to the last, has a capstone 8 feet square, and a sidestone 9 feet long, 5½ feet high (downhill side). The mean interior height under the capstone is only 3 feet, and the breadth 3½ feet. There is an endstone as well.

No. 117, lower down the northern side of the slope, not far

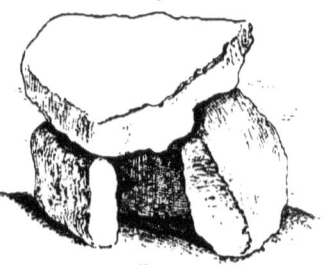

*No. 116.*

from the valley bed, is a remarkably fine specimen, well-built of slabs, which may have been hewn. It has a capstone, two sidestones, an endstone, a floorstone, and a small stone resting on one sidestone and on the endstone. The capstone is 8 feet long, 7½ feet wide, 2 feet 3 inches thick. The sidestones are each about 9½ feet long, 6½ feet high. The floorstone is

5 feet by 3 feet 3 inches, and 1½ feet thick. Thus the interior chamber is

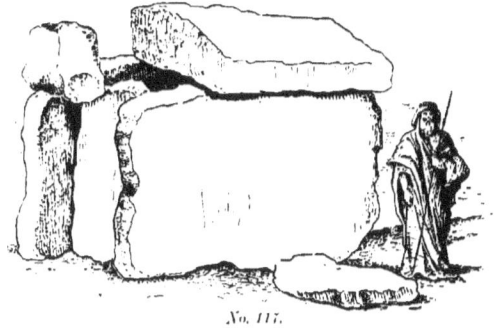

No. 117.

5 feet high, 9 feet long, and 3½ feet wide. The chief peculiarity of this example consists, however, in the well-cut cup-hollow in the upper surface of the floorstone. This is 1 foot in diameter and 6 inches deep, very well shaped. It was possible, by lying flat, to see under the floorstone, but there was no appearance of any hollow in the rock, such as a sunk grave. The monument stands on bare slippery rock near the valley bed.

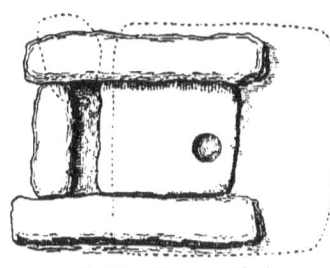

No. 117.—Plan ground level.

No. 118, about 23 paces south-east of the last, is a demi-dolmen, on the rocky slope; the stone which forms the table is 7 feet long,

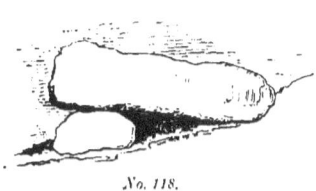

No. 118.

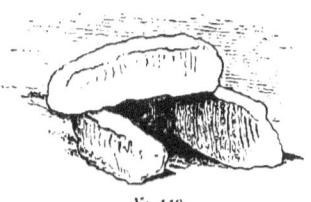

No. 119.

No. 119, about 50 paces east of No. 117, is a comparatively small specimen; one of the sidestones measured 5 feet by 3½ feet.

No. 120, about 50 paces further east again than the last (see sketch),

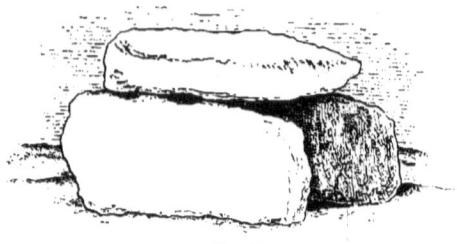

*No. 120.*

is a well-shaped dolmen. The chamber is 5 feet high, 3 feet wide; the sidestone 5 feet high, 9 feet long.

No. 121.—Crossing over the rocky bed of the ravine northwards, this specimen is found about 120 yards east of the last. The clear height under the capstone is 4 feet, the width 3 feet; the sidestones are 7 feet long (see sketch).

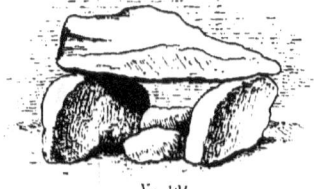

*No. 121.*

No. 122, close to the last, is a fallen specimen.

No. 123, 60 yards west of the last, on the north side of the ravine, is rather larger than No. 121.

Nos. 124 and 125, about 50 paces south of No. 120. These are very remarkable specimens, as indicating that the flat stone is the real

*No. 124.*

*No. 125.*

*ratio entis* of these monuments; they occur on the hillside, 50 paces south of No. 120, higher up. The flat stones are about 7 feet long.

No. 126, about 70 or 80 yards north of No. 117. The topstone has a hole in it 2 feet 9 inches by 1 foot 9 inches, and 6 inches deep; the sidestone is 4½ feet high, and 11 feet long. This is so high up as to command a view extending to Mount Gerizim.

*No. 126.*   *No. 127.*

No. 127.—This is a demi-dolmen, south of the last (see sketch). In the upper stone there is a slit 2 feet long, 8 inches wide, 8 inches deep—a sort of channel; perhaps, however, not artificial.

No. 128, about 50 yards west of No. 117, is fallen.

No. 129, about 30 paces south-west of the last, is also fallen.

No. 130, close to the last, is merely a small stone, raised on one yet smaller at one end. There are a good many single stones lying about on the hillsides here, which were probably connected in some way with the dolmens.

Nos. 131, 132, 133, on the eastern slope of the Kûeijiyeh hill, are all fallen.

No. 134 is a fine specimen on the same slope. As usual, the sidestones have their length parallel to the contours. The uphill stone is 4½ feet high, 9 feet long. There is an endstone 5½ feet high, 3½ feet broad. The capstone is broken; beneath it is a clear interior height of 4 feet, and there is a floorstone 6 feet long, 3½ feet wide, 1 foot 3 inches thick. In this is a hollow, partly broken away, about 10 inches in diameter, and the same in depth.

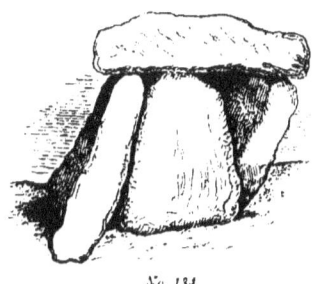

*No. 134.*

No. 135.—This is the first of a group which occurs south of No. 113, and north-east of the Rujm el Meseiyik, on the edge of the Belka plateau; with the next, it was not measured, but was about the size of No. 113.

No. 136.—See the last.

Nos. 137, 138, 139, 140, near the last, are fallen, making a group of six in this direction.

No. 141 is on the north side of Wâdy Jideid, and south of the Kûeijiyeh hill. It is of medium size.

No. 142, at the bottom of the great descent along the road to Hadâ-nieh from the east, just before crossing Wâdy Jideid. A small low dolmen, very rough but quite distinct, all by itself.

No. 143, with the rest following, was measured and sketched by Lieutenant Mantell. It belongs to a conspicuous group south of el Kûeijiyeh, low down at the head of Wâdy Jideid. This is the most eastern, and partly ruined, the topstone having fallen. It was 9 feet by 8 feet, by 2 feet in thickness. The sidestone was 9 feet long, 4 feet high, 1 foot thick.

No. 144. W. Jideid.

No. 144, about 30 yards south of the last (see sketch), is a magnificent dolmen, the topstone 12 feet by 9 feet, and 20 inches thick. The sidestone is 11 feet long, 6 feet high, 2 feet thick. In the upper surface of the capstone are three holes, each 3 or 4 inches in diameter, and about 2 inches deep. There is a floorstone in this specimen.

No. 146. W. Jideid.

No. 145, about 30 yards south of the last, and lower down. This is fallen, the topstone measuring 10 feet by 8½ feet, by 1½ feet thick.

No. 146 has a capstone much tilted, 10 feet by 9 feet, and one of the sidestones is 8 feet high, 10½ feet long, 1½ feet thick.

There are in this last group, south of the Kúeijiyeh knoll, sixteen other fallen specimens, making a total of 162 dolmens measured and examined in this valley.

The observations concerning the groups of el Kurmiyeh and el Kalûa apply equally to the present larger group, which presents no peculiarities, save in Nos. 117 and 134, where the cup-hollow is in the upper surface of the floorstone. The channels of No. 113 may be compared with those in the great southern dolmen at 'Ammân.

As regards the present group generally, it will be observed that the space beneath the table is rarely more than 4 feet high, and about 3½ feet wide. This allows of anyone standing by the dolmen being able to reach the upper surface of the table. The trilithons cannot be considered to be very appropriate forms for huts or for tombs, and such specimens as Nos. 124 and 125 are very instructive. They are evidently small specimens of the same class, but cannot be either tombs or houses, as they are too small and low; they seem clearly to be intended as tables for some purpose.

There seems to be no arrangement of the dolmens, but the probable centre is the great circle of Hadânieh.

Explored September 21, 23, 27, 28, 1881.

Wâdy el Jindil (وادي الجنديل, 'the valley of hard rock').—Omitted from the reduced map for want of space.

Wâdy el Jôfeh (وادي الجوفه, 'valley of the hollow').

Wâdy Jôfet el Ghazlâniyeh.—See under Jôfeh.

Wâdy el Jorfeh (وادي الجرفه, 'valley of the bank').

Wâdy el Jûeismeh.—See el Jûeismeh.

Wâdy Kedîsh (وادي كديش, 'valley of the pack-horse').

Wâdy el Kefeir.—See Kefeir.

Wâdy el Kefrein.—See el Kefrein.

Wâdy Kerâdeh (وادي قرادة, 'valley of goblins').—See Khûrbet Kerâdeh.

Wâdy el Khaneizir (وادي الخنيزير, 'valley of the little pig').

Wâdy el Kittâr (وادي الكطّار, the root means 'to drip').—Omitted from the reduced map for want of space and as valueless.

Wâdy Kuseih.—See Râs Kuseib.

Wâdy el Mâhfeh (وادي الماعْفه).

Wâdy el Makâbalein.—See el Makâbalein.

Wâdy Manatt Faras Barkât (وادي منطّ فرس بركات, 'valley of the place of the jump of the mare of Barkât').—Barkât ('blessings' or 'increase') is a common Arab name, and another name of the famous black hero, Abu Zeid, 'father of increase,' son of Rizk, 'sustenance,' and Khadra, 'the green or fertile one.' The legend of Abu Zeid is localized by the Belka Arabs in the Jordan Valley (see Mensef Abu Zeid), and the present name is probably connected. The Arab heroes (Abu Zeid, Zir, etc.) are represented as being so heavy that no ordinary horse was able to support them; but the feat may, perhaps, have been that of an actual Arab rider, or of his mare.

This name applies to the first valley north of Kefrein, which runs due west into Wâdy Jôfet el Ghazlâniyeh. It is too long a name to write on the reduced map.

Wâdy Mâsûh.—See Khŭrbet Mâsûh.

Wâdy Mebna Beit el Maganyeh (وادي مبنا بيت المغنيه, 'valley of the building of the rich man's house').

Wâdy Medeisesât (وادي مديْسسات, 'valley of hiding-places').

Wâdy el Mehatteh (وادي المحطّه, 'valley of the camp').

Wâdy el Mehterkeh (وادي المحترقه, 'valley of the place burnt with fire').

Wâdy el Mejeddrin (وادي المجدّرين).—This means in Arabic 'valley of the persons afflicted with small-pox,' or similar pustules, and may take its name from some such outbreak in an Arab camp.

Wâdy el Mekheiyit.—See Rujm el Mekheiyit.

Wâdy Mensef Abu Zeid.—See Mensef Abu Zeid. Omitted from the reduced map as unnecessary.

Wâdy el Merkeb.—See Râs el Merkeb.

Wâdy el Meshabbeh.—See 'Ain el Meshabbeh.

Wâdy el Mesheiyideh.—See el Mesheiyideh. Omitted as unnecessary on the reduced map.

Wâdy el Mes-hûr (وادي المسهور, 'the enchanted valley').—The *Sin* and *Sad* are hardly distinguishable among the Arabs, as all the Syrian educated persons affirm. This may perhaps, therefore, be مصمور, 'flat.'

Wâdy el Minhar (وادي المنحر, 'valley of the place of sacrifice,' according to Moslem custom).

Wâdy el Mubrakah (وادي المبركه, 'valley of the kneeling-place').—See Rujûm Mubrakat Nâket en Neby.

Wâdy el Mujerr (وادي المجرّ, 'valley of the place of pasture').—May, however, be a Bedawin corrupt pronunciation of the next. It is omitted from the reduced map as doubtful.

Wâdy el Mukerr (وادي المكرّ, 'valley of the plain').

Wâdy el Mureijib.—See el Mureijib.

Wâdy el Musheirfeh.—See Râs el Musheirfeh.

Wâdy Nââûr.—See 'Ain Nââûr.

Wâdy Naheir (وادي نهير, 'valley of the little stream').

Wâdy en Nâr (وادي النار, 'the valley of fire').

Wâdy en Nefiâiyeh (وادي النفيعيه, 'the fruitful valley').

Wâdy Nimrin.—See Tell Nimrin.

Wâdy en Nûeijis.—See Kusr en Nûeijis.

Wâdy en Nusûry.—See 'Ain en Nusûry.

Wâdy el 'Oshir.—See Rujm el 'Oshir.

Wâdy Rafiâh.—See Rujûm Rafiâh.

Wâdy er Râmeh.—See Tell er Râmeh.

Wâdy er Rameileh (وادي الرميله, 'the sandy valley' diminutive).—This is omitted for want of space, and as of no value, on the reduced map.

Wâdy er Ramleh (وادي الرمله, 'the valley of sand').

Wâdy er Rishshâh (وادي الرشّاح, 'the valley of high herbage').

Wâdy er Rûâk.—See 'Arâk er Rûâk.

Wâdy Shafâ (وادي شفع, 'the equal valley').

Wâdy Shâib (وادي شعيب, 'valley of the little hill-spur').

Wâdy esh Shita (وادي الشتا, 'valley of rain or of winter').—It is the winter camping-ground of the 'Abbâd Arabs. It has a fine perennial spring in its bed, which supplies a stream turning mills (now ruined in part) near el 'Areimeh (see 'Ain el Bahhâth and el 'Areimeh). Probably, therefore, the name refers to winter residence, not to any supply of torrent-water.

Wâdy es Sir (وادي السير, 'valley of the sheepfold,' but see under 'Arâk el Emir, the probable derivation).

Wâdy Umm Haleilifeh.—See Umm Haleilifeh.

Wâdy Umm Kaleib (وادي ام قليب, 'valley of the water-pot').

Wâdy Umm Luweizeh.—See Umm el Lôz.

Wâdy Umm er Rumam.—See Umm er Rumam. This is omitted, as not required, on the reduced map.

Wâdy Umm Shûâmir (وادي ام شوامر, 'valley mother of hemlocks').—This is a small valley leading down west to Wâdy Hesbân, from the ridge west of el 'Âl, just south of Shûnet Sukr. It is not named on the reduced map. A small solitary dolmen was found in it, consisting of a rough stone some 5 feet long, supported on two smaller blocks, the upper surface being about 2 feet from the ground. This small example is at a spot whence the Kurmiyeh hill can be seen. There are several single blocks near it—compare el Kurmiyeh.

*Dolmen in W. Umm Shûâmir.*

Wâdy Umm Suweiwineh.—See Umm Suweiwineh.

Wâdy Zerka Mââin.—A magnificent gorge 2,000 feet deep, forming the south boundary of the work. See Hammâm ez Zerka, and 'Ain ez Zerka.

At length we reached the brink of the gorge—here some 1,700 feet deep—the stream being, near the springs, still 1,600 feet above the Dead Sea. Tawny cliffs of limestone capped with chalk rise on the north, and are seamed with gulleys, where the marl has been washed down like snow-streaks left in summer, beneath the cliffs. On the south, a steep brown precipice with an undercliff of marl, and a plateau stretching thence to another and yet another ridge; beyond and above this plateau (on which are the stone heaps of

Machærus), appeared the shining waters of the lake and its western cliffs, fading away into a blue mist on the south. But the central feature of this ghastly scene of utterly barren wilderness was the great black bastion projecting from the southern cliff, and almost blocking the gorge—an outbreak of basalt which shows like a dark river in the valley of Callirhoe, as seen from the west side of the Dead Sea. It resembles the high spoil-heaps of an English coal-mine, and bears witness to the volcanic action which has made the springs in this gorge of boiling heat, and which no doubt accompanied the sudden depression of the enormous fault now known as the Jordan Valley.

It took a full hour to reach the bottom of the gorge, and the scene beneath was wonderful beyond description. On the south, black basalt, brown limestone, gleaming marl. On the north, sandstone cliffs of all colours, from pale yellow to pinkish purple. In the valley itself the brilliant green of palm clumps, rejoicing in the heat and the sandy soil. The streams, bursting from the cliffs, poured down in rivulets between banks of crusted orange sulphur deposits. The black grackle soared above, with gold-tipped wings, his mellow note being the one sound re-echoed by the great red cliffs in this utter solitude. The brooks (which run from ten springs in all) vary from 110° to 140° F. in temperature, and fall in little cascades amid luxuriant foliage, to join the main course of the stream, which is far colder and fresher, flowing from the shingly springs higher up the valley, and forming pools beneath white rocks of chalk, which we found full of fish, and hidden in a luxuriant brake of tamarisk and cane. The weather being very hot, the thermal streams were not smoking, but a strong smell of sulphur was very perceptible at times. Crossing three rivulets, from each of which our horses, apparently aware of the heat of the water, shrank back in fear, we reached the principal hot-spring, which has formed a ledge of breccia-like deposit in the valley, just north of the basalt cliff. Here the chasm is narrowest, and the main stream below could be seen winding among the black boulders, which impede its course, with the dark precipice frowning as though about to fall, like Sinai in the 'Pilgrim's Progress.' The stream has bored through the sulphurous breccia, and runs in a tunnel of its own making, issuing from this hot shaft at out 100 feet lower, in the gorge itself. Here our Arab friends stripped and steamed themselves, sitting on a frail platform of retem boughs, over the boiling spring, which is surrounded with incrustations, white, yellow, or orange, of pure sulphur. Here we heard again the legend of Solomon's black demon slave, who discovered this healing bath for his master, and we observed remains of a channel, leading probably to the baths, now buried beneath the incrustations from the stream. And of all scenes in Syria, even after standing on Hermon, or among the groves of Banias, or at Engedi, or among the crags of the Anti-Lebanon, there is none which so dwells on my memory as does this awful gorge, 'the valley of God' by Beth Peor, where, perhaps, the body of Moses was hid—the fair flowing stream which Herod sought below the gloomy prison of John the Baptist at Machærus—the dread chasm where the Bedawin still offer sacrifices to the desert spirits, and still bathe with full faith in the healing powers of the spring.—Conder's 'Heth and Moab,' p. 145, 1st edition.

Watât en Nâm (وطابس النعم, 'the smooth lowlands').—This applies to the plateau below Nebo, on the west.

El Weibdeh (الويبده, 'the pass').—This is a ruined village with remains of rough walls and rock-cut cisterns. It stands on a pass by which the road from 'Ammân to es Salt crosses.

El Yâdûdeh (اليدودة).—This is a site beyond the Survey—a conspicuous mound on which are remains of an ancient town. Two small modern houses have also here been built by a man from es Sâlt, who has recently settled here.

Yâjûz (يجوز).—This is an important site which some writers have supposed to represent Jahaz,* but erroneously, as the two names have not a single letter in common. It stands high on the south side of a valley among hills covered with scattered oaks, and has a quarried cliff to the south. On the east is the ancient circle of Kôm Yajuz, described under that name. On the north-west is the spring of 'Ain Yâjûz (see under that head), with a few ruins. The ruins are those of a Roman or Byzantine town. Vaulted substructures with round-arched tunnel vaults (compare Kefeir el Wusta) remain. The arches are, however, rough. The mortar joints are packed with stone chips—a common feature of Byzantine masonry. A rough square cistern is cut in rock and surrounded with troughs. It was apparently intended for rain-water. Some drafted stones of large size were noted, as at all Byzantine ruins of any importance. The site is on the north edge of the Survey. The principal building in the place may very probably have been a Roman temple. It measures about 230 feet by 80 feet, and is divided in two by a wall. On the west side are two chambers, and the rock-cut cistern above mentioned is to the west again. The walls are standing to a height of 10 feet or more. A fine group of oaks occurs beside the building.

Visited October 10, 1881.

El Yiserah (اليسرة).—This might, perhaps, be the place called

* The site of Jahaz has long been sought, but no identification made, since neither Yajûz nor Visera bear any resemblance to the Hebrew word, which is יַהַץ, or יָהְצָה, that is in Arabic Yakhsah, or Yahsah. As regards its position (see Deut. ii. 32; Num. xxi. 23; Josh. xiii. 18; Jer. xlviii. 21), it was in the vicinity of Heshbon, and in the wilderness (Midbar). It should, apparently, be sought east of the Survey district in the Beni Sakhr country. Among the names collected beyond the Survey is that of Rujm Makhsiyeh (مخصية), which contains the necessary root. The site is not shown on any map, but it is in the vicinity of Jâwah and Yâdûdeh, or just where Jahaz might be expected to lie, in the Midbar, or waterless country east of Heshbon. This appears to be the nearest approach to a discovery of Jahaz yet made. Ziza, the site suggested by Rev. Selah Merrill, though in the right direction, cannot be considered identical, as not one letter of the root is found in the name of Jahaz.

Jessa (Ιασσα), between Medeba and Heshbon, known to Eusebius (see Reland, 'Pal.,' ii., p. 825), which he supposed to be Jahaz. The site is that of a ruined village on a knoll in low ground. On the north is a rock-cut cistern which had just been cleared in expectation of the rains. The masonry is small and rude. Some rude vaults and round arches of unshaped stones remain standing.

Visited September 26, 1881.

Ez Zâby (الزعبي, 'the dwarf').—This is a sacred spot near Khûrbet Kefrein. A circle exists here resembling the other modern circles of the Arabs (see 'Ain Hesbân, etc.), but with its trilithon on the south instead of on the west, as is usual. Ez Zâby is said to have belonged to a tribe inhabiting the Haurân, who are said to place the lintel-stones of their circles on the south. The name is omitted for want of space on the reduced map.

Zejibet el 'Al (زجيبه العال). This is an Arab mispronunciation for Zekibet el 'Al. زقب means 'an entrance,' and the name applies to a site north of el 'Al, where there are rocks and caves. The word also means 'a narrow road,' and may apply to the road here ascending by Umm el Kenâfid).—The vicinity is described under Umm el Kenâfid. The name is omitted on the reduced map.

Ez Zellâkah (الزلاقة, 'the slippery place').—Omitted, as not of value, on the reduced map.

Ez Zerânik (الزرانيق, 'the runlets' of water).

Zârah (زارة).—This is south of the Survey, on the Dead Sea shore. The spelling was ascertained carefully, and proves that there is no connection with the Hebrew Zoar. It might, perhaps, be Zareth Shahar (צרת השחר, Josh. xiii. 19, 'in the mount of the valley,' הר העמק), as the Tzadi does occasionally become Zain—e.g., Hazzûr for Hazor.

# APPENDIX A.

### ACCOUNT OF THE SURVEY OPERATIONS.

THE Survey party reached Palestine in the spring of 1881, and were engaged first in a tour through Northern Syria, which led to the recovery of Kadesh on Orontes, secondly in organization and in shifting the base from Beyrout to Jerusalem—a step necessitated by the outbreak of a rebellion in the Haurân.

When all was finally ready on June 1st, the Turkish authorities refused to allow the Survey to be commenced, and this necessitated a delay due to reference home. During this time a great deal of revision work was done in Judea between Bethel, Hebron, and Ramleh. Finally, on August 16th, Captain Conder and Lieutenant Mantell, with half the native party, marched down to Jericho, where they met Sheikh Goblân en Nimr, and crossed Jordan on the following day.

A contract having been arranged with the 'Adwân Arabs, the rest of the party was ordered over Jordan. Messrs. Black and Armstrong arrived at 'Ain Hesbân on August 26th. The interval had been occupied by Captain Conder and Lieutenant Mantell in reconnaissance and the exploration of ruined sites. The triangulation commenced in very hot weather on August 30th. The base-line was measured and remeasured on September 2nd and 4th. In consequence of a skirmish between the 'Adwân and the Beni Sakhr, the camp was moved to 'Ain Fudeili on September 10th. On the 20th it was again moved south to Wâdy Jideid, and on the following night the Governor of es Sâlt arrived at the old camp with the intention of ordering the suspension of the work. On the 23rd a Turkish officer was sent to Wâdy Jideid to inquire into the proceedings of the Survey party, and on the 27th private intelligence was received of the intention of the Turkish Government to compel the party to desist from their work.

On September 29th the camp was again moved to 'Ain Minyeh, and the survey of the 'Adwân country was carried to the extreme southern limit. An attempt was made to come to terms with the Hameideh, in order to go yet further south; but this failed, as the Hameideh could not be induced to select any representative chief, the whole district being in a state of anarchy. It was, therefore, determined to extend the Survey northwards.

On October 5th the camp reached 'Ammân, and on the 7th a peremptory summons was received from the Governor of es Sâlt, ordering the party to desist from work and to leave the country. The matter was referred to Jerusalem and Damascus, and the party meanwhile continued its operations. On October 16th Mr. Black was invalided home in consequence of repeated attacks of dysentery, and left for Jerusalem. On October 20th the camp was moved to 'Arâk el Emir, and on the 23rd another summons was received from es Sâlt. The Waly of Syria, in spite of the representations made to him by the Consul at Jerusalem, refused to allow even a temporary continuance of the Survey while referring the matter to the Porte, and ordered that the party should be directed to withdraw.

On October 25th the camp was removed to Kefrein, and survey operations were continued until the 28th, when the whole party recrossed the Jordan.

The indoor operations commenced November 1st, and were continued during the winter. On November 10th and 17th, the Siloam tunnel was explored and carefully surveyed. On November 28th, after a severe storm, the party took refuge in Jerusalem, and the native staff were dismissed. The party was fully employed all the winter in the reduction of the field-work.

In February of the following year, by direction of the Committee, Captain Conder visited Constantinople, and obtained the promise of a new firman, which has not yet been signed.

Returning to Jerusalem in March, Captain Conder was honoured with the invitation to attend their Royal Highnesses Prince Albert Victor and Prince George of Wales on their tour through Palestine. The royal party visited the Hebron Mosque on April 5th, 1882, and a report and plan drawn up by Captain Conder and approved by Colonel Sir C. W. Wilson, K.C.B., R.E., was sent to H.R.H. the Prince of Wales, who gave it to the Committee of the Palestine Exploration Fund (see 'Memoirs Western Palestine Survey,' vol. iii., p. 333).

The royal party crossed the Jordan on April 10th, camping at 'Arâk el Emir. On the 11th, 'Ammân was reached; on the 12th, es Salt; on the 13th, Jerâsh; on the 14th, the Jabbok River; on the 15th, the royal party recrossed the Jordan. Opportunity was taken of this tour to clear up various points which had arisen during the course of the office-work in Jerusalem. The royal tour continued to Baniâs, where, on April 25th, an interesting discovery was made of basalt dolmens not noticed by the surveyors in 1877. The Princes finally left Beyrout on May 6th, and the Survey party was withdrawn soon after.

Captain Conder was appointed to the staff in Egypt on August 5th, and invalided home on October 1st. In consequence of illness he was unable to rejoin the Palestine Exploration Society until May 10th, 1883, when he was employed on the present Memoir and its plans.

C. R. C.

# APPENDIX B.

## THE TRIGONOMETRICAL AND BAROMETRICAL OBSERVATIONS.

*Base-line.*—This extends from Kefeir el Wusta on the south to Hesbân on the north. The construction was as shown, the portion A C being obtained by construction as the ground is rough, and the point A is on a Tell raised considerably above the plain on which the base is measured.

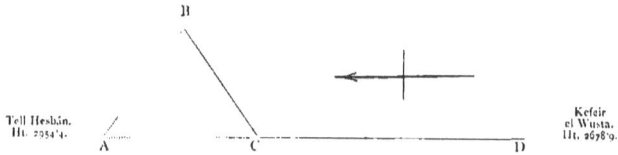

The reason of the adoption of this construction was the convenience of obtaining a good view from each end of the trigonometrical base. From D a fine view is obtained on rising ground in a flat open plateau, but C is in a hollow between low hills, whereas A is a very conspicuous point on a high Tell visible from all sides. The ground along the line B C is flat and at the same level as C, while from C to D the plateau is well suited for the measurement of a base conveniently directed with reference to the general direction of the Survey. It will be seen from the triangulation diagram, that a very good extension was obtainable from the base—large well shaped triangles springing from the first lines, and connecting the Eastern Survey with old stations west of Jordan.

The south end of the base was marked on the headstone of a grave on the low knoll west of the ruins of Kefeir el Wusta. A whitewashed cairn was built over this point after the observations had been taken. The north end was marked on a large stone on the Tell at Hesbân, over which, when the operations were complete, another cairn of about the same height (5 feet) was constructed.

The line C D was twice measured from its southern end with a light chain, which on each day of use was carefully compared, both before and after the measurements had been taken, with a standard steel-chain marked for the mean summer temperature by day for Palestine. The corrections due to the stretching of the chain were applied, and the results of the measurement and remeasurement of C D were :

|  |  |
|---|---|
| First measurement | 28,704·6 links. |
| Second ,, | 20,876·6 ,, |
| Difference | 2 links = 1·3 feet. |

The mean length used was therefore 28,705·6 links.

The triangle A B C is an equilateral triangle, in which the side B C was measured, and the angles A B C carefully observed and made equal each to 60° with theodolites. The three sides being equal, a careful measurement of B C gives the length of the remainder of the base, viz. A C. The line B C was twice measured with a steel tape corrected by the standard. This operation was carried out by Captain Conder and Lieutenant Mantell, while Messrs. Black and Armstrong were measuring the line C D. The results were :

|  | Ft. | In. |
|---|---|---|
| First measurement | 1,485 | 3 |
| Second ,, | 1,485 | 1 |
| Difference |  | 2 |

These measurements give a total of 30,955·9 links for the line A D—the trigonometrical base.

The base-line thus measured was afterwards reduced to the level of the sea, giving a difference of 2·74 feet in the whole length ; but as all the trigonometrical stations were at a considerable elevation above the sea this reduction was not used in calculating the triangulation.

The total length above given is 3·87 miles, which is rather shorter than the Jaffa base, and shorter by more than half a mile than the Esdraelon base west of Jordan. The difference of the two measurements of the Jaffa base was ½ link. The two measurements of the Esdraelon base differed by 3 links. The eastern base is thus quite equal to those west of the river, and the character of the triangulation is better, because the theodolites used were two new 8-inch instruments, those used for the Western Survey being 7-inch.

*Triangulation.*—This was carefully worked out in 1883 by Mr. T. Black. The stations east of Jordan, from and to which observations were taken, are 21 in all,* including the tree on Neby Oshâ, the elevation of which was ascertained to be 3,597 feet above the Mediterranean. The height of Mount Nebo was the most important point to ascertain. It was found to be 2,643·8, which is 300 feet higher than the elevation given on Baedeker's maps, which give the height of Heshbon correctly. The longitude of Mashita was ascertained by several lines to be about a mile further west than that given on Canon Tristram's reconnaissance map. His latitude is approximately correct. The eastern triangulation was connected with the old stations at Rujm el Bahr, Kasr el Yahûd, Neby Samwîl, Kurn Sartabeh, etc. Observations were taken during the winter of 1881 from Neby Samwîl and Kasr el Yahûd to the cairns erected by the surveyors east of the river, and the connection of the station of el Haud with Kasr el Yahûd is thus made complete, while a very fine triangle is obtained between the latter point and Zabbûd and Kurn Sartabeh, the longest side being more than 24 miles in length.

The result of the calculations was that each trigonometrical station is fixed to within a circle of 20 feet radius at the very extreme on plan. A calculation of the eastern base from the length of the old line between Kasr el Yahûd and Kurn Sartabeh differs only by 8·9 feet from the mean measured length. These limits of error are of course invisible on plan, since to the scale of 1 inch per mile a length of 20 feet is represented by $\frac{1}{264}$ of an inch. The position of the stations east of Jordan is thus fixed absolutely in connection with the Admiralty longitude and latitude of Jaffa, on which the Survey of Western Palestine depends.

The methods of the Eastern Survey were exactly the same used west of the river and described in the 'Memoirs' (vol. i., pp. 31-39), with

* Outside the Survey the position of the hill above the important ruined palace of Mashita has been fixed, giving the line of the Hâj road, and the corner of Kal'at Ziza is also fixed.

exception that mercurial barometers and the sextant for astronomical observation were not used in 1881. It is therefore not necessary again to enlarge on this subject.

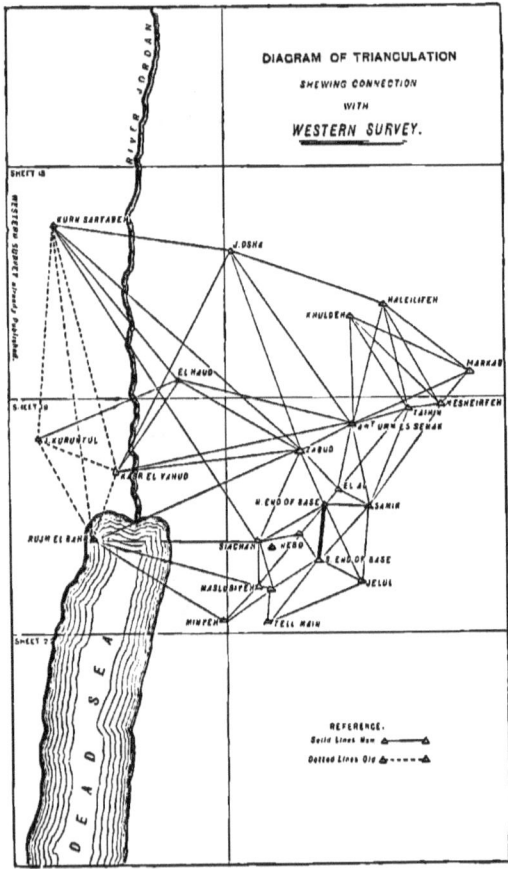

*Heights.*—The elevations of the trigonometrical stations were obtained with the theodolites; and Mr. Black's calculations show that they were extremely accurate.* None of these heights can be considered to be more than 5 feet in error either way when the corrections for curvature and refraction have been applied. A traverse 60 miles long from station to station, when closed on the original station, gives a difference of only 10 feet. The absolute elevations above the Mediterranean depend on the old observations at Rujm el Bahr and Kasr el Yahûd. The former of these is checked by comparison with the line of levels run by Sir C. W. Wilson from the Mediterranean to the Dead Sea, and a traverse thence to the Kurn Sartabeh gave the old height within a very few feet.

As regards *Aneroid Readings*, the experience of the Western Survey showed that the mercurial barometer does not give satisfactory results in fixing the heights of camps when they are as frequently changed as is necessary in rapid survey, especially on account of the autumn storms and of the great difficulty of getting simultaneous observations at sea-level. It was therefore determined that the height of the camps should, whenever possible, be ascertained by levelling from a trigonometrical station, or by comparison of the barometrical readings at such stations. The camp at 'Ain Minyeh was fixed by levelling as being 225·1 below the station at Talât el Benât, but the other camps being in deep valleys, where they were (purposely) hidden from view, this method could not be employed. The aneroids were therefore read at all the trigonometrical stations, and the camp heights made to depend on these readings. This method, which was found also west of Jordan to be better than the use of the mercurial, gives very fair results when the proper corrections for aneroid index error and for temperature are applied. The places fixed by aneroid observations may, it is considered, be relied on within 30 or 40 feet at least. Our observations do not, it is true, agree always with heights given by former explorers; but as the heights in question are found to be incorrect within 100 and even 200 feet at points which are now fixed by trigonometry within 5 feet, it has not been considered necessary to take former observations into consideration, as they evidently

---

\* Outside the limits of the Survey the following heights are also fixed by vertical angles:

| | |
|---|---|
| Jebel Osh'a | 3,597 feet. |
| Jelûl | 2,701 ,, |

The former is north of the Survey, the latter is south-east of the south end of the base, and its position was fixed by the triangulation.

either do not apply to the same exact spot, or else are less accurate than those now obtained.

The number of the aneroid observations is 219 in all, in an area of 500 square miles.* It has been found to lead to great confusion if any attempt is made to take readings at any places not easily recognisable by name or otherwise on the Survey sheets.

*Rate of Progress.*—This was about 250 square miles per month, including the measurement of the base-line and the special survey of 'Ammân. The rates west of the river were from 50 to 330 square miles per month (the latter in the Philistine plains in 1875), but the average was not over 200 square miles per month. The reason of the increase was that the country east of the river is easier to survey. At this rate the Survey, if not interrupted, would have reached 2,000 square miles per annum, and would have been complete possibly in two more years.

C. R. C.

* Forty-six are omitted from the map from want of space.

# APPENDIX C.

### THE ARAB TRIBES EAST OF JORDAN.

THE country surveyed belongs to the dominant tribe of the 'Adwân. Their south boundary is the Zerka Mââîn, their north limit is the Zerka Shebîb, or Jabbok; on the west they extend to Jordan, and on the east they are bounded by the Survey limits, viz., Wâdy el Habîs, Sâmik, 'Ameirch, el Kahf, and thence by the Hâj road. This gives a total area of 1,000 square miles. There are many tribes allied by marriage to the 'Adwân, and all of these as far north as Heshbon are collectively known as Belka Arabs. They belong to older tribes, among whom the 'Adwân grew up, and the power of the latter now depends on their alliance with these small tribes, whom they call *Tab'a*, or ' belonging ' to them. The Ghawârni, in the Ghor, are real serfs of the 'Adwân, but the Belka Arabs have their own chiefs, and are not now serfs. The 'Adwân sheikhs have also black Nubian slaves, who have lived with them for several generations, and some of these sheikhs have, I believe, black wives, as well as Arab consorts.

The Belka plateau, from the 'Adwân boundary eastwards to the Hâj road, and southwards to the Arnon, belongs to the powerful tribe of the Beni Sakhr (also called the Sakhûr), who, when not at feud with the 'Adwân, send their numerous flocks of camels to drink at the streams of 'Ammân and Heshbon, in the 'Adwân country. This tribe is generally on bad terms with the 'Anazeh tribes, who inhabit the deserts east of the Hâj road, and extend northwards to Damascus and Palmyra. There are some Beni Sakhr families also in the Hauran, and they claim a sort of supremacy over the country of the Hameidi, which, by right of the strongest, they enter at will.

The Hameidi include various small clans, or families, which range south of the Zerka Mâain as far as Kerak. They have no recognised supreme chief, and their character is very bad. They are allied to the notorious Sheikh Mujelli of Kerak. Like the Belka Arabs, they sow a little corn, which they take on donkeys to the market at Jerusalem.

In the midst of these tribes a colony of native Christians is established at Mâdeba. They were converted at Kerak in 1880 by Jesuit missionaries from Jerusalem, and established themselves early in 1881 at the ruined town of Mâdeba. North of the Survey is found the town of es Salt, and from this town northwards the Gilead hills are full of villages with a settled population. The Arabs of this district are various clans of the Beni Hasan and small tribes of the Sukr (found also at Beisân), and of the Beni Kaleib (a famous old Arab tribe). The latter are mostly thieves, and are found on the east shores of the Sea of Galilee.

In enumerating these elements of the population, we must not forget the Circassian colony established by the Sultan at 'Ammân about 1879, which is, however, neither prosperous nor likely to become so.

## THE 'ADWÂN.

The 'Adwân (عدوان, 'enemies') trace their descent from a certain Fowzân Ibn es Suweit (الصويت ابن فوزان), who belonged to the Defîr tribe (ضفير), in the Nejed. He fled on account of a blood feud, having slain his cousin, and found refuge with the tribe of the Kordah (قرضه), at Sâmik. This information, with all that follows, was obtained from Sheikh Kablân en Nimr. The Defîr tribe, in the Nejed, is said now to be reduced to a single family, though in the time of Fowzân it was large and important. The present representative is Hamed el Heiyâdreh. The tribe was destroyed by the Southern Sakhûr and by the Hajaiyir Arabs, who are found south of Kerak. Fowzân married a daughter of Sheikh Abu Heider, of the Kordah tribe. He had two sons, from whom sprang the present two divisions of the tribe; the elder was Sâleh, whose descendants form the 'Ashîret es Sâleh, or 'Sâleh tribe.' His second son was Jedid, from whom are descended the 'Ashîret en Nimr, or 'Leopard tribe.' The chief of the eldest branch, now in power, is 'Aly Diâb (son of Diâb), who is a sort of Government official recognised by the Turks in the 'Adwân country. The chief of the younger branch was the aged Sheikh

Kablân en Nimr, who was very anti-Turkish, and a great favourite with the Belka tribes, who hate 'Aly Diâb. The tents of 'Aly Diâb in summer are pitched in the plateau anywhere north of el 'Âl ; in winter he descends by 'Arâk el Emir to Nimrin. The tents of Sheikh Kablân were pitched sometimes near Jubeihah, and later on at 'Ain Fudeili, whence in winter the tribe descends to Kefrein. The two families are allied, but not very friendly, and the lands in the Jordan Valley are regularly owned, and are marked out by boundaries. Maize is grown in the Seisebân by the Ghawarni serfs of the 'Adwân, and corn is sown further north, especially near the Jabbôk. A few mud huts are also used instead of tents at Kefrein, Nimrin, etc., in winter.

The 'Adwân pedigree was thus given by Sheikh Kablân :

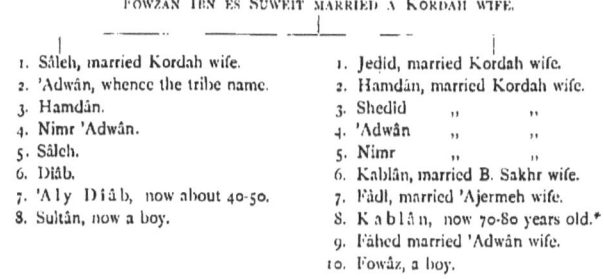

FOWZÂN IBN ES SUWEIT MARRIED A KORDAH WIFE.

| | |
|---|---|
| 1. Sâleh, married Kordah wife. | 1. Jedid, married Kordah wife. |
| 2. 'Adwân, whence the tribe name. | 2. Hamdân, married Kordah wife. |
| 3. Hamdân. | 3. Shedid ,, ,, |
| 4. Nimr 'Adwân. | 4. 'Adwân ,, ,, |
| 5. Sâleh. | 5. Nimr ,, ,, |
| 6. Diâb. | 6. Kablân, married B. Sakhr wife. |
| 7. 'Aly Diâb, now about 40-50. | 7. Fâdl, married 'Ajermeh wife. |
| 8. Sultân, now a boy. | 8. Kablân, now 70-80 years old.* |
| | 9. Fâhed married 'Adwân wife. |
| | 10. Fowâz, a boy. |

This pedigree may not be absolutely accurate, as one would expect more instead of fewer generations in the earlier branch. As the Arabs cannot write, it was handed down by memory. If we allow 30 years for a generation, it would appear that Fowzân must have fled from the Nejed some 200 years or more ago, or in the seventeenth century.

The subdivisions of the Belka tribes allied by marriage to the 'Adwân are as follows :

1. 'Arab el 'Ajermeh, at Hesbân, Sâmik, as far south as Kabr 'Abdullah and east to Umm el Hanâfish. The principal chiefs are Sheikh Mustafa esh Shehwan, Sheikh Fâleh el Hasan, Sheikh Selim Abu 'Afâsh.

* Since dead, 1888.—C.R.C.

The 'Ajermeh are perhaps the oldest Belka tribe : they are subdivided into three clans—the Sifa, the Harafish, and the Muteriyin (مطريين). They march with the Dâjah, on the north, near el Baniyât, and Merj el Hamâm.

2. 'Arab esh Shawâbkeh, at Mushukkar and el Jereineh, and a few near Minyeh. Sheikh Dâibis (دعيبس) and Sheikh 'Abd el Kâder. They are related to the 'Ajermeh, and both are very ancient Belka tribes.

3. 'Arab el Yezâideh (اليزايده), near Mâdeba and Hanina and el Maslûbiyeh. Sheikh Felâh Abu Kharaibeh.

4. 'Arab el 'Awâzim (العوازم), at Minyeh and eastwards to Mââin. Sheikh 'Aly Abu Wundi, now about 70 years old. They are a very courteous and fine-looking tribe. Another branch of the 'Awâzim is said to camp near 'Ammân. Their southern branch has 40 tents, and the northern 60, making 100 in all. These northern 'Awâzim were found in 1882 encamped at Jubeihah under Sheikh Hasein.

5. 'Arab es Suwââyir (سواعير), at Abu Nukleh ; are allied to the 'Ajermeh. Sheikh Barkât en Nâfiâ.

6. 'Arab el 'Afeishât, also 'Ajermeh. Sheikh Selim Abu 'Afâsh and Sheikh Sâleh Abu Jâbr. They are found near Nââûr and Umm es Semmak.

7. 'Arab el Ghaneimât, at Jebel Neba, Wâdy Jideid, 'Ayûn Musa, el Kefeir, as far north as Kabr 'Abdallah. They have 100 tents, and their chief is Sheikh Marzûk Abu el Ghanem. We found them courteous and communicative.

8. 'Arab ez Zafâfi (الزفافي), near Jâwa and Khareibet es Sûk, and some also at Abu Zagheileh, near the Zerka Mââin. The southern group has 40 tents ; the northern are under the principal chief, Sheikh Sâil Abu Hadîd ; the southern under Sheikh 'Aid el Melûsh. Another chief of the north branch is Sheikh Heleil el 'Amiân. These, with the next (No. 9), are collectively known as the 'Arab Ibn Hadîd. In all, there are six clans, viz., Zefâfeh, Juâmseh, Diât, Haneiteiyin, Rakkât, and Bareikât. They have black slaves, called Dhareiwât (ذريوات).

9. 'Arab Abu Jámús, or Juámseh, west of 'Ammân, and at Ammân, are related to the Dájah. Their chief is Sheikh Felâh el 'Aís.

10. 'Arab ed Dájah, in the Merj el Hamâm, under Sheikh Dîâb esh Shawârbeh.

11. 'Arab el 'Abbâd, round 'Arâk el Emir, a large tribe. The 'Abbâd, in fact, are a third branch of the 'Adwân, having the Mutluk thrice repeated as a Wusm, as is explained later in treating of tribe-marks, and occupying the slopes north of Wâdy Nââûr. Their sub-divisions are :

'Arab el Munásir (مناصير), under Sheikh Sáid 'Abd el Muhdi, in the Ard et Tubkah, west of 'Ammân.

'Arab el Fokâha (فكاها), under Sheikh Felâh esh Shedâd, at 'Arak el Emîr.

'Arab ez Ziûd, under Sheikh Ruweiyij el Muflâh, north of the last, near Mahas and Belâl.

'Arab el Bukkûr (بكّور) and 'Arab el Rahâmneh, under Sheikh Shâyid, north-west of es Sâlt, at 'Aireh and Burkah.

'Arab el Jurûm, under Sheikh Mûsa Abu Náim, at Serhân and Allân, north of es Sâlt.

'Arab el Hajâhjeh (الجاهجه), under Sheikh el Judeiâ, at Meiserah, north of es Sâlt.

'Arab es Sinâbreh (السنابره) and 'Arab el Lehwârât, under Sheikh Feiyâd es Sinâbreh, at Jilâd and Kuseib, north of es Sâlt.

'Arab Abu Jâbr, east of el Baniyât, appear also to belong to this same tribe.

12. 'Arab et Towâbiyeh, north of 'Arâk el Emir.

These clans may be considered to average at most 100 tents each. The encampment of 'Aly Diâb consists of 80 tents, and the total of the Belka tribes, together with the 'Adwân, consists of not more than about 2,200 tents, or 11,000 souls, in an area of 1,000 square miles, or eleven souls per square mile, which is less than the average of America, but a very probable result for a deserted district like Moab.

## Beni Hasan.

The subdivisions of this tribe were thus stated by Sheikh Kablân:

1 and 2. 'Arab el Khaleileh and 'Arab ez Zuwâherah, under Sheikh 'Aly esh Shehâdeh, at Kamsheh, Mersâ, Rummân, and Birin.

3. 'Arab el Khawâldeh, under Sheikh 'Aly el Ibrahim, are north of the Jabbok, in the Ard el Haweish.

4. 'Arab el 'Amûsh, under Sheikh Kâsim el Kallâb, at el Ghuweirah and Belâmah.

5. 'Arab el Khazââleh, under Sheikh Muhammad en Nimr, at Tejâniyeh and Belâmah.

6. 'Arab el Beni Helîl, under Sheikh Muhammed el Hirhashi, near Nâimeh.

7. 'Arab el Meshâlkhah, in the Jordan Valley, north of the Jabbok, near the tomb of the Moslem general, Abu 'Obeideh Ibn el Jerrâh (time of Omar). They were formerly a large tribe, and their chiefs were called Emirs. Their present leaders are Sheikh Sâleh el Faûr and Sheikh Fâdl er Robiâ.

## Beni Sakhr.

The leading family of this tribe (بني صخر, 'sons of the rock') is that of Fâiz. The celebrated chief, Fendi el Fâiz, who exacted blackmail from Tiberias as late as 1878, died soon after on a journey, and was buried in the 'Adwân country in the Jordan Valley (see under the head Kabr Fendi el Fâiz). He left eight sons, and these quarrelled, half the tribe allying itself to the 'Adwân, half (under Satm) making a league with the 'Anazeh. Satm was killed in a skirmish with the 'Adwân in May, 1881, and the tribe became reunited in September, 1881, under his brother Satâm, who is on good terms with the Governor of es Sâlt, and who gave information to Muhammed Saîd Pasha, while conducting the Hâj, of the presence of the Survey party in the 'Adwân country.

The divisions of the Beni Sakhr, according to Sheikh Kablân, are:

1. 'Arab ez Zebn, in the vicinity of Wâdy Themed, north-east of Dibon, include:

| | | |
|---|---|---|
| The Faraj | 40 tents. | |
| Muslim | 30 „ | |
| Othmân | 50 „ | |
| Mehârib | 30 „ | |
| Shemânit | 65 „ | Total 215 tents. |

2. 'Arab el Ghubein, round Ziza and Umm el 'Amed, including:
   Hâmid             .      40 tents.
   Meteir            .      60   ,,
   Dagheim           .      40   ,,
   Jabâwasheh        .     100   ,,
   Faiz (the ruling family) .   20   ,,
   Dabâmisheh        .      50   ,,      Total  310 tents.

3. 'Arab el Hakeish (هكيش), including:
   Sâlim             .      40   ,,
   Saheim            .      50   ,,
   Bishir            .      40   ,,
   S'âdneh           .      30   ,,
   Belâûneh          .     100   ,,
   Zeidân            .     150   ,,      Total  410 tents.

4. 'Arab el Khadir (خضر), including:
   Kanowah           .      70   ,,
   Berâdh'ah         .     100   ,,
   Fadl              .     200   ,,
   Reiy'aneh         .     200   ,,      Total  570 tents.

                                         Grand total 1,505 tents.

These are all inhabitants of Moab, making 7,500 souls. There are other branches of the Beni Sakhr in the Haurân, called 'Arab el Khareisheh and 'Arab es Sirhân.

### NOTE ON THE LOCAL DIALECT.

One of the greatest difficulties respecting the nomenclature arises from the peculiar pronunciation of certain letters by the Arabs, which renders their dialect difficult for townsmen to understand. They use also peculiar words, but this does not materially affect the nomenclature.

*Dhal* is pronounced generally like *Zain*, or else like *Dal*, by both the Bedu and the Fellahin. This is an archaism, and in words like *Idhn*, the 'ear,' the sound is in the mouths of the Fellahin the same as in Hebrew.

*The* is pronounced like *Sin*, and like *Te*, which are also archaisms.

*Sad* is not distinguishable from *Sin* among the Bedu, and very rarely among the Fellahin. This is the opinion of Syrian educated persons, and has been noticed by Landberg and other scholars.

*Qaf* is pronounced in five ways in Syria. Among the Bedu it is generally a hard *g*; but in some words, such as Rafik, or Kurn, it is indistinguishable from the *Jim*, which is pronounced by Fellahin and Bedawin like the English *j*, and by some townsmen like the French *j*, and never hard, like *g* as in Egypt.

*Kaf* is almost invariably pronounced like *ch* in 'chaff,' and is thus easily distinguishable in both Bedu and Fellahin dialects.

*Lam* and *Nun* are interchanged, and so are *Mim* and *Nun* in certain cases, among both Bedu and Fellahin. *Lam* and *Re* are also interchanged.

*Waw* is often pronounced when it does not really occur by the Bedu (see back, el 'Ameireh).

*Ye*. The vowel-point accompanying this letter is very vaguely pronounced by the Arabs, who attach no importance to the difference between the sounds *ay*, *ey*, or *i*.

## TRIBE-MARKS OF THE ARABS (A u s â m).

The Arabs are not always willing to tell these, but the following were collected, and are of interest, as showing the Arab derivation of the tribes :

I  Called Wusm el Mutluk. The mark of the elder 'Adwân branch is the Himyarite numeral one.

II  The second, or younger 'Adwân branch, bear the Himyaritic numeral two.

III  The 'Abbâd, the third branch of the 'Adwân, bear the Himyaritic numeral three.

ᓄ  The Ethiopic Gimel is the tribe-mark of the 'Ajermeh. It is combined with one, two, or three strokes for either of the three subdivisions of the tribe.

∧  Another 'Ajermeh mark; is possibly a Lamed, as in Ethiopic.

O  The mark of the Dâjah is the 'Ain, as in so many Semitic alphabets.

ᓂ  The Beni Hasan mark resembles the Himyaritic Resh.

ϙ  The Mihmasah, or 'coffee-spoon,' is the mark of the Beni Sakhr. It is the Himyaritic Yod.

ϙ  The mark of the Fâiz family is the Himyaritic Tza. It occurs with a single stroke for the eldest son of the family.

✕ The mark of the Jibbûr, said to be Beni Sakhr. This is the Himyaritic Tau.*

Ψ Called Rijl el Ghuráb, or 'raven's foot;' is also said to be a Jibbûr mark. It is the Himyaritic Cheth.

☉ The mark of the Khurshân Beni Sakhr; approaches the Himyaritic Vau.

O O Another mark of the Belka Arabs is the old Ethiopic Vau.

⚥ Said to be the mark of the Sherârât, who are Beni Sakhr; is the Himyaritic Tzadi.

⊂⊃ A mark of the Shâlân, who belong to the 'Anazeh clans. It is like a Himyaritic Beth badly formed.

⊃ A mark of the Kowâbkeh, who are also of the 'Anazeh; approaches the Nabathean and Palmyrene Beth.

⁊ A mark of the Shawâbkeh; is very like of that of the 'Ajermeh, to whom they are akin.

⊓ Called el Bâb, 'the door,' is a mark of the Khadir branch of the Beni Sakhr. It is the Himyaritic Beth, and retains the name.

The Arabs cannot write; they seem unaware of the fact that these marks are letters, which show their own origin. Other indications of the Himyaritic origin of these tribes are noted under the heads Jineinet Belkis and Kusr en Nûeijis. These indications agree with the history of the Beni Ghassan, who settled in the Haurân, and who were probably the subjects of Zenobia. Their chief, Thalaba, was descended from 'Amr Muzeika, the Azdite, who migrated north in 120 A.D., and who was descended from Kahlan, brother of Himyar, descended from Kahtan of Yemen. The Beni Ghassan were converted to Christianity, and from them originates the Melchite sect in Syria.

Our comparison has been with the South Semitic alphabets, and the forms ⚥ Ψ ⚥ have no relation to any North Semitic letters, but are distinctly Sabean. The | might be a Nabathean Zain, but it is evidently used as a

---

* Concerning this mark and another ✚, which is the Ethiopic Tau (see Kal'at Ummeh), Sheikh Kablân denied strenuously that it was intended for the Christian cross. He did not know it was a letter, but said it was a very old Arab mark. It will be seen that he was quite right, but the cross is found built into an Arab tomb at 'Ain 'Ammân, as described under that head. There seems, however, reason to suppose that the Christians of Sâlt sometimes use the cross as a *Wusm*.

numeral, as in Sabean. These marks belong to the Beni Sakhr and 'Adwân, who are of South Semitic origin. Some of the other marks may, however, be compared with Nabathean and Thamudite alphabets of Eastern Palestine. Thus, ꓘ is the Abushadhr Daleth, ⋀ is the Thamudite Samech, ⊃ is the Thamudite Beth, and ⚲ is used by Thamudites, as well as by Sabeans, for Yod; while ꓘ, as above-mentioned, is Nabathean, rather than Sabean. These marks, excepting ⚲, which is Beni Sakhr, and probably of Sabean origin, belong to the older tribes, 'Ajermeh, Beni Hasan, Kowâbkeh, and Shawâbkeh, which may probably be of Nabathean origin. The fiercer Nejed tribes found them in possession when they invaded the Peræan deserts.

C. R. C.

# APPENDIX D.

## GEOLOGICAL NOTE.

THE Moab plateau was not visited by Dr. Hull during his geological expedition, but the general structure is well understood, being a continuation of that found east of the great fault in the Arabah, a fault which runs north to the Huleh Lake.

The Nubian sandstone forms the base of the Moab plateau up to a level of about 1,000 feet above the Mediterranean; at its foot are white marls similar to those on the west side of the valley, where they rest on the crystalline limestone, which appears in the Koruntul cliffs. These marls are unconformable to the dip of the sandstone, and are fairly horizontal in bedding. They rise in some of the foot-hills to a level 500 feet above the Mediterranean, belonging to the oldest of the Jordan Valley or Dead Sea formations, and their occurrence is evidence of the deposits which followed the formation of the Jordan Valley fault (see 'Tent Work in Palestine,' vol. ii., pp. 40-44).

Above the Nubian sandstone east of Jordan comes a hard crystalline limestone, which is the same found west of the river. This, on an average, rises to about 2,500 feet above the Mediterranean; *i.e.*, with a thickness of 1,500 feet. This formation dips westward, and copious springs are thus found on the western slopes of the Moab plateau all along the surface of this formation. The cliffs and gorges are similar to those of the Judean desert, where the same formation occurs at a lower level, due to the contortion of the strata on the west side of the Jordan Valley in consequence of the fault.

Above the crystalline limestone comes the softer cretaceous limestone found in Western Palestine, where the Nummulitic beds form part of the series. This formation on the surface of the plateau is worn away eastwards, so that the water-courses are deflected from a ridge running north and south close to the western edge of the plateau. The formation is pervious, and no springs occur. The level attained is about 3,000 feet above the Mediterranean.

Alluvial deposits and recent gravel-beds and marls occur in the Jordan Valley east of the river at the same levels as on the west.

Volcanic formations occur on the south side of the Zerka Mââin, where are numerous hot-springs (see Wâdy Zerka Mââin), a fine black basaltic outbreak forming a cliff in this gorge just south of the principal hot-spring. On the plateau north of this valley there are also basaltic centres at 'Ain Hamârah (So' F.) and at the Hammet Minyeh. Further north basalt occurs at Tell Iktanu, near which is the hot spring of el Hammâm (see under that head). The surrounding rocks are here all hard limestone.

The general result of observations made by the present writer on both sides of the Jordan Valley and throughout Palestine, Moab, and Northern Syria in the years 1872-3, 1881-2, confirmed the views of the French geologists as to the formation of the valley, and was further confirmed by the professional visit of Dr. Hull.

C. R. C.

# APPENDIX E.

### GENERAL REMARKS ON THE RUDE-STONE MONUMENTS.

THE discovery of so many dolmens and menhirs within the limits of the Survey is the more remarkable because they are not found in Western Palestine, except in a few cases in Galilee. They occur in Gilead, north of the Survey, and in Bashan. In 1882 I found a group near the sources of Jordan. They are also known in Asia Minor, in Armenia, in Cyprus, in Phœnicia, in Arabia, in the Sinaitic desert, and on the south shores of the Mediterranean, as well as in Europe, Persia, India, etc. The probable reason of their absence in Palestine is that they have been purposely destroyed.

The monuments found include cairns, stone circles, menhirs (or single standing stones), dolmens (or stone structures, with a capstone supported on upright stones), and demi-dolmens on hillsides, one end of the capstone resting on the ground. These are described under the heads 'A i n e l M i n y e h (p. 11), 'A m m â n (p. 22), H a d a n i e h (p. 99), e l K a l û a (p. 125), e l K u r m i y e h (p. 159), e l M a r e i g h â t (p. 185), M e n s e f A b u Z e i d (p. 193), N e b a (p. 202), S e r a b i t e l M u s h u k k a r (p. 212), T e l l e l H a m m â m (p. 229), S û m i a (p. 226), T e l l e l M a t â b à (p. 231), W â d y J i d e i d (p. 254).

Another peculiarity of these dolmen-fields in Moab consists in the great number of the monuments discovered at each of the centres. In some cases the dolmens nearly touched each other. In England such monuments are found singly or scattered. In Algiers the dolmens are, perhaps, as numerous as in the country beyond Jordan, and, like those discovered by Herr Schumacher in Bashan and by Lieutenant Mantell in the Jordan Valley, the Algerian dolmens stand on stepped terraces or platforms. No holed dolmens were found in Moab, but Irby and Mangles appear to describe correctly certain dolmens near the mouth of the river Jabbok which have a hole in the endstones resembling the holes in stone chambers—apparently tombs—which are supposed to have been intended to allow entry and exit to the soul of the person buried.

The question of the origin of these structures is treated at some length in 'Heth and Moab,' chapters vii. and viii. Some antiquaries regard dolmens as tombs, though the use of dolmens not covered by a mound for such purpose is unproven, while the mounds of prehistoric tumuli existing in so many countries show how improbable is the theory that such mounds may be washed away. The position of many dolmens, especially at el Maslûbiyeh, is inconsistent with the idea that they were once covered with mounds. These monuments seem more probably to have been either habitations or altars. The following facts as to the Moabite dolmens are important to antiquaries :

1st. They do not appear to have been ever covered by mounds.

2nd. They stand on bare rock, and have no excavated grave beneath.

3rd. They occur in large groups almost invariably in the vicinity of a spring or stream.*

4th. Their stones are generally unhewn, but in some cases chipped rudely into shape.

5th. They very rarely occur on hilltops, being usually on the slope.

6th. The stone is that of the immediate vicinity—limestone—except near Tell el Kâdy, where basaltic stones were found.

7th. There is no orientation, the sidestones being usually parallel to the hill contour.

8th. Many of these monuments are very small, suitable neither for sepulture nor for a dwelling, but better adapted for the purpose of a sacrificial table.

9th. Cup-hollows occur in some cases, generally very rudely formed. At 'Ammân, etc., the cups are connected by channels.

* Stonehenge stands on the down as near as possible to the Avon. Kitt's Cotty House is on the slope above the Medway fords, and so in other cases. There was a British village by Stonehenge, and it is possible that in Moab—as in England—the reason for the vicinity of dolmens to water is that they belonged to an ancient inhabited site.

10. No ring-markings were found in connection with these cups.*

11. The dolmen builders were apparently illiterate, and probably uncivilized. It is doubtful if they knew the use of metal.

12. They were not able to deal easily with heavy weights, as is evident from the stones having been, as a rule, moved downhill, and to no great distance.

The Arabs call the dolmens بيوت الغول—B i y û t e l G h û l ('houses of the ghouls'), believing them to be inhabited by evil spirits. The less superstitious, however, regard them as مناطير—*Munátír*, or 'watch-towers,' which is an unfortunate explanation, because the dolmens hardly ever occupy a commanding position, being usually on low ground or on hill slopes.

The dolmens do not appear to have been regarded with dislike by either Romans or Arabs, since they are not thrown down by the latter, and since they occur in the immediate vicinity of the Roman city at 'Ammân.

The standing stones of el Mareighât, are among the most remarkable specimens of such erections, and the circles at 'Ain el Minyeh are equally valuable to the antiquary. The monuments described under the head el Kurmiyeh include some in which the topstone is supported on horizontal slabs instead of sidestones. These clearly were not graves, but rather resemble the 'rocking-stones' of our own islands.

* The peculiar holes in sides of menhirs have been already noticed (see 'Ammân menhir N, note). They occur also in British monuments, where they appear to be 'swearing-holes,' where the persons swearing by the stone placed their fingers or arms in the stone.

C. R. C.

www.ingramcontent.com/pod-product-compliance
Lightning Source LLC
Chambersburg PA
CBHW031854220426
43663CB00006B/614